THE

PURITANS AND QUEEN ELIZABETH.

THE PURITANS:

OR

THE CHURCH, COURT, AND PARLIAMENT OF ENGLAND,

DURING THE REIGNS OF

EDWARD VI. AND QUEEN ELIZABETH.

BY

SAMUEL HOPKINS.

"The Liberties of our House it behooveth us to leave to our Posterities in the same freedom we have received them."

Committee of the Puritan Commons to the Lords, 1575–6.

IN THREE VOLUMES.

VOL. II.

BOSTON:
GOULD AND LINCOLN,
59 WASHINGTON STREET.
NEW YORK: SHELDON AND COMPANY.
CINCINNATI: GEORGE S. BLANCHARD.
1860.

University Press, Cambridge:
Electrotyped and Printed by Welch, Bigelow, & Co.

CONTENTS.

CHAPTER I.

THE PARLIAMENT OF 1575-6.

CHAPTER II.

THE GOVERNESS AND THE PRIMATE. (A. D. 1576.)

CHAPTER III.

TREASON AND PRÆMUNIRE. (A. D. 1576, 1577.)

CHAPTER IV.

BISHOP AYLMER AND THE MAGICIANS. — PRESBYTERIAN ORDINATION RECOGNIZED. (A. D. 1577-1579.)

CHAPTER V.

THE DYING SOLDIER. (A. D. 1576.)

CHAPTER VI.

COURTSHIP AND BLOOD. (A. D. 1579-1582.)

CHAPTER VII.

THE PARLIAMENT OF 1580-1.

CHAPTER VIII.

THE JESUITS. (A. D. 1580, 1581.)

CHAPTER IX.

AYLMER, BISHOP OF LONDON. (A. D. 1579-1592.)

CHAPTER X.

THE INITIATION OF PRESBYTERIAN DISCIPLINE.

(A. D. 1582, 1583.)

CHAPTER XI.

ROBERT BROWN. (A. D. 1581-1583.)

CHAPTER XII.

EDMUND, ARCHBISHOP OF CANTERBURY. (A. D. 1583.)

CHAPTER XIII.

WHITGIFT'S THREE ARTICLES. (A. D. 1583.)

CHAPTER XIV.

THE COURT OF HIGH COMMISSION. (A. D. 1583, 1584.)

CHAPTER XV.

"SCANT CHARITABLE." (A. D. 1584.)

CHAPTER XVI.

THE PARLIAMENT OF 1584-5. (THE PURITANS.)

CHAPTER XVII.

THE PARLIAMENT OF 1584-5. (THE CATHOLICS.)

THE PURITANS.

CHAPTER I.

THE PARLIAMENT OF 1575-6.

Anabaptists burned. — Grindal elected Archbishop of Canterbury. — Parliament assemble. — The Commons contend with the Lords. — The Queen avows her Pleasure to be the Guide of Church Discipline. — Peter Wentworth contends for the Right of the Commons to Free Debate. — He is sequestered, and ordered under Arrest to answer. — His Examination before a Committee of the Commons. — Is committed to the Tower during the Pleasure of the House. — The Commons liberate him at her Majesty's Suggestion.

A unit had been added to the congregation of the dead; yet the world was no whit weaker or sadder. The great sea of life, with its burden of wrong and sorrow, of oppression and emulation, tossed and fell and rolled on, as it had done. The funeral of the Archbishop, like the bubble where a stone goes down, was but the commotion of a moment. When his tomb was closed, even the Church was as hale and as placid as though she had not lost her Primate, — a youthful widow ready for another Consolation.

On the third day of April, 1575, certain Dutch Anabaptists had been arrested and imprisoned.[1] On

[1] "Anabaptist," — literally, a *re*-baptizer. It is a term used to designate those who hold that the application of water in the name of the Divine Trinity to infants is *not* baptism; and that such application is baptism *only* when the subject has arrived at years of discretion. They

the fifteenth day of May, a few of them, clad in sheets and with fagots on their backs, had recanted their errors at Paul's Cross, and asked the prayers of the congregation. On the twenty-first, eleven were condemned by the Consistory of St. Paul's to be burned for their heresy. Of these, one woman "was converted," and so saved. The Dutch church in London, although detesting their opinions, interceded for them. But of the Church of England only two had the courage and Christian charity to do so, and they — were Puritans; the one, a Conformist; the other, a Non-conformist. The latter, in an eloquent

who hold this opinion very properly disown the name of *ana*baptists, because, when administering the rite to one who may have received it in infancy, they consider that they do *not re*-baptize.

Large numbers who held this opinion joined themselves to an insurrection in Germany, which commenced in 1521, and which was provoked by the intolerable oppressions of the nobles upon the lower orders. These insurrectionists soon came to be called Anabaptists, — their prominent leaders being of that sect, — although the most of them were Roman Catholics and other dissimilar sects and parties. They were religious fanatics; although others of the same name (in Switzerland, for example) were very sober and good men. They maintained, — That the good order of society was to be upheld only by the impulse or guidance of the Divine Spirit within each individual: That, therefore, all civil magistracy was not only needless, but a wrong to the Christian man: That all inequality of rank and of property was contrary to the Gospel: That the first should be abolished, and that a community of goods should be substituted for the latter: And that neither Nature nor the Bible forbade a plurality of wives.

Some of them, at least, held also the notion that the body prepared for the Messiah, although enwombed within the Virgin Mary, did not derive its substance from hers. That this opinion was held by those mentioned in the text is evident from Holingshed's record of their confession and recantation.

Hence the Anabaptists, so called, of the sixteenth century were regarded, not only as religious, but also as political, heretics and disorganizers, dangerous to society as well as to the Church. (Fuller, Bk. V. p. 229. Burnet, III. 177. Rapin, II. 14, note. Mosheim, IV. 424 -468. Robertson's Charles the Fifth, Bk. V. Buck's Theol. Dictionary, articles "Anabaptists" and "Mennonites." See also *ante*, Vol. I. p. 482, note 1.)

letter, "distinguished by the classical Latinity of which he was no mean master," conjured the queen, "for the sake of Christ who was consecrated to suffer for the life of many," to spare the convicts from so horrible a fate. This was John Fox, whom her Majesty used to call "my father Fox," and who *had* thought of writing her "monuments." But, notwithstanding her esteem for him, "she gave him a flat denial;" fearing lest, "having formerly punished some traitors, if now she should spare these blasphemers, the world would condemn her as being more earnest in asserting her own safety than God's honor."

The other intercessor was Edmund Grindal, Archbishop of York, who pleaded with Lord Burleigh as follows, in a letter dated ten days before the condemnation of the eleven: "If your lordship will give me leave to say mine opinion, I would think it convenient that such as will recant their errors in the Dutch church openly, and yield themselves to be members of that church, and to communicate with that congregation, in word, sacraments, and prayer, that they are to be tolerated and still remain in this realm; but such as will refuse thus to do, in mine opinion, it is most necessary that they be utterly expelled out of this realm, and if they return, to lose their lives for it." [1]

Yet the intercession of these good men — probably with some concession on the part of the culprits — seems not to have been in vain; for the punishment of eight was commuted for banishment, — seven women being thrust through the streets by the offi-

[1] Wright's Elizabeth, II. 11.

cers, and a man being "whipped, tied to a cart," all the way from Newgate to the water. Two men, continuing obstinate in their opinions, were roasted alive at Smithfield, on the twenty-second day of July, dying "with great horror, crying and roaring." Thus was the writ *de heretico comburendo* issued for the first time in this reign; the statute in point having slumbered seventeen years.[1]

Rebellious as certain Anabaptists had been in Germany, *these* offenders seem to have been peaceable; their only crime, that of worshipping God by themselves; their only dangerous doctrine, that civil government was an usurpation; and their only "blasphemy," a strange hypothesis about the incarnation of Christ. We find no further intimation of Fox's Acts and Monuments of her whom, in his letter upon this occasion, he styled "The most Serene and Blessed Princess, the most Illustrious Queen, the Honor of her Country, the Ornament of the Age."

Under "Church and State," heresy is whatever the dominant party disbelieves. Hence, in perpetrating this atrocity, the Consistory, the Privy Council, the queen, — all who shared in it or tacitly assented to it, — did most infamously and publicly justify the tortures of the Spanish Inquisition, the butcheries of Bonner and Mary, and the wholesale slaughter of St. Bartholomew's day in Paris. In this connection it is worthy of remark, that, by the statute 1 Eliz. Cap. I. Sec. XX., all that was necessary to expose one to the stake, was a vote of Parliament at any day, having the assent of the Convocation, that this or that

[1] Stow's Annals, 680. Fuller, IV. 326-328. Strype's Annals, III. Bk. IX. pp. 104, 105. Holingshed, 564.

opinion was heresy, which no one yesterday doubted to be orthodox.[1]

Queen Elizabeth liked vacant bishoprics. They filled her purse.[2] Thus it was not until the tenth day of January, 1575–6, that Edmund Grindal, the Archbishop of York, was elected, upon her nomination, to the vacant chair of Canterbury;[3] and not until the fifteenth day of February that he was confirmed therein,—nine months after the death of Archbishop Parker.[4] This prelate having "kept as hard a hand on all sects and sectaries, and more particularly on those of the Genevian platform, as the temper of the times could bear,"[5] and the new incumbent having always manifested a different spirit, and having maintained a fraternal correspondence with Calvin, Beza, Zanchy, Bullinger, Gualter, and "others of the Switzers," the Puritans "promised themselves forbearance, if not protection," under his primacy.[6] We shall soon see how far this reasonable expectation was realized.

The Parliament assembled on the eighth day of February, 1575–6, after having been several times prorogued since their adjournment in 1572. It being the second session of the same body, the two Houses resumed business without preliminary formalities, as though their recess had been but for a day.[7]

In the House of Lords, a bill was introduced

[1] Coke, VII. 57. Blackstone, IV. 48, 49.

[2] Strype's Parker, 86. Warner, II. 447. Zurich Letters, p. 69.

[3] Strype's Grindal, 192.

[4] Strype's Grindal, 193. Holingshed, IV. 329.

[5] Heylin's Presb., Bk. VII. Sec. 13.

[6] Ibid. Lingard, VIII. 145.

[7] D'Ewes, 227, 236.

providing that whoever would not receive the communion and attend church should pay yearly a certain sum of money. Upon its second reading, it was referred to a Committee, where it seems to have rested when the Parliament was prorogued.[1]

During the session, an altercation occurred between the two Houses, showing the spirit of each, and highly creditable to the Commons. To canvass this difference, a Committee of the Commons made application at the door of the Upper House. The Lords, *after a great pause,* came forth to the antechamber, and complained, with no little tartness, that they could not but greatly mislike the dealing of the Commons concerning a certain bill, and that the Commons did not use that reverence toward the Peers which was due. They concluded by demanding the reasons for such proceedings. To such a complaint and such a demand the Committee promptly refused to make any reply without special instructions from the Commons. Their report of this conference "moved all the House greatly, and gave them occasion of many arguments and speeches; all generally misliking this kind of dealing with them, *thinking their liberties much touched.*" The Committee were sent back with new instructions.

"The House of Commons," they said to the Lords, "do not want consideration of the superiority of your lordship's estates in respect of your honorable calling, which we do acknowledge with all humbleness. And we do protest that we will continue unto your lordships all dutiful reverence, *so far as the same be not prejudicial to the Liberties of our House, which it behooveth*

[1] D'Ewes, 228. Lodge, II. 137; Talbot to Shrewsbury.

us to leave to our Posterities in the same freedom we have received them. . . . . . Touching the manner of our proceedings to which your lordships have excepted, we could not have done otherwise than we have done, without breach of our Liberties; . . . . . and, touching the matter, we have acted upon good deliberation, not hastily or inconsiderately, but upon great and sufficient reasons moving us thereunto. Nevertheless, to declare those reasons in particular unto your lordships upon *requisition,* that were *to yield an account* of our doings and of things passed in our House, which *we cannot in any wise agree unto, being so prejudicial to our Liberties.*"

For a Message so decided and manly, the Lords were not prepared; for they consulted apart for considerable time before making their reply. At length the Lord Treasurer said: ". . . . . Because the Commons are the truest reporters of their own actions, and the best interpreters of their own meanings, the Lords do accept of their answer in the first part thereof touching the manner of their proceedings. But touching the other part, the matter, we do once again press upon you, the Committee, to show the reasons which have moved the House."

"We do humbly thank your lordships," replied one of the delegation, "that it hath pleased you so well to accept of our answer to the first part; but for the second, which concerneth the matter itself, and the *reasons* that have moved the House, we have no further authority to deal."

Whereupon the Lords, worsted and doubtless chagrined, returned to the Upper House; and the Committee, to the Commons. Upon their report of their proceedings, "the House was much satisfied, seeing that so great a storm was so well calmed, and the Liberties of the House so well preserved."[1]

Certain motions were made in the Commons for reformation in the Church. A Committee appointed to agree upon a Petition to her Majesty upon the subject, after reporting the same, to which they joined a bill for the reformation desired, presented the Papers to the Privy Council for the queen's consideration. To this her Majesty returned answer, "that at the beginning of this session her Highness had given in charge of the bishops to see due reformation of discipline in the Church; that her Majesty thinketh they will have good consideration thereof according to her pleasure and express commandment in that behalf; that, should they neglect so to do, her Majesty, by her supreme power and authority over the Church of England, will speedily see such good redress therein as may satisfy the expectation of her loving subjects to their good contentation."

This "Message and report" meant only that her Majesty would have the Church discipline "according unto her pleasure;" yet, framed in so fair-spoken a way, no exception could be taken to it without reflecting indecorously upon her Majesty's sincerity. It was, therefore, "most thankfully and joyfully received by the whole House with one accord." And there this matter, also, rested.[2]

These occurrences in the House of Commons claim attention particularly, because the Puritans were a majority.[3] But the event for which this session is memorable occurred on the first day of their assem-

[1] D'Ewes, 263, 264. [2] D'Ewes, 251, 252, 257. [3] Carte, III. 540.

bling, and in the Lower House, as soon as business had commenced by the reading of one bill for the first time.

Peter Wentworth, Esquire, — who retorted with so much spirit upon the servile Speech of Sir Humphrey Gilbert in 1571, — was the most mature and intrepid Puritan of the day who had any share in the business of State. Immediately after the reading of the bill alluded to, he gave vent to the fire which he had long suppressed in a Speech so remarkable for its boldness and for its defence of Parliamentary Privilege against the encroachments of the Crown, that we shall present it almost entire, — a noble monument of the principles and manliness of political Puritanism.

"Mr. Speaker," said this champion of Civil Rights, "I find written in a little volume these words in effect, — 'Sweet is the name of Liberty; but the thing itself, a value beyond all inestimable treasure.' So much the more it behooveth us to take care lest, contenting ourselves with the sweetness of the name, we lose and forego the thing itself, — of the greatest value that can come unto this noble realm. The inestimable treasure is, the use of it in this House. . . . . . I was never of Parliament but the last" — in 1571 — "and the last session; at both which times I saw the liberty of free speech — the which is the only salve to heal all the sores of this Commonwealth — so much and so many ways infringed, when also I saw so many abuses offered to this Honorable Council, as hath much grieved me even of very conscience and love to my prince and State. Wherefore to avoid the like, I do think it expedient to open the

Commodities that grow to the prince and the whole State by free speech used in this place; at the least, so much as my simple wit can gather."

After having stated how evils would be avoided and benefits accrue to prince and people by free discussion, he proceeded: —

"So to this point I conclude, that in this House which is termed a place of free speech, nothing is so necessary for the preservation of the prince and State. Without free speech, it is a scorn and a mockery to call this a Parliament House. Without free speech, it is no Parliament-House; but a very school of Flattery and Dissimulation; and so, a fit place to serve the Devil and his angels in; not, to glorify God and benefit the Commonwealth.

"Now to the impediments of this freeness. By God's grace and my little experience, I will utter them plainly and faithfully. . . . . . Amongst others, Mr. Speaker, two things do great hurt in this place. The one is, a rumor which runneth about the House, and this it is: 'Take heed what you do. The Queen's Majesty liketh not such a matter. Whosoever preferreth it, she will be offended with him.' Or the contrary: 'Her Majesty liketh of such a matter. Whosoever speaketh against it, she will be offended with him.' The other thing that doeth great hurt here is, sometimes a Message is brought into the House" — from the queen — "either of commanding or inhibiting, very injurious to the freedom of speech and consultation.

"I would to God, Mr. Speaker, that these two were buried in Hell! I mean Rumors and Messages; for wicked undoubtedly they are, — the Devil the author of them, from whom proceedeth nothing but wickedness. Now I will set down reasons to prove them wicked.

"If we be in hand with anything for the advancement of God's glory, were it not wicked to say, 'The queen liketh not of it?' or to say, 'She commandeth that we shall not deal in it?' Greatly were these speeches to her Majesty's dishonor; and an hard opinion were it, Mr. Speaker, that to dislike or to hinder such things for the advancement of God's glory should enter into her Majesty's thought. Much more wicked and unnatural were it, that her Majesty should like or command anything against God, or hurtful to herself and the State. The Lord grant this thing may be far from her Majesty's heart! Here this may be objected, that if the Queen's Majesty should have intelligence of anything perilous or beneficial to her Majesty's person or State, would you not have her Majesty give knowledge thereof in this House, whereby her peril might be prevented, and her benefit provided for? God forbid! then were her Majesty in worse case than any of her subjects. . . . . . In every cause, we ought to proceed according to the matter, and not according to the prince's mind. Always to follow the prince's mind, is perilous. Many times it falleth out, that a prince may favor a cause perilous to himself and the whole State. In such a case, what are we if we follow his mind? Are we not unfaithful unto God, our prince, and our State? Yes, truly; for we are chosen of the whole realm, of a special trust and confidence by them reposed in us, to foresee all such inconveniences. My opinion herein is, that whoso dissembleth to her Majesty's peril is to be counted as an hateful enemy, for that he giveth to her Majesty a detestable Judas's kiss; and he that contrarieth her mind to her preservation, yea, though her Majesty were much offended with him, is to be adjudged an approved lover, for 'faithful are the wounds of a lover,' saith Solomon, 'but the kisses of an enemy are deceitful.' And 'it is better,' saith Antisthenes, 'to fall amongst ravens than amongst flatterers; for ravens do but devour the dead corpse; but flatterers, the living.' And it is both traitorous and hellish through flattery to seek to devour our natural prince, as flatterers do.

"But there is another grave matter that riseth from this grievous rumor of what the queen liketh, or liketh not. What is it, forsooth? It is this. Whatsoever thou art that pronounceth such a rumor, thou doest what lieth in thee to pronounce the prince perjured! . . . . . The Queen's Majesty is the Head of the law, and must of necessity maintain the law. The king ought not to be under man, but under God and under the law. . . . . . He is God's Vicegerent here upon earth; that is, his Lieutenant to execute his will, which is,—Law and Justice; and thereunto was her Majesty sworn at her coronation. . . . . . But free speech and conscience in this place are granted *by a special law,* as that without which the prince and State cannot be preserved or maintained. What, then, *is* the grave matter that riseth, as I say, from the grievous rumor about the queen's liking which would stop free speech? What is it, forsooth? It is this. Whatsoever thou art that pronouncest that her Majesty misliketh to have free speech, which speech the law granteth, and which law her Majesty is sworn to, thou dost pronounce such rumor to thine own discredit, and dost what lieth in thee to pronounce the prince perjured! So that I would wish every man that feareth God, regardeth the prince's honor, or esteemeth his own credit, to fear at all times hereafter to pronounce any such horrible speeches, so much to the prince's dishonor; for in so doing he sheweth himself an open enemy to her Majesty, and, so, worthy to be contemned of all faithful hearts.

"Yet there is another inconvenience that riseth on this wicked rumor. The utterers thereof seem to put it into our heads, that the Queen's Majesty hath conceived an evil opinion — diffidence and mistrust — towards us her faithful and loving subjects; for if she had not, her Majesty would then wish that all things dangerous to herself should be laid open before us, assuring herself that loving subjects, as we are, would without schooling and direction, with careful minds to our powers, prevent and withstand all perils that might happen to her Majesty. And this opinion I doubt not but her Majesty hath of us; for undoubtedly there never was prince that had faithfuller hearts than her Majesty hath here, and surely there were never subjects had more cause heartily to love their prince for her quiet government. So that he that raiseth this rumor still increaseth but discredit in seeking to sow sedition, as much as lieth in him, between our merciful queen and us her most loving and faithful subjects; the which by God's grace shall never lie in his power, let him spit out all his venom and therewithal show out his malicious heart.

"Now the other matter of which I have spoken besides this rumor was a Message Mr. Speaker brought the last session into this House, that we should not deal in any matters of religion, without first receiving them from the bishops.[1] Surely this was a doleful Message; for it was as much as to say, 'Sirs, ye shall not deal in God's causes; no ye shall in no wise seek to advance his glory.' . . . . . Truly I assure you, Mr. Speaker, there were divers in this House that said with grievous hearts, immediately upon this Message, that God of his justice could not prosper the session; and let it be holden for a principle, Mr. Speaker, that that Council which cometh not together in God's name cannot prosper. . . . . . Well; God, even the great and mighty God, whose name is the Lord of Hosts, great in council and infinite in thought, and who is the only good Director of all hearts, was the last session shut out of doors. But what fell of it, forsooth? His great indignation was therefore poured upon this House; for he did put into the Queen's Majesty's heart to refuse good and wholesome laws for her own preservation" — meaning laws for proceeding in the degree of High Treason against the queen of Scots — "the

[1] Sir Simon D'Ewes says (p. 241) that "the message Wentworth meant was that sent by her Majesty to the House of Commons in the fourteenth year of her reign, upon Wednesday, the 28th day of May, by Sir Francis Knollys, inhibiting them for a certain time to treat or deal in the matter touching *the Scottish queen*." This message is on page 219.

Wentworth himself must be supposed to have known best what message he meant; and *he* said: "A message Mr. Speaker" — Bell — "brought the last session into the House, that we should not deal in any matters *of religion*, but first to receive of the bishops." (page 238.) This message was delivered on the 22d day of May, 1572. (D'Ewes, 213.)

which caused many faithful hearts for grief to burst out with sorrowful tears, and moved all Papists, traitors to God and her Majesty, who envy good Christian government, in their sleeves to laugh all the whole Parliament to scorn. And shall I pass over this weighty matter so slightly? Nay. I will discharge my conscience and duties to God, my prince, and my country. So certain it is, Mr. Speaker, that none is without fault, no not our noble queen, sith then her Majesty hath committed great, yea, dangerous, faults to herself. Love, even perfect love void of dissimulation, will not suffer me to hide them to her Majesty's peril, but to utter them to her Majesty's safety. It is a dangerous thing in a prince unkindly to abuse his or her Nobility and People. And it is a dangerous thing in a prince to oppose or bend herself against her Nobility and People, yea, against most loving and faithful Nobility and People.[1] And how could any prince more unkindly intreat, abuse, oppose herself against her Nobility and People than her Majesty did the last Parliament? Did she not call it of purpose to prevent traitorous perils to her person, and for no other cause? Did not her Majesty send unto us two bills, willing us to make choice of that we liked best for her safety, and thereof to make a law, promising her Majesty's royal consent thereunto? And did we not first choose the one, and her Majesty refused it, yielding no reason; nay, yielding great reasons why she

[1] We have here the best possible proof of Hume's error in intimating that the severity devised in the last session of Parliament was distinctively Puritan. The queen's opposition to it was against the wishes of both Lords and Commons, Puritans *and Churchmen*. See above, Vol. I. p. 427, note 4.

ought to have yielded to it? Yet did we not nevertheless receive the other, and agreeing to make a law thereof, did not her Majesty in the end refuse all our travails? And did not we, her Majesty's faithful Nobility and Subjects, plainly and openly decypher ourselves unto her Majesty and our hateful enemies? And hath not her Majesty left us all to the[1] open revenge? Is this a just recompense in our Christian queen for our faithful dealings? The Heathen do requite good for good; how much more then is to be expected in a Christian prince? And will not this her Majesty's handling, think you, Mr. Speaker, make cold dealing in any of her Majesty's subjects toward her again? I fear it will. . . . . . And hath it not marvellously rejoiced and encouraged the hollow hearts of her Majesty's hateful enemies and traitorous subjects? No doubt but it hath. I beseech God that her Majesty may do all things that may grieve the hearts of her enemies, and may joy the hearts that unfeignedly love her Majesty. And I beseech the same God to endue her Majesty with wisdom, whereby she may discern faithful advice from traitorous, sugared speeches; and to send her Majesty a melting, yielding heart unto sound counsel; that Will may not stand for a Reason. Then her Majesty will stand when her enemies are fallen; for no Estate can stand where the prince will not be governed by advice.

". . . . . But was this all? No; for God would not vouchsafe that his Holy Spirit should all that session descend upon our bishops; so that at that session nothing was done to the advancement of

[1] *Sic.* Qu. *their?*

God's glory. I have heard of old Parliament men, that the banishment of the Pope and Popery, and the restoring of true religion, had their beginning from this House, and not from the bishops. I have heard, that few laws for religion had their foundation from them. And I do surely think — before God I speak it! — that the bishops were the cause of that doleful Message," — that we should not deal in any matters of religion, but first to receive them from the bishops. "I will show you what moveth me so to think. I was amongst others the last Parliament" — in 1571 — "sent unto the Bishop of Canterbury for the Articles of Religion that then passed this House. He asked us why we did put out of the Book the Articles for the Homilies, consecrating of bishops, and such like? 'Surely, sir,' said I, 'because we were so occupied in other matters, that we had no time to examine them how they agreed with the Word of God.' 'What!' said he, 'surely you mistook the matter! You will refer yourselves *wholly to us* therein?' 'No, by the faith I bear to God!' said I, 'we will pass nothing before we understand what it is; for that were but to make you Popes. Make you Popes who list, for *we* will make you none!'

"And sure, Mr. Speaker, the speech seemed to me to be a Pope-like speech; and I fear lest our bishops do attribute this of the Pope's canons unto themselves, — *Papa non potest errare;* for surely, if they did not, they would reform things amiss, and not spurn God's people for writing therein as they do. But I can tell them news. They do but kick against the prick, for undoubtedly they both have and do err, and God will reveal his truth, maugre the hearts of them and all his enemies.

". . . . . The writ, Mr. Speaker, that we are called up by is, chiefly to deal in God's cause; so that our commission both from God and our prince is to deal in God's causes. Therefore the accepting such Messages, and taking them in good part, do highly offend God, and is the acceptation of the breach of the Liberties of this Honorable Council; for is it not all one thing to say, 'Sirs, you shall deal in such matters *only*,' as to say, 'You shall *not* deal in *such* matters?" and so as good to have fools and flatterers in this House, as men of wisdom, grave judgment, faithful hearts, and sincere consciences?

". . . . . It is a great and special part of our duty and office, Mr. Speaker, to maintain the freedom of consultation and speech; for by this, good laws are made that do set forth God's glory and are for the preservation of the prince and State. St. Paul saith, 'hate that which is evil, cleave to that which is good.' Then with St. Paul, I do advise you all here present, yea and heartily and earnestly desire you, from the bottom of your hearts to hate all messengers, talecarriers, or any other thing whatsoever it be, that in any manner of way infringes the Liberties of this Honorable Council. Yea, hate it or them as venomous and poison unto our Commonwealth; for they are venomous beasts that do use it. Therefore I say again and again, hate that which is evil and cleave unto that which is good. And this, being loving and faithful hearted, I do wish to be conceived in the fear of God and in love to our prince and State. We are incorporated into this place to serve God and all England; not to be time-servers; as humor-feeders; as cancers that would pierce to the bone; or as flatterers that would fain beguile all the world. Let us show ourselves a people endued with faith; I mean a lively faith that bringeth forth good works, and not as dead. And these good works I wish to break forth, not only in hating the enemies before spoken against, — messengers, tale-carriers, and such like, — but also in reproving them as enemies to God, our prince, and our State, — for they are so. I would have none spared or forborne that shall henceforth offend herein, of what calling soever he be; for the higher place he hath the more harm he may do. Therefore, if he will not eschew offences, the higher I wish him hanged. I speak this in charity, Mr. Speaker; for it is better that one should be hanged, than that this noble State should be subverted. Well; I pray God with all my heart to turn the hearts of all the enemies of our prince and State, and to forgive them that wherein they have offended; yea, and to give them grace to offend therein no more. Even so do I heartily beseech God to forgive us for holding our peaces when we have heard any injury offered to this Honorable Council. For surely it is no small offence, Mr. Speaker; for we offend therein against God, our prince, and our State, and abuse the confidence by them reposed in us. Wherefore God for his great mercy's sake grant that we may henceforth show ourselves neither bastards nor dastards therein; but that as rightly begotten children we may sharply and boldly reprove God's enemies, our prince's, and our State's. So shall every one of us discharge his duties in this our high office wherein God hath placed us. . . . . . I am thus earnest, I take God to witness, for conscience sake;

for love; for love unto my prince and Commonwealth, and for the advancement of justice. . . . . . Thus have I holden you long with my rude speech; the which — since it tendeth wholly with pure conscience to seek the advancement of God's glory, our Honorable Sovereign's safety, and the sure defence of this noble isle of England, and all by maintaining the Liberties of this Honorable Council, the Fountain whence all these do spring — my humble and hearty suit unto you all is to accept my good will herein; and that this that I have spoken out of conscience and great zeal unto my prince and State may not be buried in the pit of Oblivion, and so no good come thereof."

This Speech seems to have been written, and uttered *memoriter*. We have transcribed it almost entire, as it stands upon the pages of the Journal; although it was not all pronounced.

As a Puritan, Wentworth was taller than his fellows. Not that they were less jealous than he of any encroachment upon their rights, or less resolute to preserve them. But when they heard his unvarnished and burning resentment, his stinging deprecation of a wrong done by the Crown; when they looked up and saw him touching the anointed of the Lord with the rod of his correction; the plea for Liberty was lost in their consternation. They heard only "unreverent and undutiful words."[1] They "stopped his further proceeding before he had fully finished;"[2] perhaps, to forestall unpleasant strife with the queen;[3] perhaps, purely "out of a reverend regard of her Majesty's honor," which he seemed to

[1] D'Ewes, 236. [2] Ibid., 241. [3] Hallam, 151.

have impugned. After excluding him from their presence, the House ordered him under arrest, "to be examined for the extenuating of his fault." The same day he was called to do so in the Star-Chamber, before a Committee consisting of all the Privy Council who were of the House and fourteen other members.[1] This examination was no less remarkable than the Speech.

"Where is your Speech which you promised to deliver in writing?"

"Here it is; and I deliver it upon two conditions. The first is, that you shall read it all; and if you can find any want of good-will to my prince and State in any part thereof, let me answer all as if I had uttered all. The second condition is, that you shall deliver it unto the Queen's Majesty. If her Majesty, or you of her Privy Council, can find any want of love to her Majesty or the State therein, also let me answer it."

"We will deal with no more than you uttered in the House."

"Your Honors cannot refuse to deliver it to her Majesty, for I do send it to her Highness as my heart and mind; knowing it will do her Majesty good. It will hurt no one but myself."

"Seeing your desire is such, we will deliver it to her Majesty."

"I humbly require"—request—"your Honors so to do."

The Speech being now read entire, the examination was resumed by the question,—"You have

[1] D'Ewes, 241.

spoken, here, of certain rumors about the Queen's Majesty. Where and of whom heard you them?"

"If your Honors ask me *as Councillors to her Majesty*, you shall pardon me; I will make you no answer. I will do no such injury to the place whence I came. I am now no private person. I am a public man; a Councillor to the whole State in that place where it is lawful for me to speak my mind freely. It is not for you as Councillors to her Majesty to call me to account for anything that I do speak in the House. But, if you ask me *as a Committee from the House*, I will make you the best answer I can."

"We ask you as a Committee from the House."

"I will then answer. Your question consisted of two points,—where, and of whom, I heard these rumors? I heard them in the Parliament-House; but of whom, I assure you I cannot tell."

"This is no answer, to say you cannot tell of whom; neither will we take it for any."

"Truly your Honors must needs take it for an answer, when I can make you no better."

"Belike you have heard some speeches in the town of her Majesty's misliking of Religion and Succession, but are loath to utter of whom."

"I assure your Honors, I can show you that Speech at my own house written with my hand two or three years ago. So that you may thereby judge that I did not speak it of anything that I heard since I came to town."

"You have answered that. But where heard you it, then?"

"If your Honors do think that I speak for excuse's sake, let this satisfy you. I protest before the living God, I cannot tell of whom I heard these rumors. Yet I do verily think that I heard them of a hundred or two in the House."

"Then of so many, you can name some."

"No, surely; because it was so general, I marked none. And I assure you, if I could tell, I would not. For I will never utter anything told me, to the hurt of any man, when I am not enforced thereunto; as in this case, where I may do as I choose. Yet I have willed to deal plainly with you; for I have of my free will told your Honors as I have. And, if your Honors do not credit me, I will *voluntarily* take an oath, if you offer me a Book, that I cannot tell of whom I heard these rumors. But if you offer me an oath *of your authorities*, I will refuse it; because I will do nothing to infringe the Liberties of the House. But what need I to use these words? I will give you an instance to your satisfying, whereupon I heard these rumors; even such an one as, if you will speak the truth, you shall confess that you heard the same as well as I."

"In so doing we will be satisfied. What is it?"

"The last Parliament" — 1571 — "he that is now Speaker of the House uttered a very good Speech for calling in of certain Licenses granted to four Courtiers, to the utter undoing of six or eight thousand of the Queen's Majesty's subjects. This Speech was so disliked by some of the Council, that he was sent for, and so hardly dealt with that he came into this House with such an amazed countenance that it daunted all the House in such sort, that for ten, twelve, or sixteen days, there was not one that durst deal in any matter of importance. And in those simple matters that they did deal in, they spent more words and time in their preamble, begging that they might not be mistaken, than they did in the matter they spake unto. By the Council's hard handling of the said good Member, grew this rumor in the House: 'Sirs! you may not speak against Licenses. The Queen's Majesty will be angry. The Council, too, will be angry.' This rumor, I suppose there is not one of you here but heard it as well as I. I beseech your Honors to discharge your consciences in this case as I do."

"We heard it, we confess; and you have satisfied us in this. But how say you to the hard interpretation you made of the Message that was sent unto this House?"

Here Wentworth's comment in his Speech upon that Message was recited.

"We assure you, we never heard a harder interpretation."

"I beseech your Honors, was there not such a Message sent unto the House?"

"We grant that there was."

"Then I trust that you will bear me record that *I* made it not. And I answer you, that so hard a Message could not have too hard an interpretation. Can there by any possible means be sent a harder Message to a Council gathered to serve God, than to say, 'You shall not seek to advance the glory of God?' I am of opinion that a Message more wicked than that was cannot be."

"You may not speak against Messages, for none sendeth them but the Queen's Majesty."

"If the Message be against the glory of God, against the prince's safety, or against the Liberty of this Parliament-House, I neither may, nor will, hold my peace. I cannot, in so doing, discharge my conscience; whosoever doth send it. And I say that I heartily repent me, for that I have hitherto held my peace in these causes; and I do promise you all — if God forsake me not — that I will never during life hold my tongue, if any Message is sent wherein God is dishonored, the prince perilled, or the Liberties of the Parliament impeached. And every one of you here present ought to repent you of these faults, and to amend them."

"It is no new precedent to have the prince send Messages;" and two or three instances were cited.

"Sirs! you do very evil to allege precedents in this way. You ought to allege good ones, to comfort and embolden men in good doing; and evil ones, to discourage and terrify men from doing evil."

"But what meant you to make so hard interpretation of Messages?"

"Surely, I marvel what you mean by asking this question. Have I not said, so hard a Message could not have too hard an interpretation? And have I not set down the reason that moved me in my Speech; to wit, that for the receiving and accepting that Message, God hath poured so great indignation upon us that he put it into the Queen's Majesty's heart to refuse good and wholesome laws for her own preservation; which caused loving and faithful hearts to heave with grief, and traitor Papists to laugh the whole Parliament to scorn? Have I not thus said? and do not your Honors think it did so?"

"Yes, truly. But how durst you say, that the

Queen's Majesty had unkindly abused herself against the Nobility and People?"

"I beseech your Honors, tell me how far you can stretch these words of her doing so? Can you apply them any further than I have done; that is to say, in that her Majesty called the Parliament of purpose to prevent traitorous perils to her person, and for no other cause, did not her Majesty send us two bills to that effect, of which we chose first the one, and she refused it, and then the other? And did not her Majesty in the end refuse all our travails? Is not this known to all here present, and to all the Parliament also? I beseech your Honors, discharge your consciences herein, and utter your knowledge simply, as I do; for in truth her Majesty *did* abuse her Nobility and subjects, and *did* oppose herself against them."

"Surely we cannot deny it. You say truth."

"Then I beseech your Honors, show me if it were not a dangerous doing to her Majesty; first in weakening, wounding, and discouraging the hearts of her Majesty's loving and faithful subjects, and thereby making them less able to serve her Majesty; and second, in encouraging her enemies to any desperate enterprise to her Majesty's peril?"

"We cannot deny that it was very dangerous to her Majesty in those respects."

"And is it not a loving act of a subject to give her Majesty warning to avoid danger?"

"It is so."

"Then why do your Honors ask *how I dare* tell a truth, to give the Queen's Majesty warning to avoid her danger! I answer you thus: I do thank the Lord my God, that I never found fear in myself to give the Queen's Majesty warning to avoid her danger. Be you all afraid thereof, if you will; but I praise God I am not; and I hope never to live to see the day when I shall be. Yet I assure your Honors, that twenty times and more, when I walked in my grounds revolving this Speech to prepare against this day, my own fearful conceit did say unto me that this Speech would carry me to the place of prison whither I shall now go, and fear would have moved me to put it out of my purpose. Then I weighed whether in good conscience and the duty of a faithful subject, I might keep myself out of prison and not warn my prince from walking in a dangerous course. My conscience said unto me, that I could not be a faithful subject, if I did more respect to avoid mine own danger than my prince's danger. Herewithal I was made bold; and went forward as your Honors heard. Yet when I uttered those words in the House, 'that there was none without fault, no not our noble queen,' I paused and beheld all your countenances, and saw plainly that those words did amaze you all. Then was I afraid with you for company, and fear bade me to put out those words that followed; for your countenances did assure me that not one of you would stay me up in my course. Yet the consideration of a good conscience and of a faithful subject did make me bold to utter that which followed in such sort as your Honors heard. With such heart and mind I spake it; and if it were to do again, I would with the same mind speak it again."

"Yea; but you might have uttered it in better terms. Why did you not?"

"Would you have me to have done as you of her Majesty's Privy Council do, — utter a weighty matter in such terms as she should not have understood herself to have made a fault? Then it would have done her Majesty no good; whereas my intent was to do her good."

"You have answered us."

"Then I praise God for it."

The Master of Requests here remarking, with some petulance, that Mr. Wentworth would never acknowledge himself to be in fault, nor be sorry for anything he had spoken, he replied:

"Mr. Seckford, I will never while I live confess it to be a fault to love the Queen's Majesty; neither will I be sorry for giving her Majesty warning to avoid danger while the breath is in my body. If you do think it a fault to love her Majesty, or if you be sorry that her Majesty should have warning to avoid her danger, say so; for I cannot. Speak for yourself, Mr. Seckford."

Here the examination ended; an examination of the Committee, quite as much as of the Member from Tregony.

The Committee reported, that the offender "could not say anything for the extenuating of his offence;" and, upon the order of the House, — which, however, was not taken without "sundry disputations and speeches," — he was committed to the Tower until *they* should further consider his case.[1] There he remained until the twelfth day of March, when her Majesty signified that "she did remit her displeasure against him, and *did refer his enlargement to the House.*"

[1] D'Ewes, 236 - 244.

In lauding this act of royal grace, Sir Walter Mildmay, Chancellor of the Exchequer, observed, "that liberty of speech was indeed an essential privilege of Parliament; but that it consisted simply in delivering one's opinions freely; that it became licentiousness when one uttered them impertinently, rashly, arrogantly, and irreverently, without respect of person, time, or place.[1]" Mr. Wentworth was then brought to the bar of the House, where he acknowledged his fault upon his knees, and was "restored to his place, *to the great contentment of all* that were present."[2]

For his positions, he had been justified, in conference, by the Committee; for his character and opinions, he was welcomed back by the House; for the *style*, or "terms," in which he had "uttered" those opinions, he was censured, and craved pardon. He who could say, "no one is without fault, no, not even our noble queen," could also say, "no, not myself." The posture in which he did so, though to us indicative of abjectness, was by no means so in that day. Under like circumstances it was adopted by men of the noblest blood and the proudest spirit. The final proceeding was evidently understood by all parties only as a matter of form, by which no one's principles were compromised, but which was necessary for the adjustment of a difficulty in which all were involved.

We have given this Speech and examination in detail, not only because they reflect the form and features of a large-minded man, but because, in all their prominent points, they are characteristic of the stout and full-blooded Puritan. We here see — conscience trampling upon fear; fearlessness braving sov-

[1] D'Ewes, 259. [2] Ibid., 260.

ereign power; the loyal Commoner withstanding royal encroachment, defending, for a bequest to posterity, his own right to think and to speak, and God's right to a place in the Council of a nation. This was heroism; a heroism which we cannot but respect and admire, however it may have been sometimes goaded to rudeness and asperity of speech.

Such was Puritanism, a child, in 1576. In 1676, in boyhood, it drew the sword on the banks of the Potomac. In 1776, in manhood, and on the Delaware, it threw away the scabbard.[1]

[1] It was Puritanism in the Virginia Company which devised and transmitted to the Colony of Virginia their free and popular Constitution. It was the Puritanism of the Virginia Company, showing itself in freedom of debate, which excited James against them, and made him rob them of their Charter. See Stith's Virginia.

CHAPTER II.

THE GOVERNESS AND THE PRIMATE.

Julio Borgarrucci and the Earl of Leicester. — The Italian enraged against Archbishop Grindal. — Leicester's Sympathy. — The Prophesyings. — Plot to induce a Quarrel about them between his Grace and her Majesty. — Julio engages to Poison the Lady Douglass and the Earl of Essex, for Leicester's Convenience. — The Queen berates the Archbishop, and orders him to suppress the Prophesyings and to reduce the Number of Preachers. — He replies by a Letter, in which he reasons and refuses. — The Queen is angered. — She resorts to her own Prerogative to suppress the Prophesyings. — The Plot successful. — The Archbishop disgraced. — Remarks upon the Supremacy.

1576.

"Have I not carried myself as a godly man, my lord? Have I not forsaken the Religion in which I was baptized? Have I not sought the promoting of the new Religion, these fourteen years in England? And am I to have only a bishop's buffet for my seemly zeal for the Word of God?"

The Earl of Leicester was reclining moodily upon a couch, his face flushed, his lips compressed, his eye fixed upon space as if peering for some one upon whom he would vent his wrath. He made no answer; but turned upon the speaker a look which signified "Proceed."

"For my so much godly example and service to the Church, his Grace of Canterbury giveth me thanks and favor? Not a morsel! By the rood! he balketh me of my wife! In my country, my lord, we use dagger or goblet to avenge such wrong!"

"This is not Italy, most religious sir. Blood leaveth a mark, and telleth tales. An his Grace of Canterbury die of a sudden, — beware of Walsingham![1] Thy drugs and comfits and perfumes be not more subtle in their execution, than he, in tracking whom he will. I tell thee, man, he can find the footprints of a spirit; be they on the ground or in the air! Thou art expert with thine alembics; but had I not been as wary in the manner and circumstance of using thy compounds and distillings, thou hadst long agone given up the ghost, and thy name for godliness. But no wariness of mine can suffice for thy screening, if an English Primate falleth. Smother thy wrath, as I do."

[1] Sir Francis Walsingham had been employed by Elizabeth in several important embassies to foreign Courts, but was at this time of the Privy Council, principal Secretary of State, high in her Majesty's favor, and a servant watchful over her safety. "In his intercourse with others he was reserved and yet insinuating. He saw every man, and none saw him. It was his first maxim, 'Knowledge is never too dear.' He was no less dexterous to work on men's passions than to convince their reason. He would say, he must observe the joints and flexures of affairs; and so could do more with a story than others with a harangue. . . . . . He outdid the Jesuits in their own bow, and overreached them in their own equivocation and mental reservation; never settling a lie, but warily drawing out the truth. As the close room sucketh in most air, so this wary man got most intelligence, being most of our Papists' Confessor before their death, as they had been their brethren's before their treason. To him men's faces spake as much as their tongues, and their countenances were indexes of their hearts. He would so beset men with questions, and draw them on, and pick it out of them by piecemeals, that they discovered themselves whether they answered or were silent. Fifty-three agents did he maintain in foreign Courts, and eighteen spies. For two pistoles an order, he had all the private papers of Europe. Few letters escaped his hands whose contents he could not read and not touch the seals. Bellarmine read his lectures at Rome one month, and Reynolds had them to confute the next. . . . . . He would

"My lord, I cannot."

"Thy purpose, then."

"My lord, I will not. Revenge is an element of my life. It is the air I breathe. It is the blood of my veins. Without it, I die. But I have not vented my tale of wrong. These ten years, through your lordship's favor, have I been known at Court; and in that time, after this fashion hath run my history:—'Good Doctor Julio, ease me of my gout!'—'Most kind Doctor Julio, my child hath the sweating sickness! Help, for the love of God!'—'Most dear Doctor Julio, thy skill is beyond compare; give me a love-potion for a cold-hearted mistress!'—And so, forsooth, Julio Borgarrucci—the wonderful doctor, the kind doctor, the *dear* doctor—hath been their slave; snaring hearts for them; and easing pain; and cheat-

cherish a plot some years together, admitting the conspirators to his own and the queen's presence familiarly, but dogging them out watchfully. His spies waited on some men every hour for three years; and lest they could not keep counsel, he despatched them to foreign parts, taking in new servants. His training of Parry, who designed the murder of Queen Elizabeth, the admitting of him, under the pretence of discovering a plot, to the queen's presence, and then letting him go where he would, only on the security of a dark sentinel set over him, — was a piece of reach and hazard beyond common apprehension. It is a likely report (saith one) that they father on him at his return from France,"—in April, 1573, — "when the queen expressed her fear of the Spaniard's designs upon that kingdom: 'Madam, be content not to fear. The Spaniard hath a great appetite and an excellent digestion; but I have fitted him with a bone for this twenty years, that your Majesty shall have no cause to doubt him; provided, that if the fire chance to slack which I have kindled, you will be ruled by me, and now and then cast in some English fuel which may revive the flame.' . . . . . The queen of Scot's letters were all carried to him by her own servant whom she trusted, and deciphered to him by one Phillips, as they were sealed again by one Gregory, so that neither that queen, or her correspondents, ever perceived either the seal defaced, or the letters delayed, to her dying day." (Lloyd's State Worthies, pp. 512–517.)

ing death. Anon the slave turneth beggar in his turn. The poor foreigner craveth a boon. To one, he complaineth that it contrarieth the Word of God, and the law of Nature, and the law of the land, and the law of hospitality, and the law of good manners, that that mutual due benevolence and that near conjunction of life that ought to be between man and wife should be so many years disturbed. To another, he prayeth with tears, that his wife may no longer be retained from him by a powerful and crafty man nourishing her up in his Popish superstitions. But what booteth it? Who careth for the stranger? Who interposeth with my lord of Canterbury to prevent his decree? This be the return for my services, — I am barred from my wife! The gout is eased; the sick child is made ruddy; the mistress, complaint; and the *dear* doctor may go to the devil! Were I a dog, I might have my mate! Revenge, — my lord! revenge!"

"But the known wife of another man!"

"S' death! Courtiers can away with such paltry impediment, an they will have a mind to!"

"Thou liest in thy throat! I myself did use solicitation for thee with his Grace to my uttermost! So, too, did her Majesty."[1]

"Pardon, my lord! for my thought and speech were of others. I am not ungrateful; but I am boiling for revenge, and in my heat do outrun all but my wrong. His Grace giveth sentence against me; and, by rebuking me openly for having another's wife, hath added insult!"

[1] Strype's Grindal, 297. Nugæ Antiquæ, II. 18, 19.

"A pill too bitter even for a physician to digest."[1]

"Without the sauce of vengeance, — yes, my lord! But for whom ask I vengeance? The sentence was not against Julio only; but against Leicester! The insult was to Julio *and* to Julio's patron! The vengeance I crave is for both!"

"Fool!" shouted the Earl. "Thinkest thou I have not felt the sting! Dost count thy lord and master a dolt that knoweth not, and a craven that resenteth not, when he is brow-beaten and spurned! Thou criest to me for vengeance. Thou shalt have it! not for thine own sake, but mine; not in thine own kind, but mine. No blood. No drug. But revenge, — by God's death I swear it! Peace then! Thy stomach shall be fed."

"Thanks, my lord!" and the Italian's face glowed like the dark cloud on the horizon when the lightning flashes from below; for he knew that his patron's pride was stung, and that his own purpose would be compassed. He ventured to ask, "How?"

"Wouldst know — how? The blow shall come from the Highest."

"From the Queen's Majesty?"

"Troth! She hath raised him up. She shall dash him down. I will pit the Mitre against the Crown; the Crown against the Mitre. Hast thou not known me damn and yet befriend?"[2]

"Throckmorton! 'T was dexterously done!"[3]

[1] Fuller, Bk. IX. p. 163.

[2] Strype's Grindal, 224 – 226, 297. Lodge, II. 157. Life of Hatton, 52. Hayward, 89. Nugæ Antiquæ, II. 18 – 20. Fuller, Bk. IX. pp. 130, 163. Camden, 287.

[3] "We have lost on *Monday* our good friend, Sir Nicholas Throckmorton, who died at my house, being there taken suddenly in great extremity on the *Tuesday before.* His lungs were perished. But a sudden

"Hist, knave! Walls have ears!" and the Earl looked nervously around. "His Grace shall have no grace. He shall forfeit grace by his zeal for grace. He shall fall from grace by dispersing grace."

"My lord speaketh riddles."

"Tush! 't is as clear as a sunbeam."

"Gramercy! yet the sunbeam dazzleth."

"Out upon thee for a flattering knave! Is it not the vocation of my lord of Canterbury to disperse the grace of God?"

"I' sooth, it is."

"And chiefly, withal, by prophesyings. Now through these will I strike him, so that he shall lose her Majesty's grace in behalf of the grace of God."

"Call you prophesying of her Majesty's death dispersing God's grace, my lord?"[1]

"Troth! I do marvel at thine ignorance of godly

cold he had taken was the cause of his death. God hath his soul; and we, his friends, great loss of his body." (Leicester to Walsingham, Feb. 14th, 1570–1; Digges, 47.)

"He had been a great creature of the Earl of Leicester. Some apprehended his sudden death came by poison; but whether by Leicester's means, being in his house when he died, is uncertain." (Strype's Annals, III. 85.)

"As he was feeding hard at supper on salads, he was taken, as some report, with an imposthume of the lungs; as others say, with a violent catarrh; and died not without suspicion of poison." (Camden, 152.)

"He died at supper, eating of salads, not without suspicion of poison; the rather because it happened in the house of one no mean artist in that faculty;" (Fuller's Worthies, III. 280. Lloyd, 544.) "Robert, Earl of Leicester. His death as it was sudden was seasonable for him and his, whose active (others will call it turbulent) spirit had brought him unto such trouble as might have cost him at least the loss of his personal estate. He died, in the fifty-seventh year of his age, February 12, 1570"—1571. (Ibid.)

"It was a tradition in the Throckmorton family, that Sir Nicholas, before he died (which was six or seven days after being taken ill at table), accused the Earl of having poisoned him." (Biographia Britannica.)

[1] *Ante*, Vol. I. p. 202.

affairs, most learned and religious leech! I betoken not *fond and fantastical* prophesyings, such as the statute doth inhibit.[1] Wot you not of prophesyings touching the Scriptures that be now in vogue with the godly?"

"Not I, my lord."

"Hearken, then, good sir. Sundry persons — as well clergy as otherwise — do meet together at set times, by authority and command[2] of the bishop of a diocese, to exercise themselves in expounding of the Scriptures. Thus the ministers — ignorant both in Scripture and divinity[3] — be obliged to study; and the people that be present hearing are instructed in religion.[4] This hath been aforetime in most of the dioceses,[5] and hath been thought of much profit; there being great confluxes of people to hear and learn, and the ministers being forced to read expositors and commentators that so they may acquit themselves in public;[6] for particular texts of Holy Scripture are allotted to them beforehand for them to handle and interpret severally, one after another.[7] All is done in order, and under a Moderator — one of the gravest of them — appointed by the bishop.[8] These exercises I wot of five years gone by.[9]

"But it hath been said, that the Puritans have taken their advantage of these concourses, by broaching their doctrines,[10] to vent controversies concerning

[1] 5 Eliz. Cap. XV.

[2] Strype's Annals, IV. Appendix XXIII. p. 494.

[3] Strype's Annals, III. 472.

[4] Ibid., 133, 325.

[5] Ibid., 472. Strype's Grindal, 296.

[6] Ibid., 219.

[7] Strype's Parker, 460.

[8] Ibid. Strype's Annals, III. 472; IV. 544.

[9] Ibid., III. 133. Strype's Grindal, 175.

[10] Strype's Annals, III. 325.

matters of Church discipline and to call in question the establishment of this Church by Episcopacy;[1] that sometimes a layman doth speak; and that afterward the people do fall to arguing and disputing much upon religion.[2]

"Her Majesty, hearing of these exercises two years agone, did utterly mislike of them, and commanded Archbishop Parker to put them down;[3] which was done. But now, forsooth, our new lord of Canterbury no sooner findeth himself warm in his seat[4] than he setteth himself contrarywise to her Majesty's will, and doth earnestly revive these prophesyings, setting down new rules and orders for the same.[5] Right well he knoweth that great numbers of the clergy are both empty-headed and lazy,[6] and that the people have great need of more frequent preaching for their instruction in the grounds and truth of religion[7] than such dumb dogs can supply. He reckoneth the prophesyings to be colleges, as it were, in the which to store the brains and loosen the tongues of ministers to the edifying of the Church and the saving of souls. In other words, dear doctor, learned doctor, he doth call the business of prophesying the business of God.

"It chanceth that I know his Grace to be a lamb in his own cause; but a lion in God's;[8] and, whatever the Queen's Majesty may be in God's cause, I know her to be a lioness in her own, which is — her

[1] Strype's Parker, 460. Fuller, Bk. IX. p. 122. Heylin's Presb., Bk. VII. Sec. 15.

[2] Strype's Grindal, 220.

[3] Strype's Parker, 460. Strype's Annals, III. 477.

[4] Strype's Grindal, 296.

[5] Ibid., 220.

[6] Ibid., 219, 296.

[7] Ibid., 219.

[8] Fuller, Bk. IX. p. 130.

Supremacy in the Church. An I do rouse her against the prophesyings, I do but rouse him in their defence. It is a quarrel. Neither yields. The weaker falls."

"Bravo! my lord. It will be a heavy fall for his Grace."

"O, Hate! I love thee! A sweeter revenge, methinks, Signor Julio, than sending one to heaven by a drug. It lasts, — it *lasts!* One can *see* one's victim the while. Ha!"

The Italian gloated over this refinement of revenge; and when he had exhausted his praise and thanks, the Earl turned upon him, saying, "There is one on whom thou must do me service to the death, — nay, two.

"You have but to name them, my lord."

"The Lady Douglass."

"The other?"

"Essex, — now in Ireland."

"Speedily?"

"Speedily. They hinder me from the Lady Lettice. I cannot brook it."

"Enough, my lord. Grant me a favor in return."

"Speak it."

"To *touch* my lord of Canterbury."

"What meanest thou? That is arranged."

"I would touch him only with a light affliction; a mild medicament."

The Earl eyed his creature as though he would read his soul; then coolly replied, "And the Lord said unto Satan, Behold he is in thine hand; touch his bone and his flesh, but spare his life."

"My lord, Satan hath misdoubtings touching his Grace, lest he be smitten, — mayhap with impotence of limb, or with loss of hearing, or with a rheum of the eyes, or with some like malady of *bone* or *flesh*." [1]

The fruits of this conference soon began to appear. Leicester, exasperated that his letters to the Archbishop — first, to grant a dispensation to his infamous minion; then, to mitigate the sentence [2] — should have failed, now proceeded to stir the quarrel which he had devised between the Governess and the Primate of the Church. It was in 1574, that the queen had ordered the "prophesyings," or "exercises," to be suppressed; and it was almost immediately upon his accession to the See of Canterbury that Grindal, impressed with their usefulness, revived them under such regulations as he believed would render them inoffensive to her Majesty.[3] The Earl now took advantage of this to bring her jealousy of her Supremacy into conflict with the Prelate's regard for the

[1] This infamous man is thus described by Strype, and in the same way uniformly by all historians who mention him.

"He seems to have been a man of good learning, wrote a good hand,"— an unusual accomplishment in those days, — "and a good Latin style. For his learning the great Earl of Leicester also gave him countenance, and made him his physician: and for some other reason, too (if you dare give credit to the author of Leicester's Commonwealth), namely, for his skill in poisoning; and that he could make a man die in what manner and show of sickness you would, sometimes by a Flux, sometimes by a Catarrh: for which art the Earl was said to make use of him in poisoning of many." (Strype's Grindal, 225.)

I do not discover *what* was the Archbishop's decree against him. Probably it was trifling, for we find a common priest, in 1571, punished only by public penance in a white sheet "for having four wives alive." (Strype's Annals, III. 145.) Besides; in 1578, we hear of Julio in good repute; having pupils committed to his charge; and being "a suitor to the queen *for the reversion of a parsonage* in regard of his pains and labor," — in which he seems to have been successful! (Strype's Annals, IV. 207, 208), — and, in February, 1578–9, as a correspondent of the Countess of Shrewsbury. (Lodge, II. 206.)

[2] Nugæ Antiquæ, II. 18.

[3] Strype's Grindal, 220, 221.

Church of God. This covert mode of proceeding seems to have been resolved upon some time in the month of July; and about the close of September, "the Earl incensed the Queen's Majesty against the good Archbishop. But *all was put on the account* of his favoring these factious meetings."[1] The Earl "filled her Majesty's ears with complaints"[2] that her new Primate was trespassing upon her Prerogative, by being "a great patron" of the very sort of religious services which she had prohibited, and "which, if permitted to take place, would in fine prove the bane of the Church and Commonwealth,"[3] "having too much Presbyterian analogy and classical constitution."[4] She was easily led to apprehend that these "exercises" would excite the people to inquire into, and judge for themselves, matters concerning the State as well as those concerning religion; and that such investigations would indispose them for an absolute submission to her will.[5]

She took occasion, therefore, when the Archbishop next appeared at Court, to reprove him, not only with sharpness, but with anger.[6] She told him that by these meetings the laity were drawn away from their secular occupations; that they were fairs which brought the regular religious market-days into disrepute; that those inclined to Puritanism were trained by them to dislike the established religion, were filled with self-conceit, and with notions which tended to sedition; and that she was resolute to have no more

[1] Fuller, Bk. IX. p. 163. Camden, 287.

[2] Fuller, Bk. IX. p. 130.

[3] Ibid., 121.

[4] Pertaining to Classes or Conferences. Ibid., 130.

[5] Warner, II. 450.

[6] Strype's Grindal, 296. Heylin's Presb., Bk. VII. Sec. 16.

exercises of the sort.[1] She added that the pulpit was grown too common; that there were too many preachers; that she was offended with their numbers; that three or four to a county were sufficient; and that the reading of Homilies was all the people needed for their religious instruction. She then peremptorily required the Archbishop to put down the prophesyings, to abridge the number of preachers, to have Homilies read instead of sermons, and to issue special orders to his Clergy accordingly.[2]

These speeches "exceedingly dismayed and discomforted" the grave Archbishop; "not so much that they sounded very hardly against his own person, ... but most, that they might tend to the public harm of God's Church, whereof the queen ought to be a nursing-mother; and also, to the heavy burthening of her conscience, should they be put in strict execution."[3] But, as neither the time nor her Majesty's temper permitted a full reply, he retired to Lambeth House, "not a little afflicted;" and declared himself unto her Highness by letter. This letter was too remarkable, and too much to Archbishop Grindal's honor, to justify a brief description only. We shall therefore present its most important parts.

"I write," said he, "with mine own hand, that you alone may read it. First of all, I must and will during my life confess, that there is no earthly creature" — the Archbishop had never been a husband[4]" — "to whom I am so much bounden as to your

[1] Fuller, Bk. IX. p. 122. Strype's Grindal, 221, 296. Collier, VI. 567.

[2] Heylin's Presb., Bk. VII. Sec. 16. Strype's Grindal, 221. Collier, VI. 567.

[3] Strype's Grindal, Append. p. 74.

[4] Fuller, Bk. IX. p. 163.

Majesty. . . . . . I do therefore bear towards your Majesty a most humble, faithful, and thankful heart, and that knoweth He who knoweth all things. Neither do I ever intend to offend your Majesty in anything, unless, in the cause of God, or of his Church, by necessity of office and burden of conscience, I shall thereunto be enforced.

". . . . . Surely I cannot marvel enough how this strange opinion should once enter into your mind, that it would be good for the Church to have few preachers.

"Alas, Madam! is the Scripture more plain in any one thing, than that the Gospel of Christ should be plentifully preached; and that plenty of laborers should be sent into the Lord's harvest, which, being great and large, standeth in need, not of a few, but many workmen?"

After having cited the directions of Christ and the practice of the Apostles, and asking, "If the Holy Ghost prescribe expressly that preachers should be placed in every town or city, how can it well be thought that three or four preachers may suffice for a shire?" he continued.

"Public and continual preaching of God's Word is the ordinary mean and instrument of the salvation of mankind. . . . . . By preaching, also, due obedience to Christian princes and magistrates is planted in the hearts of subjects; for obedience proceedeth of conscience; conscience is grounded upon the Word of God; and the Word of God worketh his effect by preaching. So as generally where preaching wanteth, obedience faileth.

"If your Majesty come to the city of London

never so often, what gratulation, what joy, what concourse of people! Yea, what acclamations, and prayers to God for your long life, and other manifest significations of inward, unfeigned love, joined with most humble and hearty obedience! Whereof cometh this, Madam, but of the continual preaching of God's Word in that city?

"On the contrary,—what bred the rebellion north? Was it not Papistry and ignorance of God's Word through want of often preaching? and in time of that rebellion, were not all men of all States[1] that made profession of the Gospel most ready to offer their lives for your defence? Insomuch that one poor parish in Yorkshire, which by continual preaching had been better instructed than the rest, was ready to bring three or four thousand able men into the field to serve you against the rebels. How can your Majesty have a more lively trial and experience of the contrary effects of much preaching, and of little or no preaching?

". . . . . Now where it is thought that the reading of the godly Homilies may suffice, I continue of the same mind I was when I attended last upon your Majesty. . . . . . The godly preacher can apply his speech according to the diversity of times, places, and hearers; which cannot be done in Homilies. Exhortations, reprehensions, and persuasions are uttered with more affection, to the moving of the hearers, in sermons than in Homilies. Besides; Homilies were devised by the godly bishops in your brother's time only to supply necessity, for want of preachers; and are, by the Statute, not to be preferred, but to

[1] Estates; ranks.

give place, to sermons whensoever they may be had.

". . . . . Now for the second point, which is concerning the learned exercise and conference amongst the ministers of the Church. I have consulted with divers of my brethren, the bishops, by letters; who think the same as I do, *viz.* a thing profitable to the Church, and therefore expedient to be continued. And I trust your Majesty will think the like, when your Highness shall be informed of the *manner and order* thereof; what *authority* it hath of the Scriptures; what *commodity* it bringeth with it; and what *incommodities* will follow, if it be clear taken away."

After disposing of the first two points, the Archbishop proceeded to state "the profits and commodities" of these exercises as follows:

"1. The ministers of the Church are more skilful and ready in the Scriptures, and apter to teach their flocks.

"2. It withdraweth them from idleness, wandering, gaming, &c.

"3. Some afore suspected in doctrine are brought thereby to open confession of the truth.

"4. Ignorant ministers are driven to study, if not for conscience, yet for shame and fear of discipline.

"5. The opinion of laymen touching the idleness of the clergy is removed.

"6. Nothing by experience beateth down Popery more than that ministers (as some of my brethren do certify) grow to such a good knowledge, by means of these exercises, that where afore were not three able preachers, now are thirty, meet to preach at St. Paul's Cross; and forty or fifty besides, able to instruct their own cures. So as, it is found by experience the best means to increase knowledge in the simple, and to continue it to the learned. Only backward men in religion and contemners of learning do fret against it."

After stating evils which would result from the discontinuance of these exercises, the Primate addressed himself directly to the issue between himself and the queen.

"I trust, when your Majesty hath considered and well weighed the premises, you will rest satisfied, and judge that no such inconveniences can grow of these exercises as you have been informed, but rather the clean contrary. And for my own part, because I am very well assured that the said exercises are both profitable to increase knowledge among the ministers, and tend to the edifying of the hearers, I am *forced*, with all humility and yet plainly, to profess, that *I cannot with safe conscience, and without the offence of the Majesty of God, give my assent to the suppressing of the said exercises. Much less can I send out Injunctions for the utter and universal subversion of the same.* . . . . . If it be your Majesty's pleasure, for this or any other cause, to remove me out of this place, I will with all humility yield thereunto, and render again to your Majesty that I received of the same. . . . . . Bear with me, I beseech you, Madam, if I choose rather to offend your earthly Majesty than to offend the Heavenly Majesty of God. And now, being sorry that I have been so long and tedious to your Majesty, I will draw to an end, most humbly praying the same well to consider these two short petitions following:

"The first is,—That you would refer all these

ecclesiastical matters which touch religion, or the doctrine and discipline of the Church, unto the bishops and divines of your realm, according to the example of all godly Christian emperors and princes of all ages. For indeed they are things to be judged in the Church, or a synod, not in a palace. When your Majesty hath questions of the laws of your realm, you do not decide the same in your Court, but send them to your Judges to be determined. Likewise for doubts in matters of doctrine or discipline of the Church, the ordinary way is to refer the decision of the same to the bishops and other head ministers of the Church. . . . . . Would to God, your Majesty would follow this ordinary course! You should procure to yourself much quietness of mind, better please God, avoid many offences, and the Church should be more quietly and peaceably governed, much to your comfort and the commodity of your realm.

"The second petition I have to make to your Majesty is this: That when you deal in matters of Faith and Religion, or matters that touch the Church of Christ,—which is his Spouse, bought with so dear a price,—you would not use to pronounce so resolutely and peremptorily, *as if by authority*, as ye may do in civil and extern matters. But alway remember, that in God's causes, the will of God—and not the will of any earthly creature—is to take place. It is the antichristian voice of the Pope, 'So I will have it. So I command. Let my will stand for a reason.' In God's matters all princes ought to bow their sceptres to the Son of God, and to ask counsel at his mouth, what they ought to do. Remember,

Madam, that you are a mortal creature. . . . . . And although ye are a mighty prince, yet remember that He which dwelleth in the heavens is mightier; He is terrible; and He who taketh away the spirit of princes, and is terrible above all the kings of the earth.

"Wherefore I do beseech you, Madam, *in visceribus Christi*, when you deal in these religious causes, set the Majesty of God before your eyes, laying all earthly Majesty aside. Determine with yourself to obey His voice; and with all humility say unto Him, 'Not mine, but thy will be done.' God hath blessed you with great felicity in your reign, now many years. Beware you do not impute the same to your own deserts or policy, but give God the glory. And as to instruments and means, impute your said felicity, *first*, to the goodness of the cause which ye have set forth, I mean Christ's true religion; and, *secondly*, to the sighs and groanings of the godly in their fervent prayer to God for you, which have hitherto, as it were, tied and bound the hands of God that he could not pour out his plagues upon you and your people, most justly deserved. . . . . . I beseech God, our Heavenly Father, plentifully to pour his principal Spirit upon you, and always to direct your heart in his holy fear. Amen."[1]

The yoke of which the Archbishop here com-

[1] Strype's Grindal, Append. pp. 74–85. Heylin's Presb., Bk. VII. Sec. 17. P. Soc.'s Remains of Grindal, 376–390.

There is an evident typographical error in the date of this letter as given by Strype,—"December 20,"—for Grindal, in a letter dated December 16th, 1576, mentions it as having been written "about eight days ago." (P. Soc.'s Remains of Grindal, 391.)

plained, and under which he revolted, had chafed the necks of the Hierarchy from the beginning. So early as 1560 and 1561, it had drawn forth a grave remonstrance from all the bishops. Perceiving her Majesty's bent, they jointly besought her by a written address, that she would not "*strain* them to assent to that which in *their* learning and conscience did tend to the ruin of souls;" and that, instead of arrogating to herself the sole right of settling questions concerning religion according to her own will, it would please her Majesty that such questions "might be referred to be discussed and *decided* in a synod of the bishops and other godly learned men, according to the example of Constantine and other Christian Emperors."[1] Again in 1573, when the Lords of the Council, acting for the queen, restored Mr. Deering to the reading of his Lecture, "without consulting and advising with spiritual men," the act was resented by the Bishop of Ely, and reported surlily by even Parker and Sandys,[2] as a trespass upon the province and functions of the clergy. In complaining to Lord Burleigh of that encroachment, the Bishop cited authorities to show that "it is the proper office of priests to *determine* concerning religion; and of princes, to *assist* them, and to promote and defend true religion."[3] Doctor Cox in this letter doubtless expressed the opinion of all his brethren. But the yoke was keyed; and, until now, no one had protested against its imposition with a resolute tone and spirit and with unvarnished honesty.

When compelled to sit in Commission, Grindal had

[1] Strype's Parker, 97. Strype's Annals, I. 332.

[2] Strype's Parker, 433.

[3] Ibid., 426, 427.

been officially, but with grief and even with tears,[1] involved in the doing of wrong to good men and true; but, against his Mistress's order to level his shaft at the vitals of religion, he rebelled.

The intrepid Prelate went further. He struck the axe at the root of the tree. To justify his refusal, he signified that the queen was infringing upon his office, and questioned the Pope-like authority and tone which her Majesty had come to assume habitually in all the affairs of the Church. In other words, he reflected severely upon her *ecclesiastical* supremacy. He virtually declared in his two petitions — but did it in courtly phrase — that, *as she understood and exercised* it, it was the substitution of her private will and caprice for ecclesiastical precedent, synod, law, and decency; a Prerogative taller than statute, Bible, and conscience; an usurpation; a despotism; and thus the petitions were understood.

So well did the Earl of Leicester affect the friend toward the man whose ruin he plotted, that the Archbishop committed this letter to his hands;[2] believing doubtless that when delivering it to her Majesty he would soften its effect by conciliatory representations. By executing this commission, and by other pretences of sympathy and good-will, the Earl so com-

[1] Strype's Parker, 184.

[2] This fact is sufficient to show the error of the statement made by Fuller and Heylin, that Leicester sought to wrest Lambeth House from the Archbishop, and sought his ruin because he withstood the attempt. Had this been the case, there must have been such *open* variance between them, that the Earl would have been the last person whom the Archbishop would have trusted to do him a friendly office, and especially in so delicate an affair.

Fuller, however, on page 163 (Bk. IX.), states that Leicester was incensed against the Archbishop by the matter of Julio; and therefore stirred the queen about the prophesyings.

pletely imposed upon his victim as to draw from him a special letter of thanks![1]

Of course her Majesty was angered. Leicester had succeeded. The Archbishop was doomed. But, although her Majesty did not conceal her displeasure, she deferred punishment because she needed the culprit's official service in consecrating Whitgift, Master of Trinity College in Cambridge and Dean of Lincoln, as Bishop of Worcester.[2] This done in April, and the Archbishop still refusing to issue orders for the suppression of the prophesyings, the queen assumed the task of doing so in her own name; and on the seventh day of May, 1577, issued a circular accordingly, and under her royal signet, to all the bishops in the realm. "At these assemblies," said her Majesty, "which in some places they call Prophesyings, and in some other places Exercises, are disputations and new-devised opinions upon points of divinity *far unmeet for vulgar* people, who ought to be otherwise occupied with honest labor for their living, but are hereby brought to idleness, ... and encouraged to the violation of our laws and the breach of common order. . . . . . Wherefore, considering . . . . . that by the increase of these, through sufferance, great danger may ensue, even to the decay of the Christian faith, besides the other great inconveniences, to the disturbance of our peaceable government, ... and furthermore considering . . . . . that the aforesaid assemblies, called Exercises, are not nor have not been appointed nor warranted *by* US, or

[1] Strype's Grindal, 222, 224. P. Soc.'s Remains of Grindal, 391; Grindal to Burleigh.

[2] Ibid., 229. Sir George Paule's Life of Whitgift, p. 17, sec. 33.

by our laws,—We will and straitly charge you, that you do cause the same forthwith to cease, and not to be used; but if any shall attempt, or continue, or renew the same, We will you not only *to commit them unto prison*, as maintainers of disorders, but also to advise Us, or our Council, of the names and qualities of them, and of their maintainers and abettors; that thereupon, for better example, their punishment *may be made more* sharp for their reformation.

"And in these things We charge you to be careful and vigilant; as, by your negligence, if We should hear of any person attempting to offend in the premises without your correction or information to Us, We be not forced to make some example in *reforming of you* according to your deserts."[1]

[1] Strype's Grindal; Appendix No. X. pp. 85, 86. P. Soc.'s Remains of Grindal, 467–469. Cardwell's Documentary Annals, I. 373–376.

I am constrained to notice a very singular paragraph in a work entitled "Memoirs of the Life, Times, and Administration of Lord Burleigh," by Rev. Edward Nares, D. D., Regius Professor of Modern History in the University of Oxford. Three vols. 4to. London, 1829–1831.

In stating the queen's interference to suppress the prophesyings, Dr. Nares seems to have had no knowledge of the queen's circular which I have given in the text; for he quotes another letter of her Majesty, "which," he says, "she addressed nominally to the Bishop of Lincoln, but intended probably as a circular for the direction of all the bishops. In this letter," he continues, "she speaks of 'the presumption of some who, by singular *exercises* in public, after their own fancies, wrought no good in the minds of the multitude, easy to be carried away with novelties [and in a manner *schismatically divided among themselves* into a variety of dangerous opinions], which for divers good respects, therefore, she judged requisite to be forborne.'"

Upon the basis of this *pretended* quotation Dr. Nares charges Mr. Neal with misrepresenting the queen's publicly avowed purposes; and with "assurance," in saying that "the queen put down the prophesyings for *no other* reason, but because they *enlightened* the *people's minds* in the Scriptures, and *encouraged* their inquiries after truth." (Vol. III. p. 83.)

The letter which I have given in

Thus were the prophesyings again suspended by royal order. But it is to be particularly noticed in connection with Leicester's agency in this affair,— who always liked the working of Puritan leaven in the Church,—that no sooner was disgrace *fastened* upon Archbishop Grindal, than the obnoxious exercises were revived. Sandys, Archbishop of York, enjoined them upon his clergy in 1578,[1] though "not allowing the laity to be present *promiscuously*.[2] "So that it appears hence," says the biographer of Grindal, "that these Prophesies were still countenanced and practised; and the bishops thought them still the best means for begetting a faculty of preaching, and increasing of learning in the clergy; especially being secured from confusion."[3] In 1581, they were maintained by Chaderton, Lord Bishop of Chester, and continued in his diocese, at least so long as 1585, and "in pursuance of letters from the Privy Council."[4]

the text is sufficient to justify Mr. Neal. But were it not, his "assurance" by no means equals that of the Regius Professor, who, *to make out a point*, has taken the liberty to *interpolate and to italicize words of his own* in the queen's letter to the Bishop of Lincoln. These words I have designated by including them in brackets; and *all* the italics are as in Dr. Nares's work. The letter of the queen to the Bishop is in Strype's Annals, Vol. II. Appendix, Bk. II. No. IX. folio edition; Vol. IV. p. 612, Oxford edition.

This remarkable interpolation is so significant to the student of Puritan history, and the reasons for its exposure must be so apparent, that I forbear comment.

1 Cardwell's Documentary Annals, I. 374, note.

2 Strype's Annals, IV. 164, 165. Strype's Grindal, 299.

3 The Bishop of Ely expressed himself clearly on this point in a letter to Burleigh, dated June 12th, 1577. The letter is in Strype's Annals, IV. 611. He thought them "not unworthily by authority abolished," *because* "not by public authority established." Yet he urged that "her Majesty should considerately weigh the thing, and be moved to further consideration of the matter," as a necessary corrective of "the great ignorance, idleness, and lewdness of the great number of poor and blind priests in the clergy."

4 Desiderata Curiosa, Bk. III. No.

Whitgift having been consecrated Bishop of Worcester, and the royal inhibition of Prophesyings having been issued, her Majesty was prepared to "express her displeasure against the Archbishop in a more public manner."[1] By order of the Lords of the Star-Chamber in June, he was suspended from exercising the functions of his office for six months, and ordered to keep himself in his own house during the same time, — a term allowed by grace for reflection, repentance, and confession. The jurisdiction of the See was de-

XXIX. Strype's Annals, III. 481; IV. Append. pp. 544 – 547, Nos. XXXVIII., XXXIX.; V. 477.

Hallam says, "The prophesyings were never renewed after the queen's circular letter" (p. 121); and Neal the same, "Thus *ended* the prophesyings, or religious exercises of the clergy" (page 144). Warner, too, uses the same language (II. 449). But the documents to which I have referred in the text prove the contrary.

In May, 1581, Archbishop Sandys wrote to Chaderton, Bishop of Chester, "admonishing him for giving way to the Exercises." (Preface to the Letter.) "My lord, you are noted to yield too much to general Fastings, all the day preaching and praying. Verily a good exercise in time and upon just occasion, when it cometh from good authority. But (when there is none occasion, neither the thing commanded by the Prince or a Synod) the wisest and best learned cannot like of it, neither will her Majesty permit it. There lurketh matter under that pretended piety. The Devil is crafty; and the young ministers of these our times grow mad." (Desiderata Curiosa, Bk. III. No. XXIX.)

Why Archbishop Sandys should then condemn the exercises which he had himself cherished only three years before, and while the queen's circular was yet unrepealed, I cannot understand; unless, indeed, Chaderton, unlike his Grace of York, allowed the "laity to be present *promiscuously*." The note is worth citing. It shows how far the repellant elements of Episcopacy and Puritanism operated even then. While the Puritan came to dislike even the commemoration of our Saviour's nativity, *because* the rigid Churchman strictly observed it, the Churchman fancied that "there lurked matter" under "general Fastings, all the day preaching and praying," that they were "pretended piety," that "the Devil" was in them, *because* they were sustained by the Puritan. The like prejudice, on both sides, has obtained to the present day. Happily, however, each is discovering more of the image of his Master in the other; becoming less sensible of antipathies; and more, of affinities.

[1] Strype's Grindal, 229.

puted to others.[1] When the probation expired, his Grace, "still esteeming himself not to have done amiss, would not ask pardon, which supposed a fault." Nor did he appear in the Star-Chamber except by letter; in which he declared the innocence of his doings, and asked a remission of further harshness.[2] The Bishop of Ely had interceded for him with Lord Burleigh and with the queen;[3] so had Hatton, the queen's favorite.[4] But in vain. The royal ban was not removed.

The Archbishop continuing the same in January, 1577–8, the queen was minded to inflict greater punishment; and "there was much talk of depriving him," — degrading him absolutely from the Primacy. This created a great and general sensation. "If her Majesty will be safe," wrote Sir Francis Knollys, "she must comfort the hearts of those that be her most faithful subjects even for conscience sake. But if the Archbishop of Canterbury shall be deprived, then up starts the pride and practice of the Papists, and down declineth the comfort and strength of her Majesty's safety. . . . . . And the thinking thereof doth so abhor me, that I am more fit to die in a private life than to live a Courtier; unless a preventing heart may enter into her Majesty betimes."[5] It was so evident that the degradation of the highest Dignitary of the Church, only for a fault of thinking and of conscience, would excite popular disgust and even resentment, that the design was abandoned; and the queen, who always had an eye open to her

[1] Ibid., 231, 239. Heylin's Presb., Bk. VII. Sec. 18. Collier, VI. 581.

[2] Strype's Grindal, 235, 236.

[3] Strype's Annals, IV. 611, 612.

[4] Life of Hatton, 52.

[5] Knollys to Secretary Wilson, Jan. 9th, 1577–8; Strype's Grindal, 238. Wright, II. 75.

popularity, was fain to content herself with the Archbishop's suspension.[1]

In 1582, his Grace, in a letter to the Lords of the Council, made "a declaration of himself," which seems to have occasioned his partial restoration to his official functions, though not to her Majesty's favor.[2] In this "declaration"—which cannot with propriety be called a "submission"[3]—he stated that while, by reason of scruple of conscience, he had indeed refused to *execute* her Majesty's commands, yet he had never presumed to *resist* or to *counteract* them, when once issued by her circular to the bishops; that from that time he had made no attempt to *maintain* the prophesyings. He "confessed, however, that he was most heartily sorry that her Majesty *had been offended* with him."[4] Soon after this, the good Archbishop became blind.[5]

"He that would not hold by Leicester's favor, must fall by his frown; Archbishop Grindal not excepted." And, "as many in the Earl's time died that knew not

[1] Strype's Grindal, 238, 239.

[2] Ibid., 238. P. Soc.'s Memoir, xiii.

[3] Pierce, 96.

[4] Strype's Grindal, 272.

So only do I understand the document. I therefore think Mr. Strype to be right in saying that the Archbishop "was endued with an immutable constancy of mind in persisting in a thing he reckoned his duty" (p. 300); right also in saying that "he would never be brought to give forth his orders for the putting down of the prophesyings" (p. 296). Mr. Pierce contradicts both these assertions. He must have read Grindal's letter with too little carefulness, or he would never have said, as he has done, "'t is plain, by his submission,"—meaning this letter,—"*he gave out such orders* for his own diocese." Grindal's words are, that "he himself did, in his own bishopric, suffer no such exercises to be used, after the time of her Majesty's commandment." This is very different from giving out *orders against* the exercises. He never did it. The whole paragraph of Pierce is irrelevant; based on a wrong interpretation of words, and therefore, though unintentionally, unjust to a good, consistent, heroic, Christian man.

[5] Strype's Grindal, 277.

their own disease, so many fell" — as Grindal did — "that saw not the hand that pulled them down."[1]

We may have dwelt more upon the particulars of this case than even its intrinsic interest has required; but if we have done so, it has been because these particulars so well illustrate the relation of the Sovereign to the Church. The Supremacy which Elizabeth claimed in ecclesiastical affairs was no idle toy. It was an Autocracy; a sway unshared, irresponsible, unlimited; a power to decree, to inhibit, to require, to punish, according to her own sole will, irrespective of the spiritual profit or loss of her subjects, of ecclesiastical canons, constitutional rights, or statute law. She claimed it, when she insisted that the Act of Uniformity should recognize and designate her right to ordain further ceremonies. She claimed it, when she ordered to prison the *lay* Separatists of 1567, — contrary to the statute.[2] She claimed it, whenever she forbade her Commons to deal with religion. She claimed it, whenever she allowed her Commissioners in her name to impose subscriptions, oaths, fines, imprisonments which the law did not warrant. She claimed it in express words. Most conspicuously did she claim it, when she announced to her highest ecclesiastical Dignitary, that her Will should be his Rule. Most shamelessly did she claim and proclaim it, when she confined his person, and forbade him to use his sacred office who had committed nor breach nor contempt of ecclesiastical canon or act of Parliament.

Nor was this all. What Elizabeth claimed as Governess of the Church had been conceded. By Parlia-

[1] Lloyd, 519, 520. [2] 1 Eliz. Cap. II. Sec. III.

ment, when they conferred upon her the power to ordain rites at will. By her Commissioners, whenever they enforced, by arbitrary terrors, and under color of the power aforesaid, *whatever* she "ordained;" whenever, as her agents, they exceeded statutes and trod upon the necks of freemen. It was conceded, inasmuch as after a while no convict ecclesiastic had remedy in the civil courts against even an illegal sentence. It was emphatically and deplorably conceded when no Court, ecclesiastical or civil, could offer refuge or righteousness to the Prime Functionary of the Church, innocent even of technical wrong.

And when *religious* offenders were arraigned in civil Courts, and the watchword "The queen willeth" constructed the panel, shaped the proceedings, distorted statutes, excluded defensive evidence, swayed Judges, and determined Juries, — it was disgracefully conceded.[1] This we shall see by and by. As we review the past and as we advance upon the future, let us keep in mind the following questions. If, in affairs purely secular, Elizabeth's government was "a limited monarchy," by what, by whom, and when, was it ever "limited" in administering the affairs of the Church? If, in civil cases, her Will was sometimes checked by bold and resolute Judges, when did they ever check it, or attempt to check it, in religious? If, in the former, she sometimes "discreetly receded" before the Majesty of the Law, when did she ever do so, in the latter?[2] Was not her letter to the Bishop of Ely a concise, but exact, transcript of her *ecclesiastical* Supremacy, — "If you do not instantly comply with my wish, by God! I will unfrock you!"

[1] Hallam, 125, 138, 139, note. [2] Ibid., 163, 164, note.

CHAPTER III.

TREASON AND PRÆMUNIRE.

The Convocation of 1576. — A new Ecclesiastical Commission. — The State Policy of Lent. — "Golden" Manor. — Francis Tregian and Cuthbert Mayne. — The Act 13 Eliz. Cap. II. aroused. — The Arrest. — The Trial and Execution of Mayne. — The Trial of Tregian. — Sentence, to have incurred a Præmunire. — Confiscation and Eviction. — The True Wife. — Twenty-eight Years in Prison.

1576, 1577.

The Convocation over which Archbishop Grindal presided, immediately upon his Confirmation in February, passed certain articles, having the authority of ecclesiastical orders, or canons, "touching the admission of fit persons to the ministry, and the establishment of good order in the Church." The most important were, — "that those who were *to be* made ministers must give an account of their faith in Latin, and subscribe the Articles of Religion made in the Synod of 1562–3; that all licenses for preaching dated before the eighth day of that present month should be void, but such as were thought meet for that office, to be admitted again without difficulty or charge."[1]

It is to be observed, that this Convocation — unlike that of 1571 — did not require, in express terms, a

[1] Strype's Grindal, 195.

subscription to "The Articles of Religion" as a condition of *renewing* licenses. It was left for each bishop to judge for himself who in his own diocese *were* "meet." He might insist upon a subscription to *all* the Articles as a test of meetness, or he might not. Yet the words "without difficulty" seem to imply that he should not. This was fortunate; and it was also fortunate that many of the bishops did not; else there would have been a far more deplorable dearth of preachers,—for "in most places the ministry did stand and consist of old Popish priests, tolerated Readers"—of Prayers and Homilies—"and many new-made ministers, whose readings were such that the people could not be edified; and the few of these who could or would preach were such ruffianly rakehells and common cozeners by whose preachings the Word of Truth was become odious in the eyes of the people."[1]

The queen issued a new ecclesiastical Commission, dated April 23d, 1576. The jurisdiction of these Commissioners was—the *whole realm*, in places exempt or not exempt; and they, or *any three* of them were empowered to inquire of all religious offences, "as well by the oaths of twelve good and lawful men, as also by witnesses, and *all other* ways and means *they could devise*." They were also commanded, and any three of them empowered, to punish every

[1] "Discours of the Troubles at Frankfort," p. 194.

This language has the more startling emphasis, when we remember that "The Discours" was *published* in 1575. Although it appeared anonymously, no one would have ventured such a statement on its pages could it have been contradicted. Nor do I find any one of the many annalists who misrepresent the book taking exceptions to the language which I have quoted. The facts were too notorious.

offender "by fine, imprisonment, censures of the Church, *or otherwise*, or by *all* or any of said ways, as to *their* wisdoms and discretions should seem most convenient." They were still further authorized to call before themselves offenders, and persons *suspected* of offences, and persons able to give information of offences, and "to examine all such upon their corporal oaths;" also, to punish those who should disregard the summons, by ecclesiastical censures, or by fines, or by prison, until set free by order of the Commissioners themselves, — all "according to their discretions."[1]

A remarkable *English* reason for observing Fast-days, and particularly the Lent Fast, is forced upon our notice by an Order of the Council to the Archbishop on the thirteenth day of December.

It was a matter of State policy — and wise, being insular policy — that "the numbers of cattle should be increased, and that the abundance of fish which the sea yieldeth should be generally received. Besides, there should be great consideration had for the preservation of a navy and maintenance of convenient numbers of sea-faring men; both which would otherwise decay, if some means were not found whereby they might be increased."[2] King Edward VI. and his Council were of this mind. By Proclamation January 16th, 1547–8, "The king allowed that men should on Fast-days abstain from food of flesh to subdue the body unto the soul and spirit. And also for worldly and civil policy, to spare flesh and use fish for the benefits of the Commonwealth where many be

[1] Strype's Grindal, Append., Bk. II. No. VI. pp. 64 – 70.

[2] Harrison in Holingshed, I. 279.

fishers, ... and that the nourishment of the land might be increased by saving flesh, and especially at the Spring time when Lent doth commonly fall, and when the most common and plenteous breeding of flesh is, ... and that divers of the king's subjects have good livings and riches in uttering and selling such meat as the sea and waters do minister unto us."[1] These reasons were so highly appreciated, that the Parliament which met in the next November enacted a law for observing Fasting-days, which contains the very reasons given in this Proclamation.[2]

But the Puritan aversion to everything which savored of superstition and of slavery to Rome, had turned against ceremonial, periodical Fastings; and thus the Fish-days of the Church had fallen into general disrepute and desuetude. The fishermen found their occupation on the wane, and prayed to the Council for help.[3]

The Council, therefore, interfered; and in terms unusually clear set forth their reasons. Addressing a letter to the Archbishop, they wrote: "The laws for the observation of Embring and Fifty Days are not so duly observed as they ought to be, and as is requisite in policy for the maintenance of Mariners, Fishermen, and the Navy of the Realm. Her Highness hath therefore given strait charge unto her own Household for the observance of those Days; and also, to the Lord Mayor of the City of London and other her Majesty's Officers and loving subjects abroad, to the intent . . . . . the State might take such bene-

[1] Cardwell's Documentary Annals, I. 30 – 33.

[2] 2 and 3 Edward VI., Cap. XIX. Sec. I. Strype's Memorials, III. 128, 129. Fuller's Worthies, I. 33.

[3] Taylor, II. 72, 73.

fit by the laws as was at the time of making intended. Which, we can assure your Lordship, is *the only cause* why at this time the observation of the Days is so much urged. . . . . . We have thought good to require your Lordship to give order within your Province, that the Ministers and Preachers be commanded in their sermons to the people to instruct them to conform themselves and their Families to the said Laws: and further to declare unto them, that the same is not required for any liking of Popish ceremonies heretofore used, (which are utterly detested,) *but* ONLY *to maintain the Mariners and Navy in this Land, by setting men a Fishing*."[1]

Her brother Edward had two reasons; her Majesty, but one. For an island realm, it was a good one.

But we turn to a graver chronicle.

On the southern coast of England, the sea thrusts up an arm into the county of Cornwall, where it holds between the thumb and finger — the Kenwyn and the St. Allen — the small town of Truroe. The whole face of the shire is like the face of a crabbed-looking old man, with just enough of kindly light in its furrows to save him from being voted out of society. The silvery gleams which light the rough face of Cornwall are, the few rivulets which glide here and there through its narrow and verdant glens; such as the little Kenwyn, and her sister the St. Allen, which meet at Truroe, forming two of the prettiest features of a spot remarkable for its varied beauty. About five miles above, the valley of the St. Allen expands into the segment of a circle which may measure a

[1] Strype's Grindal, 226, 227. Cardwell's Documentary Annals, I. 370 – 372.

mile across its chord, and is divided into nearly equal parts by the river.

"Golden" — as this place was called in Queen Elizabeth's day — was a beautiful manor, and had received its name from the abundance and the complexion for which its harvests were remarkable. Its owner, who resided on his estate, was Francis Tregian, Esquire; a gentleman "of ancient and noble descent, and connected with the blood royal." With an accomplished and devoted wife, — a sister of Lord Stourton and a step-daughter of Lord Arundel, — with three young children, with an ample estate, and himself but twenty-eight years of age, his life was glowing with blessing and with promise. But, most unfortunately, he was a Catholic. For this, and for some private piques, certain persons in the neighborhood were bent upon doing him mischief. Nothing was easier; for although a Catholic who did not go to church and receive the sacrament might remain unmolested for years, yet he was hourly liable to arrest and capricious punishment. Besides, there was the law — the terrible law — of 1571. It had been thus far suffered to lie idle and harmless in the Statute Book, like a tiger crouching in his lair; but it was still living and hungry, watching for prey. The late arrival of many missionary priests from the English Seminaries abroad had suggested that it was high time to rouse this statute to action; and, in this particular case, there was the temptation of a fair estate, a moiety of which a conviction under the statute would transfer to those who should enter information against its owner. Of all these things Tregian was aware. They were spectres in his path.

They were thorns in his pillow. Whenever young Francis, or Adrian, or the little Mary, rounded their lips for a kiss, or his wife hung trustfully upon his arm, he would think of the cold looks of the gentry and the shy looks of the peasants, and it would seem to him that Malice was hissing at his ear in derision of his sacred pleasures.

The altered aspect of his neighborly relationships was owing in part to the popular rumor that disguised Seminary priests were scheming treason to Elizabeth and freedom for the Queen of Scots; a rumor which naturally excited fresh jealousy towards every one known as a Catholic. But towards Tregian this jealousy had been intensified by a particular incident.

Some time in the year 1576, a stranger had made his appearance at Golden, and immediately became domesticated in Mr. Tregian's family. He was a young man; of gentlemanly deportment; and had not only been received with welcome, but had been uniformly treated with a deference more than was due to his years, by the entire household. As month after month passed away, and the stories about Douay emissaries grew rife, people began to whisper, and to question one another, about this mysterious idler. It was only found that he had arrived at Truroe in a small coasting hoy from Plymouth. That his history, his nativity, his pedigree, could not be traced; that he was the honored guest of a Catholic; that he had been seen at dusk by a miner, on his knees by the woodside, knocking his breast, with a blue flame flickering over his head, — all this was enough to confirm evil conjecture. He was either from the regions below, or from Douay.

On the eighth day of June, 1577, the bolt exploded of which Tregian had been vaguely apprehensive. A troop of horsemen, armed to the teeth, advanced leisurely along the high-road from Launceston, the shire town, until they reached the avenue leading to the manor-house of Golden, whence they went by spur to the entrance of the mansion and there deployed into a line surrounding it, almost as soon as their presence was discovered. The scene within — the wondering terror of the children, the suppressed, dignified agony of the wife, the consternation of the servants — we leave to the imagination of the reader. It was but the work of a moment for the Sheriff to pounce upon Tregian and the stranger, who was described in the warrant as Cuthbert Mayne, a dangerous Romish priest. These two secured, the house ransacked, and several of the domestics also taken into custody, the whole posse hurried off with their prisoners to Truroe; leaving to tears and desolation a family, but an hour before, peaceful and happy.

At Truroe, the prisoners were arraigned before the Bishop of Exeter, who had a manor there; and, after a brief examination, the priest was committed to prison. Tregian was liberated under bonds of two thousand pounds to appear at the next Assizes for trial as a recusant.[1] It does not appear what particular disposition was made of the domestics; but they were not yet set at liberty. This arrest had been made

[1] They who absented themselves from the worship of the Established Church were called "Recusants," whether Catholics or Protestants, until the Parliament of 1592–3; when the statute 35 Eliz. Cap. II. gave rise to a legal distinction between the two, — the Protestant being called "a recusant;" the Catholic, "a Popish recusant." (Butler, I. 292, 293. Fragmenta Regalia; in the Phenix, I. 195.)

by means of certain unknown residents in the neighborhood who had moved the Privy Council to prosecute the penal laws in the county, and had then lodged information with a Justice against Tregian as a recusant and the harborer of a Seminary priest.[1]

Mayne was brought to trial before the Court of Assize in September at Launceston; and under the Statute of 1571,[2] by which it was made treason to "reconcile" any one to the Church of Rome, or to put in use any superstitious things from that See. It would seem that the offences charged against him were not satisfactorily proved. This, however, was a small impediment to conviction; for the Court charged that a *strong presumption* was equivalent to proof! The jury of course brought in a verdict of guilty. One of the Judges, to be sure, challenged the legality of the proceedings; but this also was a matter easily disposed of. It was referred to the Lords of the Council who — probably influenced less by any special nicety or scruples about "proceedings" than by the policy of showing to lurking priests the reeking teeth and talons of the law — after two months, ordered execution upon the judgment.

There was no soft-hearted delay in obeying the order. On the twenty-ninth day of November, the young priest was dragged upon a hurdle, or wickerwork sledge, from the castle-yard to the market-place of Launceston, — about one fourth of a mile, — where stood a gallows of unusual height. Beneath was a platform, on which was to be acted the closing scene of the tragedy, elevated sufficiently to be in view of

[1] Butler, II. 237, 238.

[2] 13 Eliz. Cap. II.

the crowd who had come to see the pageantry of death according to Church and State. When taken from the sledge, the young martyr kneeled in prayer during a chance moment; calmly ascended the ladder; and would have spoken, when the rope was adjusted, to declare how pure had been his mission and his heart from the taint of treason, and how, knowing his peril, he had cheerfully staked his life, only that he might minister the rites of his religion to those who lacked them and hungered for them. But he was checked, and told to give himself only to prayer. A little grace was allowed him for this; he was murmuring, "*In manus tuas Domine* —;" the ladder was turned; after a few rapid vibrations, the rope was cut; and the half-conscious man fell. Most mercifully, his head struck with great force upon the edge of the scaffold; so that he suffered comparatively little when his palpitating bowels were cut out and thrown hissing upon the fire.

Such, in part, was the punishment of treason.[1] Such, in part, was the punishment of the first Seminary priest convicted under the statute "against bringing in and using superstitious things from the See of Rome." Over a part, we draw a veil; at least for the present.[2]

[1] Holingshed, I. 311. Blackstone, IV. 92.

[2] Challoner, p. 11. Holingshed, IV. 344. Camden, 224. Fuller, Bk. IX. p. 110. Strype's Parker, 360. Carte, III. 543. Lingard, VIII. 150.

Strype and Carte say, that Mayne was "the first priest executed" in this reign, which is not true; for besides those mentioned in the first volume of this work, Thomas Woodhouse, one of Queen Mary's priests, was executed as a traitor on the 19th of June, 1573, for denying the queen's supremacy, — probably under the statute 5 Eliz. Cap. I. Sec. IX. (Holingshed IV. 323. Lingard VIII. 150, note.)

Mayne was the first of the *Seminary* priests — as they were distin-

We turn to the other victim of this prosecution. Before the sitting of the Court by which Mayne was convicted, the enemies of Tregian, unable seasonably to perfect — or, as would seem from what afterwards transpired, to *buy up* — their testimony, effected a postponement of his trial by an order for his appearance before the Privy Council. Thus he was conveyed to London; and, while waiting for his examination, was kept in confinement. At the Council Board, he was charged with recusancy, with entertaining suspected persons, and with countenancing superstitious practices. "Recusancy" was a definable offence; "suspected persons" and "superstitious practices" might have as many definitions as definers. To these two shapeless charges, Tregian seems not to have replied. But his recusancy he acknowledged; and pleaded in justification, that though loyal in his very heart to the queen and to her government, his conscience would not permit him to obey her laws pertaining to religion. This was, doubtless, the simple and sufficient truth.

When the examination was concluded, he was told by Walsingham, that he could not be discharged, because other informations against him were expected from Cornwall; which certainly implied that what had been alleged was not sufficient to detain him either in prison or under bonds. He was therefore treated with all the courtesy due to a gentleman of his station not yet convicted nor plausibly impeached. The noble-hearted Earl of Sussex welcomed him as a

guished who came as missionaries from the English seminaries abroad — who was executed *under the law of* 1571; and so, doubtless, Strype and Carte intended to have said.

guest, and advised him as a friend to the only course which would avail to his deliverance; assuring him that his prosecution should be stopped, that he and his servants should be released, and that he would probably secure the queen's special favor, if he would only *appear at church.* The proposition involved a sacrifice of religious principle, and was declined.

At length his prosecutors were ready. In the latter part of November, they preferred new and distinct charges,—that he had been present at the celebration of Mass; that he had received and dispersed *Agni Dei;* and that he had aided, comforted, and entertained those who asserted the Pope's Supremacy. Upon these charges, he was committed to close confinement in the Marshalsea prison, and even debarred from all correspondence with his family,—not only a wanton aggravation of his affliction, but a great detriment to his financial affairs. His counsel—it was rarely that such assistance was allowed to those who were prosecuted by the Crown[1]—his counsel strove hard that he should be tried in the Court of the King's Bench. But his enemies, fearing the influence of his friends in London, some of whom were in station and power, prevailed that he should be remanded to take his trial in Cornwall. They took care also, that on the long journey thither—after ten months in the Marshalsea—he should ride with the appointments befiting a vagabond, and under guard of a professed enemy; a man of brutish heart and vulgar manners, who never intermitted those annoyances and indignities which low malice

[1] Lord Auckland's Principles of Penal Law, second edition, page 198, as quoted by Butler, I. 402, 403.

can so liberally invent, until he had safely lodged him in Launceston castle. Here it was necessary that he should again wait for trial. By and by it came. Let us look at some of its particulars, — for they throw a ray or two upon the character of Elizabethan criminal courts.

"The most material witness" to support the charges was "a strolling fiddler;" and from the character of his testimony we may fairly presume, that they "who owed Tregian a malice" had manufactured it for his mouth, and that he gave it on a bribe. This man had been hired by Mr. Tregian, and allowed entertainment among his domestic servants, during the Christmas festival of 1576, and apparently upon like occasions before, to assist at the merry-makings of his neighbors and tenants. He "deposed," that he had sometimes seen Tregian go to Mayne's chamber for an hour, and that he *conjectured* it was to attend Mass! He further deposed that at Christmas, 1575, he had been Mayne's bedfellow; and that Mayne had then avowed himself to be a priest just from Rome, and the bearer of a number of Agni Dei.

Other evidence was produced; but less pertinent to the indictment. The trial hinged upon the deposition of Twig. The prisoner was graciously permitted to make exceptions. He did except. He made it appear, "by questioning," that Twig, the witness, did not even know where Mayne's chamber was; but the queen's counsel replied that "such circumstances were not material!" He then submitted to the Bench, whether Mayne, known as a cautious man, could have avowed himself a priest to a stranger and a vagabond? and further, whether a strolling fiddler would ever have been consigned as a bedfellow, in a gentleman's house, to an educated and refined man like Mayne? Moreover, he offered to prove by forty witnesses that Mayne had never been at Rome; that, during the Christmas of 1575, he was not in England, but in Douay; that he did not come over until Easter; and that, by consequence, Twig had perjured himself! But "it was an unusual thing to examine witnesses against the Crown."[1] Besides; Tregian, not anticipating such lies, was not prepared with rebutting witnesses. The Judges therefore replied, that "it was a frivolous thing to mention them, and that the trial could not be put off!" So the jury were left to consider matters as they stood.

Now, when defensive evidence was inadmissible; when to prove a witness perjured was frivolous, or, if not frivolous, a reflection upon the Crown not to be permitted; when testimony to conjectures and monstrous improbabilities was allowed and received; when "it was a common and lucrative practice for sheriffs to return juries so prejudiced and partial"—that is, so sure to the prosecution—"that they would find Abel guilty of the murder of Cain,"[2] what could Tregian do? One thing,—what the Earl of Sussex had proposed. At this critical juncture, it was proposed again. While the jury were out he was importuned *only to come to church.* It was *promised* him, that if he would do so, *the prosecution should be dropped.* Had he acceded—it would have saved him. But he held fast to his integrity, and again refused!

[1] Lord Auckland, 5th edit., p. 106, quoted by Butler, I. 378, note.

[2] Lord Auckland, 2d edit., p. 198; by Butler, I. 403.

The jury returned. The verdict was rendered;—Guilty of each article in the indictment; recusancy; being present at Mass; entertaining one who maintained the Pope's Supremacy; receiving and dispersing Agni Dei. For some reason, not apparent, judgment was deferred until the next Assize.

The unfortunate man now turned to the only remaining source of hope. The intercession of his friends who had interest at Court might avail to the mitigation of his sentence. He therefore despatched a servant to London with money to cancel certain debts, and with letters to his friends giving an account of his trial and asking them to plead that, in consideration of the kind of evidence, the extreme penalty of the law might at least be abated. His friends, however, made no effort; not because they were untrue or without influence, but because his letters were never received. It happened—*somehow*—that his servant was arrested at Honiton, less than a quarter of the way to London, rifled of everything in his possession, and shut up in prison!

At the next term of Assize, Tregian's counsel made a vigorous remonstrance against the giving of sentence. They urged that it had not been made to appear that Tregian was privy to Mayne's act of bringing in superstitious things from Rome, nor that he himself had received them, nor that he had attended Mass, nor that he had abetted or countenanced Mayne in denying the queen's Supremacy; that nothing had been produced to sustain these points, but sheer presumptions; in short, that no one fact had been made out, but *recusancy*.[1]

[1] So reads the narrative. Yet, so far as we can see, it could hardly

But this availed nothing. Judge Manwood pronounced sentence that Tregian had incurred a præmunire; that is, the forfeiture of all his estate and imprisonment for life, or during the queen's pleasure. In a few minutes, the convict found himself alone, in a filthy dungeon, without bed, stool, or glimpse of light, or ray of hope. Thus was a young husband and father blasted. But yesterday, gracing society and looking forward to years of rural quiet and domestic enjoyment; to-day, a homeless, beggared outcast! All this — for conscience sake! for religion! for serving and worshipping God as he thought he ought to do, when the State told him he might only serve and worship as he thought he ought not to do! Whatever apology may be made for a law which wrought such doom — a point to be noticed hereafter — in this case, its apologetic reasons were utterly inapplicable and its operation a wrong which cried unto Heaven. In this case, and in Mayne's, the prosecution made no pretence that there was a crime; no pretence that wrong had been done to society; no pretence that mischief had been done, or intended, to the State. Nothing was alleged but certain acts purely religious, beginning and terminating with the actors and God. At best, the punishment in the one case was a diabolical retribution for *constructive* treason; in the other, the pains and

have been denied that Tregian did, contrary to 13 Eliz. Cap. II. Sec. IV., "aid, comfort, and maintain, *after the fact*, one who had brought in superstitious things from Rome."

Although this precise point does not appear in the charges or in the verdict, it was doubtless considered to be embraced in both. The counsel seem to have evaded it, or ignored it. It is but justice to say, that the penalty prescribed by the statute for *this* offence was the penalty adjudged by the court.

penalties of a præmunire for *a constructive privity to a constructive treason.*

Such was law, such was humanity, such was baptized civilization, under the Reformed Church of England in her youthful vigor! Such are the fruits of Religion when grafted upon the State,—the body, to perdition; or conscience, to the devil! Contrary to Nature, it beareth not of its own, but partaketh of the root and fatness of the State!

As this is the only case of a præmunire which we shall adduce, we will trace further its "pains and penalties." And first, let us change our stand-point.

The voice of gladness had ceased in the Manor-House of Golden. The young wife, with the exception of occasional visits to her husband, had been engrossed by the duties of a mother, which had served to mitigate the suffering of her bereavement and suspense. When the tidings came of her husband's doom, the night which he passed in his dungeon was as sleepless to her as to him. For him, she could only weep and pray; for her children, she would act. But how? The question was quickly resolved.

The next night, at midnight, she was roused by the rapid approach of horsemen, succeeded immediately by rude and clamorous demands for admission, and by threats to force an entrance if denied. Resistance would have been folly. Bolts and chains were of course removed, and the house was immediately entered by the party who had ridden post from London to take possession of the confiscated goods and estate; so well had Tregian's persecutors been assured at what time his spoils would be ready for the gathering. The whole family were instantly thrust out of doors, and told to shift for themselves. The shock of such barbarity roused Mistress Tregian's womanly daring, and she instantly resolved upon a journey to London, — two hundred and fifty miles, — although expecting very soon to become again a mother. By some means, she procured horses, packed her three frightened children in panniers, soothed them as well as she could, and before daylight, with a man-servant and a maid-servant, resolutely commenced her journey. When about half way, she fell in labor, and gave birth to a daughter. This addition to the family, says the narrative which we follow, "was of some service — *to balance the panniers!*" With only a minimum of rest after this event, the journey was accomplished. As all Mr. Tregian's estate, even to his mother's jointure, was seized, and all his goods, his wife had no resource for support but the charity of friends! — Relying upon this, the heroic woman followed the royal Court as a suitor more than a year.

In the mean time, Tregian, after only one night in the horrible dungeon of the common jail, had been lodged again in the castle. Here, through his poverty, he was almost starved; but he alleviated his wretchedness as well as he could by religious studies and devotions, and by writing, — a pin for a pen, candle-snuff and water for ink. An apparent attempt to assassinate him — suborned by those who had been enriched by his spoils, and who feared that at some time he might be able to dispossess them — alarmed him. He feared a second attempt might succeed, and brand his name as a suicide. This nerved him to escape. He was foiled. For punishment, or for security, or for both, his prison apartment was changed. And here we are indebted to the contemporary writer, from whose manuscript this narrative is derived, for a specimen of the prisons of the time. Tregian was loaded with thirty pounds of irons, and thrust into a dungeon of the castle where were twenty felons whose persons, habits, foul language, and low malice were insufferably offensive. If we bear in mind to what sort of jests, tricks, and insults, men who have abandoned themselves to degradation profusely and laboriously resort on purpose to torment one accustomed only to the amenities of polite life, when misfortune throws him into their circle and their power, we can imagine the sufferings of Tregian in this den of vulgarity, profanity, and vice. Add to this, that the dungeon was at once lodging-room, eating-room, and *latrina*, — and the revolting picture is complete. Even the jailer was moved to relenting; and after a month restored Tregian to his former apartment above.

At length his lady obtained a warrant for his removal to the King's Bench prison in Southwark. To meet the officer's exorbitant fee of fifty pounds for transportation, the devoted wife sold her best apparel and some other valuables; and, this being insufficient, suffered the rest to be contributed by her friends. Afterwards Tregian was removed to the Fleet prison. He bore his confinement with good heart, and for the most part with unimpaired health, during twenty-eight years, — thanks to a noble and devoted wife who, after his removal from Launceston, shared his prison, nursed him when he drooped, and presented him with eleven more children while yet a prisoner.

In the Journal of the English College at Douay is the following entry: "July, 1606, one Mr. Tregian, an ancient gentleman, after thirty years' imprisonment," — an error of two years, — "arrived here on his way to Spain." When Elizabeth died, the king of Spain interceded with King James for Tregian's liberation, which was granted on condition that he would abjure the realm. This being consented to, and once more a free man, Tregian had rested at Douay on his way to the Court of his royal intercessor. Two years afterwards, he died at Lisbon.

Such is the outline history of a Præmunire.[1]

[1] Butler, II. 237 – 247; from a MS. written in 1593. Lingard, VIII. 151 and note.

CHAPTER IV.

BISHOP AYLMER AND THE MAGICIANS. — PRESBYTERIAN ORDINATION RECOGNIZED.

Sandys consecrated Archbishop of York. — Aylmer consecrated Bishop of London. — Astrology. — Necromancy. — The Pranks of Magicians against her Majesty. — Her Sufferings. — The Physicians bewildered and baffled. — Bishop Aylmer triumphs. — William Whittingham ordained at Geneva. — Installed Dean of Durham. — Excommunicated by Archbishop Sandys. — The Case referred to a special Commission. — The Commissioners disagree. — Another Commission. — Whittingham charged with being "a mere Layman." — Testimony to his Ordination by Presbytery. — The Testimony, only, questioned. — Whittingham dies while the Case is pending. — Its Points stated and considered. — The Church of England allows the Validity of Non-Episcopal Ordination.

1577–1579.

Edwin Sandys, Bishop of London, was confirmed as Archbishop of York on the eighth day of March, 1576–7, and installed in his new office on the thirteenth day of the same month; the See having been nursed for the queen thirteen months.[1]

On the twenty-second day of the same month, John Aylmer was confirmed, and on the twenty-fourth consecrated, Bishop of London.[2] This was the man who wrote the description of women, so remarkable for its classic elegance, which has been given in a former chapter.[3]

[1] Strype's Annals, IV. 42. Strype's Grindal, 228.

[2] Ibid., 228. Life of Hatton, 58. Strype's Aylmer, 28.

[3] Vol. I. p. 254.

In 1578, he distinguished himself by adroitly ending an affair which had long kept her Majesty, her Cabinet, and her whole Court in a turmoil, and had tasked men of the highest scientific attainments. Although it was in no wise ecclesiastical or political, we will relate it, because it illustrates the superstition of the day, and the transcendental importance of royal discomfort.

In January, 1577–8, one Simon Penbrooke, known as a "figure-flinger," or astrologer, was convented before a court holden in Southwark, in the parish church of St. Saviour's. This was not because he consulted the stars and cast nativities; for the highest in the realm countenanced such things. The queen herself had had recourse to the stars "to find out a lucky day for her coronation;" and the Lord Treasurer had cast her nativity to gain light upon the question of her marriage.[1] Penbrooke was convented because he was "vehemently suspected to be a sorcerer," or necromancer; one who could command the agency of spirits to work his designs, — an art generally believed, but abhorred, by Churchman and Puritan, by prince and beggar. As the Judge was entering the church, and while Penbrooke was conversing with his Counsel, he leaned his head forward upon the pew in which they two were standing, and suddenly, with a gurgling in his throat, expired. On his person were found "five devilish books of conjuration," the image of a man made of tin, and other like things; whereupon the Judge remarked that this sudden death "was the just judgment of God towards those who

[1] Taylor, I. 75, 272. Mackay, I. 153. Strype's Annals, III. 23; IV. Append., Bk. I. No. IV.

used sorcery, and a great example to admonish others to fear the justice of God;" and, adds the chronicler, it "was an illustration of Leviticus xx. 6: 'The soul that turneth after such as have familiar spirits, and after wizards, to go a whoring after them, I will even set my face against that soul, and will cut him off from among his people.'"[1]

About the same time — perhaps a little before, in the same month[2] — three waxen images were found near Islington, in the house of a priest, a reputed magician; one of them representing her Majesty; the other two, apparently, Burleigh and Leicester. Each of these images was pierced through the breast with "a great pin." This looked like a diabolical contrivance to bring about the deaths of these three personages. Her Majesty and her confidential advisers were in great alarm. Messenger after messenger was sent from Richmond, where the Court then was, for Doctor John Dee, a man about fifty years of age, in whom the queen had great confidence, and whom she had before consulted, as one versed in occult science.[3] He found the Privy Council in pos-

[1] Holingshed, IV. 344; Stow's continuation. Strype's Annals, IV. 206.

[2] Ibid. and Taylor, I. 273 compared.

[3] John Dee was born in London in 1527, and entered the University of Cambridge at the age of fifteen years. Eighteen hours every day to intense study, four to sleep, and two to refreshments, was his regular and voluntary allotment of his time. Such untiring zeal and labor would have made him a prince of learned men and a blessing to his generation, had they not been diverted, after a while, from true science and philosophy, to false. This raised suspicion of sorcery, and brought him into peril.

"On the accession of Elizabeth, a brighter day dawned upon him. During her seclusion at Woodstock, her servants appear to have consulted him as to the time of Mary's death. They now came to consult him more openly as to the fortunes of their mistress; and Robert Dudley, the celebrated Earl of Leicester,

session of the mystic image of her Majesty, to which they pointed him, requiring him "to prevent the mischief which they suspected to be intended against her Majesty's person." This he did, "within a few hours, in godly and artificial manner." The result was then announced to her Majesty by Mr. Secretary Wilson, in presence of the Doctor and the Earl of Leicester, as she sat without the Privy Park, by the landing-place. This report was "to the satisfying of her Majesty's desire;" and the anxiety of the Privy Council was abated.[1]

In the month of April, however, there was reason to fear that the influence of such diabolical machinations as those of Penbrooke and the priest had not

was sent by command of the queen herself to know the most auspicious day for her coronation. So great was the favor he enjoyed, that some years afterwards Elizabeth condescended to pay him a visit at his own house."

He lived by astrology, but expended his chief labors to find the philosopher's stone and the elixir of life. By the stone, he expected to establish intercourse with spirits, — *good* ones, — and to become their pupil in the mysteries of the universe. At last, as he fancied, the effulgent Archangel Uriel brought it to him, and he began his novitiate in diving into the secrets of futurity, by using the talisman as a vehicle of angelic instructions. The great difficulty in this case was, — he never could remember what the angels told him.

After trying vicissitudes and unremitting studies at home and in Poland, he returned, thinking he had found the secret of transmuting base metals to gold. Of course Elizabeth could well afford him kind words; for a maker of gold could not be supposed to need it. However, his wants were such that he received small sums at various times from her Majesty; and "finally, a small appointment as Chancellor of St. Paul's Cathedral, which he exchanged in 1595 for the wardenship of the College at Manchester. He was reduced at last to the precarious life of a common fortune-teller, and often sold or pawned his books for a dinner. He died in 1608, in the eighty-first year of his age, having toiled incessantly for threescore years and ten, and done no good.

The inquisitive reader will find a larger account of this man in Mackay's Memoirs of Popular Delusions, I. 152–163; from which the above sketch is taken.

[1] Taylor, I. 273; Dr. Dee's account.

been completely neutralized. Her Highness had a grievous toothache. A royal toothache makes itself felt throughout a large and important circle. It is not to be presumed that this affliction made the queen cross, but it excited commotion alike in the Privy Chamber and in the Privy Council. It not only tormented her Majesty, but her whole Court, and the whole corps of her physicians, who "differed as to the cause and as to the means of cure."[1] It being a question "whether it were the effect of this magic" mentioned above, — for Penbrooke, against whom Doctor Dee directed no countercharm, seems to have had the credit of it as much as the priest, — "or proceeded from some natural cause,"[2] of course, the proper remedy could not be determined, or, in professional phrase, "was not indicated." Some of the faculty were of the opinion that if the tooth were somewhere else it would not ache; but they were afraid to tell her Majesty. They applied to Burleigh to do it. Burleigh was afraid, and wrote to Hatton. Hatton was afraid, and only laid the letter in the queen's way.[3] The queen was afraid, and the pain continued.

The trouble occurred again in October. Walsingham persuaded her Majesty "that her own physicians should confer upon the case with some of the most experimented physicians in London."[4] This was done; and her Majesty's physician, Doctor Bayley, consulted "diligently" with Doctor Dee,[5] and probably with others. But no good resulted. Her Majesty

[1] Strype's Aylmer, 293.
[2] Strype's Annals, IV. 207.
[3] Life of Hatton, 50.
[4] Ibid., 94.
[5] Taylor, I. 273; Dee's narrative.

"took no rest for divers nights, and endured very great torment night and day."[1] What *but* magic could have defied such professional skill?

At length in December, the queen "had no intermission of the torment day nor night, and it forced her to pass whole nights without taking any rest."[2] The Court physicians were again summoned; but they still differed as to cause and cure. As a last resort, the Lords of the Council sent for a certain learned "outlandish physician who happened to be at Court," and commanded him to give his opinion in writing respecting the queen's extremity. This he did in an elaborate Latin letter. "He was overwhelmed," he said, "with a sense of his responsibility in expressing an opinion upon a case so august. It was dangerous to do so, when so many most illustrious and learned men, who were continually in the service of her Majesty, were doubtful of the cause of her affliction, and even disagreed among themselves; dangerous for him, a person of humble acquirements and who had never talked face to face with royalty." He then diffidently prescribed various remedies. "But," he concluded, "should they fail, let her Majesty deliberate whether it be not better that the tooth should be drawn even with some pain, than to pass so many sleepless nights and tormenting days." If her Majesty tried the mild applications recommended, they were ineffectual; and her case wore more and more the aspect of a diabolical one, which certainly might with more propriety, and at an earlier day, have called for the intervention of the clergy. She had a nervous horror of chirurgical implements;

[1] Strype's Annals, IV. 207.

[2] Strype's Aylmer, 292.

being of the opinion that they would hurt "acutely." It was reserved for the new Bishop of London to effect relief.

"Madam," he said one day, being in her presence, "have it out!"

Her Majesty looked up as if amazed at his audacity; then shuddered, — for Elizabeth had sensibilities.

"But I assure your Highness it will not hurt much."

The queen shook her head.

"But, Madam, I will prove it! I am an old man, and have few teeth to spare; but one I will spare to make good my word, and in hope of procuring your Majesty ease. Master Surgeon! try your skill on me. Hurt, if you can; albeit I defy you. Out with one of my teeth!"

It was quickly done. The loyal Prelate did not wince.

"See you not, Madam, it be as I told you? It be a very trifle, and is over in a twinkling!"

Her Majesty was amazed; convinced; persuaded. She instantly followed the clerical example, and the tooth and the ache were gone together, — magic or no magic. Bishop Aylmer had effected in a few minutes that which statesmen and learned doctors had labored for months, and in vain, to do. So much less effective is counsel than example.[1]

When Doctor Cox and his party had broken up the original congregation of the exiles at Frankfort, William Whittingham with some others retired to Geneva. He there married Catharine, a sister of John

[1] Strype's Aylmer, 294.

Calvin;[1] was chosen by the English congregation to be their pastor, and was accordingly set apart to the office of the Gospel ministry. He remained there with a few others, a year and a half after the accession of Elizabeth, in order to complete the publishing of "The Geneva Bible."[2] In 1560, he accompanied the Earl of Bedford on an embassy to France;[3] and, soon after, went as chaplain to the Earl of Warwick — Leicester's brother — during his defence of New Haven. Although while officiating there his influence was openly against the rites and ceremonies of the English Church, he won the highest esteem of the Earl, who procured for him, through the intervention of Leicester, the Deanery of the church of Durham. He entered upon the duties of this office in 1563; and soon after preached before the Court.[4] When Sir William Cecil was created Lord Burleigh and Lord Treasurer, he was nominated to fill his place as Secretary of State, and might have had the office had he wished it. "He also did good service against the rebels in the north in 1569."[5]

Although it was well known that he had received Orders at Geneva, this had been no objection to his preferment in the Church of England. Nor had he been annoyed, save by a temporary suspension from office in 1564[6] for his non-conformity. This was doubtless owing, in part at least, to the sympathy and protection of his bishop, Pilkington, who as well as himself had remonstrated at that time to Leicester

[1] McCrie, 427.
[2] Strype's Annals, I. 343.
[3] McCrie, 427.
[4] McCrie, 427. Strype's Annals, I. 545, II. 88. Wood's Athenæ, I. 448.
[5] Wood, I. 448.
[6] *Ante*, Vol. I. p. 238.

against the compelling of strict conformity. Pilkington died in 1576;[1] and the See of Durham was still vacant when Sandys was translated to York. Sandys is represented to have been "as strenuous a supporter of conformity as Parker, or as, in after times, Laud himself."[2] In the year 1576–7,[3] immediately upon his entrance upon his new See, he commenced a visitation of his Province in person; particularly to inspect and set in order the church of Durham, "hearing of some irregularities there, and that Whittingham was no ordained minister according to the order of the Church of England." The Dean and the Chapter denied his right of visitation there, while he claimed it as Archbishop of that Province, — the Bishopric of Durham being void. This led to a quarrel between that church and the Archbishop, which his Grace chastised by summarily excommunicating the Dean. Upon the question of the right of visitation, Fleetwood, the Recorder of London, wrote to Lord Burleigh, then absent from the city: "There is a broil of excommunication between my lord Archbishop of York and the minister of Durham about the visitation. I think my lord Bishop is in the wrong."[4] A special Commission was ordered by the queen to inquire into the case.[5] The Archbishop justified his proceeding on the grounds, — "that it was not lawful for Whittingham to hold that Deanery in respect of his defect therein; and that he was worthy of deprivation because his ministry was not warranted by the law of

[1] Strype's Annals, IV. 52.
[2] Taylor, II. 70.
[3] Strype's Annals, IV. 168.
[4] Ibid., 107.
[5] Ibid., 106, 107.

the land, being ordained by a few lay persons in a house at Geneva."[1] Upon the latter point, the Archbishop laid so strong stress, that the former, which was certainly true in law, seems to have been lost sight of entirely;[2] which is the more to be noticed because soon after — February 11th, 1577–8 — Richard Barnes, — then the new Bishop of Durham, and as rigid a Precisian as Sandys, — wrote to Burleigh that "they of the County of Durham are a stubborn, churlish people, who show but, as the proverb is, *Jack of Napes* charity in their hearts; . . . . . only that Augean stable, the church of Durham, exceeds, whose stink is grievous in the nose of God and man, and which to purge far passeth Hercules's labors." This meant, that "the clergy neglected the habits, and deviated from the orders, appointed to be used in divine service."[3]

By reason of differences of opinion between the Commissioners, they came to no result.[4] Matthew Hutton, Dean of York, whose admirable letter to Lord Burleigh has been largely quoted in a previous chapter,[5] was one of their number; and he expressed the opinion, that "Whittingham was in better sort ordained than our ministers in England, and that his ministry was much better than the Archbishop's was."[6]

Another Commission was therefore issued in 1578, dated the fourteenth day of May, "to visit the cathedral church of Durham, and to require and see the letters and muniments whatsoever of the Dean,

[1] Strype's Annals, IV. 168.
[2] Ibid., 167, 170.
[3] Ibid., 108, 109.
[4] Ibid., 169.
[5] *Ante*, Vol. I. pp. 468 – 472.
[6] Strype's Annals, IV. 168; V. 468.

Prebendaries, Canons, as well for their Orders as benefices obtained by them, and them diligently to examine and search; and, if they found any of them not sufficient in that behalf, to dismiss them from their offices and benefices." The Commissioners named were, the Archbishop of York; Henry, Earl of Huntington, Lord President of the North; Richard, Bishop of Durham; John, Bishop of Carlisle; Matthew Hutton, Dean of York; and several others.[1]

The Commissioners met on the fifteenth day of November at York.[2] Immediately upon the conclusion of the preliminary formalities, it became manifest that it was intended to deal only with the Dean at this time; against whom thirty-five articles and forty-nine interrogatorics were ready drawn to be put into court, of which none of the Commissioners — except, of course, the Archbishop — had been apprized. This led to discussing what branch of their Commission should be first taken up; in which so

[1] Strype's Annals, IV. 169.

[2] Wright, II. 95; Secretary Wilson to Leicester.

There is some obscurity in this note of Doctor Wilson; for which reason, although it indicates the sentiment at Court upon the subject in hand, I refrain from introducing it in the text as *proof* of that sentiment. I submit it here, however, interpolating the only exposition of it which I am able to give. It was dated November 9th, 1578.

"I am informed that the Commissioners appointed to deal with the Dean of Durham can hardly agree amongst themselves for his deprivation, because" — on the single ground, or for the reason alone that — "he is no minister lawfully made; whereas, for other matters," — his non-conformity, — "they are contented to deprive him, and so" — by their refusing to declare him a mere layman — "he shall be in less hazard of further loss, and the Archbishop worse liked for depriving a preacher. The fifteenth of this month is the time of his appearance at York; the Commissioners, in the mean season, being smally esteemed" — for their indecision — "of some, and they that were most forward to advance it," — the deprivation as a layman, — "almost defaced."

much time was fruitlessly occupied, that they adjourned to meet at Auckland on the twenty-fifth instant.[1] We shall state the points made in canvassing the case, without designating the particular dates when each was presented.

"It was alleged that William Whittingham, now Dean of Durham, *hath not proved* that he was orderly made minister at Geneva, according to the order of the Geneva book or office, by public authority established there.[2] The Archbishop *assumed* that, "according to the laws of the realm, Whittingham was neither deacon nor minister, but a mere layman,"[3] and demanded proof of the alleged contrary fact; an unexceptionable position, doubtless, throwing the burden of proof where it properly belonged.

To this Whittingham put in his answer, "that indeed he was neither deacon nor minister, according to the order and law of the realm;" meaning, according to the ceremonial formula prescribed by the law for consecration. "But, that he was a mere layman, he denied;" meaning, that though he had not been *ordered* — put into orders — after the form of the English ceremonial, he *had* been ordered by *some* superior authority which was recognized by the laws and statutes of the realm.[4] "I was ordered,"

[1] Strype's Annals, IV. 173.

[2] Ibid., 170.

[3] Ibid., 170, 173.

[4] To express what was unquestionably Whittingham's defensive position, I have used almost *verbatim* the words of the royal Commission, as quoted by the Archbishop's Chancellor; but which he seems to have misunderstood or distorted. That the reader may be his own interpreter, I give them: —

"If he" — The Dean — "be not ordered by some superior authority, according to" — as is required by, not in the fashion of — "the laws and statutes of our realm, then my express pleasure and command is," &c. (Strype's Annals, IV, 170, 171.)

To this command no reasonable

he added, "in Queen Mary's time, in Geneva, according to the form there used;"[1] a direct denial of the opening allegation. To prove this, he presented a certificate signed by eight persons, — "That it pleased God, by lot and election of the whole English congregation," — at Geneva, — "there orderly to choose William Whittingham to the office of preaching the Word of God and ministering the sacraments."[2] This proved nothing in point; and nothing at all, except that the congregation signified whom they desired for their minister, and that Whittingham was no adept in that precision and completeness of language which belong peculiarly to the legal profession, — a fact demonstrated by "The Discours of the Troubles at Frankfort," if indeed he wrote it.

The Archbishop — who had his lawyer at his elbow — objected, properly enough, "that this certificate might have been made in Mr. Whittingham's chamber, for aught that appeared to the contrary; and that the witnesses were not sworn." He also "laid hold of the words '*lot and election;*' offering that, neither in Geneva, nor in any Reformed Church in Europe, it could be proved that any such *orders* were ever used or allowed," — which was doubtless true. But, he added, singularly enough, "First and last only, it was seen used in Matthias, the Apostle." Respectable authority, one would suppose; nevertheless, not recognized by the laws and statutes of England, the only standard of appeal before the Court. "For the con-

exception can be taken. It meant merely, "if he is not consecrated to the office of the Christian ministry by such ecclesiastical usage and authority as are properly required by all Reformed Christendom, then let him be declared a layman and no minister."

[1] Strype's Annals, IV. 170.

[2] Ibid., 171.

firmation of his opinion, he avouched[1] Mr. Calvin, who affirmed that the election" — of Matthias — "was not, nor is to be, drawn into an example."[2] A pertinent appeal, so far as the sanction of the Geneva Church, and the recognition of its ecclesiastical character and authority by the laws of England were concerned.[3]

Afterwards, Mr. Whittingham produced a certificate more discreetly framed. It was dated at London on the fifteenth day of November. It was sworn to by the signers, upon the holy Evangelists, before a Notary Public. It read thus: "It pleased God, by the suffrages of the whole congregation," — meaning the English congregation at Geneva, — "orderly to *choose* Mr. William Whittingham unto the office of preaching the Word of God and ministering the sacraments;" to which was added, "that he was *admitted* minister," — not, be it observed, by the suffrages of the congregation, but, — "with such *other ceremonies as there is used and accustomed.*"[4]

To this it was objected by the Archbishop's lawyer,

[1] Strype's Annals, IV. 171.

[2] Ibid., 172.

[3] I think Doctor Taylor perverts this, when he says (Vol. II. 74), "Calvin himself had not permitted the case of *Whittingham* to be drawn into a precedent." Pray, when did Calvin ever publish, or have occasion to publish, or to say, anything about Whittingham's orders? The passage in Strype quoted in the text refers, almost necessarily, I conceive, to Calvin's opinion concerning the election of *Matthias* as a precedent.

In this connection I am constrained to note, that the same writer says positively, on page 66, "Whittingham was ordained by the *Presbytery* of Geneva." How, then, could Calvin have barred Whittingham's case as a precedent, without impeaching the authority of his own Presbytery? But, on page 68, Doctor Taylor says, "Whittingham had only *lay* ordination." If he judged ordination by a Presbytery to be only lay ordination, — which must have been the case unless he has flatly contradicted himself, — the Church of England did not; as will soon appear in the text.

[4] Strype's Annals, IV. 172.

"that it was no proof of *the fact;* that he knew not the witnesses, save one, whom he believed to be an honest man,"—which was simply denying that a solemn judicial oath was of itself entitled to credit, —"and that no *mention* was made of any *ordaining authority,* or functionary, or of any external solemnities, not even of that form, peculiar to ordination, the laying on of hands."[1] This was indeed crowding a man to the wall; each of these particulars being comprised, upon the most obvious construction, in the words, "such other ceremonies as *there* is used and accustomed;" it being notorious that the Church of Geneva considered the authority and action of a Presbytery, and the laying on of hands, essential to ordination. It thus became obvious that the Archbishop was bent upon disputing every inch of ground, even to the most trifling negatives. Indeed *all* his positions were negations.

What more could Whittingham do? Calvin was dead. Twenty-two years had elapsed, and probably most of the witnesses, who had not testified, were dead also. The records of the Church of Geneva were not immediately accessible. Had they been copied, certified, sworn to, and attested by a Notary Public, the Precisianism which could carp at the certificate already produced, could have invented some exception to the copy of record; could have designated something which was *not* in it. The Dean could only pawn his Christian honor, his veracity, and reiterate as he did, "that he was able to *prove* his vocation to be such and the *same that all the ministers* in Geneva use to have."[2]

[1] Strype's Annals, IV. 172. [2] Ibid., 174.

This, beyond a question, was literally true. And however captious, perhaps incredulous, Archbishop Sandys was, the known integrity of Whittingham, and the obvious meaning and trustworthiness of his certificate, commanded respect and carried conviction elsewhere; the conviction that, according to the rites and usages of the Genevese Church, his ordination was valid. The Lord President accordingly wrote to Burleigh, accepting the fact as proved; and confessing plainly "that for only the alleged cause that Whittingham was a *mere layman* he could not, in conscience, agree to the sentence of deprivation;" and adding, "that it could not but be ill taken of all the godly learned, both at home and in all the Reformed Churches abroad, that we should allow of the popish Massing priests in our ministry, and disallow of the ministers made in a Reformed Church."[1]

Hereupon the Court adjourned to receive further instructions from the Privy Council; their Commission having continuance during her Majesty's pleasure.

Before any further proceeding upon his case, Mr. Whittingham died, on the tenth day of June, 1579, aged fifty-five years.[2]

This case is of singular importance as showing what was *then* considered by the Church of England essential to valid ordination. For this reason only, it has been thus minutely detailed.

The question mooted was not, what Dr. Taylor asserts it to have been,[3] whether "a call," or the suffrages of a congregation, "could be considered as

[1] Strype's Annals, IV. 173, 174.

[2] Neal says, in his sixty-fifth year; yet on the same page dates his birth truly in 1524; Vol. I. 145. Possibly a typographical error.

[3] Vol. II. 74.

an equivalent to an ordination;" for neither Whittingham, nor any one else concerned, made pretence to this, or believed it. He only asserted and sufficiently proved, that the congregation at Geneva chose him *to become* their minister, and that he became such by *ordination*, which ordination was effected according to the usages of the Church of Geneva; the latter point being all it was necessary for him to establish.

Nor was it a question, whether the Orders conferred by a *Presbytery* were valid; for Archbishop Sandys himself admitted that they were. He admitted it, indirectly, in the first Item which he laid before the court, "That it was not proved, that Whittingham *had* been made minister according to the order established at Geneva." He admitted it point-blank over his own signature. "This Durham matter breedeth a great broil. The Dean hath gotten more friends than the matter deserveth. The discredit of the Church of Geneva is hotly alleged. Verily, my lord, *that Church is not touched.* For he hath not received his ministry in that Church, or by any authority or order from that Church, *so far as yet can appear.*"[1] His Grace could only deny *the fact* of Presbyterian ordination. He could not call in question its validity without impeaching Parliament, the highest authority in the realm, and without offending the sentiment, then universal, of the English Church,— including, of course, his own.

The real question was,—and here we resort again to the language of the queen herself in her Commis-

[1] Sandys to Burleigh, April 4th, 1579; Strype's Annals, Append., Bk. II. No. XIII.; Vol. IV. 620.

sion, — "Has the Dean, or has he not, been ordered by some superior authority, according to the laws and statutes of the realm?" Yet, it will be perceived, not one word was said about his having been, or his not having been, ordered in the *mode* or *fashion* prescribed by the laws; except that, on the very threshold of the inquiry, Whittingham himself avowed that he had not. Had *this* been the main point at issue, there could have been no controversy. The case would have been settled upon the moment, and by the very words of the first replication. The real point was back of the English, episcopal mode, and had no relation to it. It was, whether Whittingham's ordering had been — according to the laws of the realm — by *some superior authority;* superior to his *own* when about to receive Orders; superior to that of a layman. On both sides, and by the Court, it was tacitly conceded that, if his ordering had been after the usages of the Genevan Church, then it had been by a "superior authority." In other words, by all parties, it was a point tacitly conceded, — not at all argued, or agreed to, or held in suspense, or even mentioned, — that ordination according to the Presbyterian forms of the Church of Geneva was *equivalent* to ordination according to the Episcopal forms of the Church of England, — or, to ordination by a bishop.

And why conceded? We have anticipated this question by saying, — that nobody doubted it, and that the highest authority of the realm had settled it. And here, be it distinctly observed, we are obliged to exclude the Bible from the "authorities of the realm;" because, in all matters of ecclesiastical government and discipline, the Dignitaries of the

Church had not only ignored, but publicly repudiated, the Bible. In such matters, Parliament, and the Fathers, as Parliament might read them, were their only admitted standards.

Hence it was, that the controversy resolved itself into a simple question *of fact.*

Let us consider how the highest authority of the realm had settled it; we mean Parliament, for Tradition and the Fathers were rated below the Parliament even in religious matters. We turn to the act entitled "An Act to reform certain disorders touching ministers of the Church."[1] Its first section orders, "that every person under the degree of bishop who doth, or *shall* pretend to be a priest or minister of God's holy Word and Sacraments, by reason of ANY *other form* of institution, consecration, or ordering, than the form set forth by Parliament in the time of the late king of most worthy memory, King Edward the Sixth, or now used, ... shall . . . . declare his assent, and subscribe, to all the Articles of Religion which ONLY concern the true Christian Faith and the doctrines of the Sacraments comprised in a Book imprinted, entitled Articles . . . . . agreed by the Archbishops," — *et ceteri,* — "in the year of our Lord God a thousand five hundred sixty and two, ... upon pain of being *ipso facto* deprived and his ecclesiastical promotions void as if he were naturally dead."[2]

[1] 13 Eliz. Cap. XII.

[2] On a blank leaf of the volume of Strype's Annals now before me, I find written: "A specimen of Neal's fibs in the case of Dean Whittingham, p. 175." On page 175 is a corresponding note, by the same hand, in the margin, where Strype says that, "by the Act 13 Elizabeth, their ordination was allowed who had been ordered by another order than that which was

But why should *not* one who claimed to be priest or minister by virtue of other than Episcopal consecration — the form elected for use in the Church of England — be deprived, and his promotions be void, as if he were naturally dead? The answer seems to lie upon the very face of the statute: "Because, of such an one, we need only to be assured of his *doctrinal* qualifications; because, his *canonical* qualifications are what they should be; because, the particular form of ordering which the national Church has seen fit to adopt is not essential to constitute one a minister of the Word and Sacraments; because, the right to such ministry is as truly conferred by the ceremonials and officials of one Christian Church as by those of another; by the Romish mode and officials, or by the Presbyterian, as by the English."

Nor is this all. The incidental, informal way in which this inwrapped opinion is indicated, shows that it was held as an axiom by the framers of the statute; as an opinion so far from doubt as not to

here established." I am unable to discover, in this text of Strype, any disclosure of fibs by Mr. Neal, who, through his entire narrative of Whittingham's case, relies wholly upon Strype; appears faithfully to have followed him; and, on the matter of the statute, does nothing but use *his very words.*

I am indebted, however, to the memoranda. They have modified my own representation of this case throughout. They have made me utterly refrain from alluding to a writer thus scandalized in secret places, by even the softest word which courtesy can give as a synonyme for falsehood. They have made me rely wholly upon Strype. They have made me scrupulously watchful lest I should misunderstand him. They have made me more than usually careful to cite him step by step; and to distinguish explicitly between his words and representations and my own. They have made me do all I can to avoid fibbing myself. And they will now deter me from appealing even to Strype in commenting upon the statute before us; which itself cannot fib, and is the best and sufficient authority.

require even a declaration. The sufficiency of any other form of ordination is not here imparted, or pretended to be imparted; but is supposed, — supposed, too, with a significance peculiarly intensive.

This view of the statute corresponds with, and accounts for, the very noticeable fact that, in the controversy between Archbishop Sandys and the Dean of Durham, the statute was not even alluded to. The validity of Presbyterian ordination, no one had occasion to advocate; for no one questioned it. It was, as said before, conceded. An examination of the statute, and the silence of the parties about it, show the *reason* of the concession. In this view of the statute, we see why it was not cited; a fact for which, under the circumstances, we can account in no other way.

But more. The practice of the Church had corresponded with the underlying sentiment of the law. Thousands of Romish priests had been retained in the service, and were permitted to enjoy the revenues, of the Church, on the simple condition that — even with a lie in their right hands — they should underwrite the doctrines of Protestantism. Thus the validity of *their* ordination, which had been by other form than that of Edward the Sixth, had been admitted by the functionaries of the Church of England. And if hitherto there had been no acknowledged case of a minister in her service who had received *Presbyterian* ordination, we have not far to go to find one.

On the sixth day of April, 1582, — Archbishop Grindal being still suspended from the functions of his office, — John Morrison, a Scotchman, was licensed by Aubrey, Vicar-General for the Province of Canterbury, to exercise the Gospel ministry within the Province; apparently the first license of the kind to such a party. We transcribe all of it which is pertinent to the matter before us. "Since you, the aforesaid John Morrison, were ordained by the General Synod or Congregation of the said county of Lothian, ... according to the laudable form and rite of the Reformed Church of Scotland: We, therefore, ... approving and ratifying, as much as lieth in us, and as by right we may, your ordination and preferment, ... grant to you a License and Faculty, with the consent and express command of the most Reverend Father in Christ, the Lord Edmund, by the Divine Providence, Archbishop of Canterbury, ... that in such Orders by you taken you may, ... throughout the whole Province of Canterbury, celebrate divine offices, minister the Sacraments,"[1] &c.

Whether other like licenses were issued, or not, one such high official document is sufficient for our purpose; as decisive as fifty. Yet, in addition to this, if we may credit Mr. Neal,—and we have reason to, although he gives no voucher for the statement,—there were, in that same year, "some scores, if not hundreds, in the Church, who had only been ordained according to the manner of the Scots or other foreign Churches."[2]

So clear it is—both from the Statute Book and from the practice of the English Church that,—at least until 1582,—the general sentiment of that Church "approved and ratified" other fountains of

[1] Strype's Grindal, 271, and Appendix, Bk. II. No. XVII.

[2] Neal, I. 152.

priestly virtue than its own; and acknowledged other than the hands of *mitred* heads as having ordaining power. So clear it is also *why* Archbishop Sandys — determined to laicize his antagonist — could not touch him with his lance while trenched within a Presbyterian wall. So clear also *why*, first of all, he strove to force him thence.[1]

[1] In his "History of the Martin Mar-Prelate Controversy," (which I shall have occasion more particularly to notice hereafter,) Mr. Maskell says: "Nevertheless he" — Whittingham — "was not rejected, and retained his dignity till his death." He adds, in a foot-note: "Many years afterwards, Whitgift said, 'if he' — Whittingham — 'had lived, he would have been deprived.' The fact remains, Dean Whittingham was not deprived." (London edit., 1845, p. 63.) True; Whittingham did retain his dignity till his death. True, also; Whitgift did *say* as Mr. Maskell represents. (Strype's Whitgift, 252.) Yet I submit whether — as Whittingham deceased before his case was adjudicated — there is, or is not, something very disingenuous, unfair, and deceptive, in the language which Mr. Maskell has been pleased to employ and to quote. I submit, also, whether, in view of the facts stated in the text, it is not almost certain that, had Whittingham lived, he would have been *confirmed* in his dignity. I cannot doubt that the validity of his ordination would have been declared by the Commissioners; notwithstanding the opinion of Whitgift.

Will the candid reader be pleased to compare this singular language of Mr. Maskell with the remarkable interpolation of the Regius Professor of Modern History in the University of Oxford as stated above, p. 64, note 1?

CHAPTER V.

THE DYING SOLDIER.

Walter Devereux. — The sick Earl and his Page. — Sir Nicholas White, Master of the Rolls. — The Earl's joyous Anticipation of Death. — His Paroxysms. — Suspicions of Poison. — The Archbishop of Dublin. — The Earl suspects the Cause of his Death, and significantly mentions the Earl of Leicester. — The last Agony. — The Name of Jesus. — The Soldier's loving Reliance upon his "Saviour Christ."

1576.

The massive castle of Dublin, a fortification of great strength and capacity, had long stood captivated by the rare beauties which Nature had just there lavished. With the most beautiful harbor in Europe on the east, with the faithful Liffey pouring the liquid offerings of a thousand upland fountains at its feet, and with a phalanx of hills in emerald costume ever in respectful attendance, it had been contented with its home for more than three hundred and sixty years.

One of its most spacious and pleasant apartments commanded the eastern view; whence, seven miles distant, could be seen a strip of the sea or channel which separated from the English coast. This room was also one of the most richly furnished in the castle — its walls hung with tapestry; its floor clad with rich carpet; its movable furniture elaborately wrought by English hands and of English oak. The fine arts of Spain and Italy also had their specimens here; while a few of the more elegant weapons of the chase and of the battle-field had their posts of honor. Yet the chamber had a sombre aspect; for it was with difficulty that the light could struggle through the narrow openings which served as windows in those thick walls, even when, out of doors, the sun was shining in his strength.

On the fifteenth day of September, 1576,—we go backward in our narrative only for a little while,—before one of those windows, which had been materially modernized, sat a man about thirty-five years of age, gazing silently and intently toward the sea. Though evidently a great invalid, and dependent upon cushions to prop him in his spacious chair, and though suffering was written distinctly upon his brow, his cheek had the roundness and complexion of health.[1]

This was Walter Devereux, Earl of Essex, and Earl Marshal of Ireland; "a nobleman of ancient lineage and great personal valor."[2] For his services in the Northern rebellion of 1569 he had been rewarded with the Garter and an Earldom.[3] He had afterwards adventured his whole estate in a great scheme for the colonization of Ulster (for which scheme he had first received a grant from the queen); "a large price," says Fuller, "to pay for a bear's skin, before it was known how the bear was to be killed." For this grant he had been indebted, in no small degree, to the exertions of Leicester, who was jealous of his influence with the queen, and therefore wished him

[1] Wright, II. 35. Sidney State Papers, I. 141. Camden, 217.

[2] Taylor, I. 234.

[3] Ibid.

away,[1] — for "the shadow doth not more naturally attend the sun, than envy doth favor,[2] — and no less, to the influence of his wife's beauty, which Leicester had begun to covet. In Ireland, he had operated as general of the queen's forces[4] against the Irish, who had resisted his enterprise and harassed him by constant fighting. In the midst of successes which were promising him speedy triumph, "The Heart of the Court" had interfered, and Essex was ordered to return to England in 1575.[5] After a short residence at Court, he had quarrelled with Leicester, of whom he was jealous, as the author of his disastrous recall, and had openly threatened him. Leicester, who feared him, and whose love for the Countess Lettice had become inflamed, was as familiar with the sly wisdom of those times, to cripple or to kill men by honors, as he was with the art of "poisoning with oil."[6] He therefore resorted to the Court trick of procuring orders for Essex's return, with the airy title — for it conferred no political power — of Earl Marshal of Ireland.[7] He had since buffeted the hardships

1 Taylor, I. 235.

2 Lloyd, 486.

3 Ibid. Wotton's Reliquæ, 185.

4 Strype's Annals, III. 576.

5 Ibid.

6 Wotton, 185.

7 Camden, 217. Ellis, 1st Series, Vol. II. 280; from Dugdale's Baronage, II. 178. Strype's Annals, III. 576; White to Burleigh. Carte, III. 542. Taylor, I. 235, 236.

In constructing the text just preceding, the testimony of Camden was overlooked. Under date of 1573 he says: "Walter Devereux (whom Queen Elizabeth had lately created Earl of Essex) craved leave to undertake an expedition; following therein the counsel of those who desired above all things to have him farther off, and to plunge him into dangers under pretence of procuring him honor. Which he knew well enough; but being a stirring man, and one not unacquainted with warlike discipline from his very youth, he held on his resolution, and made an agreement with the queen that, upon certain conditions, the one half of Clandeboy," — apparently a part of Ulster, — "if he drove out the rebels, should be granted to him

of a soldier life in a barbarous country, until the second day of October, 1576, when he had yielded to a disorder of the bowels, which had seized him four days before.[1]

He sat now, looking out upon the harbor and the distant sea, with an earnest seriousness upon his face, which betrayed that his thoughts were of home. At

and his soldiers; for the defence whereof he should maintain, at his own charge, two hundred Horsemen and four hundred Foot. And to furnish himself for the war, he borrowed of the queen ten thousand pounds of English money, mortgaging his lands in Essex for the same." (Page 201. Also — pp. 212, 213 — under date of 1575.) "In the midst of his course of victory he was again, beyond his expectation, commanded to resign his authority, ... and through Leicester's cunning dealing nothing was omitted whereby to break his mild spirit with continual crosses, one in the neck of another."

[1] Sidney State Papers, I. 140.

The story which Doctor Taylor indorses, that Essex had heard of the actual seduction of his wife by Leicester, and was taken sick when hastening to England for revenge, I cannot but consider apocryphal. It seems to have no better foundation than "Leicester's Commonwealth;" and cannot be reconciled with the letter of Sir Nicholas White, who was with him, nor with that of Sir Henry Sidney, — in both which Essex's movements, for the three or four days preceding his prostration in Dublin castle, are described as indicating anything but a purpose to return home.

The two letters referred to are, so far as I can find, the only documents of the day which contain reliable testimony respecting the circumstances of Essex's death; and that of Sidney, as will appear, is open to serious objections. I should add, perhaps, the funeral sermon by the Bishop of St. David's, so far as its statements respecting the Earl's condition of mind are concerned, which statements he received from ear-witnesses. The letter of E. W., also a contemporary paper; which, however, I cite by itself on a single point only. I derive my account of Essex's last days chiefly from the two letters and the sermon; and my references to them are under their own names, instead of to the authors in whose writings or collections they are contained.

White's letter, which was addressed to Lord Burleigh, is preserved in Wright II. 35; in Ellis, 1st Series, Vol. II. 280, taken from MS. Lansdowne, No. XXI. num. 33 original; and in Strype's Annals IV. 83, 84. It is dated September 30, 1576. The letter of Sir Henry Sidney, Lord Deputy of Ireland, was addressed to Mr. Secretary Walsingham, and dated October 20, 1576. It is in the Sidney Papers, I. 140–142. The Sermon is in Holingshed, IV. 331–336.

a respectful distance behind the Earl stood a young attendant, of about sixteen or seventeen years of age; now and then turning a sly and sinister look toward his master.

"Albert!" said the Earl, rousing from his reverie, "a cup of water!"

The page took cup and tankard from a bracket of polished oak, and having first and unseen thrown into the cup a powder almost invisibly minute, he placed both vessels upon a silver salver, and, gracefully bowing upon his knee, presented them to the Earl.[1] After a slight attempt to raise the tankard, Essex dropped his hand, saying, with a sigh, "Nay, boy; it passeth my weakness. Do the office thyself!"

Albert poured out the water, which the Earl conveyed to his own lips with an evident effort. It is no wonder that the page looked intently as his lord eagerly drank the cool, clear water,—it was so strange to see one so weak, yet with every token of fresh health in the color of his face, the clearness of his skin, and the fulness of his flesh.

"God bless it to your lordship!" he murmured, as he received the cup again.

"Amen!" answered the Earl, devoutly. "Nevertheless, my lad, I misdoubt me there be nothing shall make me sound again!"

"Avaunt such misdoubtings, good my lord Earl; and count thee many a bright day and year to come. It be but weakness. Where be sign of disease? Thy color be rather better than impaired;[2] thy hand full and round as aforetime. Troth! it be *but* weakness, my lord, after disease be spent."

[1] Osborne, 43, note.

[2] Sidney's Letter.

As the Earl instinctively raised the hand which had been described, the youth put it to his own lips and kissed it softly and with profound respect.

"Albert! I am dying!"

"Hush, my lord!" Yet did the merest blink of satisfaction flit upon his features.

"Nay, boy! it be so; and God's will be done! There be life before *thee,* Albert, and a chance to do thy devoir for the queen under belt and golden spur. By thy sword, thou mayest yet win honor. Serve well thy queen; but forget not thy God. When Death looketh in at thy window, the memory of the last will do thee good. But when Death looketh in at the window, and the Good Shepherd calleth his sheep, one *feeleth* that the honor which a queen conferreth is froth. With nothing else, lad, you will be beggared when you come to die. Lay up treasure in heaven, Albert! So may God make thee rich!" and as he said the last words, he laid his hand upon the boy's head, as gently and devoutly as a father would. The page drooped his eye under the benediction, and was spared the embarrassment of a reply which he thought would have choked him. A rap at the door of the antechamber, he obeyed with unwonted speed; and in a moment the Master of the Rolls stood beside the sick man. With the anxious look of a sincere friend, he said, "How fareth your lordship?"

"Ah! Sir Nicholas? Welcome! As yet, poorly enow; albeit, the better for thy kind look. *Lend* it me awhile; and thy voice too, kind friend. They will cheer me. 'Awhile,' I say, Sir Nicholas; not long. The malady hath touched the springs of life."

Sir Nicholas White looked grave. After a moment's silence, he replied, "My good lord, I purpose to be more about you than afore sithence your sickness. An my poor presence can comfort you, a comforter shall not be lacking. Howbeit, my lord, I tell you plainly, — to my seeming you will need a better."

The Earl looked up to read the meaning of Sir Nicholas's last words; which he quickly did. "A better *Comforter!*" he replied, with a quiet smile. "Troth, troth, Sir Nicholas! We think alike of my ailing; you, for its mystery and stubbornness; I, for something here," — laying his hand over the vital regions, — "which I cannot describe. And there is another reason." Then, dropping his voice, he murmured, "Can it be always so — with others?"

"What, my lord? What reason? What is always so?"

"These new eyes, I have; these new sights."

"My lord?"

"Nay; not new eyes, not new sights. But things I have seen aforetimes and loved to see, — but loved too faintly. I see them now so clearly, that while I joy in what I see, I be so sore grieved with the remembrance of my former unthankful life,[1] that I know not betimes whether be the greater, — the grief or the joy. That other Comforter, Sir Nicholas, — it is what He is doing within me that makes me think I am about to die. I mistrust what be God's way of giving grace; that He giveth not till the time of need, as He feedeth the young ravens; that He giveth not grace to die with, till dying be at hand. So when one feeleth a new, unwonted incoming of

[1] Sermon.

grace such as exactly befitteth a dying strait, he may be sure that dying be not far off."

Then pausing a moment for weariness, he resumed: "The Comforter taketh the things that be of Christ, and showeth them unto us. It be his office-work. Now this stricken, helpless Walter Devereux hath never been so weak, and yet so stout of heart, as now. My exceeding sinfulness seemeth more than ever to exceed. Doth this make me writhe? Not at all. The blacker and bigger my sin seemeth, the larger and the richer and the lovelier seemeth that Christ whom the Comforter revealeth. So precious, and so exceeding fit for sin, be the cross and Him who hangeth thereon, that I do but drop my sin there, to look up and trust and give thanks. I say, the more helpless and wicked this Walter Devereux be, the more glorious and precious Walter Devereux's Christ. I could prize him but half so much, were I but half so big a sinner. Troth! wot you not, Sir Nicholas, He who showeth the things of Christ, hath been showing them to me, — showing just such a Christ as I, Walter the sinner, Walter the lost, Walter the helpless do need? This maketh me to think that He be getting me ready to die, — praised be His name!"

"Amen!" ejaculated White; "God be praised! God be praised!"

"It hath come to pass, my good Sir Nicholas, that mine eyes be so full of Christ's beauty, my soul hath such sweet confidence in His precious passion, as bringeth to me forthwith manifold more health of soul than I lose health of body. I may say, in troth, that I be so filled with joy in the Holy Ghost, that all my delight be in meditation of the joy of the world to come and the fruitions of the presence of God forever.[1] I shall wrap my mantle around me and lie down to sleep."

Sir Nicholas had grasped the Earl's hand, so drawn to him was he by these wondrous words. Once or twice he had tried to speak; but now he sat looking into that strange sick face glowing with Gospel light, the tears streaming down his own; and himself constrained and content to keep silence. Sir Walter seemed exhausted; and so the two friends sat holding each other's hands, and letting out beams of silent sympathy from each other's eyes.

From the inner door of the anteroom peered the page, — a look on *his* face akin to Satan's when he first espied the peace and love of Eden.

A change soon came over the sick man, and suddenly; another terrible fit of acute pain, such as had been his scourge from the first of his attack, with irregular intervals of ease. He was instantly removed to a couch, and all was confusion. Three physicians, who were constantly within call, were by his side; an Irish physician, Doctor Trevor; Mr. Chaloner, physician to the Lord Deputy Sir Henry Sidney; and Mr. Knell, not only "a professor of physic, but an honest preacher."[2] They were evidently bewildered by the strange and terrible phenomena of the case. But little had been done except to use clysters to such a degree as seemingly to have produced inflation.[3] But little was done now; and that little was evidently without benefit. The agony was more excruciating and more protracted than upon any like

[1] Sermon. [2] Sidney's Letter. [3] White's Letter.

occasion before; but his heroic fortitude was in proportion to his torture. Every limb and every feature was contorted; but in every lull of suffering, while his servants stood pale and weeping, and the page knelt at the foot of the couch and sobbed, the Earl, to nerve his flagging patience, would exclaim, "Courage! courage! I am a soldier! under the banner of my Saviour Christ I must fight!" These words were constantly on his lips, in the times of his extremity.[1]

Upon this occasion, when one of his most violent paroxysms was at its height, one of his attendants burst forth, "By the Mass! my lord, you are poisoned!"[2] The page Albert started at the words, and looked up with an expression of terror upon his face. But so did all the others. The thought of poison had been *whispered* before. But it was the first time the page had heard it spoken, and with the terror on his face was alarm,—*not* betokened by the others. But it passed in a moment, and at that time caused no remark.

When the fit was over, the servants of the household retired; and for a long while the Earl was left entirely to quiet repose. When he had rallied, and while his physicians were yet present, he requested the Master of the Rolls to summon the yeoman of his cellar. When the man made his appearance, Essex addressed him mildly, and told him that words had been spoken there of his having been poisoned, and that he must question him upon the point; "which I shall do," he added, "not to burden but to excuse you." The servant answered modestly, yet

White's Letter. Sidney's Letter. [2] Sidney's Letter.

positively, "that neither in his wine, water, or sugar *could* poison have been infused."[1]

The Archbishop of Dublin having entered during this conversation, now changed the current of questioning to the patient himself.

"What think you yourself, my lord?"

Seriously, though not with energy, the Earl answered, "My lord, I *think* I am not;" and this he repeatedly affirmed afterwards. The physicians, being asked what they thought, spake doubtfully; saying that it *might be he was* poisoned. (Yet afterwards they affirmed that they never thought it; but for *argument's* sake, and partly *to please the Earl!* Moreover, that they never ministered anything to him against poison.[2]) Soon after the physicians had thus expressed themselves, the matter was dropped; much to the relief of the page Albert, who had watched every eye, syllable, and intonation during the inquisition.

His Grace now addressed the sufferer as his spiritual counsellor.

"I would know, my lord Earl, whether you rest

[1] Sidney's Letter.

[2] Ibid.

I have scrupulously adhered to the very words of the letter. It is valuable testimony on some points; but, unlike White's, was made up from hearsays gathered more than three weeks after the Earl's death, and by one whose family were interested to invalidate the rumors of Leicester's complicity in the tragedy of Dublin castle. On the one subject of Essex's sickness the letter contains statements strangely inconsistent. "The physicians *thought* he might be poisoned." "They *never* thought so." "The Irish physician affirmed, before good witnesses, that he *was not* poisoned." "They *never* gave him medicine against poison." "Doctor Knell, upon suspicion of *his being* poisoned, *gave* him medicine" — accordingly — "*several times.*"

Strange statements to be found over the same signature! Had there been *no foul play,* could such clashing testimony have been gleaned?

your hope of acceptance with God, *in any* measure upon trentals, masses, diriges, pardons, or any other such papisticals."

Essex looked at the Bishop in amazement, and answered with no little vehemence, "God forbid! I do contemn them utterly! Nay, my lord, in my very soul do I hold them to be wicked, and blasphemous against the death and passion of Christ."

"And your trust is — where?"

"For my salvation, I do repose my affiance and sure trust in the blood of Jesus Christ."

"Eschewing all and any trust in your own works and deservings?"

"Utterly, my lord; utterly! I have no *good* deservings. My life — my unthankful life — be no ground of trust, but of grief; of grief only. I do apprehend, lay hold of, and embrace, remission of sins, *only* by mine invincible faith in the merits of the sacrifice of Christ's body, offered upon the cross for the sins of the world."[1]

More conversation of this sort followed; and when the Archbishop retired, meeting Sir Nicholas White returning after a brief absence, he caught him by the arm, and said with tremulous emotion, "Sir Nicholas, let us bless God for his grace! The Earl showeth himself more like an angel from heaven than a man compassed with flesh and blood. I do greatly admire at his heavenly speeches. They will serve me for sermons as long as I live,[2] — such arguments of hearty repentance of his life; so sound charity with all the world; such assurance to be partaker of the joys of heaven through the merits of Christ's passion; such

[1] Sermon. [2] Ibid.

joyful desire speedily to be dissolved and enjoy the same,—when have I ever heard the like![1] Sir Nicholas! an you would hear sermons, sit under the pulpit of my lord of Essex!"

As the Earl became more and more convinced of the speedy termination of his life, so did he the more pant for the life to come. Thither almost all his thoughts and conversation now turned. To his friends when visiting him, "he ministered godly admonitions" freely and tenderly; and "his heavenly lessons and exhortations to his servants were such, that they reported they should never forget, and should be the better for while they lived."[2]

On the twentieth day of September, he was anxious to arrange his worldly affairs. "Tell his Honor the Lord Treasurer," he said to Sir Nicholas White, "that I have thought I was born to do him, and his, good. But now I must commit the oversight of my son and all to him. I would also have his Honor moved that your son may still attend upon the person of my son, as he hath done, and that they two may be brought up together. Tell my lord of Sussex, that I do think of him and speak of him most lovingly.[3] Let my son Robert be straitly charged ever to be mindful of the moment of time assigned both to his father and grandfather, the eldest having attained but to six and thirty years; to the end that — in consideration of the short course of life that he by nature must look for[4] — he may so employ his

[1] Sidney's Letter.

[2] Sermon. Sidney's Letter.

[3] White's Letter.

[4] Robert, the son and heir of Walter Devereux, was at this time about ten years of age. His father's apprehensions were realized. From the pinnacle of royal favorit-

tender years in virtuous studies and exercises, that he may in the prime of his youth become a man well accomplished to serve her Majesty and his country as well in war as peace. And I do enjoin upon him my commandment to bend all his endeavors to this."[1]

He also spake respecting his patents in Ireland, how "they should be turned to a reasonable commodity to his son;" and directed that such of his servants as had served him most diligently and patiently in his sickness should receive favor. He then added:

"One word will I say, Sir Nicholas, touching my sickness. Whereas I have said truly and at divers times, that I have *thought* I have not been poisoned, now my heart misgiveth me. Verily, Sir Nicholas, I doubt I *have* been poisoned; because of the violent evacuations I have had."[2]

"Think you, my lord, that any one here would do so foul a thing?"

"Nay, nay, Sir Nicholas! *Of that suspicion* I do acquit *this* land. No, not Tirrelaghe Lunnaghe himself[3] would do villany to my person."[4]

"Touching this matter, my lord, I can only say,

ism, Elizabeth sent him to the scaffold, near the close of her reign, when he was thirty-four years old.

[1] E. W.'s Epistle to Robert, the young Earl of Essex; Holingshed, IV. 339.

[2] I place no confidence in Sidney's statement in his letter, that Essex attributed the grief of his body to grief of mind. Partly, because of the character — already shown — of the letter itself, and the object for which it was evidently written. But chiefly, because Sir Nicholas White makes no allusion to any such saying of the Earl. Considering the intimacy of the two at the time, and considering all that had passed upon the subject of poison, it is unaccountable that White should have omitted to mention any such speech, had it been uttered; or any such opinion, had it been entertained.

[3] The chief of the rebels in Ulster.

[4] White's Letter; *verbatim.*

that, either through the ignorance of your lordship's physicians, or *some violent cause* beyond their skill, your life is sacrificed." [1]

Essex mused, as if deliberating whether to say more. At length he said, "I repeat it,—of the *suspicion* I do acquit this land. Nor do I *accuse* any one elsewhere. But this I know, that Robert Dudley, Earl of Leicester, is my enemy.[2] May God forgive him, as I do!" [3]

On the twenty-second day of the month came the closing scene. The agony of the morning was dreadful; yet his memory and speech were perfect, and he often called to himself, "Courage! courage! soldier of my Saviour Christ!" [4] But about eleven o'clock, with the name of Jesus, half finished, upon his lips, he suddenly lost his speech. Still he continued conscious, and of clear mind; for whenever *that* name was mentioned, he would raise his hand in token of happy and trustful recognition. Soon after, "his ghost sweetly and mildly departed, by all Christians to be hoped, into heavenly bliss." [5]

"O noble Earl of Essex! in thy time the pearl of nobility! the mirror of virtue and worthy qualities! the child of chivalry! the beautiful flower of England! the precious jewel and comfort of Wales! the trusty stay of Ireland! Thy life was most honorable: thy worthiness incomparable: thy death precious in the sight of God, for thou diedst in the Lord, a right inheritor of the everlasting kingdom of Heaven!" [6] Such was the lament of "the right rev-

[1] White's Letter; *verbatim.*
[2] Lloyd, 486
[3] Sermon.
[4] White's Letter.
[5] Sidney's Letter.
[6] Sermon.

erend father in God, Richard, Bishop of St. David's, at the burial of this right honorable Earl of Essex, in the parish church of Caermarthen, in Wales."[1]

Of outward signs of poison upon the Earl's person there were none; unless, indeed, a fair flesh and a fresh complexion, and "a color rather *better* than impaired," should be considered such, when continuing, under racking torments, through more than three weeks, and even withstanding death itself. The body was examined; and Sir Nicholas was *told* — for he "could not abide" to be present — that "all the inward parts were sound, saving that the heart was somewhat consumed, and the bladder of the gall empty," — a second-hand testimony, which amounts to nothing.[2]

Thus the Earl of Essex "might have lived longer, if his wife had not had at Court more favor than himself. Abraham was afraid of, and Sir Walter was undone by, his Sarah's beauty. This is certain, he was *no sooner* in his grave, than the same great man, whom he declared his enemy at his death, was his successor in his marriage-bed."[3]

We have digressed to notice the dying hours of

[1] Holingshed, IV. 331.

[2] Ellis says: "The suspicion of poison having been administered to the Earl by Leicester's means seems to be *done away* by White's letter"! (1st Series, Vol. II. 280,) — a remark which I cannot appreciate. Nor do I think the reader can, if he chooses to review the extract which I have made under date of September 20th. "I doubt I *have* been poisoned, *because* of the evacuations I have had. But, of *that suspicion* I do acquit this land," &c.

It is remarkable that Essex seems not to have made the least allusion during his sickness to the Lady Lettice, his Countess. Is it possible that his dying declaration of Leicester's enmity had reference, in part, to that Earl's bearing toward her?

[3] Lloyd, 486.

this Christian nobleman, because the case stands in immediate connection with, and is explanatory of, incidents at Court in 1579, and about to be narrated. We have done this with the more heartfelt satisfaction, because it is peculiarly refreshing to turn from the strifes of religious parties, and from the wrongs inflicted by the Established Church, to note the presence and beauty of that evangelical piety which has ever been fostered under her wing. With all her precisianism, formality, and semi-Romish cumbrances, she has retained God's Truth in its pureness; and we may, perhaps, be forgiven for stepping aside to study closely so beautiful an illustration of its spiritual power in one of the most chivalrous of her courtly nobility.

In Christ Jesus there is neither Churchman, nor Puritan, nor Papist, Jew nor Greek, circumcision nor uncircumcision, Barbarian, Scythian, bond nor free; but Christ is all and IN ALL. The same Lord over all IS RICH UNTO ALL that call upon him.[1]

[1] Romans x. 12; Galatians iii. 28; Colossians iii. 11.

CHAPTER VI.

COURTSHIP AND BLOOD.

French Proposals to Elizabeth for Marriage. — The Duke of Alençon proposed. — When the Duke of Anjou, he sends Simier to woo in his Behalf. — The Queen coy, but yielding. — The Council tasked with framing a Treaty of Marriage. — Leicester's Hypocrisy about it. — His Attempt to Poison the Lady Douglass, his Wife. — She marries Sir Edward Stafford. — Leicester privately marries the Lady Lettice, the Dowager Countess of Essex. — Her Father, Sir Francis Knollys, compels a Repetition of the Marriage Rite. — Simier discloses the Marriage to the Queen. — Her Anger. — The Duke of Anjou visits the Queen privately. — Popular Disturbance about the Queen's Marriage. — "The Gapinge Gulphe," a Pamphlet by John Stubbes. — The Queen denounces it. — Stubbes and his Associates arrested, convicted, and sentenced. — Execution of the Sentence. — His History afterwards. — The last Acts in the Royal Courtship.

1579-1582.

"We are resolved, for the benefit of our realm and contentation of our subjects, to marry with some person of kingly blood and quality, ... and we are free from all manner of impediments to marry where we please. . . . . . In the beginning of our reign, it is not unknown how we had no disposition of our own nature to marry. . . . . . Nevertheless, after some course of years passed, we confess that the state of our realm, the continual and urgent solicitations, not only of our counsellors, but also of the whole estates of our subjects being many times assembled in our Parliament, did stir us up to some further consideration by the weight of their reasons, than naturally of ourself we had been inclined unto. . . . . . This our resolution is now indeed not only necessary for them, our realms and dominions, but also convenient for ourself. . . . . . She"—the Queen Mother of France—"now knoweth our resolute determination towards marriage, and with what manner of person."

Such were Elizabeth's instructions on the twenty-fourth day of March, 1571–2, to Sir Francis Walsingham, then her ambassador at the Court of France.[1] They seem to have been given in reply to a proposition from Catharine de Medicis, the Queen Mother, and Charles IX., King of France, for Elizabeth's marriage with Henry, the Duke of Anjou.

In 1565, Catharine, desirous of securing the English queen, who was considered the Head of the Protestant party, in an alliance which would preclude her from aiding the Huguenots, had made the same offer of her son Charles; but had met with no encouragement.

In 1568, she had indirectly proposed the hand of her second son, the Duke of Anjou, and from the same motive;[2] but not formally, until the latter part of the year 1571, just when the fate of the Duke of Norfolk, and that of Mary, Queen of Scots, were under discussion.[3] The time was judiciously chosen; for the subsiding uneasiness produced by the rebellion in the north and by the Papal bull of excommunication, was revived and immeasurably enhanced by the plans of Norfolk and the Scottish queen. It was, therefore, from a policy befitting the crisis, that Elizabeth encouraged the overture by the instruc-

[1] Digges, 62–64. [2] Camden, 107. [3] Ibid., 159.

tions we have just quoted. But the Duke of Anjou himself refused the advances of the English queen; partly because sensitive to the scandal which had attached to her fame, and partly on the score of religion.[1]

Two days before the massacre in Paris in 1572, Catharine had offered to the virgin queen her youngest son, the Duke of Alençon, sixteen years of age, and about twenty-three years younger than Elizabeth. Her Majesty "modestly excused herself," alleging their difference in religion and their disparity of age.[2] Although suspended briefly by the horrible news from Paris, the matter was soon renewed and kept in agitation. The only obstacles suggested by the English Court were presented in the following words: "Her Majesty cannot accord to take any person to her husband whom she shall not first see. Nor can she assent that any person which shall be her husband, shall, with her authority and assent, use any manner of religion in outward exercise that is, in her conscience, contrary and repugnant to the direct Word of Almighty God, and so consequently prohibited by the laws of the realm. . . . . . If Monsieur de Duc will obtain her his wife, without sight of him, her Majesty cannot be had; and yet therein her Majesty is very loath *he should think* that she desireth his coming."[3]

Hereupon the Duke began to talk of wooing in person, and to write "many love-letters;" while Elizabeth smiled and listened and read;[4] and the

[1] Taylor, I. 74, 75. Life of Hatton, 16.

[2] Camden, 188.

[3] Burleigh to Walsingham, March 20th, 1572-3; Digges, 335.

[4] Camden, 194, 195.

matter was thus kept in motion until the death of Charles IX. in May, 1574, when Henry, the Duke of Anjou, exchanged the throne of Poland, to which he had been elected, for that of France, and Francis took the title of Duke of Anjou in lieu of that of Alençon.[1] "Then followed a deep and long silence concerning his marriage."[2]

In 1576, the French ambassadors "began to tickle Queen Elizabeth's ears with love-stories about her marriage with Anjou;[3] and in 1578 the Duke resumed his wooing in earnest, by a special agent, Monsieur Simier, whom he sent over to plead his cause. Simier was "a choice courtier, a man thoroughly versed in love-fancies, pleasant conceits and court dalliances." He was accompanied by many of the nobility of France and was courteously and even kindly welcomed by her Majesty to the hospitalities and entertainments of her Court,—then at Richmond.[4] Her Majesty, though coy for "a long time," became impressible under the skilful "amorous wooings" of the deputy; "continued her very good usage of him and all his company;" and in February, 1578–9, he had so well prospered, that "he had conference with her Majesty three or four times a week; and she was the best disposed and the pleasantest when she talked with him (as appeared by her gestures) that was possible."[5] There began also to be a rumor that the Duke, and even the Queen Mother herself, would soon make their appearance at the English Court.[6]

[1] Life of Hatton, 80. Camden, 204.

[2] Ibid., 203, 204, 207.

[3] Ibid., 213.

[4] Ibid., 227.

[5] Ibid., 232. Lodge, II. 205; Talbot to Shrewsbury, Feb. 13th, 1578–9.

[6] Ibid. Strype's Annals, IV. 163.

The Privy Council were now so much burdened with the matter, that from the thirty-first day of March to the fourth day of April inclusive, — and perhaps longer, — "they sat in conference from eight o'clock in the morning until dinner time; and presently, after dinner and an hour's conference with her Majesty, to counsel again, and so till supper time; and all about the matter of the Duke's coming; his entertainment; and what demands should be made unto him in the treaty of marriage and such like."[1] Thus the affair had every appearance of progressing to a consummation.

It had been Leicester's uniform policy to affect the furthering of the queen's marriage;[2] but only because "by promoting the queen's match he could hinder it.[3] In his heart he was opposed to it.[4] Pro-

[1] Lodge, II. 212; Talbot to Shrewsbury, April 4th, 1579.

[2] "My lord of Leicester, finding just occasion thereto, doth, by all good means, to my knowledge, further the marriage." (Digges, 72; Burleigh to Walsingham, March 25th, 1571–2.)

"For the other greatest matter," — the marriage, — "you shall shortly receive her Majesty's full resolution. It appears that her Majesty hath good liking to proceed, if reason take place in the conditions. God send such speed as may be to the glory of Almighty God, and her Majesty's good satisfaction." (Digges, 82; Leicester to Walsingham, "Good Friday," 1572.)

"The Earl of Leicester, Mr. Hatton, and Mr. Walsingham, have earnestly moved her Majesty to go forward with the marriage as her most safety." (Lodge, II. 223; Sandys to Shrewsbury, March 5th, 1579–80.) To this Mr. Lodge appends the following note: "It is remarkable that these three ministers should be usually mentioned together in history as the most vehement opposers of the marriage." Yet the fact — admitting, on the mere opinion of Archbishop Sandys, that it *was* a fact — only shows that in this instance historians have looked behind the outward seeming of ministers, — which the Archbishop did not. As for Leicester, *his* seeming is sufficiently accounted for by Lloyd, as quoted in the text; and also by Fuller (Bk. IX. p. 139), who represents him as habitually carrying one face at the Council Board, and another elsewhere.

[3] Lloyd, 519.

[4] Camden, 232. Strype's Annals, IV. 244.

voked by Simier's apparent success, he gave rise to a rumor, — fitted better than anything else that could have been devised in those days to excite popular horror, — that Simier had gained an ascendency over the queen's affections in favor of the Duke, by means of love-potions and other unlawful arts.[1] Simier was enraged, and retaliated. To explain this fully we must turn to incidents of previous occurrence.

In July, 1575, Leicester had entertained her Majesty at his castle of Kenilworth for nineteen successive days, in a style of unparalleled magnificence.[2] This may have been merely for the sake of display, and out of gratitude for two hundred thousand crowns given to him the year before by the queen; and it may have been for the purpose of making an impression upon her, — the hope of obtaining her hand for himself not having then been abandoned. But not long afterwards, "he sounded her disposition in

[1] Camden, 232.

[2] Strype's Annals, III. 380 – 386.

"Fourteen Earls and seventeen Barons, besides the Ladies of the Queen's Household, were lodged in the castle, and attended on by four hundred of Leicester's servants, all in new liveries; his gentlemen, clad in velvet, waiting at table; sixteen hogsheads of wine, forty of beer, and ten oxen were consumed every day. The plenty of provisions, fruits, and comfitures was prodigious; and the order which reigned in every part of the entertainment was admirable, not only at the banquets, but at the huntings and other sports in the fields; and in the comedies, plays, and dancings within doors, in which there was not a day's intermission; for, after the queen had been with the company at church on the Sunday mornings to hear prayers and sermons, this patron of the Puritans entertained them with the like sports and pastimes as on other days in the afternoons. Among other solemnities, her Majesty touched *and cured nine persons of the King's Evil.*" (Carte, III. 546.) "For the kings and queens of this realm, without other medicine, (save only by handling and prayer,) only do cure it." (Strype's Annals, III. 585.)

The formula of religious ceremonies used at the healing of the king's evil — or scrofula — may be found in Sparrow's Collections, pp. 165, 166.

choosing him for a husband; and, not receiving a favorable answer, abandoned all thoughts thereof."[1] He had long before silenced by his threats the importunity of the Lady Douglass for an avowal of their marriage. Yet their intimacy — evident enough to the courtiers in 1573[2] — had continued until after the queen's refusal of his hand. Enamored of the Lady Lettice, Countess of Essex, he had then resolved to possess her person; and, to obviate all difficulties, had arranged for the murder of her husband and his own wife, when he conspired with Julio for the disgrace of Archbishop Grindal. We have seen how he succeeded with Essex. But in his experiment upon the Lady Douglass, Julio had failed; mistaking either the strength of his potion or the vigor of her constitution. Yet the poison was so far effectual as to cause the loss of her hair and nails; and she, knowing sufficiently well the author and the reason of her illness, and that the only way to insure herself against another like attempt would be to render Leicester's apprehensions of her interference impossible, contracted open marriage with Sir Edward

[1] Sidney State Papers, I. 48, 49. The following letter sustains the statement in the text. "Her Majesty, I see, is grown into a very strange humor. . . . . . Your lordship hath been best acquainted, next myself, to all my proceedings with her Majesty, and I have ere now broken my very heart with you, and have offered, for avoiding such blame as I have generally in the realm, mine own exile, that I might not be suspected a hinderer of that matter," — the queen's marriage, — "which all the world desired and were suitors for. . . . . . *And as I carried myself more than a bondman many a year together, so long as one drop of comfort was left of any hope*, as you yourself, my lord, doth well know. *So, being acquitted and delivered of that hope, and, by both open and private protestations and declarations discharged*, methinks it is more than hard to take such an occasion to bear so great displeasure for," &c. (Wright, II. 103; Leicester to Burleigh, November 12, 1579.)

[2] Lodge, II. 100.

Stafford; and thus, by adultery, saved her life.[1] Immediately after the death of Essex,[2] Leicester forsook the Lady Douglass; *more* openly than *before* showed his love for the Lady Lettice; and soon[3] married her privately at Kenilworth.[4] But Sir Francis Knollys, her father, knowing well the infidelity and arts of Leicester, and "fearing he might put a trick upon his daughter," was not satisfied with this clandestine marriage, and caused the ceremony to be performed again at Wanstead, in Essex, on the twenty-first day of September, 1578,[5] in presence of himself, the Earl of Warwick, Leicester's brother, the Lord North, a Notary Public, and several other witnesses.[6] This transaction, though generally known at Court, was carefully concealed from the queen;[7] for, "everybody being either within the obligation of his courtesies or the reach of his injuries,"[8] no one dared to make him his enemy by revealing a fact which would bring the Earl under the royal displeasure. But Simier — a foreigner and a visitor — was beyond all such considerations of profit or loss. He had only his own mission to perform, with which Leicester by his whispering about philters was interfering. To revenge himself, and to prostrate the greatest seeming barrier to the Duke's wishes, Simier promptly informed the queen of her favorite's marriage with the Countess of Essex. Her Majesty

[1] Carte, III. 543. Biographia Britannica; Article Robert Dudley, note E. Lodge, I. 309, note. Taylor, I. 75. See also above, Vol. I. Chap. X. note 5.

[2] Dugdale's Baronage; quoted in Ellis, 1st Series, II. 280.

[3] Fuller's Worthies, III. 524.

[4] Carte, III. 542. Fragmenta Regalia, 193.

[5] Sidney Papers, I. 69. Birch, I. 74.

[6] Carte, III. 542. Camden, 218.

[7] Taylor, I. 80.

[8] Lloyd, 519, 520.

was greatly incensed, and ordered the Earl to confinement in the castle of Greenwich. She would have sent him to the Tower but for the intercession of his greatest but most noble-hearted enemy, the Earl of Sussex, who "first moderated the queen's passion with reason, and then overcame it with the jest, 'You must allow lovers their jealousies;'[1] thus gallantly hinting that Leicester's slander of Simier was more the fault of her Majesty's transcendent charms than of the susceptible and disappointed Earl. This was notoriously the way to soften Elizabeth;[2] and in consequence Leicester

[1] Lloyd, 494. Camden, 233. Sidney State Papers, I. 49. Carte, III. 553, 554.

Sussex's detestation of Leicester never abated. "It is confidently affirmed, that, lying in his last sickness, he gave this caveat to his friends: 'I am now passing into another world, and I must now leave you to your fortunes, and to the queen's grace and goodness; but beware of the Gipsy' (meaning Leicester,) 'for he will be too hard for you all. You know not the Beast so well as I do.'" (Naunton; Fragmenta Regalia, in the Phœnix, p. 194.)

[2] "Elizabeth, even in age, had a great conceit of her personal beauty." (Osborne, 49.) But I have said "notoriously." The truth of this is apparent from the following anecdote: "A purveyor having abused the County of Kent, upon her remove to Greenwich (being, as I have heard, the first air she breathed), a countryman, watching the time she went to walk, which was commonly early, and being wise enough to take his time when she stood unbent and quiet from the ordinary occasions she was taken up with, placing himself within reach of her ear, did, after the fashion of his coat, cry aloud, 'Which is the queen?' and continuing still his question, she herself answered, 'I am your queen. What wouldst thou have with me?' 'You,' replied the fellow, 'are one of the rarest women I ever saw, and can eat no more than my daughter Madge, who is thought the properest lasse in our parish, though short of you! But that Elizabeth I look for devours so many of my hens, ducks, and capons, as I am not able to live.' The queen, no less auspicious to all suits made through the mediation of her comely shape (of which she held a high esteem after her looking-glasses, long laid by before her death, might have confuted her in any good opinion of her face), than malignant to all oppression above her own, inquired who was

was soon liberated, although for months her Majesty treated him with lofty coolness.

In May, the Privy Council were still engaged in their deliberations upon the engrossing question of the proposed marriage; and on the third day of that month, a point was settled which may be quoted as indicative of the double-facedness which characterized the whole transaction. "It was by common consent concluded that the article for the matter of religion should remain in suspense until that Monsieur should come to her Majesty, and upon their mutual liking, the same should be concluded; and if there were not a mutual liking, then the cause of breaking off from conclusion of marriage should be imputed only upon the difference arising upon the article of Religion."[1]

Soon after, "the secret opinion was that the matter of Monsieur's coming, and especially the marriage, was grown very cold;"[2] and within a month, when Simier pressed her Majesty for a decision, she replied only that she must *see* her suitor. The hint was taken.[3] In August, the Duke suddenly presented himself to her Majesty at her Court in Greenwich; having come in the style of a private gentleman with only one or two attendants.[4] After only a few days'

purveyor, and, as the story went, suffered him to be hanged." (Ibid., 54, 55.)

[1] Murdin, 320; Report to the Council by Burleigh.

[2] Lodge, II. 217; Talbot to Shrewsbury, May 15.

[3] Lingard, VIII. 126.

[4] Camden, 233.

I do not find the date of the Duke's visit stated by any writer but Lingard, who — if his marginal date be correctly printed in the very inaccurate edition before me — assigns it to the month of September. I fix upon August, because it appears from Harrington's account (Nugæ Antiquæ, Vol. I.) that Stubbes's book against the marriage came out in August; and be-

wooing, and having been seen by but very few, he returned, sanguine of success.[1]

That the queen should have conducted herself towards him with cordiality, and even with the outward signs of ardent affection, confirmed and seemed to justify the supposition that she had been plied by some unworthy art. His face was disfigured by the small-pox,[2] and by a nose so monstrous that it had the appearance of being doubled.[3]

Much and long as the English people had desired their queen's marriage, the present overture was most unwelcome. The suitor for her Majesty's hand was reputed to be a man of debauched life;[4] he was certainly a Frenchman, a Catholic, a scion of that royal House whose sympathy was notoriously with the Queen of Scots, and which, but just now had whelmed the Protestants of France in blood and mourning. Add to all this, the rumor of Simier's sorcery, and the confirmation of that rumor by the queen's amorous grace towards a man of repulsive features, and we cannot wonder that the general opposition to the match was serious and the popular excitement great. "I do assure your lordship," wrote Leicester to Burleigh from Kenilworth, "since

cause Strype says (Annals, IV. 232) that "it came forth while the Duke was here in his courtship;" i. e. in 1579.

[1] Camden, 233. Carte, III. 554.

[2] Taylor, I. 76. Mackintosh; who refers to Digges, not now before me.

[3] "When he went to Flanders, the following epigram was circulated, in which his nose is whimsically made a type of the duplicity of his character:

Good people of Flanders, pray do not suppose
That 't is monstrous this Frenchman should double his nose;
Dame Nature her favors but rarely misplaces;
She has given two noses to match his two faces."

(Taylor, I. 76.)

[4] Strype's Grindal, 242.

Queen Mary's time the Papists were never in that jollity they be at this present in this country.[1] . . . . . They be here, and in more places than here, upon their tiptoes."[2] If such was the "jollity" of the Papists in anticipation of the projected marriage, it was but of course that the aversion of the Protestants should be in like measure. The popular excitement ran high and burst forth. It was manifested "especially by those that were of the Puritan party;" and "made a considerable shock at Court."[3] The invectives uttered from the pulpit against the match were vehement in the month of March, when her Majesty interfered and "gave express commandment that none of the preachers should hereafter preach upon any such text as the like might be inferred;" a pretty large interdict upon the Bible.[4] How well this was obeyed at this time is doubtful; for afterwards "the Lord Mayor of London was commanded to reprimand the city clergy for their sermons about the queen's marriage."[5]

[1] County?

[2] Wright, II. 102.

[3] Strype's Aylmer, 63, 64.

[4] Lodge, II. 212, 213; Talbot to Shrewsbury, April 4th, 1579.

Simultaneous with this commandment of the queen was the following curious letter, to which no signature appears, but which Peck supposes to have been written by Burleigh:

"The queen's Majesty dislikes sermons discussing matters of Government in the hearing of vulgar people, who are not apt" — qualified — "to hear such things. She will receive private advice to herself or Council. The vulgar, by such hearing of sermons, catch lightly occasions to think sinisterly or doubtfully of the Head of her Government. If preachers desire amendment in things properly belonging to herself, I assure myself she will willingly hear any by speech or writing. . . . . . I wish in my heart no jot of the authority of preachers diminished; and yet wish them not to presume upon their authority to condemn others without some *growethe*," — *sic.* — "March 24, 1578–9. To Dr. Chaderton, my very loving friend, Master of Queen's College." (Peck's Desiderata Curiosa, Vol. I. Bk. III. No. VII.)

[5] Life of Hatton, 235.

But the most true exponent of the popular sentiment respecting the marriage was given through the press. In the month of August a tract was published in London, entitled "The Discoveringe of a gapinge gulphe, whereinto England is like to be swallowed by another French marriage, yf the Lord forbid not the banes by lettinge her Majestie see the sin and punishment thereof." The author was John Stubbes, a student at law of Lincoln's Inn; the printer, —— Singleton; and the publisher, or disperser, William Page.[1] Stubbes was a Puritan; thirty-seven years of age; held in high esteem by his associates at Lincoln's Inn, "who were of the more learned and ingenious sort;" a man of bold and earnest spirit; and of so much talent and loyalty as to have commanded the respect and confidence of Lord Burleigh.[2] His tract, although styled at the time "a lewd and seditious libel," was characterized not only by "a smart and stinging style,"[3] but by good sense and unfeigned loyalty.[4] Its burden was the danger to religion which would ensue, should the marriage take place, — an apprehension by no means singular, for it had its parallel in the opposing sect in France.[5] It contained many sincere expressions of loyal affection for the queen, but spared not the Duke. It inveighed against his clandestine mode of courtship as "an unmanlike,

[1] Strype's Annals, IV. 239. Camden, 270.

[2] Strype's Grindal, 242. Strype's Annals, IV. 305.

[3] Camden, 269.

[4] Hallam, 139.

The original MS. was in existence in 1804. (Nugæ Antiquæ, I. 143.)

[5] "The news of the espousals had equally alarmed the zealots of both Religions. In France it was pronounced from the pulpit that the marriage of the presumptive heir to the monarchy with an heretical princess portended nothing less than the speedy downfall of the Church." (Lingard, VIII. 132.)

unprincelike, needy, French kind of wooing." It contained also the following words: "This man is a son of Henry II., whose family, ever since he married with Catharine of Italy, is fatal, as it were, to resist the Gospel, and have been every one after other, as a Domitian after Nero, as a Trajan after Domitian, and as a Julian after Trajan. Here is, therefore, an imp of the Crown of France to marry with the crowned nymph of England."[1]

The queen took offence at this book, partly because she thought it would mar her popularity; partly because it tended to thwart her political intrigues; and partly because "she believed these kind of things proceeded from the Puritans, or Inno-

[1] Nugæ Antiquæ, I. 154.

Dr. Lingard says (VIII. 132) that Stubbes "described the marriage as an impious and sacrilegious union between a daughter of God and a son of the devil." He seems to refer to the passage which I have quoted. If he does, I am at a loss to know what he means by such a representation. The word "imp" originally signified *to graft;* and scions, or twigs fit for grafting were called "*imps.*"

Thus, in "The Abbot," by Sir Walter Scott, close of Ch. XXIII.: "Come to aid me in my garden, and I will teach thee the real French fashion of *imping*, which the Southron call grafting."

Again, in Shakespeare's King Richard II. Act II., close of Scene I.:

"If then we shall shake off our slavish yoke,
Imp out our drooping country's broken wing," &c.; —

which Stevens explains thus: — "When the wing-feathers of a hawk were dropped, or forced out by accident, it was usual to supply as many as were deficient. This operation was called to *imp* a hawk."

In Elizabeth's day it had a secondary or figurative meaning; denoting a hopeful youth on the eve of puberty. So Chaucer, and other ancient English poets. Thus James of Scotland, in his boyhood, was described by one of his own loyal subjects as "Their chief earthly jewel, the goodly young *imp* their king." (Lodge, II. 200; Aleyn to the Lord Bishop of Carlisle, November, 1578.) So Lord Cromwell, in his last letter to Henry VIII., prays for the *imp his son.* So, also, we find the expression "*godly* and *virtuous imp*," in Fox's "Acts and Movements," II. p. 129, fol. edit. 1684. The word is also used in the same sense in "Love's Labor Lost," Act I. Scene II.:

vators,"[1] "whose opinions and favorers," she told Malvesier in this very connection, "she *would root out*."[2] She denounced the book as "containing a heap of slanders against the Duke, bolstered up with manifest lies; as maliciously and rebelliously stirring up her subjects to fear their own ruin, a change of government, and an alteration of religion, by her Majesty's marriage; and as interlacing flattering glosses towards her to cover the manifest depraving of her Majesty and her actions to her people;" and as further censurable because "there *was not* once, in any one sentence of the libel, any so much as a supposal touched of any motherly or princely care to be in her Majesty for the profit, peace, or policy of the realm. And therefore her pleasure and commandment was, that no person should esteem the said

"ARMADO. *Boy*, what sign is it when a man of great spirit grows melancholy?
MOTH. A great sign, sir, that he will look sad.
ARM. Why, sadness is one and the selfsame thing, *dear imp*."

Once more. In the Invocation which Spenser has prefixed to his "Faerie Queene," Stanza III.:

"And thou, most dreaded *impe* of highest Iove,
Faire Venus' sonne, that with thy cruell dart," &c.

Therefore Stubbes, instead of calling the Duke "a son of the devil," as Lingard says, only designated him as a *scion* of the Crown of France. Even a common English Dictionary would have taught the Catholic historian this; it being supposed that the English Dictionaries are as full and explicit as the American in their definitions of the English vocabulary.

It is *modern* usage which has consigned the word to Satan, as designating the younger members of *his* family. Mr. Lodge (Ibid., note) thinks that the word was used in a bad sense by the Earl of Shrewsbury in his letter of November 9th, 1585, on page 319. He was at odds with his Countess, to be sure; and there calls *her* children "her imps." But that he used the word "as a term of reproach," or that it was ever so used at so early a date, admits of question.

This explanation is not only due to correct Dr. Lingard, but is necessary to understand rightly the sense in which the word is used in quotations from Papers of the day on previous pages of this work.

[5] Camden, 270. Strype's Annals, IV. 233; Queen's Proclamation.

[2] Strype's Annals, IV. 242.

book otherwise than as a traitorous device; and that the foresaid book or libel, wherever found, should be destroyed in open sight of some public officer; and that the favorers or withholders thereof should be attached to answer according to their demerits."

Such were the chief points of a Proclamation issued by her Majesty on the twenty-seventh day of September.[1] On the same day the Council ordered the Lord Mayor of London and his associates to be present at the publishing of the queen's Proclamation.[2] On the fifth day of October, they addressed a letter to his Grace of Canterbury, "requiring him to assemble his chief clergy to hear the Proclamation; to signify unto them her Highness's firm determination to maintain Religion unchanged; and to admonish them not to intermeddle in their sermons with any such matter of State, which pertained not to their profession, and wherewith they ought to have nothing to do at all."[3]

Early in October — apparently[4] — the parties concerned in this offensive book were arrested and put upon their trial under the statute 1 and 2 Philip and Mary, Cap. III., entitled "An Act against seditious words and rumors." Sentence was given against them, that their right hands should be stricken off, as prescribed by Section IV. of that act for the first offence of "maliciously devising, writing, printing, or setting forth any manner of book, ... containing clause or sentence of reproach and dishonor to the King and Queen."[5]

[1] Strype's Annals, IV. 232 – 238.

[2] Nugæ Antiquæ, I. 143.

[3] Strype's Grindal, Append., Bk. II. No. XIII. p. 92. P. Soc.'s "Remains of Grindal," 410.

[4] Camden, 270.

[5] Camden says that some lawyers were reprehended and punished for saying that the sentence was void on the ground that the Act

During his imprisonment, between his trial and the execution of sentence, Stubbes addressed a petition to her Majesty. We give it almost entire, because its style challenges comparison with that of Sir Philip Sidney — accounted the most accomplished gentleman and scholar of the day — in his remonstrance to her Majesty against this same marriage;[1] because it is as fair an exponent of Puritan loyalty as was the book itself of Puritan anti-papacy; and because it shows that the man in "the simplicity of his heart"[2] had not dreamed of giving offence, although he had so stung her Majesty's pride.

was only temporary, and died with Queen Mary. If this *was true*, a certain lawyer and a certain Judge, one would think, must have been strangely ignorant of the statutes. The Act 1 and 2 Philip and Mary, Chap. III., was indeed enacted to be only in force until the end of the *next* Parliament, and no longer." (Sec. X.) But it was renewed from time to time until the Parliament of 4 and 5 Philip and Mary, — the last under that reign, — when it was again continued "until the last day of *the next* Parliament." "The *next* Parliament," — by the grace of God, — was 1 Eliz.: by which (Chap. VI.) it was enacted that "the said Act be expounded . . . . . to *extend* to the Queen's Highness that now is, as fully . . . . . as though it had by express words extended to the heirs and successors of the said late queen; *any question, ambiguity, or doubt, ... hereafter happening to grow . . . . . to the contrary in anything notwithstanding.*"

Does not this explicitness cast a doubt over Camden's statement? If the statute 1 and 2 Philip and Mary could be said, technically, to have "died" *at all*, it must have died, according to its own words, at "the end of the Parliament 2 and 3 Philip and Mary. But, *before* the end of the Parliament 2 and 3 Philip and Mary, it received a new lease, or rather a fresh element, of life; and so, again, at the next Parliament; and so, again, from the Parliament 1 Eliz. I cannot see, therefore, that, even in the most rigid, exacting, and technical sense, it *had ever died*. Timely renewals of vital force were always furnished on the eve of expiration.

[1] It is in Cabala, 330–338; and in Strype's Annals, IV. Appendix, Bk. II. No. XIX. pp. 641–652.

In this letter Philip Sidney says: "How their hearts will be galled, if not aliened, when they shall see you take a husband, a Frenchman, a Papist, in whom (howsoever fine wits may find further dealings or painted excuses) the very common people well know this, that he is the son of a Jezebel of our age," &c.

[2] Hallam, 139.

"If my lot, most Dread and Gracious Sovereign, when it was at the best, was yet so low as I never was worthy one least look of your Majesty's eyes, how should I (now that I am in bodily bonds) and (which is the great captivity of mine afflicted mind) in this high indignation of your Majesty) be yet so hardy to crave that patience of your royal ears as to have my humble words hearkened unto? Surely, even this emboldeneth my panting heart, that, as the King of kings, the Lord of heaven and earth, doth take to his singular recommendation, and readily heareth, burdened minds out of their deepest dungeons, ... even so that princes, which are his visible Majesty among men, do endeavor to resemble the Lord of lords not only in chiefest authority and sovereign commanding, but chiefly in that which he saith is over all his works, — that is, mercy and forgiveness. Whereunto comes, as an addition of sustaining me in this heartening, that my prince is a Christian lady whose natural inclination to pity, religion hath also taught to have compassion. . . . . . And as those prayers which have any promise of hearing from God must be qualified with a sorrowful acknowledgment of the sins we have committed, and of his gracious pardon to be bestowed upon us undeservedly, even so am I the bolder to offer this supplicatory submission and petition into your Majesty's hands, because it is the very true and unfeigned witnessing of my prostrate heart, laden with grief to have by this act incurred your princely displeasure, and to have disquieted or troubled your gracious heart. . . . . . If I had supposed this thing would have reached so highly, either in offence or disquiet to the mind of my natural Queen, or in so heinous breach of the laws of your Majesty's peace, I would most willingly have redeemed the pain for one hand, with both hands; and rather to have had no life, than to fall in my prince's thought for a suspect subject of doubtful loyalty, or to be recorded in so high a Court of this land for a miserable turbulous wretch, seeking to interrupt her peace and that State by whom I stand. . . . . . Submitting myself, therefore, in all truth and humbleness of heart upon my knees, to the high censure of your royal wisdom, and to that judgment which is given against me by law, as touching my outward fact and every circumstance thereof, I crave (by your most gracious favor) pardon to say these few words for myself; the contrary whereof I cannot say though it were to save my head: That is, that my poor heart never conceived malicious thought, or wicked purpose, against your Majesty's person or State; but joyed and rejoiced in your high life, health, honor, and peace; judging the contrary to be the greatest calamity earthly that could befall either to this Commonweal or my private estate. . . . . . Whereupon, if there might ensue first and principally some better conceiving, or at least not so evil opinion, of my single-hearted allegiance, and, secondarily, some mitigation of your great indignation, I would reckon but as in the third place, and for an accessory benefit, the pardon of my hand. The which, unless it may like your gracious Majesty, of your free mercy and accustomed pity, to give me again, there is nothing in me already to move you, neither can I promise any new and worthy recompense of service due for so great a grace; for alas!

what can *my* poor hand perform? . . . . . This, then, can be the only use of it, — even to bear it about with me while I live, for an evident gage of your prince-like, lady-like, Christian, free mercy towards me; provoking others, as it were, by the lively speaking thereof, to deserve well of her, by well-doing, who is so ready to do well without desert, and to be graciously merciful to so grievous an offender. The Lord God cut off both their hands and shorten their arms, who do not with all their heart pray for your everlasting life in heaven, after your godly, long, happy, honorable, healthful, and joyful life here on earth. Amen.

JOHN STUBBES."

In the gray of the morning, on the third day of November, a party of mechanics were busily at work in the market-place of Westminster; and when the sun had fairly risen they had just completed a rude but substantial platform of some ten feet square, and elevated seven or eight feet from the ground. The men had wrought rapidly, but with none of those signs of contentment and good cheer usual to their vocation, and with no more words than necessary for the accomplishment of their task. Even in the construction of a gallows, rough-handed and rough-hearted men, such as these were, are wont to choke unbidden and unpleasant thoughts by bits of ballads, or by jokes and repartees. But this was evidently no scaffold for death, and yet the last plank was laid, and the last nail driven, in silence; and the men went quickly and sulkily away. Boys came and pointed at the structure, spoke in low monosyllables and exclamations, and ran home with sober faces. Country-men and country-women, servant maids, smart prentices, burghers, scullions, and beggars,—all looked askance at that platform as they passed along; and when, near midday, there was a vast and surging crowd around it, there was no noise there, and no sign of tumult. When two men came and placed upon the plank a sort of butcher's block; and another, wearing a smutted face and leathern apron, threw beside it a butcher's cleaver and a mallet, there was an evident sensation among the people, but no more outward sign of it than a suppressed murmur and a slight swaying of the mass as each shifted his place to view the doings on the stage. "The king's wrath is as messengers of death, and as the roaring of a lion;" how much more a queen's!

The silent crowd opened a way for the Sheriff and his attendants, in whose custody Stubbes, the loyal writer of treason, and Page, the publisher of his writing, mounted the scaffold to receive execution of their sentence. Singleton, the printer, had been pardoned.[1] The Sheriff read his warrant with official rapidity, and then gave a permissive sign to the convicts. Stubbes moved to the verge of the scaffold, and, in a firm, manly voice, addressed the multitude as follows:

"What a grief it is to the body to lose one of his members, you all know. I am come hither to receive my punishment according to the law. I am sorry to lose it by judgment; but most of all with her Majesty's indignation and evil opinion, whom I have so highly displeased. Before I was condemned, I might speak for my innocency; but now my mouth is

[1] Camden, 270.

stopped by judgment, to which I submit myself, and am content patiently to endure whatsoever it pleaseth God, of his secret providence, to lay upon me, and to take it justly deserved for my sins. And I pray God it may be an example to you all, that, it being so dangerous to offend the laws, without an evil meaning, as breedeth the loss of a hand, you may use your hands holily, and pray to God for the long preservation of her Majesty over you, whom God hath used as an instrument for a long peace and many blessings over us, and specially for his Gospel, whereby she hath made a way for us to rest and quietness of our consciences. For the French I force not;[1] but my greatest grief is, in so many weeks' and days' imprisonment her Majesty hath not once thought me worthy of her mercy, which she hath oftentimes extended to divers persons in greater offences. For my hand, I esteem it not so much, for I think I could have saved it and might do yet; but I will not have a guiltless heart and an infamous hand. I pray you all to pray with me, that God will strengthen me to endure and abide the pain that I am to suffer, and grant me this grace, that the loss of my hand do not withdraw any part of my duty and affection toward her Majesty; and because, when so many veins of blood are opened, it is uncertain how they may be stayed, and what will be the event thereof."

Then turning to the block and kneeling beside it, he continued: "I beseech you all to pray for me, that it would please God to forgive me my sins. I crave pardon of all the world, and freely forgive every one that hath offended me; and so, with mercy to deal

[1] I. e. "I lay *no stress* on matters between them and me."

with me whether I live or die, I may live or die his servant. My masters! if there be any among you that do love me, if your love be not in God and her Majesty, I utterly deny your love."

He then laid his hand upon the block; and, while the executioner was making ready, said repeatedly to the people, "Pray for me! pray for me now my calamity is at hand." The executioner laid the edge of the cleaver upon the victim's wrist. A heavy blow with the mallet,—the hand rolled from the block, and Stubbes, bounding with agony to his feet, his quivering stump spouting blood, his face ashy pale, took off his hat with his left hand and said in a loud voice, "God save the queen! God save—" tottered a step or two, and fell in a swoon.[1]

Our annalist, William Camden, was present;[2] and he records: "The multitude standing about was deeply silent, either out of an horror at this new and unwonted kind of punishment, or else out of commiseration towards the man as being of an honest and unblamable repute, or else out of hatred of the marriage which *most* men presaged would be the overthrow of Religion."[3] Probably for each reason.

Page, who seemed a man of stouter mould than Stubbes, now stepped forward and said, "I am come hither to receive the law according to my judgment,

[1] Even Bishop Warburton declares, that "this was infinitely more cruel than all the *ears* under Charles I., whether we consider the punishment, the crime, or the man." (Vol. XII. p. 381, London edit., 1811.)

[2] Yet he has mistaken the date of the occurrence by two years; stating that it took place in 1581. The letter of the Lords of the Council to the Archbishop of Canterbury, respecting "a certain libel entitled "The Gaping Gulph," is suffieient proof of this, being dated "the 5 October, 1579."

[3] Camden, 270.

and thank God of all; and of this I take God to witness, that knoweth the hearts of all men, that, as I am sorry that I have offended her Majesty, so did I never mean harm to her Highness's person, crown, or dignity; but have been as true a subject as any was in England, to my ability, except none. This right hand"—holding it up—"did I put to the plough, and got my living by it many years. If it would have pleased her Majesty to have pardoned it, and to have taken my left hand or my life, she had dealt more favorably with me; for now I have no means to live. But God which is the Father of us all will provide for me. I beseech you all to pray for me, that I may take this punishment patiently. I pray you," turning to the executioner and laying his hand upon the block, "despatch me quickly."

At two blows the hand flew. The sufferer held the stump upward, eyed the severed member a moment, pointed at it and said, "I have left there a true Englishman's hand." He then went from the scaffold "very stoutly and with great courage." [1]

Such was the barbarity of the law. Such, the terrible punishment for uttering that "the marriage," to which "the minds of the *best* men in England were averse" "would be the overthrow of Religion,"—a result "which *most men* presaged." [2] Such, the punishment for uttering what, by construction only, came within the range of the statute. Such, the *earnest* of her Majesty's intent to "*root* out Puritanism." Such, her pitiless severity, when only "*a little* more in-

[1] The Petition of Stubbes to the queen, and the speeches of the two men on the scaffold, I find in Harrington's Nugæ Antiquæ, Vol. I. pp. 143–158.

[2] Camden, 270.

censed against those from whom she easily believed these kind of things to proceed."[1] We shall soon see that it was thought too *mild;* and in this instance satisfying the law did not satisfy the queen.

From the scaffold, Stubbes was sent, "a double-close prisoner" to the Tower,[2] whence he addressed a petition to one of the Privy Council, dated "The House which is my prison, the 3 of December." In the course of this Paper he expressed himself thus: "If I should reckon up my long imprisonment, my painful wound, my weak, wretched body, my want of ability to bear these exceeding extraordinary expenses and the present shipwreck of my poor estate, — all these are but the sour fruits growing by my own offence, whereof I have not had a light taste of palate, but digested them into every vein of my heart. Something it may speak for me, that my poor wife and little child (two helpless innocents in mine offence)[3] have yet their great part in all these mine adversities. . . . . . Most unhappy do I esteem myself in doing anything that might have troubled the long peace of her Majesty's estate which hath nourished me in my youth, and wherein I desire to wax old, and after which I neither wish to live, nor fear to die."[4] His wife also, in a petition to the queen, "dared avouch upon her life, that his meaning and intent in writing what had incurred her Highness's most grievous and fearful displeasure, was, the glory and honor of God; next, the pres-

[1] Camden, 270.

[2] Strype's Annals, IV. 304. Nugæ Antiquæ, I. 159; Stubbes's Petition.

[3] In the original, "ij sillie innocents;" "silly" used in a sense now obsolete.

[4] Nugæ Antiquæ, I. 165.

ervation and safety of her royal person and the public weal and benefit of his country."[1] Stubbes continued in prison at least until August, 1580; and we have no sign of his liberation until July, 1581.[2]

That his loyalty was no pretence; that it was in no wise abated by the harshness of his sovereign; and that he was a person of no mean ability; are evident from the fact that Lord Burleigh intrusted to him, in 1587, the responsible task of answering Cardinal Allen's Reply to Lord Burleigh's pamphlet entitled "The Execution of Justice in England," &c. Allen's "popish libel was thought by the Papists to be for workmanship unmatchable and for sound matter uncontrollable." "But, God be thanked!" wrote the two learned civilians Doctor Byng and Doctor Hammond to Lord Burleigh, — "God be thanked! it is ripped in sunder by Mr. Stubbes's treatise in defence of English Justice; and the rottenness of every member in such sort discovered as all the shifting surgery of the Romish faction will never recure it. Touching the work, it is more than time, in our opinion, it were abroad; not only for the better staying of weak ones, but for repressing the insolent vaunts of petty Romish pamphleteers."[3] One-handed as he was, Stubbes not only served her Majesty devotedly in the cabinet, but in the field. He wielded the sword, as well as the pen, for the honor and support of her Government; distinguishing himself as "a valiant commander in the wars of Ireland."[4] Was he, or was he not, the same John Stubbes whose

[1] Strype's Annals, IV. 239, 240.
[2] Ibid.
[3] Ibid., IV. 306. Hallam, 94, note.
[4] Neal, I. 147. Brook, I. 42.

name afterwards appears in D'Ewes as a member of the House of Commons?[1]

The royal courtship — in some of its particulars rather comical — concerns us no further. Yet we will indulge ourselves in tracing its outline onward. Soon after the Duke's departure, the queen ordered Burleigh, Sussex, Leicester, Hatton, and Walsingham, to estimate the advantages and disadvantages of the proposed marriage, — a task which seems to have perplexed them.[2] On the sixteenth day of April, 1581,[3] a splendid embassy came from France, seriously to prosecute the marital negotiations, and were entertained in princely style. Articles of contract were drawn up; the queen, however, warily interposing a reservation which kept the contract incomplete. Difficulties were started. The negotiations became complicated and embarrassed. On the first day of November,[4] the Duke made his appearance in state; and made love seemingly with great effect. Tender scenes occurred, — exciting scenes, — lovers' pledges, — lovers' tears, — lovers' misunderstandings, — lovers' reconciliations, — paroxysms of grief among the Ladies of the Bedchamber, — and sleepless nights on the part of the queen.[5] The affair had so much the aspect of real love, that the Duke, after a rupture and a taunt upon faithless islanders, was soothed and induced to remain three months longer.[6] Her Majesty even took her pen as if to sign the final contract; when "she suddenly

[1] D'Ewes, 431, 436, 440.
[2] Camden, 233. Carte, III. 555.
[3] Cecil's Journal; Murdin, 781. Holingshed, IV. 435.
[4] Holingshed, IV. 447.
[5] Camden, 265 – 268. Carte, III. 566, 567.
[6] Lingard, VIII. 133.

threw it away in great fury, asking the Lords of the Council in a reproachful manner, 'If they were so blind as not to see that after her death they would be cutting one another's throats, or did not know that marriage would soon put an end to her days?' which was generally interpreted of some bodily infirmity that rendered conception and childbearing exceeding dangerous,"[1] and which, having been "objected by her physicians and gentlewomen, did many times run in her mind, and very much deterred her from thoughts of marrying."[2] Yet she wept when the prince left in February, 1581–2; required of him a promise to return in a month;[3] and on her return from Canterbury,[4] to which place she accompanied him, "would be long in no place in which she lodged as she went, neither would she come to Whitehall, because the places"—by her avoiding them—"should not give cause of remembrance to her of him with whom she so unwillingly parted."[5]

[1] Carte, III. 568.

[2] Camden, 269.

[3] Lingard, VIII. 134.

[4] Holingshed, IV. 461.

[5] Lodge, II. 258; Talbot to Shrewsbury, Feb. 12th, 1581–2.

Mr. Lodge makes a mistake in his comment upon this letter, in supposing that "all writers on this period inform us that the Queen and Monsieur *parted* on ill terms." The quarrel about the ring, to which he refers, is stated to have taken place on the anniversary of the queen's accession, the 17th of November, almost three months *before* "the queen and Monsieur *parted.*" A reconciliation had taken place; and even Camden, whose story, particularly, Lodge repudiates, states that on the fifth day of February (Holingshed, IV. 461), they "parted" on *good* terms. (Compare Camden, 267, 268, with 273.) "Either part" — the French and English companies — "took their leave of the other" at Canterbury, "not without great grief and show of very great amity, *especially between her Majesty and the Monsieur.*" (Holingshed, IV. 461.) "The departure was mournful between her Highness and Monsieur; she loath to let him go, and he as troubled to depart; and promised to return in March." (Strype's Annals, IV. 318.)

Thus ended this diplomatic farce, by which, for ten years, Elizabeth humored and vexed her subjects, perplexed her ministers, contrived to bait the most formidable power in Europe, and to keep at bay all attempts in behalf of the Queen of Scots.[1]

[1] Dr. Lingard says (VIII. 135, note), "It cannot be, as some writers have imagined, that all the tokens of attachment which she lavished on the Duke were dictated by policy only, and not by affection."

That Elizabeth had a maudlin passion for this youth of repulsive aspect, which in its heats sometimes made her forget the risk to her life which would accrue upon her marriage, may be freely admitted; and yet, that she ever seriously resolved upon it may be doubted, and the entire negotiation with France may be fairly regarded as a political game, conducted with consummate art, and available, while it lasted, to the interests of the English Crown.

Elizabeth's assertions, quoted at the opening of this chapter, that "she was free from all manner of impediments to marry," and that "it was her resolute determination to do so," are not worthy of a moment's consideration; for the woman who could fib so outrageously as she did to Sir James Melvil (*ante*, Vol. I. p. 276), could, for a like diplomatic purpose, or for any other, do the like again.

While the matter of the marriage was pending, it was one day urged, "that England might enjoy a sound and joyful security" — in regard to the succession — "by means of the queen's children." (Camden, 234, 267.) Another day, there was a cry made about "her perils by conception and childbearing" (ibid., 269); and again, Hatton is found expostulating with her Majesty to her face, that "she was not likely to have *any* children." (Carte, III. 568. Lingard, VIII. 131.) Again: while "a great sort of wise men verily thought the marriage would come to pass, yet nevertheless there were divers others, like St. Thomas of Jude,* who would not believe till he had both seen and felt." (Lodge, II. 212; Talbot to Shrewsbury.) Castelnau, the French ambassador, was one of the sceptics; "believing that Elizabeth's *sole* object was to prevent any interference in behalf of Mary, Queen of Scots, and to perpetuate disunion between the Courts of France and Spain." (Taylor, I. 83, 179.) At the Court of France, too, the new propositions made in 1580–1 were considered "as intended only to amuse the Duke." (Carte, III. 569.) Villeroy, Secretary to the French King, "pronounced the scheme of marriage to be, on the part of Elizabeth, a systematic scheme of dissimulation and policy." (Mackintosh, III. 280, London edit. 1831.) "I know a man," wrote Sir Gilbert Talbot, in 1579, to his father, the Earl of Shrewsbury, "may take a thousand pounds, to be bound to pay double so much when

* Judæa.

Monsieur cometh into England, and treble so much when he marrieth the Queen's Majesty; and if he do neither the one nor the other, to gain the thousand pounds clear;" the odds at that time being considered, by some one, to be three to one against the marriage. (Lodge, II. 217, 218, and note.)

Even the remarkable paper in Murdin (p. 336; Oct. 7th, 1579), in which Elizabeth is represented as having been "much troubled" because her Council did not make "universal request to her to procede in this marriage," upon which occasion "she shed many tears," may fairly be regarded as describing an act of dissimulation. For two reasons: 1. Her sagacious Council could generally detect, and always chose to advise according to, her wishes; 2. At this very time, "she thought not mete to declare to us whether she would marry with Monsieur or no."

What was said merrily in 1567, upon proposals for the queen's marriage with the Archduke Charles, doubtless expressed the *sober* sentiment of "most men," of "the best men in England," of the queen herself, — that "where these three, Honor, Power, and Riches, are respected in marriage, the Devil and the World are the Matchmakers and Brokers." (Camden, 101.)

In view of these things, I have ventured to regard the whole affair of her courtship as a diplomatic game on the part of Elizabeth.

CHAPTER VII.

THE PARLIAMENT OF 1580-1.

Puritans disciplined. — Scarcity of Preachers. — Precisianism about the Sacramental Bread. — Parliament reassemble January 16, 1580-1. — A Motion by Paul Wentworth for a Day of Fasting, and for daily Preaching for the Commons. — The Motion carried. — Her Majesty's "Admiration." — After Debate, the Commons acknowledge their Fault. — The State of the Church shown by Petitions to Parliament. — The Commons, by a Committee, petition the Queen for Reformation in Matters of Religion. — The Report of their Committee. — Its Falsehood. — The Queen's real Answer. — The spurious Report considered. — The Influx of Seminary Priests in Disguise. — Foreign Plots against the Queen. — The first Jesuit Missionaries. — The "Act to retain the Queen's Majesty's Subjects in their due Obedience." — Reasons for it. — The "Act against Seditious Words and Rumors against the Queen's most excellent Majesty." — History of the Passage of both these Acts. — Framed to bear upon the Catholics only.

The authors of the "Admonition to Parliament," — Field and Wilcox, — after being discharged from prison at some time not specified, resumed the preaching of the Gospel. The former, as minister of Aldermary church in London; the latter, here and there as he had opportunity, but chiefly at Bovington in Hertfordshire. In 1577, they were cited before the Commissioners ecclesiastical for "entering into great Houses and teaching God knows what;"[1] when Aylmer, Bishop of London, to punish them for their "obstinacy," suggested a novel expedient, — that they should be sent to the most barbarous parts of the

[1] Strype's Aylmer, 55, 56; Aylmer to Burleigh.

realm, where they might be useful in reclaiming ignorant Papists. We only learn, however, that Mr. Field was separated from his people, who again and again petitioned in vain for his restoration. We are left in ignorance of the censure passed upon Wilcox.[1]

In 1578, the same prelate committed to prison Francis Merbury, minister at Northampton — a non-conformist of moderate principles and deportment — as "an overthwart, proud, Puritan knave." It was his third commitment for the same sin.[2] Several other clergymen were in the London prisons at the same time.[3]

Aylmer exercised his ecclesiastical lordship with rigor. His administration will come more particularly under notice in another chapter.

At least nine clergymen were suspended about the same time in the diocese of Norwich.[4]

With these exceptions, and perhaps some others, there seems to have been but little done from 1576 to 1581[5] in the way of disciplining the non-conforming Puritans; partly because there were so few of them left in the service of the Church, and partly because — as we shall soon see — the attention of both Church and State was particularly engrossed by the stealthy aggressions of Popery. There seems indeed to have been a reaction, to some extent, *in favor* of the ministers silenced from preaching. In 1578, the county of Norfolk[6] was disturbed by the discovery of some papistical practices there; which seems to have suggested the necessity, or at least

[1] Brook, I. 322, 323; II. 191.
[2] Brook, I. 228.
[3] Neal, I. 148.
[4] Brook, I. 238, 450.
[5] Fuller, Bk. IX. pp. 135, 138. Lodge, II. 188.

the policy, of some counteracting influence. "Shortly after, a great sort of good preachers, who had been long commanded to silence for a little niceness, were licensed and again commanded to preach; a greater and more universal joy to the countries and *the most of the Court*, than the disgrace of the Papists. And the gentlemen of those parts being great and hot Protestants" — Puritans? — "(almost before by policy discredited and disgraced)" — for their Puritanism? — "were greatly countenanced."[1]

So thoroughly had the work of purgation been performed by the Precisians, that the scarcity of officiating clergy who were capable of preaching was most deplorable. Since Mr. Merbury was sent to the Marshalsea prison "to cope with the Papists" there, the large and populous town of Northampton had not a single preacher, — the people crying aloud meanwhile for the bread of life. Of one hundred and forty clergymen in the county of Cornwall, not one could preach a sermon. Even in the city of London half the churches had no preachers; and of the incumbents of the other half, hardly one in ten "made conscience to wait upon his charge."[2]

Yet the ministers who were deprived of their livings still retained their connection with the Established Church, worshipping in her assemblies, and partaking in her sacraments. Some of them, so long as their licenses continued, occupied the pulpits of incumbents to whom the legal duty of reading service on Sundays and administering the sacrament twice a year was a drudgery. For a pittance allowed

[1] Lodge, II. 189; Topclyffe to Shrewsbury, Aug. 30, 1578.

[2] Neal, I. 146.

from the livings, to which the people added their voluntary contributions, the ejected ministers not only assumed the task of these "lazy drones," but preached fervently from the pulpit, and taught, reproved, counselled, and exhorted from house to house.[1] Others, respected for their knowledge of the Scriptures, for their Christian piety, and exemplary lives, were received as tutors and chaplains into the families of the nobility and gentry; and, being thus sheltered in "places exempt" from ordinary ecclesiastical jurisdiction, could serve their Master without molestation from the prelates.[2]

It has been before stated that the paramount principle of Elizabeth's ceremonial policy was, to preserve as close a resemblance as possible to what was visible in the Romish Church. Perhaps no one thing discloses this more clearly than a discussion, renewed in 1580, of the grave question whether the sacramental bread should be leavened or unleavened, thick or thin, round, square, oblong, or broken. In this there had been no uniformity for many years, if indeed at any time since the queen's accession. How this should have happened, Archbishop Parker "could not tell," except by attributing it to "the practice of the Devil."[3] The only authority upon the subject was the queen's injunction, which directed the sacramental bread to be like that "which heretofore served for the use of *the private Mass*."[4] By the

[1] Neal, I. 139.

[2] Ibid., 151.

[3] Strype's Parker, 309.

[4] Sparrow, 85.

The words of the injunction I give in full:—

"*Item.* Where also it was in the time of King Edward the Sixth used to have the sacramental bread of common fine bread, it is ordered for the more reverence to be given to these holy mysteries, being the

second rubric of Edward VI., common wheaten bread was *allowed* for this purpose; but the queen's injunction was mandatory, and — by the declaration, "the Queen's Majesty may . . . . . ordain and publish such further rites and ceremonies as may be most for . . . . . due reverence of Christ's holy mysteries and sacraments," — the injunction had the authority of a Parliamentary statute.[1] Aside from this mandate, Archbishop Parker considered it of no importance which kind of bread was used. Even at Court, the common bread had come to be used in 1570, although offence was there taken at the same innovation elsewhere.[2] In July, 1580, when the same matter was again in agitation, the Lords of the Council wrote to Chaderton, now Bishop of Chester: "Touching the Lord's Supper with wafers or common bread, the remedy we think meet to refer to the next session of Parliament, where the necessary reformation is only to be had. In the mean time, for appeasing such division and bitterness as may arise of the use of both kinds of bread, we think meet that where

sacraments of the body and blood of our Saviour Jesus Christ, that the said sacramental bread be made and formed plain, without any figure thereupon, of the same fineness and fashion round, though somewhat bigger in compass and thickness, as the usual bread and wafer, heretofore named singing-cakes, which served for the use of the private Mass." (Sparrow's Collections, pp. 84, 85.)

[1] 1 Eliz. Cap. II. Sec. XIII. Sparrow, 117. Strype's Parker, 310; Parker to Cecil.

In 1573 this question was brought to trial in Norfolk; when Mr. Serjeant Flowerdew charged "that *common* bread was to be used, by authority of Statute" (Strype's Parker, 453); referring, doubtless, to King Edward's second Service-Book. "An opinion," says Dr. Taylor, very justly (Vol. II. 72), "not legally sustainable, for it treated a permissive rubric as if it had been mandatory." I cannot understand, however, with what reason he says that "the queen's injunctions had *not* Parliamentary sanction."

[2] Strype's Parker, 309.

parishes use common bread, and others the wafer, they *continue* as at present.[1] In August, Burleigh and Walsingham wrote to him: "It were good to teach them that are weak in conscience, in esteeming of the wafer bread, not to make difference. If their weakness continue, it were not amiss, in our opinions, charitably to tolerate them, as children with milk."[2]

These citations are sufficient to show that, by itself, it was considered immaterial, even by strict Churchmen, which usage obtained; and that the *only* determining consideration was her Majesty's commandment. On the other hand, the prevailing Puritan sentiment was, that whether the bread should be leavened or unleavened was not worth the striving for; yet that it would seem more fit to use common bread, because, although our Saviour at the institution of the Supper used that which was *un*leavened, it was common bread notwithstanding, — "there not being a man in all Jewry who, at that hour, used any other."[3] This idea of *fitness*, however, operated sufficiently, with *them*, to produce a corresponding practice.

In this case, had her Majesty by her injunctions ordered the common bread, perfect uniformity in one thing would have been attained, for the Puritan preference would have been met, while the precise ministers and the whiffling priests, like spaniels, always obeyed their Mistress's whistle. Thus the sole cause for this diversity was her Majesty's will; and uniformity, in this instance, could not have been her motive. There could have been none other, in ordering the bread to be like that "which heretofore

[1] Desiderata Curiosa, Vol. I. Bk. III. No. XVII.

[2] Ibid., No. XX.

[3] "Discours," 207.

served for the use of the *private Mass*," and in ordering this, in these significant words, than that of humoring the superstition of the restive Popish populace. If such was her determining reason in a particular which needlessly precluded uniformity, are we not justified in judging that it was *not so much* uniformity upon which her Majesty was intent, as a time-serving resemblance to Rome? Are we not justified in saying, that *hence* it was that the English Establishment became fettered with so many observances in honor of saints, and with so many *symbols* of Romish doctrines? and, that *hence* it is, notwithstanding the plump antagonism in the theology of the two communions, that a man may glide from either to the other, almost unawares?

The attack of Robert Bell upon Monopolies, in the Parliament of 1571, had impinged upon the purses of four favored courtiers. Therefore he had been excessively frighted by the Council; and then — somehow — reconciled to the Court before his election as Speaker of the Commons in 1572.[1] Then Robert Bell, Esquire, became Sir Robert Bell; and then, Lord Chief Baron of her Highness's Exchequer.

The Parliament of 1572 had never been dissolved; and since their last session in 1575–6, Sir Robert had deceased, — one of the hundreds of the victims of a sudden and terrible scourge which we shall notice hereafter. Consequently, when they next convened on the sixteenth day of January, 1580–1, the Commons were without a Speaker. To supply this defect, they made choice of Mr. John Popham, her

[1] Hallam, 150.

Majesty's Solicitor-General, "with full consent of voices."[1] When the new Speaker was presented to her Majesty on the twentieth day of the month in the Upper House, had disabled himself, was approved, and had made the usual petitions, the Lord Chancellor, Sir Thomas Bromley, in her Majesty's name and behalf, granted his petitions, but "concluded with a *special* admonition that the Commons should not deal or intermeddle with any matters touching her Majesty's Person, or Estate, or Church Government."[2]

The next day, Mr. Paul Wentworth — the Puritan who first in the Parliament of 1566 challenged the encroachment of the Crown upon the liberties and privileges of the House — moved the appointment of a day for a public fast by the Members of the Commons House, and that they should assemble daily at seven o'clock in the morning to hear preaching; that so, through their acknowledgment of dependence upon God, "He might the better bless them in all their consultations and actions." Although propounded by a Puritan, and expressive of Puritan sentiment, the motion was opposed by Sir Francis Knollys. After many arguments on either side, the motion prevailed by one hundred and fifteen voices to one hundred. Upon which, Sunday, the twenty-ninth instant, was appointed, for "as many of *the House of Commons* as could conveniently assemble," as a day of "Preaching, Prayer, Humiliation, and Fasting, for the assistance of God's Spirit in all *their* consultations during this Parliament, and for the preservation of the Queen's Majesty and her realms."[3]

1 D'Ewes, 277-281.

2 Ibid., 268, 269.

3 "Mr. Norton showed precedents that there had been fasts in

The appointment of preachers for that day was referred to "such of her Majesty's Council as were of the House."[1]

A candid construction of this language, taken in its connection with the pending negotiations for the queen's marriage with a Catholic prince, and with the known fact that Romish emissaries were lurking about in great numbers, leaves no room to doubt that this measure was prompted, not by any affectation of godliness, but by a noble sense of dependence upon God in a time of peculiar danger to her Majesty, to the realm, to the Reformed Religion, — a danger which suggested the first and most important enactment of the session.

"Her Majesty's admiration of the rashness of the House was great; they had committed an apparent contempt against her express command by the Lord Chancellor at the opening of the session; a fast without her pleasure first known was an innovation;

London by order only from Council." "By which," remarks D'Ewes, "it seemeth that he intended to infer that *a Parliament* might much rather appoint it." This is simply an inference of the intention of an inference, and the result of Sir Simon's uncareful reading of his own record; from which record it will be perceived that no other inference could have been indicated by Mr. Norton than that *the Commons* might appoint. It is evident that by "a *public* fast," in this instance, was not intended a fast for the public, nor indeed a fast for Parliament, but only for those by whom it was appointed, — the House of Commons. Carte has taken his cue from D'Ewes; and signifies, somewhat tartly, that the Commons were silly enough to mistake themselves for the Parliament; a sneer which the language of the Journal shows to be gratuitous, and as vapid as a host of others which have been lavished upon the Puritans. Hume misstates the Journal when he says that "Wentworth moved the appointment of a *general* fast." In D'Ewes the words are, as I have given them, "a public fast;" but the action of the House shows that this was understood to mean only a fast for the Commons *in a public way*, — "in the Temple church."

[1] D'Ewes, 282, 283.

the allowing of fasting and prayer was in her own person; she imputed their offence, however, not to any evil or malicious intent, but partly to her own lenity, at the last session, towards the brother of him who made this rash motion."

Such was her Majesty's message on the twenty-fourth day of the month, by the Vice-Chamberlain, Sir Christopher Hatton. She did not say that she was as afraid of the pulpit as of the press. She did not say that preaching, upon such an occasion, and when the French courtship was uppermost in everybody's mind, would be likely to excite "vulgar people, who were not qualified to hear such things," against her subtle policy of state. But that she had weighed these considerations, no one could doubt. Sir Christopher, having uttered the Message, concluded by advising the House to acknowledge their fault, to ask pardon, and to promise better behavior. After debate *pro* and *con*, this was "agreed to by consent of the whole House."[1] The next day, her Majesty sent "answer of her most gracious acceptation of the submission; with one special note, that they do not misreport the cause of her misliking, — which was not for that they desired fasting and prayer, but for their *intruding upon her authority ecclesiastical*."[2]

"A mean, abject spirit," says Mr. Neal,[3] "in the representative body of the nation." But it should be remembered that this interference of her Majesty was only with the private wishes and personal rights of the members; and was not an attack, such as had before called for resistance, upon any *Parliamentary* privilege. It should also be remembered, that

[1] D'Ewes, 284. [2] Ibid., 285. [3] Neal, I. 147.

the boldest man in the nation was there in his place, — Peter Wentworth;[1] that he held his peace; and that — if the record be *literally* true — he did not vote against the submission. The future will show that *he* had not put on "a mean and abject spirit;" and it has before been showed that he not only knew when to speak, but also when to keep silence. There were doubtless prudential reasons, consistent with manliness, for which the Commons saw fit to retract.

We have said above, that the lack of properly qualified ministers was deplorable. It was more: to the people it was intolerable. They could no longer endure it in silence, and therefore implored Parliament for relief. "We are above the number of fourscore and ten thousand souls," said the people of Cornwall in their supplication, "which, for the want of the Word of God, are in extreme misery and ready to perish, and this neither for want of maintenance nor place; for besides the impropriations in our Shire, we allow yearly nine thousand and two hundred pounds, and have one hundred and sixty churches. But the *greatest part* of these are supplied by men who are guilty of the greatest sins. Some are fornicators; some, adulterers; some, felons bearing the marks in their hands for the said offence; some, drunkards, gamesters on the Sabbath day, &c. We have many non-residents who preach but once in a quarter; so that, between meal and meal the silly[2] sheep may starve. We have some ministers who labor painfully[3] and faithfully in the Lord's husbandry; but these men are not suffered to attend their callings, because the mouths of Papists, infidels,

[1] D'Ewes, 288. [2] Weak, or helpless. [3] Severely.

and filthy-livers are open against them, and the ears of those who are called lords over them are sooner open to their accusations — though it be but for ceremonies — than to the others' answers. Nor is it safe for us to go and hear them; for though our own fountains are dried up, yet, if we seek for the waters of life elsewhere, we are cited into the spiritual courts, reviled, and threatened with excommunication. Therefore from far we come, beseeching this Honorable House to dispossess these dumb dogs and ravenous wolves, and appoint us faithful ministers who may peaceably preach the Word of God, and not be disquieted by every apparitor, registrar, official, commissioner, and chancellor, upon every light occasion."[1]

From the city of London, also, was sent a petition to Parliament, a part of which was as follows: "May it please you, therefore, for the tender mercies of God, to understand the woful state of many thousand souls, dwelling in deep darkness and in the shadow of death, in this famous and populous city of London; a place in respect to others accounted as the morning star, or rather as the sun in its brightness, because of the Gospel supposed to shine gloriously and abundantly in the same, but, being nearly looked into, will be found sorely eclipsed and darkened through the dim cloud of unlearned ministers, whereof there be no small number. There are in this city a great number of churches, but the one half of them at the least are utterly unfurnished of preaching ministers, and are pestered with candlesticks, not of gold, but of clay, unworthy to have the

[1] Neal, I. 146.

Lord's light set in them; with watchmen that have no eyes; with clouds that have no water. In the other half, partly by means of non-residents which are very many, partly through the poverty of many meanly qualified, there is scarcely the tenth man that makes conscience to wait upon his charge. Whereby the Lord's Sabbath is ofttimes wholly neglected, and for the most part miserably mangled; ignorance increaseth, and wickedness comes upon us like an armed man. As sheep, therefore, going astray, we humbly on our knees beseech this honorable assembly, in the bowels and blood of Jesus Christ, to become humble suitors to her Majesty that we may have guides. As hungry men bound to abide to our empty rack-staves, we do beg of you to be means that the bread of life may be brought home to us; that the sower may come into the fallow ground; that the pipes of water may be brought unto our assemblies; that there may be food and refreshing for us, our poor wives and forlorn children. So shall the Lord have his due honor; you shall discharge good duty to her Majesty; many languishing souls shall be comforted; atheism and heresy banished; her Majesty have more faithful subjects, and you more hearty prayers for your prosperity in this life and full happiness in the life to come, through Jesus Christ our alone Saviour. Amen."[1]

In confirmation of what has been largely manifest in the preceding pages, that this dearth of religious instruction, and this patronizing of clerical vice, were not owing to the want of qualified instructors, but to the requisition of precise conformity to every

[1] Neal, I. 146.

ceremonial iota, we have the testimony of another petition presented to Parliament at this session, from certain students of Cambridge. They stated, "that there were in the University many able and well-qualified men ready and willing to engage in the Gospel ministry, but who could not get into places; that unlearned men, nay, the scum of the people, were preferred before them;[1] so that in this great want of laborers they themselves were standing idle in the market-place all the day; that this was because they could not in conscience yield to the subscriptions urged by the bishops, approving the Romish hierarchy, and all the effects of that government, as agreeable to the Word of God. They then offered a conference or disputation, as the queen and Parliament should agree, to put an amicable end to these differences, that the Church might recover some discipline, that simony and perjury might be banished, and that all who were willing to promote the salvation of souls might be employed."[2]

The Commons had by no means forgotten their own Petition to her Majesty for reformation in the Church, presented at their last session; nor her answer, that if her bishops did not see due reformation according to her pleasure, she would. But these loud cries from their constituents doubtless stimulated them to action. Notwithstanding her Majesty's "special admonition, that the Commons should not deal or intermeddle with any matters touching Church Government," some bill upon Religion was drawn by them, repeatedly conferred upon by joint Committees of both Houses, and, after various amend-

[1] Compare Strype's Aylmer, 32. [2] Neal, I. 147.

ments, was read once in the Commons. But no further trace of it appears upon the Journal.[1]

On the third day of March, however, various motions and arguments were made upon reformation in matters of Religion, with particular reference to the Petition of the House during the last session. Sir Walter Mildmay, the Chancellor of her Majesty's Exchequer; Hatton, her Vice-Chamberlain and favorite, and her two Secretaries, were appointed a Committee "to confer with the Lords Bishops touching the griefs of the House for some things very requisite to be reformed in the Church; as, the great number of unlearned and unable ministers, the great abuse of excommunication for every matter of small moment, the commutation of penance, the great multitude of Dispensations and Pluralities, and other things very hurtful to the Church." They were also instructed "further to impart unto their Lordships the earnest desire of the House for the redress of these griefs; and to desire their Lordships to join with them in petition to her Majesty for the same." This commitment was accompanied with a special protestation, that "the arguments and speeches upon the subject should be deemed in every man to proceed of good and godly zeal, without any evil intent or meaning at all." [2]

Four days afterwards, this Committee reported that they had obeyed their instructions; that some of the Lords Bishops admitted, and were ready to redress, the grievances alleged, and had willingly joined with them in humble suit to her Majesty

[1] D'Ewes, 289, 294, 295, 299, 301.

[2] Ibid., 301, 302. Strype's Whitgift, 92.

for the same;[1] that her Majesty had graciously replied, that at the last session she had committed these matters unto some of her Highness's clergy, who had not performed them, and that she would eftsoons commit the same unto such others as should see the same neither delayed nor undone.[2]

On what authority the Committee made this report is open to conjecture. *But such was not her Majesty's answer.* When the Petition of the Commons was communicated to her, she sent for Sandys, the Archbishop of York,—his Grace of Canterbury being "under a cloud,"—and directed him to frame an answer, and to consult with three or four bishops in the work, if he wished advice. This he did; and together they "set down what things they thought good and to which they could gladly yield; and some reformations they specified which could not be effectual without the action of Parliament." When this was presented to her Majesty, she retained the Paper, saying that she would consider of it. When at length Hatton and the others of the Committee pressed his Grace for an answer,—for the queen seems not to have met them upon the subject in person—he repaired to her Majesty, who replied through him, "That her Highness *was sufficient of herself* to deal with the clergy in matters ecclesiastical; and that the Parliament-House should not meddle therein; neither could her Majesty yield unto alteration of any ecclesiastical law." *This* was her Majesty's answer to the Petition,—a flat denial; a curt inhibition; an assertion of her abso-

[1] Strype's Whitgift, 93.

[2] D'Ewes, 302, 303.

lute Supremacy. The Committee "much misliked of it," and reported to the Commons as has been stated.[1]

[1] Desiderata Curiosa, Vol. I. Bk. III. No. XXIX.; Sandys, Archbishop of York to Chaderton, Bishop of Chester.

This letter stands in such a relation to the record in D'Ewes's Journal that I transcribe it:—

"The Parliament men of the nether House found themselves greatly offended with the bishops of this realm, as negligent in their office and abusing the ecclesiastical jurisdiction. They made mean to her Majesty for reformation. They appointed Mr-Vice-Chamberlain, the two Secretaries, and Sir Walter Mildmay, to move her Majesty in it. It pleased her Majesty to send for me, to open the matter unto me, and to require me to make answer; and, if I liked of it, to call unto me three or four bishops to assist me in this action. I called unto me the Bishops of St. David's, of Lincoln, of Sarum, of Bangor, and of Worcester. The things wherein they sought reformation were, especially, four: the ordering of unworthy ministers, Excogitations, Dispensations, and Commutations. We set down touching these four things that which we thought good, and could gladly yield thereto. I delivered the same book to her Majesty. Some reformations we set down which could not be effectual without act of Parliament. Her Majesty kept the book to herself, saying that she would consider of it. Mr. Vice-Chamberlain, with others, pressed me for an answer. Whereupon I repaired to her Majesty and prayed answer. The answer was, that her Highness was sufficient of herself to deal with the clergy in matters ecclesiastical; and that the Parliament-House should not meddle therein; neither could her Majesty yield unto the alteration of any ecclesiastical law. Yet we bishops concluded upon some reformations, and acquainted her Majesty with the same. Her Highness liked thereof; commanded the bishops of the Province of Canterbury to monish their fellow-bishops of the same; and that I should impart this thing to the bishops of my Province; requiring them to be dutiful in their offices and service in punishing of sin, and that our negligence should be no more complained of. The execution of sharp discipline" — against complainers, the puritanical — "will stop the mouths of their cries against us. Thus I write at large the occasion and . . . . . * these orders, which, withal, I send you, not doubting but that your lordship will diligently see them put in execution. . . . . . And thus I bid your lordship right heartily Farewell. Bishoppthorpe, this ii. of May, 1581.

"Your lordship's in Xt.,

"EDWIN EBOR."

I find no writer who notices this remarkable letter, so contradictory to the Committee's Report, and which gives to the whole transaction a character truly painful. Strype, Collier, and Hallam follow D'Ewes; and seem to have been ignorant of

* The Lacuna is in the original.

Not dreaming of any imposture, and having again, as they supposed, the royal word that the delay of reform was entirely owing to the negligence of the bishops, and that thenceforth she would secure its accomplishment, the House could do no less than acknowledge the royal complaisance. They therefore directed their Speaker, "in his Oration upon the last day of the session,[1] in their name to yield unto her Highness their most humble and dutiful thanks, with their like"—i. e. humble and dutiful—"remembrance and continuation of their most humble and lowly Petition for *speedy* execution and accomplishment thereof." [2]

This spurious reply to the Commons is too remarkable and suggestive to be passed without comment.

It should be remembered that all of the Committee were courtiers. Probably not one of them sympathized with the Puritan spirit of the House. Yet they all "much misliked of" her Majesty's answer delivered by Archbishop Sandys. Therefore they suppressed it and reported another,—of their own devising, it is to be presumed; one which they knew would satisfy the Commons for the time, and which, particularly because it threw the burden of negli-

what occurred between the queen, Sandys, and Hatton.

I do not forget that the queen could afterwards have directed the answer which was given to the House. But I cannot believe that she did; for had she done so, it seems next to impossible that Archbishop Sandys, in *such* a letter, should not have mentioned it.

[1] This was done upon a motion of Sir Walter Mildmay, *who made the Report.* Did he make the motion because he would not have the queen previously acquainted with the report as given? His motion was certainly very peculiar: "That not this whole House, nor any chosen or selected number of the same, but Mr. Speaker, in his Oration upon *the last day* of the session, do .... yield thanks," &c.

[2] D'Ewes, 303, 310.

gence and of future responsibility upon the prelates, they as well knew would be acceptable to her Majesty. Why did they mislike her reply? Why suppress it? Why falsify it by inventing a "gracious" one? We are not at a loss for reasonable answers. Because they knew the temper of the House. Because they knew that an imperious and querulous denial of *such* a petition would not have been tamely received. Because they feared that it would have kindled a fire in her Majesty's Parliament which would have been dangerous, and which might not have been quenched so easily as that of 1566. Five years the queen had delayed to convoke them; her chief reason being, probably, "her dislike of their Puritanical temper;"[1] a temper not abated by the return of new members in lieu of some deceased, some sick, and some in her Majesty's service.[2] Had there been "a mean and abject spirit in this representative body of the nation," would the Committee have feared to confront it with her Majesty's *very* answer?

Again: this reporting of a false answer throws suspicion upon all other messages of a conciliatory kind professing to be from her Majesty's lips; and particularly upon the answer to a similar petition at the last session, which answer *also* was reported by Sir Walter Mildmay. We cannot tell whether it was, or was not, the reply given by the queen.

This peep behind the curtain reveals also that the sufferance of evils in the Church was not entirely owing to the negligence of the bishops; that even the most rigid, Sandys and Whitgift, — one of the five with whom Sandys "consulted," —were willing

[1] Hallam, 127.

[2] D'Ewes, 279, 282.

to yield on some important points; that it was Court policy to make her Majesty's bishops bear the odium, as far as could be, of her Majesty's sins; that courtiers felt themselves authorized, by her Majesty's connivance, to represent her opinions and purposes as might best suit and soothe the humor of the Commons; that her bishops were never directed to make reforms; and that they never dared to attempt it. With the example of the Archbishop of Canterbury, pilloried before their eyes for years, — how could they dare? "Proud prelate! an you do not my pleasure, by God! I will unfrock you," made other ears to tingle than the Bishop of Ely's.

But we "see greater things than these." Bad as was the condition of the Church, it was as the queen would have it. "She disliked preaching." "The Homilies were enough." "There were too many preachers already." There must be public worship; there must be ministers to read the service and to administer the sacraments; but *preaching* ministers were a nuisance, if allowed "to the vulgar sort." It was *her choice*, therefore, to have ministers who were ignorant and incapable of preaching; although it was obvious that even Catholic Gentry, who were brought to outward obedience only, might "become inwardly in heart as conformable as they were outwardly in body were there only a competent number of good, learned preachers."[1] She knew that her people were starving for lack of spiritual food. She knew that they were in anguish for themselves, their wives, and their children. She knew that a

[1] Desiderata Curiosa, Vol. I. Bk. III. No. XVIII.; Walsingham to the Bishop of Chester, July 31st, 1580.

large part of her ministering clergy were "infamous in their lives and conversation." She knew that by means of clerical neglect, incapacity, and immorality, "ignorance increased and wickedness was coming upon the people like an armed man." We cannot plead for her Majesty that she was ignorant of these facts; for the plaints from Cornwall, London, Cambridge, and "other places," were not mumbled in a corner; nor was the special Petition of the Commons to her Majesty in 1571. She resented the interference of Parliament in religious matters, not merely as "an intrusion upon her authority ecclesiastical," but because she would not have reform; because, at all hazards, at whatever spiritual cost to her people, she *would stint* the preaching of God's Word.

Can we wonder that a Puritan, smarting under the lash of persecution, should have said in an hour of bitter anguish, that "the queen was perjured, because she had sworn to set forth God's glory directly as by the Scriptures are appointed, and did not?"[1]

The queen and her government were constantly on the alert to detect and baffle any suspicious movements of her Catholic subjects. The arrival of priests, Englishmen by birth, but educated at Seminaries abroad for the express purpose of religious operations at home, has been repeatedly mentioned. Their presence was known; but as they kept themselves concealed and under disguise, and operated with great caution, it was difficult to discover and arrest them. Their influence, however, had been suf-

[1] Strype's Annals, IV. 187. Neal, I. 153.

ficiently manifest, for they had made many proselytes from the divine service of the established worship.[1] In consequence of this, the operation of the law had been revived, and many, both priests and lay Catholics, had been committed to prison.[2] In 1579, there were about one hundred in the various prisons of the realm; and two in the private custody of bishops.[3] Some had been set at liberty. Many others, however, had been unmolested and "winked at, while they remained quiet;"[4] and others still, who were "*stirring* Papists" too, although annoyed by the Commissioners, "got favor at Court by interest made with the queen."[5]

But in 1580, the Government became alarmed at the greater incoming of Seminary priests, whose precautions against discovery kept pace with their increase of numbers. They now changed their disguises almost daily. "He who on Sunday was a Priest, or Jesuit, was on Monday a merchant, on Tuesday a soldier, on Wednesday a courtier, &c., and with the shears of equivocation (constantly carried about with him) he could cut himself into any shape he pleased."[6] The knowledge of these operations had roused the queen to issue Commissions for new inquisition and rigor against "those of the Romish persuasion." The first which we find was dated on the eighteenth day of June.[7] On the same day, the Bishop of Ely had despatched notice to Lord Bur-

[1] Strype's Grindal, 253, 256, compared. Strype's Whitgift, 90.

[2] Lodge, II. 188.

[3] Strype's Annals, IV; appendix Bk. II. No. XXI.

[4] Strype's Grindal, 254, 256.

[5] Strype's Annals, IV. 339, 340.

[6] Fuller, Bk. IX. p. 130. Camden, 245. Strype's Grindal, 256. Butler, I. 370.

[7] Strype's Grindal, 254.

leigh of information just received by him from "the godly brethren" in Helvetia, of new plots against her Majesty, in which the Pope — Gregory XIII. — had conspired with the King of Spain, whom he was to furnish with twelve thousand Italian soldiers. A few months afterwards, Gualter, one of the chief divines of Zurich, wrote from Rome, that this conspiracy was for the purpose of invading England.[1] Walsingham had also been informed by his spies in Rome, — men who carried themselves so cunningly as to draw pensions even from the Pope, — that a new onset, preparatory to an invasion by arms, was to be made upon England by a secret mission of the Jesuits;[2] and that two Englishmen, Robert Persons and Edward Campian, had received commissions for that purpose from the General of the Society of Jesus.[3] The spies had also given information of the time of the departure of these men from Rome, and of their projected route. They had also forwarded their portraits; copies of which had been furnished to all the queen's officers at her custom-houses, and a strict watch had been kept for them at every port. Yet they had escaped detection, and had arrived safely in London in the latter part of June.[4] The queen and her Council were chagrined and otherwise disturbed. Special efforts had been ordered for the apprehension of the two Jesuits; and detective officers were stimulated both by promises and by threats.[5] The queen

[1] Howell, I. 1058, 1063. Strype's Annals, IV. 338, 339; Append., Bk. II. Nos. XXVII., XXVIII.

[2] Fuller, Bk. IX. p. 117.

[3] Lingard, VIII. 152.

[4] Gee's Introd. to Persons's Memorial, p. 21. Taylor, II. 147. Butler, I. 360.

[5] Lingard, VIII. 152. Butler, I. 371.

had also issued a Proclamation requiring the speedy return of such of her subjects as had gone abroad for education; ordering "that no man should entertain in his house, or harbor, any priests sent forth of the aforesaid Seminaries, or Jesuits, or cherish or receive them;" and declaring "that whosoever did to the contrary should be accounted a favorer of rebels and seditious persons, and be proceeded against according to the laws of the land." [1]

It was also known that fugitive Englishmen were laboring at Rome and at the Courts of Catholic princes, to further an invasion of their own country; and that they had published tracts declaring the conspiracy of the Pope and the Spanish King to reduce England by force of arms to the domination of the Papal See.[2]

Such had been the movements in 1580, both at home and abroad, of those who were hostile to the Protestant Religion, and of those enemies of the State who aspired to wrench the sceptre from Elizabeth. With a clear knowledge of all which we have stated, — and doubtless of much more, — and with a serious conviction of the necessity for prompt and vigorous measures against the insidious operations of Popery, — the Parliament had again come together. The first bill which they passed was the act 23 Eliz. Cap. I., entitled "An Act to retain the Queen's Majesty's subjects in their due obedience." Its important branches we condense.

Sec. I. Where sithence the Statute made in

[1] Camden, 246. Lingard, VIII. 152. Carte, III. 558.

[2] Camden, 247.

the thirteenth year of the Reign of the Queen.... against.... Bulls, Writings,.... and other superstitious Things from the See of Rome, divers evil affected persons, contrary to the meaning of the said Statute, have practised by *other* means.... to withdraw divers of the Queen's Majesty's Subjects from their natural obedience to her Majesty, to obey the said usurped authority of Rome,.... and to withdraw their due Obedience to her Majesty's laws established for the due service of Almighty God: For Reformation whereof, and to declare the true meaning of the said Law, Be it.... enacted,.... That all persons whatsoever which.... shall put in practice to absolve.... the Queen's Majesty's Subjects.... from their natural Obedience to her Majesty, or to withdraw them *for that intent* from the Established to the Romish Religion, or to move them to promise any obedience to the.... See of Rome,.... or shall do any overt Act to that Intent or Purpose, shall.... suffer and forfeit as in the case of High Treason. And if any person, after the end of this Session of Parliament, *shall be* willingly absolved, withdrawn, or reconciled as aforesaid, or shall promise any such obedience, ... that then every such person, their procurers and counsellors thereunto, shall suffer and forfeit as in cases of High Treason.

Sec. II. To aid or maintain such offenders, knowing them to be such, or to conceal their offence twenty days, to be counted misprision of treason.

Sec. III. To say or sing Mass, punishable by amercement of two hundred marks and by imprisonment one year, and until the said sum of money be paid. Willingly to hear Mass, punishable by a fine of one hundred marks, and a year's imprisonment.[1]

Sec. IV. Every person above the age of sixteen years who shall forbear to attend church as required by the Act of Uniformity, shall forfeit for every month[2] after the end of this session of Parliament which he or she shall so forbear, twenty pounds of lawful English money; and upon so forbearing for the space of twelve months, shall give bonds in the sum of two hundred pounds at the least for good behavior until he shall conform and come to church according to the true meaning of the said Act.

Sec. V. To employ a schoolmaster who shall not repair to church as aforesaid, or be allowed by the Bishop or Ordinary of the diocese, shall be subject to a forfeiture of ten pounds a month; and such teacher shall be disabled to be a teacher, and suffer imprisonment one year.[3]

[1] Upon this Fuller remarks: "If the Mass were lawful, let it freely be permitted; if unlawful, let it be wholly prohibited. It is a sad case to make men pay dear for their damnation, and to sell them a license to do that which the receivers of their money conceive to be unlawful. (Bk. IX. p. 131.) Neal quotes with approbation (I. 148). Is there no difference between a fine and a remuneration for a permission? Is there no punishment in a fine? Why is not imprisonment — except for the time being — as much a permission or license to sin as a hundred marks? — each inflicted after the fact.

[2] Butler seems to find fault with this when he says, "Every fourth Sunday of absence was held to complete the month; and thus thirteen months were, in relation to these penalties, supposed to occur every year." (Vol. I. 292.) So they were, in relation to everything else cognizable by the temporal Courts. "A month in law is always a lunar month, or twenty-eight days, unless otherwise expressed." "In *all* acts of Parliament where months are spoken of without the word 'calendar,' and nothing is added from which a clear inference can be drawn that the legislature intended calendar months, it is understood to mean lunar months." (Blackstone, II. 141, and note 3.)

"Although '*schoolmaster*' may seem of the common gender, and

Sec. VIII. Of all forfeitures of money by this Act, ... one third part shall be to such person as will sue for the same. And every person forfeiting moneys by virtue of this Act, and who shall not be able, or shall fail, to pay the same within three months, shall be committed to prison until he pay or conform.

Sec. IX. excepts, on certain conditions, such as have the Divine Service as by law established in their own private Oratories, from the pains and penalties of this Act for not repairing to Church.

Sec. XII. provides that this Act shall not take away or abridge, the Authority or Jurisdiction of the Ecclesiastical Judges; who may do as before the making of this Act they might lawfully have done.

This Act was evidently based, not only upon the opinion expressed in its first section, that obedience to the See of Rome was incompatible with loyalty to the queen, — which it was, so far as the bull of Pius V. was considered binding, — but upon the distinct conviction, that the fresh arrival of Seminary priests, and the auxiliary mission from the Society of Jesus, were for the express purpose of using the powerful apparatus of Religion to subvert the authority of the queen, and to prepare the minds and swords of her subjects to act with the Vatican and the Escurial for her dethronement and death. "The act was thought most needful for the assurance and safety of her Majesty's person and realm."[1] "It was thought

inclusive of both sexes, yet, by the letter of the law, all *she-teachers* (which did mischief to little children) evaded the punishment. Thus when authority hath carefully shut all doors and windows imaginable, some little offenders will creep through the crannies thereof." (Fuller, Bk. IX. p. 131.)

[1] Desiderata Curiosa, Vol. I. Bk.

highly necessary," because it was not doubted that such priests and Jesuits, though "pretending only to administer the Sacraments of Religion and to preach to Papists," did "whisper in corners, that Elizabeth, being a heretic and excommunicate, had no regal title and authority;" and that her laws, in the eye of God and man, were therefore null and void.[1] "The appearance of such men in any Protestant State, was held a sure presage (as the playing of porpoises above water) that foul weather was to follow."[2] Yet by some it was held, "That not all sinners are Devils, nor are all Devils Beelzebubs; that some Priests and Jesuits"—at whom particularly this law aimed its highest curse—"were of a milder temper and better metalled, who by moderation might be melted into amendment."[3]

How far the prevailing opinions, by which this act was shaped were justifiable, or otherwise, we reserve for future consideration.

The only other important act passed at this session of Parliament was 23 Eliz. Cap. II., entitled "An Act against seditious words and rumors uttered against the Queen's most excellent Majesty." After reciting that the previous laws respecting this offence did not provide sufficient punishment, it enacted,—

Sec. I. That if any person, after the end of forty days next ensuing the end of this present session of Parliament, shall advisedly and with malicious intent,.... speak any false, seditious, and slanderous

III. No. XXXI.; The Lords of the Council to Chaderton, May 28th, 1581.

[1] Camden, 245, 272. Fuller, Bk. IX. pp. 130, 131. Strype's Grindal, 256. Strype's Annals, V. 53. Strype's Whitgift, 90. Coke's Reports, Vol. III. Part V. p. xxxviii.

[2] Fuller, Bk. IX. p. 132.

[3] Ibid.

news, rumors, sayings, or tales .... against the Queen's Majesty that now is, ... every such person shall for every such first offence be .... set openly upon the pillory, ... and there to have both his ears cut off; or, at his election, pay two hundred pounds .... within two months after judgment, ... and also suffer imprisonment six months.

Sec. II. enacted for giving currency to any such seditious and slanderous reports,— after the forty days aforesaid,— the pillory and the loss of one ear; or, if the offender should so choose, the payment of two hundred marks within two months after judgment, and imprisonment for three months.

Sec. III. For the second of either of the offences aforesaid, death and forfeiture, as in the case of felony.

Sec. IV. If any person, after the end of the said forty days, either within this realm .... or in any other place, ... shall advisedly and with a malicious intent against our said Sovereign Lady, devise, write, print, or set forth any manner of book .... or writing containing false, seditious, and slanderous matter to the defamation of the Queen's Majesty that now is, ... or to the encouraging, stirring, or moving of any insurrection or rebellion within this realm ..... or shall advisedly and with malicious intent against our said Sovereign Lady procure or cause any such book .... or writing to be written, printed, published, or set forth .... he shall suffer such pains of death and forfeiture as in case of felony is used.

Sec. XIV. repeals the acts on this subject of 1 and 2 Philip and Mary, Cap. III., and 1 Eliz. Cap. VI., during the continuance of this Act, which, by the next and last Section, is limited to the natural life of the queen.

It has been alleged that these two acts, at the time of their progress through Parliament, were considered as sharp against the Puritans as against the Papists; that by the first, particularly, "the queen *and her Parliament* tacked the Puritans to the Papists, and subjected them to the same penal laws, as if they had been equal enemies to her person and government, and to the Protestant Religion." [1]

There were more than a score of acts passed at this session; but the two great matters of legislative business which engrossed the minds of the Parliament were, — a Subsidy and the Papists. With the first, we have nothing to do. The absorbing interest which attached to the second was manifested by the manner in which Paul Wentworth's proposition was met by the Commons; and, so soon as things were in a proper train, was distinctly avowed by Sir Walter Mildmay in an elaborate Speech in the Commons House. The burden of this was, to show "the principal cause of their assembly." In doing this, he stated the *dangers* of the realm, and the *provision* to be made against them. The *dangers*, he said, were "the secret practices of the Pope and his secret ministers within the realm;" in consequence of which "the obstinate and stiff-necked Papist is so far from being reformed, as he hath gotten stomach to go backward, and to show his disobedience, not only in arrogant words, but also in contemptuous deeds. To confirm them herein, the Pope doth comfort their

[1] Neal, I. 148.

hollow hearts with absolutions, dispensations, and reconciliations; he hath sent hither a sort of hypocrites, naming themselves Jesuits, a rabble of vagrant Friars newly sprung up, whose principal errand is, by creeping into houses of men of behavior and reputation, not only to corrupt the realm with false doctrine, but also under that pretence to stir up sedition. . . . . By these practices many, yea very many, of those which divers years together did yield to conform themselves in their open actions . . . . sithence the swarming hither of a number of Popish priests and monkish Jesuits, have and do utterly refuse to be of our Church, or to resort unto our preaching and prayers. The sequel whereof must needs prove dangerous to the whole State of the Commonwealth."[1] Then, passing to the second point proposed, he said, "And seeing that the lenity of the time, and the mildness of the laws heretofore made, are no small cause of their arrogant disobedience, it is necessary that we make a *provision* of laws more strict and more severe, to constrain them to yield their open obedience, at least, to her Majesty in causes of Religion; . . . . letting them find how dangerous it shall be for them to deal with the Pope or anything of his, or with those Romish priests and Jesuits; and therewith also, how perilous it shall be for those seditious Runagates to enter into the land to draw away from her Majesty that obedience which by the laws of God and man are due unto her. This, then, is one of the *provisions* which we ought to take care of in this Council."[2]

Here we have, from a competent and trustworthy

[1] D'Ewes, 286. [2] Ibid. 287.

source, the *reasons* for which both the first and the second statutes of this session were framed, and the *objects* which they aimed to secure. The reasons,—the seditious operations of Romish priests, and the refusal of the *Catholics* to resort to preaching and prayers. The objects,—to intimidate and keep out the priests, and to compel the *Catholics*—not the Protestants, be it noticed—to attend the established Service.

The argument of Sir Walter Mildmay was approved and pursued by Mr. Norton,—a Member before known to us as a Puritan; and upon *his* motion a Committee was appointed to consult upon bills necessary to "restrain and correct the *evil affected* subjects, and to maintain forces" against any attack by arms.

Thus originated the bill for a Subsidy, and the two bills under our consideration,—a preparative outline of which was penned by Mr. Norton under order of the Committee.[1]

On the sixth day of March, the bill "to retain the Queen's Majesty's subjects in their due obedience," was read the third time and passed *without any opposition or debate*, and sent to the Upper House "with *special recommendation* unto their Lordships."[2]

But another "provision" was needed against the practices of the Catholics. "Naughty papistical books" in favor of the Scottish queen and the northern rebellion of 1569, and on other matters whereby "her Majesty was touched," had been printed and circulated; and the press had at last been discovered in the summer of 1579.[3] But now,

[1] D'Ewes, 288, 289, *bis*. [2] Ibid., 302. [3] Strype's Annals, IV. 271.

"pamphlets, ballads, and seditious placards," were again making their appearance from some secret Popish press.[1] To "provide" against this form of "encouraging, stirring, or moving of any insurrection or rebellion within the realm,"[2] the bill was framed "against seditious words and rumors." This bill, like the former, had sole reference at the time of its progress *to the Papists.* "It was levelled at the books dispersed by the Seminary priests."[3] A bill

[1] Taylor, II. 148.

[2] Sec. IV. of the Act.

[3] Hallam, 124.

Mr. Neal (I. 148), speaking of the Puritan clergy who had been silenced, and could not even assemble in private to mourn over their own and the nation's sins, without the danger of a prison, adds: "This exasperated their spirits, and put them upon writing satirical pamphlets against their adversaries, ... the unpreaching clergy, ... the severity of the laws, the pride and ambition of the bishops, ... and the High Commission; which her Majesty being informed of, procured a statute this very Parliament, by which it was enacted," &c., quoting 23 Eliz. Cap. II. Sec. IV. But I do not find that any such *satirical* pamphlets had at this time appeared from Puritan pens. The editor of the edition of Neal now before me says, — referring for proof to Neal's eighth chapter, — that the author here means the satirical pamphlets which appeared over the name of Martin Mar-Prelate. If so, then both Mr. Neal and his editor are mistaken; for these satires did not appear until 1588. (Hallam, 124, note; "Puritan Discipline Tracts," Petheram's edit.) They could not, therefore, have provoked the statute now under our notice. But whether the Puritans had, or had not, at this time issued such tracts, it seems clear, not only from the facts which I have given, but from the whole burden of arguments by which the bill was brought into being, that it was a "provision" only against books of *Catholic* authorship, "*defaming the queen and inciting to rebellion.*" Such were not Puritan papers.

Mr. Hallam does indeed say, in his note to which I have referred, that "the abusive language of the Puritan pamphleteers had begun several years before;" i. e. before the appearance of the Martin Mar-Prelate tracts, in 1588. In proof of this he refers to Howell's "State Trials," page 1263, where I can find nothing in point; and to Strype's Annals, II. 193, folio edition. But the paper in Strype is a *private* letter to the Bishop of Lincoln, which I have quoted above in Vol. I. pp. 439, 440. It is an *argument;* and might reasonably have been spared from the epithet "abusive." Besides, Mr. Strype says, "I think it was *never printed.*" At any rate,

on the same subject was first introduced by the House of Lords;[1] amended by Mr. Norton in the Commons, and sent back;[2] returned with new amendments by the Lords;[3] and finally sent up to them again, as "a bill the Commons could not deal withal."[4] A new one was then drawn, and passed, in the Commons; and thence sent to the Lords.[5] Before acting upon it, "their Lordships sent certain notes in writing, to feel the opinion of the Lower House, whether they would be content to leave in force, unrepealed, so much of the Statute 1 and 2 Philip and Mary as concerned slanderous words against *Noblemen and the Lords of the Clergy.*" The Commons peremptorily refused,[6]—a wary and sagacious answer, as was afterwards demonstrated in blood. They were willing to protect their queen, and to prevent rebellion; but *no further would they go.*[7] While, with all loyalty, they were vigilant for the honor of the Crown and the peace and weal of the realm, they were careful to preserve to the subject all liberty not inconsistent with true allegiance.

Such is the history of these two bills. Each originated in the Commons. Each was constructed and passed, to "provide" against *Catholic* defection and mischief-making. The first, bearing the stamp of *pure*

no Puritan writings had been issued "defamatory of the queen nor inciting to sedition."

[1] D'Ewes, 290.

[2] Ibid., 290, 299.

[3] Ibid., 304.

[4] Ibid., 305.

[5] Ibid., 306.

[6] Ibid., 307.

[7] The Statute 1 and 2 Philip and Mary, Cap. III. Sec. I., is a renewal of a statute made in the reign of Richard II. against "speaking false things of Prelates, Dukes, Earls, Barons, and other Nobles and Peers of the Realm, ... or of any of the great officers of this realm." Punishable "*by advice of the Council.*"

antipapacy in its proeme and in almost every line before and after its fourth section, and framed — be it particularly observed — when there were no *Puritan* Separatists to whom it could apply, or so few, if any, as not to have attracted legislative attention, passed the Commons, not only without opposition, but to their peculiar satisfaction. The second — a substitute for one over which the two Houses had wrangled and which had been "dashed" — the language of which did *not* show its specific and exclusive reference to Popery, was more carefully framed; and its most terrible penalty was directed only for publications libellous of her Majesty and insurrectionary in their aim.

When, therefore, we consider who were the originators of these bills; the reasons and objects for which they were framed; the peculiar language by which the one was, almost throughout, qualified and defined; the clauses by which the intent of the other was clearly revealed and its application specially guarded — to say nothing of the refusal to insert an insidious extension of it — it seems an enormous demand upon our credulity, to be told that the *Parliament* — in one branch of which was a large, if not preponderating, Puritan corps under watch and ward of the two Wentworths — contrived machinery for the express purpose of cutting the throats of both Catholics and Puritans at a stroke. However the fourth section of the first statute reads by itself, it does not stand by itself; it is hedged in before and behind; and we read it in its connection. We interpret it by the known character of its authors, of its zealous commendators; by its specific and undeniable purpose.

The *letter* of a certain law gave both ship and cargo to a man who did not, because he was so sick that he could not, desert them when in danger of wreck; but such was not the *design* of the law.[1] The *letter* of the fourth section of 23 Eliz. Cap. I. prescribed for a *Puritan* who should forbear Divine service a pecuniary mulct; but such was not its *design*. The *letter* of the fourth section Cap. II. admitted of a forced construction by which a Puritan book against *bishops* made the author obnoxious to its penalty of death; but such was not its *design*. If any one chooses to assert otherwise, to interpret the intent of Parliament by the uses to which these sections were wrested, we are at issue with him in a matter of opinion. That is all; only we have given our reasons. That the queen and her bishops, the queen and her commissioners, the queen and her lawyers, "tacked the Puritans to the Papists" under these acts, is notorious. That is no affair of ours. But it is an affair of ours whether, in passing them, Puritans did or did not mean to unpuritanize and to hang Puritans. The supposition that they did, seems preposterous. For any undue severity of either statute against the Catholics, and for that only, they were responsible. We will talk of *this* point by and by.

[1] Blackstone, I. 61.

CHAPTER VIII.

THE JESUITS.

The Arrival of Campian and Persons. — Their published Pamphlets. — Increasing Defection of the Catholics. — Government Espionage. — Hesitation of the Queen to proceed against the two Jesuits. — She is persuaded to issue a Warrant for their Arrest. — Campian discovered and taken in July, 1581. — He is sent to the Tower. — Persons's Perils and Escape to France. — Campian tested by Disputations and the Rack. — His Trial. — The Execution of Campian, Sherwine, and Briant. — Observations upon the Character of their Mission.

1580, 1581.

Stealth is a Jesuitical grace. With the two missionaries who had just been sent from Rome it was a necessity. After having pursued their journey together as far as Calais, they had parted; thinking it prudent thus to divide the risk of their enterprise. Persons had set sail in the night, had crossed the Channel, and had assumed so well the dress, the mien, and the licentious manners of a soldier of that day, that he had passed without annoyance or suspicion to London; where he waited for the arrival of his fellow-missionary.[1]

Campian had more difficulty. After waiting at Calais four days, he had put to sea in the evening of the anniversary of John the Baptist, — the twenty-

[1] Gee; Introduc. to the "Memorial," pp. xx, xxi. Taylor, II. 147.

fourth day of June,—and landed very early the next morning at Dover, with a companion whom he styled his "little man." Here they were immediately ordered before the Mayor, who suspected them of being propagandists from Rome, and declared roundly that he would send them under guard to London. Suddenly, however, and without apparent reason, he altered his mind and dismissed them. It was because the Jesuit, when in the magistrate's presence, had silently asked John the Baptist to ask the Virgin Mary to ask the Son to ask the Father, that he might be delivered from his peril. Such was Campian's opinion. He immediately sped to London, where "a good angel led him without his knowledge to the same house which had received Persons." Here he had been warmly welcomed, reverently esteemed, and furnished with every desirable equipment for his mission.[1]

Thus had the first Jesuit missionaries effected their return to their native country in 1580; adroitly baffling all the precautions of Walsingham, and all the vigilance of his subordinate officials.[2] They neces-

[1] Fuller, Bk. IX. p. 115; Campian to Mercuranius.

[2] Robert Persons was born in Stowey, in the County of Somersetshire, of somewhat dubious parentage, in the year 1546. He entered Baliol College, Oxford, at the age of seventeen years, and was admitted Master of Arts in 1572. He was distinguished in the University as a scholar; and, particularly, for his skill in scholastic disputations. At first a zealous Protestant, he became an equally zealous Catholic, and left England in 1574. The next year he was admitted to the Jesuit College at Rome. He is described as "a fierce, bold, turbulent, busy, meddling" man. (Camden, 246, 247. Fuller, Bk. IX. p. 114. Gee; Introduction, pp. ii., xv., xvi. Wood's Athenæ, II. 64, 65, 67. Taylor, II., 145.)

Edmond Campian was born in London in 1540. At thirteen years of age he delivered an eloquent oration before Queen Mary at her accession to the throne. He took his Degree of Master of Arts at St. John's College, Oxford, in 1564;

sarily prosecuted their mission with the greatest precautions; moving about the country in various disguises; now apparelled as soldiers; now, as gentlemen; now, as ministers of the Church of England; and now, in some "antick habit;" and as frequently changing their names as their costume.[1]

Soon after their arrival, each had drawn up a Paper stating the objects of their mission.[2] In his own, Campian avowed himself to be a priest of the Society of Jesus; and declared that he came to England "to extend the Catholic faith, to teach the Gospel, and to minister the sacraments,[3] to instruct the simple, to reform sinners, to confute errors; in brief, to cry alarm, spiritually, against foul vice and proud ignorance;" and, that "he was straitly forbidden by the Father

took holy Orders in the Church of England soon after; and was a florid preacher. In 1566, he gained great applause from Queen Elizabeth and a learned auditory, for his accomplished eloquence. About 1571, he resided at the English College in Douay, where he made profession of the Romish faith, and took the Degree of Bachelor of Divinity. After being admitted to the Order of the Jesuits at Rome, in 1573, he taught philosophy and rhetoric six years at Prague, in a Jesuit College, where he preached constantly in Latin. He was "a man of admirable parts; an elegant orator; a subtle philosopher and disputant; an exact preacher in English and in Latin; of a sweet disposition, and well-polished manners." (Wood's Athenæ, I. 473–475. Fuller, Bk. IX. p. 114. Camden, 246. Howell, I. 1072.)

Thus Persons was thirty-four years of age, and Campian forty, when they entered upon their mission in England.

[1] Campian to Mercuranius. Gee; Introd., xxviii. Howell, I. 1059.

[2] Lingard, VIII. 154.

Dr. Lingard says that these Papers were "in answer to the queen's Proclamation." But this Proclamation was not issued until the tenth or twelfth day of January, 1580–1; whereas Campian's Paper had been published and was in every man's hand before October or November, 1580; or before his letter was written to Mercuranius, his General, in "the fifth month" after arriving in England. The defiance which his published Paper breathed had not, therefore, even the apology of a provocation. (Strype's Annals, V. 61. Holingshed, IV. 434.)

[3] Campian to Mercuranius.

who sent him to deal in any respect with any matter of estate or policy of the realm." He further requested audience of the queen; and permission to dispute before the Privy Council, the doctors and masters of the Universities, and the lawyers spiritual and temporal; in doing which he would "avow and justify the faith of the Catholic Church." In conclusion, he declared that "all the Jesuits in the world had made a league cheerfully to carry the cross that might be laid upon them in England, and never to despair of the recovery of the kingdom, while they had a man left to enjoy Tyburn, to be racked with torments, or consumed in prisons." [1]

Campian delivered this Paper to a friend, with directions that it should be published in case the writer should be arrested. His friend saw fit to publish it before; at which Campian seems to have rejoiced, as "something which he did not so much as hope for," because "the Paper was now in every man's hand," made his "adversaries stark mad," and "the preachers out of their pulpits answer, rending Persons and himself with railings." [2] He had also published "a neat, well-penned book in Latin, called 'Ten Reasons,' in defence of the doctrine of the Church of Rome." [3] Persons also published a book, occasioned by the queen's Proclamation against himself and his companion, over the signature of Andreas Philopater; [4] and still another "virulent one in English against Chark, who had soberly written against

[1] Strype's Annals, V. 46. 47, VI. 183-186; Append., Bk. I. No. VI. Lingard, VIII. 154.

[2] Campian to Mercuranius.

[3] Camden, 247. Strype's Aylmer, 48. Lingard, VIII. 154.

[4] Gee; Introd., xxxiii.

Campian's challenge."[1] The burden of this seems to have been an argument against conformity to the worship of the English Church.[2]

Soon after the arrival of these zealous missionaries, an increased defection of the Papists from the services of the Church had begun in Lancashire, in York, in "the northern parts" generally, and particularly in the diocese of Norwich and in the county of Southampton. "The people's hearts were stolen away mightily;" and they did "fast revolt" from the established worship, so that in one instance, "upon some secret pact, purposely wrought, five hundred persons refused to communicate."[3] These things led to the issue of special ecclesiastical Commissions from the queen, and to "privy search in sundry suspected places" for Popish books and other superstitious things, and for priests.[4] Before November, 1580, if we may credit the statements of the two Jesuits, "by wariness, by the prayers of good people, and by God's goodness, they had gone over a great part of the island, and had made innumerable number of converts, high, low, of the middle rank, of all ages and sexes." "Very many had been reconciled to the Romish Church,—in one month, fifty thousand;[5] and the prisons were filled with Catholics," some of them gentlemen of estate, and some of them priests.[6]

[1] Camden, 247.

[2] Carte, III. 559. Taylor, II. 148.

[3] Strype's Annals, IV. 339–345.

[4] Ibid.

[5] Dr. Lingard, with more modesty and more probability than Persons, gives fifty thousand as the whole number of Popish recusants in all the parishes in the kingdom, returned *by actual census*. (Vol. VIII. 154.)

[6] Fuller, Bk. IX. pp. 116, 117; Campian to Mercuranius. Lingard, VIII. 154. Taylor, II. 150; Persons to ——, in Rome. Strype's Annals, IV. 347; V. 600, 601; Persons to Allen.

Such was the condition of things when the Parliament assembled in January, 1580–1; and which occasioned the two acts of their session which have been described.

We have observed, incidentally, that the queen's Government had maintained a constant and successful espionage at important points in Catholic Europe. The agents of Walsingham, pretending to be English refugees for conscience sake, and conforming devoutly to the rites and obligations of the Romish Church, had sat as if eager learners in the halls of the Seminaries, insinuated themselves into the very sanctuaries of Catholic devotees, excited their sympathies, and gained their confidence.[1] It was thus, that the likenesses of Campian and Persons had been obtained. The same plan was adopted at home. The Secretary's spies were as busy and as sly in London as in Rome. They dogged the Catholics in highways and in byways; watched their behavior; overheard their private discourse; noted their household affairs; and had an eye to their foreign correspondence. The two pioneer Jesuits, and their co-workers the Seminary priests, aware of the toils spread around them, were as much occupied in dodging detectives as in saving souls. Not only did they move from place to place under successive disguises, — to-day, "ruffians;" to-morrow, "courtiers with feathers and all ornaments of light-colored apparel," — but, when stationary in the performance of their priestly functions, were constrained to hide in some secret cranny contrived for the purpose, in some obscure cave, or unfrequented wood. It was "in a tangled dell near Hen-

[1] Howell, I. 1069.

ley" that Campian wrote his "Ten Reasons;" being supplied the while by stealth with books and food.[1]

Queen Elizabeth was in a dilemma. The young Duke of Anjou was whispering soft words in her ear. It might obscure the sunshine of their courtship, and jostle the policy which it involved, to bring priests of her lover's own faith to her scaffolds. On the other hand, her subjects, already trembling lest the Protestant faith should be compromised and imperilled by her marriage, would be confirmed in their apprehensions, — possibly nettled to exasperation and tumult, — should not vigorous means be adopted to secure the lurking emissaries of Rome; while she could in no way so effectually appease the popular fever as by letting the law loose to let the blood of the priests. For a while, therefore, she had curbed the zeal of her Puritan Secretary Walsingham and of her Puritan kinsman Knollys, who were specially eager for the arrest of the two Jesuits. At length the two courtiers had prevailed, and a warrant was issued for the arrest.[2] This enterprise Walsingham intrusted to George Eliot, one of his most expert spies, who had served him well at Rome under the mask of a devout Catholic. Still maintaining the same profession, and probably known as a Protestant only to those in the secrets of Government, pretending also to be in danger for his religion from the very men he served, he now commenced his new commission by searching the city of London; a work which he prosecuted

[1] Harleian Miscellany, I. 143. Butler, I. 360, 361.

[2] Camden, 270. Taylor, II. 162, 169, 170. Wood's Athenæ, I. 477, note 8. Strype's Annals, V. 56; Knollys to Burleigh and Leicester, dated September, but sufficiently indicative of his previous influence.

long time, and assiduously, but in vain.[1] The wary Jesuit left no footprint where he trod.

Months rolled away; and Campian, "counting not his own life dear unto him," but that he might propagate his faith and nourish the flock of his fold, held on his course without faltering, and without discovery. In July, 1581, he was ministering to the Catholics in the county of Berkshire; by whom, as by all of his faith who knew him, he was not only welcomed as a priest, but honored and beloved as a man. Here he found shelter in the family of Edward Yates, Esquire, near to Wantage,—a town where Roman soldiers once had a fortified camp; where had once been a villa of the English kings; and where Alfred the Great was born. The mansion of Yates, situated in the fertile valley of White Horse,[2] and commanding a good view of its rural beauty, lay about thirteen miles southwest of Oxford and about sixty west of London. Here the devoted missionary rested; for once indifferent whether it should be sunshine or rain on the morrow, because he had the rare luxury of an English home; and scarcely caring whether the queen's officers were far off or near, because there was a prophet's chamber for his retreat. This was a hiding-place; so cunningly contrived as almost to defy discovery.[3] The Catholics of the neighbor-

[1] Fuller, Bk. IX. p. 117. Taylor, II. 163.

[2] Upon an eminence overhanging this valley, Alfred the Great won a decisive battle over the Danes. To commemorate this, he carved on the northern side of the hill — an almost precipitous cliff of chalk — the figure of a white horse of great size. This gives to the valley its name. It has stood there unimpaired these thousand years and more, and may now be seen by the traveller as he passes over the Great Western Railway.

[3] Butler, I. 361.

hood, careful however not to attract attention, stole thither in great numbers for confession, absolution, and divine service according to the rites of their Church.

Many of them were assembled there for religious service on the seventeenth day of the month.[1] Two priests were present besides Campian. Trusty men had been posted out of doors as sentinels.[2] Mass had been celebrated; and Campian addressed his hearers, with his usual eloquence, from the pathetic lament of our Saviour over the guilty city of Jerusalem.[3] No one listened with more seeming eagerness to his words than George Eliot. He had fled to Berkshire for safety, he said; and the Catholic gentry who had sheltered him had invited him, for his soul's sake, to attend upon the preaching of the apostle from Rome. In the midst of the sermon an alarm was given. The sheriff, with his posse, was at hand. The congregation fled; the three priests, to their hiding-place. Eliot, in the confusion, failed to track them; and the prey which he had so long hunted slipped from his very grasp.

It was a strait recess in which the priests took refuge; too low to admit of an erect position, and of sufficient capacity only for a narrow couch. Upon this they threw themselves; and engaged at once in prayer, mutual confession, and absolution. The penance which they enjoined upon one another was, to say three times, "Thy will, O Lord, be done!" and, "John Baptist, pray for us!" This latter invocation was because of Campian's remarkable deliverance at Dover.

[1] Lingard, VIII. 155. [2] Butler, I. 361. [3] Howell, I. 1063.

In the mean time the soldiers, for whom Eliot had sent just before the assembling of the people, had arrived; but, in their eagerness for Campian, had paid little regard to others. After a while, the running to and fro, the shouting, the bursting of doors, the crash of wainscoting and furniture, incident to the search, ceased. Only now and then a footfall was heard across a hall or along a stairway; and the self-imprisoned men began to think themselves safe. The silence did not last long. The tramp of the whole troop was suddenly heard, and it grew nearer and nearer. Their frequent pauses, their low consultations, indicated that they had some uncertain clew to the secret hiding-place. Campian, perceiving this, made a movement to leave his companions and deliver himself to the officers; declaring that, as he only was sought for, they would be unmolested, and that otherwise all would be taken. But his companions held him down by force, declaring, with equal positiveness, that it was impossible that their retreat should be discovered. A pause in the movements without seemed to confirm their opinion; till suddenly a single man approached with a confident step, wrenched violently a small bracket attached to the wainscot without, the panel of which flew back, and the three priests were revealed! The nervous anxiety of one of the servants of the household had led him to some indiscretion which the sagacity of Eliot had thus successfully improved.

After remaining two days in custody of the sheriff, the three prisoners were transported to London on horseback; each one with his arms pinioned and his feet tied to one another beneath his horse. Campian was distinguished from his fellows by a paper fastened upon his hat, and having upon it in large capitals, "CAMPIAN, THE SEDITIOUS JESUIT!" In a kind of triumphal procession, they entered London on the twenty-second day of the month, which was a market day; were escorted for show through those places where were the greatest crowds; and were then delivered to the Lieutenant of the Tower.[1]

Persons was also hard pressed "by Walsingham's setters." Once he had escaped by hiding in the haystack of an inn to which pursuivants had been sent for his arrest. At another time, on his way to the Red Lion on Holborn Hill, where he had an appointment at a certain hour, he became bewildered in the lanes and alleys through which he chose his way; and when at length he reached the hostel, he found it surrounded with soldiers, who thought they had entrapped him there. Crossing himself devoutly, he turned, and escaped again. Thus, "by losing his way, he saved his life." Terrified by his narrow escape, he took refuge in an obscure house on the sea-shore; was tracked thither by spies; received notice of their approach just in time to throw himself on board a fishing-smack; and so made his escape to France. "This wary bird would not be catcht to whistle in the cage to the tune of Walsingham. Wherefore over he went to Rome, and there slept in a whole skin, as good reason it was, so great a general should secure his person from danger."[2]

In the Tower, Campian had opportunity to discuss his "Ten Reasons" and — the rack. In August and

[1] Challoner, 24, 25. Taylor, II. 163, 164.

[2] Fuller, Bk. IX. p. 118. Taylor, II. 150.

September, several learned ecclesiastics held four different "conferences" with him; disputations; theological tiltings; in which it was clearly the aim of each party, not to win, but to unhorse and lance the other; and most, to make gallant flourish of his own weapons.[1] In this strife, each was victor; each, vanquished, — as is always the case in ghostly combats. In the other, ropes and levers prevailed over flesh and blood. Four stretchings made the sufferer tell who had given him the rites of hospitality, whom he had confessed, and where he had celebrated Mass.[2] This "questioning" was "favorably" done, it has been said;[3] by which we are only to understand that the victim was neither torn asunder nor stretched to death. But, favorably or unfavorably administered, "it is not a *pleasant* thing" — so wrote one in those days who had experienced it — "to be stretched on the rack till the body becomes almost two feet longer than nature made it."[4]

[1] Strype's Annals, IV. 361. Strype's Parker, 376. Strype's Aylmer, 301.

[2] Fuller, Bk. IX. p. 117. Lingard, VIII. 156. Strype's Parker, 376. Howell, I. 1060.

[3] Strype's Annals, IV. 358.

[4] Lingard, VIII. 160, note; Nichols to Allen.

"The trial by rack is utterly unknown to the law of England; though once, when the Dukes of Exeter and Suffolk, and other ministers of Henry VI., had laid a design to introduce the civil law into this kingdom as the rule of government, for a beginning thereof, they erected a rack for torture, which was called in derision the Duke of Exeter's daughter, and still remains in the Tower of London, where it was occasionally used as an engine *of state*, not of law, more than once in the reign of Queen Elizabeth. But when upon the assassination of Villiers, Duke of Buckingham, by Felton, it was proposed, in the Privy Council, to put the assassin to the rack, in order to discover his accomplices, the Judges, being consulted, declared unanimously, to their own honor, and the honor of the English law, that no such proceeding was allowable by the laws of England." (Blackstone, IV. 326.) "The common law of England admits not of torture to extort confession." (Hallam, 93.)

On the twelfth day of November, Campian and seven other priests were brought to the bar to plead to an indictment of High Treason. This indictment was not under the statute passed at the last session of Parliament, but under that of 25 Edward III.[1] The reason of this seems to have been, that the queen and her ministers might shift whatever odium might attach to the issue from their own law to one which had the sanction of venerated age. The indictment was, for having conspired at Rome, Rheims, and other places beyond the seas, the death of the Queen's Majesty, the overthrow of the religion professed in England, the subversion of the state, and for having stirred up strangers to invade the realm for these purposes; moreover, that they came to England to persuade and seduce the queen's subjects *to* the Romish religion and obedience to the Pope, and *from* their duties and allegiance to her Highness.[2] Each pleaded "Not guilty;" and on the twentieth day of the month they were brought to the bar for trial.[3]

The accounts which we have of this trial are far from satisfactory. The historian[4] labors chiefly to present Campian as a man "so fine in his quirks and fantastical conjectures, that some he won by smooth devices, and other he charmed with subtlety or choked with sophistry;"[5] the reporter, to parade

[1] Camden, 271.

"The statute of Edward the Third saith, that if any man shall compass or imagine the king's death, or shall levy war against him, or shall probably be attainted to have been an adherent to the king's enemies, he shall be adjudged a traitor." (Strype's Annals, VI. 339.)

[2] Howell, I. 1049. Strype's Parker, 376, 377.

[3] Howell, I. 1050.

[4] Holingshed's Continuator, IV. 447–455.

[5] Holingshed, IV. 456.

his acumen and to disparage the lawyers of the Crown.[1] In reading the latter, although some strong circumstantial testimony appears, one looks in vain for even respectable argument; and is at a loss to perceive how either branch of the indictment was sustained by proof sufficient, even in those days, to convict men on trial for their lives. If, however, we compare this Report with the materially different indictment given by the historian (and this authority, the writer in each case being unknown, is as good as the other) we certainly see greater reason to suppose that both the charges were at least plausibly sustained. The historian has it thus: "That, at Rome, Rheims, and divers other places, where the Pope having with other princes practised the death and deprivation of our most gracious princess, and utter subversion of her kingdom to advance his most abominable religion, these men, having vowed their allegiance to the Pope to obey him in all cases whatsoever,[2] being there, gave their consent; yea, uttermost furtherance they might, to aid him in this most traitorous determination. And for this intent and purpose they were sent over to seduce the hearts of her Majesty's loving subjects, and to conspire and practice her Grace's death, as much as in them lay, against a great day set and appointed, when the

[1] Howell, I. 1050 – 1083.

[2] Their vow of devotion to the Apostolical See was absolute, — without conditions; the consecration of themselves, their bodies, souls, and utmost services, to be disposed of for the good of the Church, to go into every country whither the Supreme Pontiff chose to send them, instantly, without discussion, condition, or reward. (Ranke's History of the Popes, Vol. I. Bk. II. Ch. I. p. 129, Philad. edit., 1841. "Loyola and Jesuitism," by Isaac Taylor, p. 124, New York, 1849.)

general havoc should be made, those only reserved that joined them."[1]

But, whatever was the precise phraseology of the indictment, after the testimony was concluded, "the matter rested in this" — we quote the words of one of the judges — "whether to believe the prisoners who spake for their lives, or the witnesses who came freely to depose as they were demanded. While the former denied whatsoever was alleged, the latter affirmed *sufficient proof against them*." Besides, at this point of the proceedings, the Lord Chief Justice generously said to the prisoners, "If you have more to say in discharge of what is alleged against you, speak; and we will hear you until to-morrow morning. We would be loath you should have any occasion to complain on the Court, and therefore, if aught rest behind that is untold, and that is available for you, speak; and you shall be heard with indifference."[2] And "they all thanked his lordship, and said they could not otherwise affirm, but that *they had found of the Court both indifference and justice*."[3] We are therefore constrained to believe, that the indictment was sustained by clearer evidence, or that the evidence was more skilfully combined by the Crown lawyers, than appears in the report.

When the prisoners were asked, in conclusion, "What can you say why you should not die?" Campian answered, "The only thing we have now to say is, that if our religion do make us traitors, we are worthy to be condemned; but otherwise are, and have been, as true subjects as ever the queen had

[1] Holingshed, IV. 447.

[2] Candor; impartiality.

[3] Howell, I. 1069, 1070.

any," — the very point in question with us; the point we shall soon discuss.

Sir Christopher Wray — the Lord Chief Justice — then proceeded to pronounce sentence. "The Court doth award, that you be had from hence to the place whence you did come, and so drawn through the open city of London upon a hurdle to the place of execution, and there to be hanged and *let down alive*, ... [1] and your entrails taken out and burnt in your sight, then your heads to be cut off and your bodies to be divided into four parts, and to be disposed of at her Majesty's pleasure. And God have mercy on your souls."

On the morning of the first day of December, "an infinite number of people" were assembled at Tyburn to witness the execution of the law upon three convict priests, — Campian, Sherwine, and Briant; the last of whom had been tried and condemned, with six others, the day after Campian's conviction.[2] Political considerations, and the presence of her French lover, restrained the queen from signing warrants for the execution of others. They were reserved until after his departure.[3]

Conspicuous in the assemblage were several of the queen's Privy Council, and many of the nobility. In

[1] The Latin reader may supply the lacuna thus, — *et verenda abscecari.* In Howell, the sentence of the Court consists largely of "*et ceteras.*" I have, therefore, transscribed the full form of the sentence for High Treason, as given in Hargrave, and in Howell also, in the case of Dr. Parry. For the words, "let down alive," the Continuator of Holingshed has, "until half dead."

[2] Holingshed, IV. 455.

[3] Ibid., 488. Lingard, VIII. 158, 159.

due time appeared the convicts; Campian, drawn upon one hurdle by himself; the others, together, on another.[1] Some of the mob shouted and jeered as they passed through their midst. Others, touched with pity, spake words of comfort to them, invoked divine support in their behalf, and wiped from their faces the viscid mire which blinded them.[2]

Campian was first brought up into the cart beneath the gallows; and when the noise of the agitated multitude had subsided he began to speak. After a few words of Latin, he said in English, "I am here brought as a spectacle before the faces of God, of angels, and of men; satisfying myself to die as becometh a true Christian and a Catholic man." He was here interrupted by Sir Francis Knollys and the sheriffs, who told him that his proper business, at that moment, was to confess his treason.

"For the treason you have laid to my charge, and I am here to suffer for, I desire you all to bear witness with me, that thereof I am altogether innocent."

"But the charge hath been proved," interposed one of the Council.

"Well, my lord; I am a Catholic man and a priest. In that faith have I lived. In that faith I intend to die. If you esteem my religion treason, then of force I must grant unto you that I am guilty. As for any other treason, I never committed it, — God is

[1] The first step in the punishment of High Treason was, that the offender be drawn, or dragged, upon the ground; not carried in any way, or permitted to walk. "But usually by connivance, — at length, ripened by humanity into law, — a sledge or hurdle was allowed, to preserve the offender from the extreme torment of being dragged upon the ground or pavement." (Blackstone, IV. 92, 377.)

[2] Holingshed, IV. 456. Challoner, 29. Taylor, II. 170.

my judge. But you have now what you desire. Prithee, have patience and let me have *my* desire. Suffer me to speak a word or two for discharge of my conscience."

"You may speak only touching your crime."

"Of all treason and conspiracy I am innocent; and to this my answer I desire credit as to one made upon my death and soul. The jury might easily be deceived. I forgive them. I forgive all concerned in my fate, as I desire to be forgiven. When I was put upon the rack, I did confess the names of some into whose houses I had been received, for it was promised me that no harm should come to them thereby. Their pardon also I crave, inasmuch as they have been made to suffer maugre the promise.[1] And whereas I did after write to Mr. Pound that it grieved me that I had offended the Catholics by this my confession, yet that I had not nor would not discover any secrets of my friends by them declared, come rack, come rope,[2] which letter was intercepted and produced against me, I do now affirm on my soul, and as I would answer before God, that the secrets were not, as has been misconstrued, matters of treason or conspiracy, or any matter against her Majesty or the state; but the saying of Mass, hearing confession, preaching, and such like duties and functions of the priesthood."

"What think you," it was asked, "of the bull of Pius the Fifth?"

To this he gave no answer.

"Do you renounce the Pope?"

"I am a Catholic."

[1] Taylor, II. 164.

[2] Howell, I. 1060.

"In your Catholicism is contained all treason."

He then began to pray in Latin; when he was interrupted by a minister, who requested him to say some prayer with him in English.[1] With a mild look, Campian replied:

"You and I are not one in religion; wherefore I pray you content yourself. I bar none of prayer. I only desire those of the household of faith to pray with me, and to say one creed when I am in mine agony."

Lord Charles Howard, afterwards Lord Admiral, who presided upon the occasion, then said,[2] "It were fitting that you should ask the queen's forgiveness."

"Wherein have I offended her? Of offence against her, I am innocent. This is my last speech. In this give me credit. I have prayed for her; and do."

"For which queen?" asked the Lord Howard. "For Elizabeth?"

"Yea, for Elizabeth; your queen and my queen."

After he had been allowed a little time for silent prayer,[3] the cart was drawn from beneath him. According to the atrocious law under which these men were convicted, they should have been suspended only *three minutes;*[4] but Lord Howard assumed an act

[1] Holingshed, IV. 459, and Challoner, compared.

[2] If this was "the Lord Howard of Effingham, High Admiral of England," to whom was intrusted the command of the English fleet which was sent out against the Spanish Armada, his service at these executions was a fact of no small significance; for — he was *a Catholic.* Not only by his function, but by his words, upon this occasion, it is made evident that *he* believed the convicts guilty of treasonable conspiracy, and worthy of death. (See Dr. Nares's "Life and Times of Lord Burleigh," Vol. III. p. 333.)

[3] Holingshed, IV. 459.

[4] The statute is not before me. My authority is "Chambers's History of the Rebellion of 1745," p. 377, Edinburgh edit., 1847. It was not unfrequently the case that consciousness was so little impaired by

of mercy in permitting them to hang until they were quite dead.

As soon as it was evident that Campian was beyond suffering, he was cut down and stripped; when the executioner completed his work as prescribed by the sentence of the Court. His hands dripping with blood, he then savagely laid hold of Sherwine, saying, "Come Sherwine, take your wages!"

The priest, "who was a scholar worthy of Exeter College, where he was educated, and a gentleman of most mild and winning deportment, took no notice of the insult."[1] He did not even look reproachfully. Nor did he shrink. "With a cheerful countenance," he embraced the brute! He kissed his bloody hands! Then quietly getting into the cart, he closed his eyes and, after continuing some time in silent prayer, said, "Do the people expect speech from me?"

Greatly moved by his remarkable composure and meekness, many of the crowd, and some of "the honorable sort," answered, "Yes." He then began an address to the Holy Trinity.

"I thank thee, O God the Father, I thank thee, O God the Son, I thank thee, O God the Holy Spirit, for the manifold mercies and blessings bestowed upon me a sinner, from the hour of my birth to this present!"

the brief suspension, that the sufferer, under the first stroke of the knife, revived sufficiently to attack the executioner; and sometimes with such fury, that the combined strength of several men was necessary to effect the sentence of the law. (Fox's Acts and Monuments, III. 1023. Stow's Annals, 766, 769. Strype's Annals, III. 124.)

This fiendish punishment was not abolished until early in the nineteenth century; and then not without opposition. (Sir J. Mackintosh's History of England, I. 369. Philad. edit., 1836.

[1] Taylor, II. 171.

Then turning to the multitude, he began to give an account of his faith, but was interrupted by Sir Francis Knollys, who exhorted him rather to confess his treason; to which he mildly replied, "I am innocent of any such crime."

Being still urged, he said in the same mild way, "I have no occasion to tell a lie. It is a case where my soul is at stake. Although in this short term of mortal life, I am to undergo the infamy and punishment of a traitor, I doubt not my future happiness through Christ Jesus, in whose death, passion, and blood I only trust. Blessed Jesus! I acknowledge the imperfection, misery, and sinful wretchedness of my nature! But notwithstanding what I am, thou knowest me innocent of all treason and traitorous practices; and that I went beyond the seas, not for such things, but for my soul's health, to learn to save my soul."

Upon this he was again urged by Sir Francis Knollys to confess that what he had done could be no otherwise than traitorous.

"Tush, tush, Sir Francis!"—words of simple reproof, not contemptuous—"you and I shall answer this before another Judge, where my innocence of treason shall appear, and you will see that I am guiltless."

"We know that you are no contriver or doer of treason, for you are no man of arms; but you are a traitor by consequence."

"If to be a Catholic only," replied Sherwine, with more energy than he had before spoken,—"if to be a perfect Catholic, be to be a traitor, then am I a traitor."

He was then forbidden to make any further speech.

"Well; if I may not address this people, you will not debar me from saying this one word, — I forgive. And this I most heartily and truly do. I forgive all who, by general presumption, or particular error, have procured my death."

After he had uttered another prayer to his "Saviour Jesus," and repeated the Lord's prayer in English,[1] some one called upon him for his opinion of the bull of Pius the Fifth. But, like Campian, he gave no answer.

"Why pray you not for the queen?"

"I have prayed for her. I do."

"For which queen? For Queen Elizabeth?" inquired Lord Howard.

With a pleasant smile, Sherwine replied, "Yea; for Elizabeth Queen, I now at this instant pray the Lord my God to make her his servant in this life; and, after this life, co-heir with Jesus Christ."

To this, one replied, "Troth! it be thy meaning that she become a Papist!"

"God forbid otherwise!"

Perceiving that the cart was about to be removed, he once more betook himself to prayer; and while saying, "Jesu! Jesu! be to me a Jesus!" he was swung off. It is said, that the spectators were affected to tears, and with one accord exclaimed, "Good Sherwine! the Lord receive thy good soul!"[2]

Before the body was submitted to the executioner's knife, Briant was ordered to the cart. He was only twenty-eight years of age, and was somewhat remarkable for his beauty. He began to give an account of

[1] Holingshed, IV. 459.

[2] Taylor, II. 172.

his Catholic education, but was ordered to desist, and to confine his words to a confession of his treason. But with somewhat of a defiant air he denied his guilt; and added that he was neither at Rome or at Rheims at the time designated in his indictment, and that he regarded the bull of Pius the Fifth as all other Catholics did. He spake little; but passed most of his time in silent prayer. While saying, "*Miserere mei Deus*," he was swung off.[1]

Such in brief was the career of the first Jesuit missionaries under Elizabeth's reign. Such was the terrible vengeance of her government, — a vengeance softened, however, in this particular instance, by deferring the butchery of the victims until, by the rope, they had become insensible to the knife.[2]

[1] Holingshed, IV. 459. Taylor, II. 172.

Except where I have given other references, my narrative of these executions is derived from Challoner. His account was taken from one written by an eyewitness, and published in 1582.

[2] Blackstone says (IV., 376, 377), "There being very few instances (and those accidental, or by negligence) of any person's being embowelled till previously deprived of sensation by strangling." I am surprised at this remark; as well as by the fact that this learned jurist does not allude to the atrocity of emasculation as a part of the penalty of High Treason.

Hallam (p. 102, note), after quoting Dr. Lingard's remark, that "the butchery of those who were executed between 1588 and the queen's death, with a few exceptions, was performed on the victim while he was in full possession of his senses," says, "I should be glad to think that the few exceptions were the other way. Much would depend upon the humanity of the sheriff, which one might hope to be stronger in an English gentleman than his zeal against Popery. But I cannot help acknowledging that there is reason to believe the disgusting cruelties of the legal sentence to have been frequently inflicted. In an anonymous memorial among Lord Burleigh's Papers, written about 1586, it is recommended that priests persisting in their treasonable opinion should be hanged, and the manner of drawing and quartering forborne. This seems to imply that it had been usually practised on the living."

Of the character, trial, and conviction of Campian we have fuller details than of those of any other Catholic priest condemned under Elizabeth's reign; and no case has been more plausibly urged than his to show that clerical emissaries from Rome were executed, not for any really treasonable acts, but for their religious faith and the celebration of their religious rites, — and for these only. The allegation lies not only against the government, but against those who approved of these its executions; against Puritans particularly, than whom none were more sternly hostile to the doctrines and practices of Rome. We suspend our judgment of the political behavior of the Jesuits and Seminary priests generally, until we shall have collected fuller means of judgment. Yet we cannot dismiss the conspicuous case of this Jesuit apostle without inspecting his pretensions to a holy martyrdom.

It will be observed that there were two counts in his indictment, "neither of which," — to use the words of the historian, — "were for facts of doctrine or religion, nor yet for offences against any late or new statutes, but," — both of which were, — "for facts such as were in truth," — i. e. not constructively, — "high treasons committed against her Majesty's royal person and against the ancient laws and statutes of the realm."[1] Either count, if sustained, justified conviction of "*treason*, by the law of England, and according to the common use of language, — the crime of rebellion or conspiracy against the government;"[2] yet neither count could have been

[1] Holingshed, IV. 458. Coke's Reports, Vol. III. p. xxxiii.

[2] Hallam, 102, note.

sustained, even in the opinion of the tribunals of that day, by merely proving that the party on trial had performed the rites of Catholic worship.

The Papacy was *at war* with England. Pius V., by his bull, had declared himself the enemy of Elizabeth, — not only spiritually, but politically her enemy; for the same document which affected to thrust her from the pale of the Church, commanded her subjects, under threat of eternal damnation, to revolt from their allegiance. He had also stirred up the rebellion of 1569; had set on foot the conspiracy of 1571; and, in each instance, had stood ready to co-operate with money, troops, and munitions of war. Gregory XIII. had done likewise, confirming[1] the anathema of his predecessor; planning, as we have seen, an invasion of England in 1579, "to deprive her Majesty of life, crown, and dignity," to raise "everywhere the general cry, — 'Queen Mary! Queen Mary!' and in Ireland, initiating the enterprise 'in his own name and under his own standard.'"[2] Although, when upon trial, Campian roundly asserted that "he did not esteem the strength of these facts worth a pennyworth of pippins,"[3] yet they were grave and relevant antecedents. Though not proofs of traitorous guilt on his part, yet, as the Lord Chief Justice said, "they were inducements to the point itself."[4]

The war which the Pope had waged against the English government was not a mere war of paper and ink; but of insurrection, of invasion, of military

[1] Holingshed, IV. 448.

[2] Ibid., 447, 450, 451, 457, 458. Howell, I. 1053, 1058. Strype's Annals, IV. 357, 368. Lingard, VIII. 152.

[3] Holingshed, IV. 448.

[4] Howell, I. 1053.

force, of dethronement. That "he was the most mortal enemy her Majesty had,"[1] and that he was her *military* enemy, were facts which "could not any ways have escaped the knowledge of Campian," although he protested that "he had not so much as the smallest inkling of them."[2] They were known the world over. Under these circumstances, he and his companion, having long before sworn fealty to his Holiness,"[3] and having "bequeathed themselves," as "men dead to the world,"[4] to the Society of Jesus, "dutifully to execute the commandment" of their general, whether to go, to come, or to do,[5] "were charged with a sudden embassage to England" as the confessed agents and pensionaries[6] of the very prince who was notoriously the queen's most mortal enemy. Born subjects of the Crown, deserters of their native land, affiliated to a power at open war with the queen, — a power whose fixed policy it was *stealthily* to instigate her subjects to revolt, — returning as its sworn and paid emissaries, operating as such and in disguise, — such a combination of circumstances could hardly fail, in a threatened commonwealth, to insure conviction of treason, even under the improved rules and generous principles which govern our modern tribunals.

It was, indeed, asserted by Campian — but asserted baldly — that he was sent to England, "not as a traitor to conspire the subversion of his country,[7] but

[1] Howell, I. 1055.

[2] Ibid., I. 1058, *bis*.

[3] Ibid., 1055.

[4] Ibid., 1054, 1056. Holingshed, IV. 453.

[5] Campian's words. Howell, I. 1058. Holingshed, IV. 451. *Ante*, p. 210, note 2.

[6] Holingshed, IV. 453, 454. Howell, I. 1056.

[7] Should we here insert, by way of paraphrase — "but as a saviour

as a priest to minister the sacraments and to hear confessions;" that he was sent "only for the saving of souls;"[1] that "he was flatly with charge and commandment excused from matters of state and government;"[2] that his acts corresponded to this injunction; that "he touched neither state nor policy;" and he added, "What reconciliation can there be to the Pope, since reconciliation is only due to God? The reconciliation that we endeavored was only to God."[3] The duplicity of this interrogation and reply is transparent.

Persons, too, soon after his arrival in England,

to subvert the *government* of the country," we should probably express the full meaning of the Jesuit. His language when on trial savors of the same nice ambiguity: "if our religion do make us traitors, we are worthy to be condemned;" which is *verbally* consistent with the opinion that the overthrow of the *government* would be the salvation of the *country*, and therefore no treason.

[1] Howell, I. 1054, 1058. Holingshed, IV. 450, 451, 453. Gee; Introduction, xxiv.

[2] Howell, I. 1059.

Cardinal Allen is responsible for a like statement, viz. that "the English Popish missionaries, of all sorts, had no commission from any source to move sedition, or to deal against the state; but only to exercise the functions of their priesthood, — *preaching*, *teaching*, catechizing, ministering the sacraments, and the like; an express clause in their instructions being, that they deal not in matters of state." (Butler, I. 357, 358. So Lingard, VIII. 159.)

I find no intimation that the commission with this prohibitive clause was ever produced, — as one may suppose it would have been, — to sustain the defence of Campian. In other words, I find no evidence of its reality but the unsupported assertions of interested parties.

If the commissions of the Jesuits *were* so limited, — of which I am not convinced, — Persons certainly violated his oath of obedience. If they were not so limited, then he "swore by his faith" to a falsehood; as will appear in the text. In either case, he perjured himself.

The same assertion of the limitation of the commission given to Campian and Persons was also made by the Jesuit Morus, — or Moor, — in his History of their Mission. (Gee; Introduction, xix., xxviii.)

It should not escape notice, — for we are dealing with Jesuits, — that "the functions of the priesthood," called "preaching and teaching," have an indefinite latitude.

[3] Howell, I. 1054.

when adverting to a rumor that he and Campian were to array parties and plots against the government under pretence of religion, "swore by his faith that they had no such intent,"[1] and then read a Paper purporting to be their Commission from Mercuranius, the General of the Jesuits, to the effect that they were ordered, explicitly, to avoid all discussion, either by word of mouth or in writing, of anything which related to the public concerns of the kingdom.[2] We shall soon see that he was far from behaving himself accordingly.

Unfortunately for Campian's plea that his mission was purely for the saving of souls, a remarkable modification of the bull of Pius V. had been granted to him upon the eve of his departure from Rome by Gregory XIII., who then filled the chair of St. Peter.

The Paper was found in possession of one of Campian's accomplices.[3] Ten years before, Campian had complained to the Cardinal of Sicily, that the bull of Pius V. bore very hardly upon the Catholics in England, whom it laid under the curse of anathema if they obeyed the queen. The Cardinal had replied, that he thought the bull might be so mitigated that

[1] The Continuator of Holingshed — probably John Stow — makes a counter-statement, and in the strongest language possible. "Campian and the rest of his fellows . . . . . bolster up one another with large protestations, ... affirming that they were not sent hither for any such intent," — i. e. "to further the death of her Majesty, and the overthrow of the realm," — "which is as untrue as we know it for truth that the Lord God liveth in heaven." (Holingshed, IV. 450, 451.) This remarkable asseveration deserves some consideration, coming as it does from a contemporary and a watchful observer of events, who must have known the details of proof showing the *true* intent of the Jesuits.

[2] Butler, I. 365, 367.

[3] Burleigh's "Execution of Justice," in Harleian Miscellany, II. 130, and in Holingshed, IV. 522.

the Catholics might acknowledge her Highness as their queen without incurring the curse.[1] Accordingly, when all was ripe for the mission of Campian and Persons, it was granted in due form by the Pope, that the bull of Pius V. should not be so binding upon the English Catholics, but that they might acknowledge, serve, and honor the queen *until* the public execution of it might be had or made.[2]

But this was not all. Light was thrown upon this modification of the bull. Hart, one of Campian's associates, and who, though condemned him with him, was spared, declared as follows: "The bull of Pius V.—for so much as it is against the queen—is holden among the English Catholics for a lawful sentence and a sufficient discharge of her subjects' fidelity, and so remaineth in force; but in some points touching the subjects it is altered by the present Pope. For where in that bull all her subjects are commanded not to obey her, and, she being excommunicated and deposed, all that do obey her

[1] Howell, I. 1057. Gee, xxiii, xxv.

[2] Holingshed, IV. 448, 453, 522. Harl. Misc., II. 130. Strype's Annals, IV. 347; V. 54.

The dispensation, modification, Grace, or Faculty granted, was in the following words:—

"Let it be desired of our most Holy Lord the Explication of the Bull Declaratory made by Pius the Fifth against Elizabeth, and such as do adhere to or obey her; which Bull the Catholics desire to be understood in this manner,—That the same Bull shall always oblige her and the Heretics, but the Catholics it shall by no means bind as affairs do now stand, but hereafter, when the public Execution of the said Bull may be had or made." Then followed other petitions of Faculties for further authorities; the whole concluding thus: "The Pope hath granted these foresaid Graces to Father Robert Persons and Edmund Campian, who are now to go into England; the 14th day of April, 1580. Present, the Father Oliverius Manarchus, Assistant." (Gee; Introduction, xxvi. Harleian Miscellany, II. 130. Camden, 246. Holingshed, IV. 522.)

are likewise innodate and accursed, which point is perilous to the Catholics, — for, if they obey her they be in the Pope's curse, and if they disobey her they are in the queen's danger, — therefore the present Pope, to relieve them, hath altered that part of the bull, and dispensed with them to obey and serve her, without peril of excommunication; which dispensation is to endure *but till it please the Pope otherwise to determine.*"[1]

Thus "the aforesaid graces" granted to Persons and Campian were simply "a permission to dissemble in hope of better opportunity to revolt;"[2] or — to adopt words published at the time upon the highest authority, and which it would have been folly to publish if untrue — "a toleration to the Catholics to keep themselves covert under pretence of temporary and permissive obedience to her Majesty, until there were force sufficient whereby the bull of her Majesty's deprivation might be publicly executed, when they should join all together with that force upon pain of curse and damnation."[3]

Such a document, — a command for rebellion when the time might serve, — was Treason under a mask. With this Paper as one of his credentials, Campian, one of "the priests appointed to win the people against the appointed time when a great army should be ready to join with them,"[4] came into England. Campian, one of the Jesuits "whose common creed it was, that it was the Pope's right to deprive kings

[1] Harleian Miscellany, II. 131. Holingshed, IV. 523. Gee, xxx.

[2] Hallam, 93.

[3] Strype's Annals, V. 298; a Paper attributed to Lord Burleigh. Holingshed, IV. 458; a Paper "published by authority" at the time.

[4] Holingshed, IV. 451; testimony of Anthony Monday.

of their crowns,"[1] came into England an agent of the Pope, a servant of the Jesuits, and with such traitorous instructions in his hands. What was he to do with them, but to use, to show, and to obey them? How could he do *this* without "preaching and teaching" treason? According to the Catholic creed; could he reconcile men to God but by reconciling them to

[1] Hallam, 92, *bis*.

We have the creed of the Jesuits upon this point, from the pen of Campian's associate.

"It is certain, and what we ought to believe, and it is the opinion of all Divines and Ecclesiastical Lawyers, that if any Christian Prince fall from the Catholic Faith, and would have others to follow him, he himself thereby doth forthwith, both by Divine and Human Law, yea, though the Pope, the Supreme Judge hath not issued forth any censure against him, fall from all his Authority and Dignity, and his subjects are freed from all their oaths of allegiance which they sware to him as a lawful Prince; and they may, nay, and ought, — if they have force enough to overcome, — to pull him down from his throne as an Apostate, Heretic, a Forsaker of Christ, and an Enemy to the Commonwealth." (Gee; Introduction, p. xxxiii. Hallam, 93, note.)

That this was Campian's creed, to which, in Elizabeth's case, he held the more firmly because of the bull of *deposition*, — deposition was understood to be included in excommunication (Lingard, VIII. 157, note), — and that, therefore, aside from any quibble on the score of absolution, he held that treason against Elizabeth was impossible, are indicated, not only by his profession as a Jesuit, but otherwise.

From the Report of his trial, it would seem that he *had* acknowledged to Elizabeth herself, that she was his Queen both by possession and *by right*. (Howell, I. 1062. Lingard, VIII. 157.) If he did, — although he had Gregory's dispensation to serve and honor her for the time, — he was false to his spiritual allegiance, for the Bull of Pius V., "for so much as it was against *the queen* remained in force." But whether he did, or did not, rests altogether upon the *verbal* accuracy of the reporter of the trial. (Compare Hallam, 92.) On this point, I submit the following.

1. We have his refusal to answer the very rigid and exact question, — "Whether her Majesty was true and lawful queen, or a pretended queen, and deprived, and in possession of her Crown only *de facto?*" — a refusal signed by his own hand, attested by witnesses, and published by the Government *at the time*. (Howell, I. 1078.)

2. On the scaffold he would only acknowledge Elizabeth as his queen; which did not necessarily mean that she was such otherwise than *de facto*, or by possession.

3. He would never answer plainly respecting "her subjects' al-

the Pope? Could he reconcile to the Pope without reconciling to the Pope's new declaration? Could he reconcile to this declaration, could he invite, commend, or even propound reconciliation to it without "teaching" that Elizabeth was no longer rightful queen, but "deposed"? without teaching that her subjects were "discharged of their fidelity"? without teaching that, "when time might serve, they

legiance due *civilly*,"—in distinction from *ecclesiastically*;—"but answered sophistically, deceitfully, and traitorously; restraining his confession of allegiance to the permissive form of the Pope's toleration." (Strype's Annals, V. 297, 298.) He had also in his possession prescribed directions from abroad "how to behave himself in England;" in reference to just such questions; "to answer *Sophistice*," reserving a paramount allegiance to the Pope; and his answers were in *literal* conformity to these directions. (Holingshed, IV. 452, *bis*. Howell, I. 1062.)

4. He refused to express an opinion of the Pope's right to depose princes; and, particularly of the deposing authority of the Bull of Pius V.; refused, before his sentence, (Howell, I. 1062, 1078. Holingshed, IV. 452, 458,) and, as I have stated, on the scaffold.

5. Had he truly considered Elizabeth his *rightful* queen, "having under God the sovereignty and rule over all manner of *persons* born within her realms" (Sparrow, 83; the queen's explication of the Oath), he could have taken the Oath of Supremacy, and thereby have saved his life, "without being reconciled in points of religion." So did three of his accomplices, who thereby received "her Majesty's grace and mercy," although still holding to the Catholic faith. (Howell, I. 1074. Lingard, VIII. 159.) So had Feckenham offered to do in 1580; though he refused to change his religion or to go to church. (Strype's Annals, IV. 354, 678.) In 1583, Andrew Oxenbridge, a Doctor of Laws, subscribed the Oath; but still holding the Catholic faith. (Ibid., V. 276.) So did others. (Fuller, Bk. IX. p. 133, Sec. 6, Col. 2.) All this shows that it was not true that Campian was offered his life on condition of going to church,—that is, of changing his religion. (Howell, I. 1055.) All this shows, and conclusively, that it was not for his religion, but for his treasonableness, that he lost his life; unless, indeed, as was said to him on the scaffold, "in *his* Catholicism was contained all treason."

6. Camden states positively (p. 271) that, "when asked whether he would take part with the Queen or the Pope, if his Holiness should send forces against the Queen, Campian openly professed and testified under his hand, that he would stand for the Pope."

ought to take up arms against her"?[1] That this was the errand upon which he was sent "was most manifestly *tried and proved*,"[2] however this proof may be lacking in the *Report* of the trial. Did he, or did he not, prosecute his errand?

His mission, his commission, the baptized treason which he carried in his hand, his Jesuitical principles about the Pope's deposing power, his paramount allegiance to his spiritual commanders, their designs upon the English government, all indicate that he did. If he did not, he betrayed his trust and was false to his spiritual oaths. If he did, he was guilty of "the crime of conspiracy against the Government." He was either a traitor to the Order of Jesus and to his spiritual prince, or a traitor to the good order of the realm and to his temporal prince. The Court, who doubtless had more light than appears in the Report of the trial, — the Court, from whom, as he acknowledged, "he had found both impartiality and justice," — declared him guilty of the political sin, — to the Catholic Church, to the Society of Jesus, to Campian himself, the milder verdict of the two. And if, as we are told upon high legal authority of a later date, *he* was one of those "who in secret corners *whispered and infused into the hearts of many*, ... that they ought not to obey the queen, ... under pain of the Pope's curse, which was High Treason by the ancient laws of England;"[3] if, as we are told by the same pen, "he *confessed* that he came into England to make a party for the Catholic cause *when need should require*,"[4] — these

[1] Holingshed, IV. 458; Paper published at the time "by authority."

[2] Ibid.

[3] Coke's Reports, Vol. III. p. xxxviii., — by error of the press numbered xxxiii.; *de jure regis ecclesiastico*.

[4] Ibid.

were "overt acts, upon the principle of the Pope's deposing power," sufficient to bring him fairly "within the statute of Edward III. for compassing the queen's death, or intending to depose her;"[1] sufficient to justify the verdict of the jury and sentence from the Court.[2]

It should also be remembered that Persons, under the same Commission and the same religious pretence, had unquestionably operated "to ripen matters" for the public execution of the bull against the queen, and "for setting her Majesty's Crown upon another head." For this, he made distinct propositions under his own hand.[3] And so vigorously did he prosecute this his vocation, that some Catholics — doubtless disbelievers in the Pope's deposing power, and therefore loyal[4] — "thought to have delivered him into the Magistrates' hands."[5] Campian was an *accomplice* of Persons, — a fact of grave import in the eye of law, in the eyes of any jury.

We do not forget Campian's solemn asseveration before the Court: "I protest, before God and his

[1] Hallam, 102, note.

[2] There is a Paper of the day which very well argues this point. It is styled "A Treatice;" showing "that such Papists as of late times have been executed were, by a statute of Edward III., lawfully executed as traitors." It is recorded at length in Strype's Annals, VI. Appendix, Bk. I. No. XLVII. It contains the following paragraph: "For the Jesuites and Seminary priests executed, to give their faith unto the queen's enemy, who sought her overthrow, her death, her crown, to persuade her subjects unto a reconcilement with the said her enemy, and so to encrease his strength and diminish her Majesty's, &c., is to compass, or at least imagine, her highness's destruction, is, in a sort, a levying or preparation of war and rebellion. And to be convicted of the premises, I am sure, is probably to attaint them for adherents unto her Majestie's enemies. And, therefore, the Jesuites and seminary priests, executed by the statute of Edward III. were traitors, and so most lawfully executed." Compare note [1], page 209, of this volume.

[3] Gee; Introduction, xxviii.

[4] *Ante*, Vol. I. p. 364.

[5] Camden, 247.

angels, by heaven and earth, and before this tribunal which, I pray God, may be a mirror of the judgment to come, that I am not guilty of these treasons contained in the indictment, or of any other whatsoever."[1] We do not forget his assertions when Death was standing at his elbow; his wary assertion, "As for any other treason than my religion, I never committed it;" and his other assertion, "Of all treason and conspiracy I am *innocent*, and to this I desire credit as made upon my death and soul." But neither do we forget that these were words (in the first instance) of one upon trial for his life; of one whose school's craft was verbal chicanery; of one who could religiously believe himself "not guilty"—"innocent"—of any crime *after ghostly absolution;* of one who, at the last moment before his arrest, for the penance of saying three times, "Thy will, O Lord, be done!" and, "John Baptist, pray for me!" had been technically purged from all guilt; and of one who believed that conspiracy against *Elizabeth* was no treason. It is, therefore, with no sneer, but with sober judgment, and deploring such religious delusion, that we count these his words of no weight.

It would be tedious to array all the recorded particulars which show Campian's complicity in treasonable preparatives. But we have given enough for our purpose; enough to show that there were other reasons for his execution than his exercise of the priestly office, and that those who were consenting unto his death—Walsingham, Knollys, and other Puritans—had a better justification before God than the impulse of religious antipathy.

[1] Howell, I. 1049.

CHAPTER IX.

AYLMER, BISHOP OF LONDON.

The gentle Tutor spoiled into a Lord Bishop. — Lord Burleigh censures his "Papal Jurisdiction." — The Bishop's "Choler." — Burleigh's Retort. — The Bishop increases his Rigor. — The Queen angry with him for Remissness. — He boasts that "on the other Side he is hated like a Dog." — Robert Wright and Lord Rich convented. — Method of Examination in Ecclesiastical Courts. — False Records of Answers. — Other sinister Proceedings. — Commissioners disgusted with their own Court. — True Reasons of the Prosecution. — The Bishop spurred again. — The Queen angry with him. — His remarkable Letter to her. — He castigates the Lord Mayor. — Mr. Wright in Prison. — The Bishop and Retribution.

1579-1592.

He is a wise man who knows what he will think, or do, or be, to-morrow. New relations give birth to new desires; new positions, to new opinions; and all, to new behavior. Adam alone, was different from Adam with Eve; and each thought, acted, became different from what they were before, when, in a new position, they saw the fruit in a new and tempting light.

John Aylmer, their son, when an exile in Strasburg and writing his "Harbor for Faithful Subjects," stoutly declaimed against the secular wealth of bishops. "Come off, ye bishops! Away with your superfluities! Yield up your thousands! Be content with hundreds! Let your portion be priest-like, not prince-like!"[1] But John Aylmer, Bishop

[1] Strype's Aylmer, 225.

of London took *his* thousands without scruple, saying, "Alack! when I was a child, I spake as a child; but when I became a man, I put away childish things!"[1]

John Aylmer, schoolmaster to Lady Jane Grey, was so gentle and pleasant that the noble maiden, by others "misordered sometimes with pinches, nipps, and bobbs, thought herself in hell till the time came that she must go to Mr. Aylmer; thought all the time nothing whilst she was with him; and, when called from him, would fall on weeping."[2] John Aylmer, schoolmaster to the Puritans, was a different man,—rude, imperious, pitiless. He was not only superintendent of ecclesiastical order and discipline in his own proper diocese; but, from the time of Archbishop Grindal's sequestration, he had also acted as such for the See of Canterbury[3] presiding over the Convocation;[4] and having jurisdiction over the "Peculiars" of Canterbury,—"those parishes dispersed through the Province, in the midst of other dioceses, which were exempt from the Ordinary's jurisdiction, subject to the metropolitan only," and which constituted the Archiepiscopal diocese in distinction from the Archiepiscopal Province.[5] In this new position, Bishop Aylmer practised such judicial severity as to call forth remonstrances, at various times, from the Lord Treasurer Burleigh — personally friendly to him — "for his urging so much some *ceremonious* points and push-

[1] Strype's Life of Aylmer, p. 269. Harrington's Nugæ Antiquæ, II. 35.

[2] Strype's Life of Aylmer, p. 5; Lady Jane to Roger Ascham.

[3] Life of Hatton, 246; Aylmer to the queen.

[4] Fuller, Bk. IX. p. 135. Strype's Aylmer, 330.

[5] Blackstone, I. 380; III. 65

ing the rigor of his ecclesiastical officers."[1] "The former," said his lordship, "be *not* of *the substance* of religion; and the ecclesiastical jurisdiction" — as it was in *practice* — "is mere papal. Such and such men there are, who ought to be permitted to preach, whom you count Disturbers."[2] The bishop was irritated by the reproof; and "gave the Lord Treasurer a *quick* answer."[3]

"It grieveth me that my Lord Treasurer is counted to have a miscontented mind towards the Bishop of London. . . . . To be plain with you, my lord, you are the man that do most discourage me. . . . . By your words and countenance, my government is hindered. . . . . It cannot be, my lord, but three words of this sort from your mouth shall more embolden them that be Disturbers, and hinder our labors, than our toil and moil shall in many years be able to help and salve. These are the things, my lord, that do discourage me, and make me weary, — that on the one side we shall be bawled on by them, and not backed nor countenanced by such great Magistrates as you are. And therewith for my part so oppressed with business (enough for three) without either help, reward, or thanks, it must needs make us desperate, as by my writing you may see I am. . . . . Very grief of mind makes me to deal with your lordship as Job did with God; toward whom in his passion he sometimes forgat himself. So I may seem to pass the limits of my duty."[4]

"My good lord," replied the Lord Treasurer, on the very same day, "your lordship's letter is too full of

[1] Strype's Aylmer, 283.
[2] Ibid., 284.
[3] Ibid., 282.
[4] Ibid., 283 – 285.

choler for me to answer directly without adding of choler: and so I should add oil to the fire. But I am otherwise disposed, both for reverence to your spiritual vocation, and for charity to mine old familiar acquaintance. For the opinion by you conceived of me, as not bearing you good-will, surely your lordship therein doth misinform yourself: and for answer, before God I protest that I bear you no kind of disfavor. . . . . . For reprehension of the common misusage by bishops' Chancellors, Commissaries, Summoners, and such like, I say, with grief of mind, that I see therein *no true use of the discipline meant* at the first erection of those offices (which I well allow of); but, *a corrupting of them to private gain, and not to the public benefit and edifying of the Church.* And it grieveth me to see the fond, light, pretended Reformers to have occasion ministered unwisely to condemn the offices, where they should condemn the misuse thereof. And so, my lord, lest in much writing I should by heat of argument stir your choler, I end, and pardon your taunts sparkled in your letters. Your lordship's, with reverence and Christian charity,

"W. BURGHLEY.

"Westminster, May 26, 1579."[1]

A characteristic letter,—cool, caustic, and clearly indicating his lordship's views of pitilessly urging "ceremonious points not of the substance of religion."

But the Bishop of London would neither submit to snaffle nor curb. Much as "it grieved him that he was not backed nor countenanced by so great a magistrate," "otherwise his very cordial friend,"[2] he did not abate his inquisitorial rigor. Only six

[1] Strype's Aylmer, 286, 287. [2] Ibid., 282.

months after, he resumed it with a "straiter hand." It was chiefly laid upon those who were averse to the Ecclesiastical Constitutions, and "by whom, for the most part, disturbances were just then moved about the queen's marriage" with the Duke of Anjou.[1] He harassed the clergy of London by summoning them no less than four times within five months — from the first of November, 1579, to the first of March, 1579–80 — to enforce upon them "a due" — that is, an exact — "conformity to the orders of the Church, by diligent inspection of their behavior, and by prescribing to them several rules in their ministry."[2] Again in January, 1580–1, apparently,[3] he held another visitation, requiring of his clergy a promise, — 1. To keep the Book of Common Prayer and Sacraments straitly; 2. Not to use invectives in their sermons against Estates, — as some had lately done against France and Spain; 3. Not to refuse wearing the surplice; and 4. Not to add or diminish anything in divine service." He also required them to answer, — 1. Whether any that had the cure of souls did not also administer the sacraments" (a point which will be explained hereafter); 2. Whether any did not observe the ceremonies to be used at baptism and marriage; 3. Whether the youth were catechized; 4. Who refused to read the Homilies; 5. What preachers called others who did not preach, 'dumb dogs.'"[4] "Those who did not subscribe, and answer the interrogatories to his lordship's satisfac-

[1] Strype's Aylmer, 64.

[2] Ibid., 64 – 68.

[3] Whether in 1580–1, or in 1581–2, is not essential. A comparison of Strype's Aylmer, p. 82, with Strype's Annals, V. 20, renders the year doubtful.

[4] Strype's Aylmer, 82. Strype's Annals, V. 20.

tion, were immediately suspended and silenced," — probably.[1]

Upon this occasion, he not only displayed his rigid Precisianism upon "ceremonious points" by insisting upon such articles and inquiries, but avowed the bitterness of his persecuting spirit, exclaiming hotly, "I will surely and severely punish offenders in these points, or I will lie in the dust for it!"[2]

In September, 1581, the queen was told that disorders were practised in the house of Lord Rich of Rochford, in Essex, — a nobleman who sympathized with the Puritans; that religious exercises were held there at variance with the Forms of the Church; and, particularly, that his chaplain had spoken against religiously observing the anniversary of the queen's accession, — the seventeenth day of November, — saying that doing so was *to make her an idol.*[3] Upon hearing this latter report, "the queen was very angry," and commanded the Bishop, through the Lord Treasurer, to put a stop to these unlawful exercises.[4]

The chaplain of Lord Rich was Robert Wright; a Cambridge scholar of high repute for his learning, but a Puritan.[5] Like Cartwright and others of the same school who were not satisfied with the English manner of inducting into Holy Orders,[6] or, more probably, who were barred by arbitrary requisitions from receiving Orders at home, he had received Presbyterian ordination at Antwerp. Being there for the purpose of observing the Polity of the foreign Re-

[1] Neal, I. 149.
[2] Strype's Aylmer, 83.
[3] Strype's Annals, V. 177.
[4] Strype's Aylmer, 83.
[5] Neal, I. 151. Brook, I. 239.
[6] Neal, I. 144.

formed churches, he had been urged by resident English merchants to enter upon the ministry in their service. Through their persuasions, he had received Orders at the hands of Villers and other ministers there.[1] After officiating accordingly, he had returned to England and had been employed by Lord Rich as his domestic chaplain; preaching and administering the sacrament, in his lordship's private chapel, and sometimes in the private chapels of others of the nobility and gentry; but doing neither in public, because he had no license from the Bishop.[2] "He had preached seven years before" going to Antwerp, "according to the order of her Majesty's Injunctions, with approbation in the University;"[3] and during some time had acted as a religious teacher in the family of *the late* Lord Rich.[4] For his seriousness, piety, and fervid preaching, he was greatly beloved by all the clergy in Essex.[5]

Upon receiving the queen's angry command, the Bishop of London replied to the Lord Treasurer in the following letter, which shows some of the antecedents of the marked case of discipline which we are about to recite:—

"I understand her Majesty is offended with certain disorders in Essex; specially, with such exercises as are had in the Lord Rich's house, one Wright the minister, ordained I cannot tell how nor where. Please your lordship inform her Highness, that in the late Lord Rich's time, I had many storms at his hand for

[1] Strype's Annals, V. 179; VI. 231. Append., No. XXIII.

[2] Ibid., V. 178, compared with VI. 231; Append., No. XXIII.

[3] Strype's Annals, VI. 230.

[4] Ibid.

[5] Ibid., 234. Neal, I. 151.

staying them; and now within a fortnight, the now Lord Rich came to my house, with his base[1] uncle and another, to entreat me to license Wright to preach in my diocese. Which because I utterly denied unless he would subscribe the Orders of the Church, his said uncle did so shake me up, as I was never so abused at any man's hand since I was born. I would have committed him, but there were not three of us[2] together, to do it according to the authority of the Commission. Nevertheless we have determined to call him at our first sitting. . . . . Wright, their preacher, I cannot come by, unless we send a power of men to fetch him out of a nobleman's house. . . . . Therefore, as we do as far as the Commission allows, I trust her Majesty will think the best of our doings, and not either suffer us to be defaced of such busy-bodies, or be grieved with us for not doing that which our authority reacheth not to. I have struggled with them in this behalf two years; and yet, unless we should pull them out by the ears, I know not how we should come by them. . . . . I have, as I think in my conscience, rather deserved her Majesty's gracious favor than discouragement; for I am hated on the other side like a dog, and am called the oppressor of the children of the Lord." This letter was dated "29 September, 1581."[3]

By some means — whether by "pulling them out by the ears" or otherwise does not appear — Lord Rich and Mr. Wright were convented before the Commissioners in October; "Lord Burleigh himself,"

[1] Illegitimate.

[2] Of us Commissioners. See the Commission; above, Chap. III.

[3] Wright, II. 154. Strype's Aylmer, 84, gives the substance of it.

perhaps by the queen's special order, "being present."[1] The immediate cause[2] of Mr. Wright's arraignment was the queen's anger upon hearing that he had said, "To have a sermon on the queen's day, and to give God thanks for her Majesty, was to make her a god."[3] He was now charged openly by the Bishop with having slandered her Majesty by saying that she was privy to the exercises in the Lord Rich's house; "for which," added the Bishop, "you deserve to lie in prison seven years." Lord Rich was charged with having earnestly seconded these and other like speeches of his chaplain. Mr. Wright answered by a simple denial of the charge.[4]

The details of his examination give us a rare and notable insight into the mode of conducting and determining the ecclesiastical prosecutions of the time. He was required to answer upon oath to any interrogatory concerning his opinions, acts, and words; even though the true answer should be an accusation of himself. Of this he complained, and with good reason; questioning whether, by the laws, he was bound to do so.[5]

This judicial sifting of *opinions* shows how little the queen's servants, — who professed and always intended, in these prosecutions, only to fulfil her wishes — acted upon what she had pledged as the rule of her government, "never to allow that any of her subjects should be molested, either by examination or inquisition, in any matter of faith, so long as they

[1] Strype's Aylmer, 85.

[2] Strype's Annals, V. 177.

[3] Ibid., VI. 233.

[4] Ibid., V. 177. Strype's Aylmer, 86.

[5] Strype's Annals, VI. 228, Append., Bk. I. No. XXIII., Oxford edit.; III. Append. p. 39, folio edit.

shall profess the Christian faith, ... assuring all her obedient subjects to enjoy her Government without any molestation to them by any person, by way of examination or inquisition of their secret opinions in their consciences, for matters of faith."[1] This rule — as we have seen in part, and as will abundantly appear hereafter — was *never* a rule in the ecclesiastical Courts. Indeed, the very Commission of the queen, under which these Commissioners acted, directed them "to inquire of offensive *opinions*."[2]

Nor was this all. Mr. Wright was compelled to answer verbally; his answers were committed to paper by the scribe of the court; and he was not permitted to determine and attest the accuracy of the register, or to protest against it.[3]

Such was the fashion of dealing with a Puritan. But — as in the cases of Campian and his associates — a conspirator, a sanctimonious traitor, being a Catholic, was permitted to scrutinize the record of his answers, and no such record was adduced against him but over his own manual attest.[4]

Nor was even this all. The record of Mr. Wright's answers was not true,[5] and this untrue record was the evidence of his crimes.[6]

It was written, — "Being examined touching the form of ordaining ministers in the Church of England, he answered that he did not know of any form appointed for the ordaining of ministers of this

[1] Haynes, 592.
[2] Strype's Grindal, Append. p. 65.
[3] Strype's Annals, as above.
[4] Howell, I. 1078 - 1084.
[5] Strype's Annals, VI. 228, Oxf. ed.; III. Appendix, p. 39, folio edit.
[6] Ibid., V. 178; Burleigh's *return* to Wright.

Church, but by hearsay."[1] His true answer was, "He remembered not that he had read and perused any such form. He had sent to the Stationers and could not get it; but he judgeth so reverently of those rites, that he acknowledgeth *there is the substance* of *the ministry*."[2] He afterwards stated that, "to his remembrance, he had never in his life thought that there were no lawful ministers in England."[3]

It was written, — "Being examined of the Book of Common Prayer whether it were good and godly, he said he could not answer what he thought of it in every particular, because he *had not read* the same!"[4] His true answer was, "To speak in general of the Book of Common Prayer, he *thought it good and godly*."[5]

[1] Strype's Annals, V. 178.

[2] Ibid., VI. 229.

[3] Ibid., 233.

This was always the opinion of the Puritans, notwithstanding Bishop Warburton, who says that "the Puritans opposed the *divine right* of presbytery to the *divine right* of episcopacy; which was the making each other anti-Christian." (Vol. XII. p. 381.) "They *never* required such as had been episcopally ordained to be re-ordained; but, *in the height of their power*, declared, — 'We hold ordination by a bishop to be for substance valid, and not to be disclaimed by any that have received it.'" (Neal, I. 152; Editor's note.)

The doctrines of the divine right of bishops, and of the invalidity of Presbyterian ordination, were as yet not *avowed*, I think, by the English Church; doctrines directly contrary to the statute 13 Eliz. Chap. XII. (See above, Chap. IV. of this volume.) They were just beginning to come into vogue; as seems to have been intimated by Mr. Wright while in the hands of the Commissioners: "I *hope* this Church will no more disallow the ministers of other Reformed Churches, (if in life and doctrine sufficient,) *than they* disallow ours." (Strype's Annals, VI. 236; Append., Bk. I. No. XXIV. Folio edit.; III. Append. p. 42.)

There were at this time some scores, if not hundreds, of ministers licensed by the bishops, and ministering the most holy ordinances of the Church under her sanction, who had received, and who were known to have received, Presbyterian ordination only. (Neal, I. 152.)

[4] Strype's Annals, V. 178.

[5] Ibid., VI. 229. Append., Bk. I. No. XXIII.

It was written,—"He confesseth that *being a layman,*" &c.;[1] whereas he declared before the Commissioners that he had been "*religiously ordained* to the Christian ministry at Antwerp"[2] by certain ministers there; and this appears lower down upon the very record itself.[3]

It was written,—"The *manner* of his admitting to the ministry he doth not answer;"[4] whereas, "he declared the manner of his admitting *so long as they would hear him,*" and avowed himself "ready to declare it at all times when it should be demanded of him."[5]

It was written,—"He confesseth that in preaching he used to say prayers of his own devising; that he *never* used to pray as in the Book of Common Prayer; and that he never prayed for archbishops and bishops."[6] His true answer was, "He prayed as preachers use to do in all places, and *altogether in prescript words*"—the words of the Litany—"saving, as the occasion fell out, in some points. Yet he *ever* prayed for the Queen's Majesty, and for the Lords of the Council, and for all ministers of God's Word, and so for archbishops and bishops, seeing *they be ministers.*"[7]

1 Strype's Annals, V. 178.
2 Ibid., VI. 231.
3 Ibid., V. 179.
4 Ibid.
5 Ibid., VI. 231.
6 Ibid., V. 178.
7 Ibid., VI. 229.

I find it written on a fly-leaf of Vol. V. of Strype's Annals,—"Puritans would not so much as pray for bishops, 494." On page "494," Strype says,—"It was a custom of the Puritans many years after to omit the mention of bishops in their prayers." But this is not *all* which Mr. Strype says. Immediately after he gives an example of what he means, in the case of Mr. Joliff, a minister of Aldermary: "That he prayed for the Queen's Majesty, but left out the *Supremacy;* and that he refused to pray for archbishops and

It was written, — "He affirmeth that every minister is a bishop."[1] His true answer was, "Every minister is ἐπίσκοπος, which we *call* bishop." But he said not, as the record was intended to represent, that "every minister is a lord-bishop." Indeed, Bishop Aylmer himself inadvertently said to the same effect as Mr. Wright, in his presence before the Commissioners. Rebuking a minister for striking one of his parishioners, his lordship cited against him the Scripture, — "a bishop must be no striker;" in which quotation there had been no reason, had not the minister been ἐπίσκοπος, — a bishop.[2]

It was written, — "He answered, that the election of ministers ought to be by the flock and congregation."[3] His true answer was, "He supposed it not to be an error, that the ministers should be chosen *with consent* of their flock; so that their flock *were first well taught.*"[4]

In our very impatience through such a series of frivolities, we have proof of their historical importance; for the more frivolous the pretences, the graver the fact that upon such only, an honest servant of Christ, a devoted preacher of his Gospel, — though in the humble capacity of a private chaplain, — should be harassed by prosecution and treated like a felon. The discrepancies between his answers and the record of a corrupt or stupid scribe we commend to the reader's righteous indignation.

bishops, — *nomine.*" That is all the truth; and therefore it is not true, that Puritans would not so much as pray for one *who was* a bishop.

So some men read history.

1 Strype's Annals, V. 179.

2 Ibid., VI. 231.

3 Ibid., V. 178.

4 Ibid., VI. 230.

At the close of this examination Mr. Wright was ordered to prison to await another summons. This was issued on the seventh day of November, when he and Lord Rich were again brought before the Commissioners. "At this second appearance," says our annalist, "great proofs were brought against them." Of what? "Concerning their speech about solemnizing the queen's day."[1] These great proofs were depositions taken and sworn to before "Commissioners appointed by special choice;" one of them a "notorious slanderer of Mr. Wright," the others, strangers to him; and all of whom, in taking the depositions, "sharply rebuked witnesses who would not speak that which they knew not against him," and would "bring in only the testimony of men that bare him displeasure." Moreover, these depositions were taken while he was not present, but shut up in prison.[2]

Yet, notwithstanding the "great proofs" of the speech about solemnizing the queen's day, "there was no such matter in the commission returned;" that is, in the depositions returned by the special Commissioners.[3] These depositions were misrepre-

[1] Strype's Aylmer, 86.

[2] Strype's Annals, VI. 232.

[3] Ibid., 233.

This appears, not merely from Mr. Wright's statement to Lord Burleigh, which is here quoted, but from the copy of the depositions themselves, which his lordship sent to him. They are in Strype's Annals; but they are *silent about "the speech."* There is no authority, but Strype's statement, for saying that Mr. Wright and Lord Rich were convicted *of*—not *for*—this speech; or even for saying that it was alleged against them in Court. Mr. Strype is not supported on this point by his own documents. I have therefore treated his statement with neglect, as being a mistake into which he was probably led by reading Wright's Paper through the words, "it had been deposed against him," but *no farther*.

The depositions were these (Strype's Annals, V. 179):—

sentations of words or of facts such as might be plausibly perverted by ill-natured persons; and none of them, even if literally true, alleging matters either

1. "That he called the preachers that followed the Book of Common Prayer, 'dumb dogs,'" — which reminds one of a schoolboy whimpering because another calls him hard names. This, although spoken, if spoken at all, with reference only to those who could not *preach* (Strype's Annals, VI. 234), came within *the letter* of the queen's Commission of 1576, under which the Commissioners were acting; but within the letter only on a *forced* construction, for it was not "against the queen's ministers *and* contrary to any the laws and statutes of the Realm." (See the Commission in Strype's Grindal, Bk. II. Append., No. VI.)

2. "That" he said that "the ministers were thieves and murderers." A misrepresentation such as any prejudiced hearer or carping spy would be likely to make of a very proper sermon which Mr. Wright preached from the words, "The thief cometh not but for to steal and to kill and to destroy." (Strype's Annals, VI. 233.) This was within the letter of the Commission, only as was the first deposition. Against this libel Mr. Wright "could bring the testimony of a score of preachers in Essex, that they loved him, and that he loved and reverenced them." (Ibid., 234.)

3. That he said, "That there were no lawful ministers in England;" an absurd deposition to swear to; for Wright claimed to be one; and the words are not, "in the *Church* of England."

4. "That the people were drawn from a sermon at the church at Rochford, ... to a sermon preached by Mr. Wright in the Hall of Lord Rich;" which might possibly come within the Commission and the statute, if true. But it was false. (Ibid., 235.)

5. That "he affirmed that he was called" — to the ministry — "by the Reformed Church."

6. "He affirmed that the Lords of the Council" — and, by implication, the queen — "did know of him and also of his preaching." This was charged against him at his first appearing. By what statute, an offence? At least Aylmer knew of him and of his preaching, and for two years did not check him. (Ibid., 236.)

7. "Preachers and ministers were taunted and rebuked by Lord Rich and Mr. Wright in the Lord Rich's house." Brotherly admonition taken as a "taunt." (Ibid.) If literally true, not comprised in the Commission, nor against "any statute."

8. "He found fault with the laws ecclesiastical, and depraved the ministry." Upon strained construction, possibly cognizable under the Commission.

9. "That preachers were openly examined and rebuked for their sermons in a great audience in the Hall of the Lord Rich, by procurement of Wright." But he rebuked them for defaming his lordship, — the former Lord Rich, — and his chaplain and their religious exercises, *in* "*their* sermons." (Ibid.)

within the scope of the ecclesiastical Commission or of any statute, but by forced construction, unless we except occasional and trifling deviations from the prescript Prayer.

These, and the matters recorded upon the examination, were certainly puerile; yet, as certainly, of great weight in the judgment of Bishop Aylmer and other Precisians. To some of the Commissioners, however, the proceedings were so "odious," that they would not be present at this "second appearance." To use the Bishop's words, — they "slipt the collar," which "weakened the proceedings of the few that did assist."[1] Notwithstanding, they had strength and servility enough to commit the Lord Rich to the Marshalsea; Mr. Wright, to the Fleet; and "one Dix, another very disordered man and a violent innovator," to the Gate-House; compounding for the sin of committing the two latter by thus giving them an opportunity "to exercise their learning against the Papists who lay in those prisons, which hitherto," says Strype, "they had broached against their brethren and against the state!"[2] We have no document, except what we have adduced, to show *of what* these men were convicted.[3]

The real ground of this prosecution and commitment was — private pique. First, on the part of certain ministers who "stomached Mr. Wright for showing a mislike of those who had two benefices," and of those who were "envious of his favor with the

[1] Strype's Aylmer, 92, 93.

[2] Ibid., 86.

[3] Mr. Strype does indeed say — for the speech about the queen's day, and "for rejecting the Book, and many other disorders." (Strype's Aylmer, 86.) But the documents do not show this.

Lord Rich;"[1] and again, on the part of the queen for the rumor which had reached her ear of exception taken to celebrating the day of her Accession;[2] to say nothing of the spleen of "the great person" — my lord of London? — "in the *late* Lord Rich's time, who desired to have his son and Mr. Wright out of his lordship's house."[3]

At this sitting, the Commissioners disposed of other cases of delinquents and "suspect persons;"[4] some, by simple admonition; others, by suspension "till they should show themselves conformable in allowing the Book."[5]

They also gave a new impulse to the practice of "sending out Apparitors, or spies, from place to place every Sunday, to see what conformity was used in every parish, and *to certify*."[6]

The case of Mr. Wright had hardly been disposed of, — to soothe the offended dignity of certain Precisian preachers and to atone for her Majesty's imaginary affront — when the Bishop was compelled "from above" to be once more astir. The queen was now told that the disorders in Lord Rich's house were not the only ones in Essex; that the clergy in that county, — which formed a large part of the diocese of London, — had all sadly "declined either on the left hand or on the right hand from the direct line limited by her laws and injunctions;"[7] and that there

[1] Strype's Annals, VI. 232.

[2] Ibid., V. 177.

[3] Ibid., VI. 233, compared with Aylmer's letter to Burleigh, above.

[4] Queen's Commission, 1576.

[5] Strype's Aylmer, 92.

[6] Ibid., 93.

Mr. Pierce is wrong (p. 99) in saying that Bishop Aylmer "*devised* the employing of spies." They were employed for the same purpose in 1567 (Strype's Parker, 260), and as early as 1564. (Strype's Annals, II. 131, 132.)

[7] Murdin, 183; the queen to Parker, in 1571.

were not seven congregations in the whole country whose divine service was alike. This implicated the Diocesan as slack in enforcing conformity; than which nothing could irritate the queen more. The Bishop soon heard of this. It stung him like a nettle. He instantly caused the county to be scoured; found not three churches in which the Service of the Book was not observed; sent up a prayer to the Lord Treasurer that he would tell her Majesty so, and also that he had been belied, that he was very faithful in detecting and curing such disorders, and that he and his colleagues of the Commission had just galvanized the whole corps of spies. He was a brisk man in such matters, and *very* touchy.[1]

But he was soon in trouble again. He had admitted Lord Rich to bail after his commitment; for which he had incurred the queen's displeasure. This stung him so keenly that he could not be content to use the Lord Treasurer's mediation, but determined to address himself directly to her Majesty.[2]

"MOST GRACIOUS PRINCE:—

"God hath placed you in His own throne of justice to deliver unto his people equal measure of indifferent judgment, as He doeth unto you; wherein you have hitherto so honorably carried yourself, as I doubt not but you shall be to all posterity a mirror of magistrates, a pearl of princes, and a true pattern of princely virtue, to be followed of many and attained of few. . . . . Your Highness is persuaded

[1] Strype's Aylmer, 201, 202.

[2] Life of Hatton, 243. Sir Harris Nicholas, the writer of Hatton's Life, gives this letter without date; but seems to assign it to April or May.

by my ill-wishers (for it cannot proceed from your own gracious nature) that my service is all in words, and nothing performed in deeds. I let pass my words. My deeds are these:—

"While I was a private man in Lincolnshire and Leicestershire, I thank God there was none whom, either by rigor of law, by gentle persuasion, or weight of argument, I brought not to church, and to the level of God's obedience and your Majesty's devotion. Since my departure from thence and my coming to this *Sea* of London (for so I may justly call it in regard of the tempests that continually afflict it), things are much altered and fallen to ruin. I suppressed the private conventicles which were very rife; and the deformed — or, as they termed them, reformed — churches, which were many and far out of order, I reduced them to conformity, agreeable to the establishment of your Majesty's proceedings. In the country where I lived, I brought the greatest towns to unity; I made the ringleaders and guides of those seditious sects build up that which their disobedience had destroyed. I made them gather where they had dispersed, and sow the seeds of obedience where they had trodden down the corn.

"I have had ever such a watch over Paul's Cross, that in my time there never came any Puritan in that place. The ministers and preachers in London are brought to that pass, that at this day they be the most staid men that commonly live in your kingdom. To speak of punishment for disorders and corrupt *opinions*, was it ever heard of that *any of my predecessors did either deprive, imprison, or banish* (?) *so many as I have done?* Did ever any man stand so much with them in disputation, or sustain by them and for them so great malice, so many slanders, yea, or so great dangers, as I have done? These be deeds, with your Majesty's favor, and no words.

"Is there any man in England whom they take to be so professed an enemy unto them as they hold me to be? Whom ever have I preferred of that faction, either by myself or by my friends on that side? I am called a Papist; a tormentor of God's children; a Bonner and butcher; a claw-back; a man-pleaser; and I am reported to *your Majesty* to be a *favorer* of them, a milk-sop, and to fear such as be their friends above the fear and reverence I owe to you.

"No, no, most Gracious Sovereign; I have learned to have but one king, one faith, and one law, and that only will I fear. . . . . Have I not sustained these five years the importable burden of both the Sees of Canterbury and London; behaving myself so in the charge as I dare justify my service before God and man? If in all this time I have stumbled but once (if it were so), shall all my former service be so soon forgotten, and this peccadillo written in marble? Your Highness thinketh that the Bishop of London may do what he will, and see everything reformed as he listeth in the government of the Church; wherein I beseech your Majesty to inform yourself better, and not to suppose my authority greater than it is, thereby to aggravate and make greater your indignation against me. I can do nothing by your Commission without two more;[1] and in these odious matters every man is commonly wont to shrink from me.

[1] See the Commission, Chap. III. above.

And we bishops, what can we do?[1] Only excommunicate them, and that they hold for an advantage to keep them from the Church. If we do imprison them, or fine them, it is a *præmunire*, or an action of false imprisonment may be brought against us. . . . .

"JOHN LONDON."[2]

Are we not justified in saying that this was a different man from him who taught Lady Jane Grey "so gently, so pleasantly?"

But we have another specimen of the tartness of this noted Disciplinarian. The command — alluded to in a former chapter — issued to the late Lord Mayor of London to rebuke the city clergy for their sermons about the queen's marriage, seems to have been used, and with zest, by the present Mayor, Sir James Harvey, to the peculiar annoyance of some whom the Bishop cared for. His Honor not only administered reprimand to them, but personal reproaches and abuse.[3] This drew upon him a prelatic castigation.

"MY LORD MAYOR: —

"I hear that you deal very hardly with the preachers and clergy of whom the charge and oversight is committed unto me by God and her Majesty's gracious direction. I must therefore needs foresee, as chief Pastor both to you and them, that in their function they suffer no injury; in which respect I am to desire you to use them as the ministers of God and as the keepers and rulers of your soul, — which,

[1] As bishops only; and not sitting in Commission.

[2] Life of Hatton, 243.

[3] Ibid., 235.

I hope, you esteem to be the better part of you, — of whom the Holy Ghost hath said that they are worthy of double honor, the like whereof cannot be spoken of you.

" . . . . You, of your goodness, are pleased to term me familiarly by the name of Aylmer, as unreverently as if I should omit the title of your office and call you Harvey; which, to teach you good manners and what you ought to do, I mean not to do, — God willing. You say, that when Aylmer was at Zurich, he thought a hundred pounds was enough for any minister. Admit he said so. So thought you, peradventure, in your prenticehood, that a hundred pounds by year had been enough for a merchant.

" . . . . Your great forgetfulness of that dutiful goodness that, both by the law of God and man, you owe to your Bishop and Ordinary; the lack whereof, though I bear it now for your office sake (which I need not unless I will), yet the next year I may haply remember it, when by God's grace I am like to be as I am, and you somewhat inferior to what you are now. . . . . If you take this in good part, as coming from him that hath charge over you, I am glad of it; if not, I must then tell you your duty out of my chair, which is the pulpit at Paul's Cross, where you must sit, not as a judge to control, but as a scholar to learn; and I, not as John Aylmer to be taunted, but as John London to teach you and all that city; and, if you use not yourself as an humble scholar, then to discipline you as your chief Pastor and Prelate. . . . . John London.[1]

" 1st March, 1581–2."

[1] Life of Hatton, 236.

Again, are we not right in saying that *this* Aylmer was not the same as he who taught the Lady Jane Grey "*so* gently, *so* pleasantly"?

We can reasonably suppose that such a man,— with an Imperial Mistress whose jealousy and wrath were roused by bail for a Puritan,—would spare no severity to bring things in the Church "to the level of her Majesty's devotion;" that such a man would readily exceed his predecessors in "punishment for disorders and *opinions;*" that such a man might with some truth be reputed "a tormentor of God's children," "a claw-back," "a man-pleaser." And, "if all the city were not humble scholars," we can easily understand *how* John London would "discipline them as their chief Pastor and Prelate."

In May, 1582, Mr. Wright was desirous to visit his wife, then three months a mother. There *may* have been some "distress" in her case, as she was still "lying-in." But however this may have been, his keeper—a man well disposed to the Puritans—received private word from Mr. Secretary Walsingham, upon the strength of which he gave Mr. Wright liberty for a single day on his mere parole, that he might go down to Essex "in the closest manner" to see his first-born child. This came to the knowledge of the Bishop, who threatened to expose the keeper of the prison to the queen. Upon this, Mr. Wright interceded with the Lord Treasurer, "that he would stand good lord unto the keeper, *that he might not be discouraged from favoring those that profess the true religion,*"—a plea which presupposes Lord Burleigh's compassion for the hardships of the Puritans. It is to be hoped that the intercession was availing.[1]

Mr. Wright was still in prison in September, 1582. The Bishop then required of him, — doubtless as a condition of liberation, — "to subscribe to his good allowance of the ministry of the Church of England and to the Book of Common Prayer." This Mr. Wright was willing to do, and probably always had been willing to do; for to both he had always held "a good allowance." But one thing more was required by his lordship, — bonds "in a good round sum, that from henceforth he should neither commit in act, nor preach, anything contrary to the same." On these conditions, the Bishop was willing to grant "further favor," if with the consent and privity of the queen.[2] It does not appear whether these conditions were complied with, or whether Mr. Wright was ever liberated.[3]

[1] Strype's Annals, V. 177, 178. Waddington's Life of Penry, Appendix M., p. 254.

[2] Strype's Aylmer, 87.

[3] I am sorry to say, — and I say it only in justification of my own narrative, — that Mr. Neal's account of this affair differs — in points materially affecting the good name of Bishop Aylmer — from that of Strype, whom only he cites as his authority.

His statement, that Wright was shut up some months before trial, is incorrect; and the clause about "the poor wife in distress" is an embellishment. Wright himself described her only as being "in a weak state." (Waddington's Penry, p. 254.)

Aylmer did *not* "confine him as soon as his noble patron was dead;" but suffered him to "continue" in the Rich mansion — so said Mr. Wright himself — "*without his check* from Christmas was *two* years till Michaelmas *last*" (Strype's Annals, VI. 236); that is, September 29th, 1581, — the very day when Aylmer, writing to Lord Burleigh, said, "I have struggled with them these *two* years," — "we have determined to call him at our first sitting."

The Bishop being applied to by the former Lord Rich for a license for Mr. Wright to preach *in public*, "the Bishop," said Wright, "when he understood that I was no minister," — he was not ordained at that time, — "would not grant it." (Ibid.) Wright also said, that

"The Lord scourgeth every son whom he receiveth;" particularly the "sons of Levi" over whom "he sitteth as a refiner and purifier of silver." Unto some men, in *this* life, "the measure they meet is measured to them again." The man after God's own heart" suffered retribution in this life, and *in kind*, for the most heinous of his sins; even though — Godward — that very sin "had been put away."[1] In other words, — "Some men's sins are open beforehand, going before unto judgment; and some men they follow after."[2]

We cannot wonder, therefore, that atonement — not indeed proportionate, but sufficient — should be imposed upon Bishop Aylmer for his sins *towards man;* that they should be visited upon him *in kind;* that when for sixteen years, "as John London," he had ridden the Church with the rowels of the state, the state, in turn, should ride and rowel him.

when the younger Lord Rich applied for a license, "my lord of London *did not utterly deny*, but said he would first see some *testimony* that I was ordained." (Ibid., 231.) — "I utterly dęnied," wrote Aylmer in his letter to Burleigh, "*unless* he would subscribe the orders of the Church." Therefore Mr. Neal is wrong in saying, "his lordship *always* refused a license *because* he was no minister, that is, had only been ordained among the foreign churches."

Nor do I find evidence in Mr. Neal's authority — Strype — that "the Bishop would not allow his Orders, and therefore *pronounced him a layman*, and incapable of holding any living in the Church." I think the probability otherwise, because such a position does not seem to have been taken by the hierarchy at so early a date; because his lordship's willingness that Wright "should have further favor" *seems* to point to privileges as an acknowledged clergyman; and because, in writing to Lord Burleigh, "Wright the minister *ordained* I cannot tell how nor where," the Bishop seems to admit, or at least not to deny, that he had been, or might have been, ordained somewhere and in some way.

There are other points in which Mr. Neal varies from his authority. But I have said enough to show that his narrative is unreliable.

[1] 2 Sam. xii. 11, 13.

[2] 1 Tim. v. 24.

"By my faith!"[1] exclaimed his lordship, "this is very strange!"[2]

"And by my faith, it is very convaynient."

"For you, sir."

"Arrah! and by that same token, a bit of a convaynience to your lordship it is. Hospitality pertaineth to the office of a bishop; and he who giveth is *more* blessed than he who recayveth. *Ergo,*—the best of the convaynience is to yourself."

The Bishop was a little man; so little "that the merchant of the ship in which he made his escape"—from Queen Mary's persecution—"put him into a wine-butt with a partition in the middle, so that he was enclosed in one end of the cask while the searchers drank wine drawn out of the other."[3] With his "long gray beard,"[4] his rising choler evident in his face, his vivid eye glancing now at an open letter in his hand and now at his collocutor, and sitting bolt upright, he formed a striking contrast to the burly, cool, roughhewn, brazen-faced Irishman who sat before him. The words seemed to open his eyes to an unpleasant prospect; for he now sunk back in his chair with a sigh. But as he scanned the bold brow of his visitor he became suspicious, and exclaimed, "A Romish priest!"

[1] Strype's Aylmer, 215.

[2] Some of the words used by Bishop Aylmer, in the progress of this affair, are too gross to be retained in my narrative. Whether such were adopted in the courtly parlance of the day, or whether they were peculiar to his lordship and indicated only *his* vulgarity, they are too indecent to be quoted in modern times by an author who would treat either his own pages, or his own readers, with respect. I have therefore supplied their places by *lacunæ*.

The specimen which I have given above (Vol. I. 244) of John Aylmer's language is hardly sufferable; but it is chaste in comparison with what I here suppress.

[3] Brook, I. 242, note.

[4] Strype's Aylmer, 295.

The fellow had spoken in a loud tone and with a familiarity which was impudence. In the same style of address, he continued.

"Nay, nay; it is only a Romish priest I *was*, your Reverence; whilom *Father* Denis, but now only *Sir* Denis Rowghan."[1]

"Prithee, *Sir* Denis Rowghan,"—after his lordship had re-examined the letter,—"why should her Majesty's Council send you to me."

"It is their Honors, sure, that must know that same best. Albeit, *I* am thinking that myself being in lack of that godly learning for which the Lord Bishop of London is famed above all others, and being myself a man of consideration, it would be his lordship's pride to take me to school,—besides the convaynience."

"I must obey their lordships," said the Bishop, dryly.

"Sure obaydience is one of your lordship's virtues; and it 's your pride that your virtue will be,—considering the quality of me and mine."

"And *yours?*"

[1] "*Sir* was a title formerly applied to priests and curates in general." Denis Rowghan, therefore, is to be understood as disclaiming his title as a *Romish* priest, but still asserting his proper title to the priesthood. "*Dominus*, the academical title of a bachelor of arts, was, at the Universities, usually rendered by *Sir* in English; so that a bachelor who in the books stood *Dominus* Brown, was, in conversation, called *Sir* Brown. In the use of the word by old dramatists and writers, the Christian name appears to have been generally used, although, at the universities, it was omitted. . . . . . Whether it was from the general prevalence of the Christian name John that we find" in the writings of the day "so many Sir Johns, I cannot tell. . . . . . The reader who is curious in the matter may consult the Notes to Reed's Shakespeare, ed. 1813, V. 7, 229; VIII. 117; XIV. 390, 482." (Petheram's note to p. 7, line 4, of his reprint of "Hay any worke for Cooper." See Vol. I. of this work, p. 203.

"The Mistress Rowghan, to be sure! the like of whom your lordship will be proud to entertain."

"Married!" exclaimed the Bishop in despair. "Their lordships say nothing of a wife!"

"And was it not because the wife is part of the man? Sure they would not be for wasting the ink to prove *that* to your Reverence,—and you a man of such learning!"

"Sir Denis, her Majesty's Council have commanded me to receive *you*, and I shall obey; but I cannot receive your wife."

"Troth! neither did they command you to receive my leg. Would your lordship tell how much of me, and which particular parts of me, you can slice away, and yet receive the Sir Denis Rowghan? But it's joking your lordship is—"

"I cannot do it, Sir Den—"

"—for two be better than one; a *double* convaynience, my lord. Sure I shall be proud to introduce your Honor to my dame; and its proud your Honor will be to entertain the like of her—"

"But, Sir Denis—"

"—for I will mention in your ear a bit of a saycret, my lord. The woman is delicate at this present, for it's not long married we've been. So, you see, Sir Denis and his wife will require great observance from the people of my lord of London; and should she be for the lying-in, it's proud your lordship will be to provide for that same,—the nurses, and the medicines, and the little delicacies, and any other convaynience."

The Bishop was stupefied. His withered cheek had turned yellow under this Irish insolence; and he sat for some moments gazing silently at the door whence Sir Denis had disappeared.

"My faith!" he at length exclaimed, "an indignity to the See! The Bishop of London to keep a coarse, noisy, voracious Irishman! to keep him in meat, and drink, and lodging! And how long? With his .... woman too; and she like to lay her burden in my house! My faith!"

There was no alternative. The order of Council was imperative. Sir Denis came with his "pretended wife," and with Arthur Connock, his servant, to boot! And then the fellow put on airs, such as a vulgar man has when he apes importance, — insolent, imperative, boisterous; and he "made such a revel rout in the house, that the Bishop and his servants were perfectly afraid of him."

In his distress, the prelate thus "bemoaned himself to the Lord Treasurer:" "Besides my charges, there is the *care* of these people. And I assure your lordship it be a great offence to my *conscience*[1] to keep such an idle couple in the house, who stir no more in reading, in working, in praying, than very dead idols. .... It hath been the wont to commit to the keeping of the bishops of London *learned* men; and not asses with their .... wives. *This* be an office, my lord, unworthy a bishop, an aged man, and a free citizen. I therefore pray your lordship that I may have help; for I am hindered in my study, my prayer, and my preaching."

True, it had been a practice of the Privy Council,

[1] The shoe pinched where it should. When the State Church required that of Puritans, which was "an offence to *their* consciences," did the Lord Bishop regard their cry?

from the close of Elizabeth's first Parliament, to commit Catholics to the hospitable custody of bishops, to be benefited — perchance converted — by the godly instructions of their orthodox hosts; and under the rule of this custom the Council had quartered Sir Denis, — a doubtful neophyte. But the imposition of a vulgar man was unprecedented. There was some mystery in it. And the more, because, though letter after letter was sent to the Council, and though the Bishop's son waited upon them time and again that his father might be "released of that most heavy and unbishop-like burden," "the Bishop could not get rid of his guest."

The case grew worse. When his lordship removed his family to his palace in Fulham, the Irishman "would not by any means go thither." So that the Bishop, as it seems, having the man in charge, was obliged to remain himself in his London house. The fellow saw that he was an object of fear; and for his own fun, began to practise pranks accordingly, — preparing pistols, sword-canes, and other weapons, betokening some bloody intent. Thus, "the Bishop's men dared not tarry about their lord, nor he himself go into his own house, but by some back way." He made a touching appeal to Burleigh. "I acknowledge that it is an honorable meaning to seek to benefit this man; but what will it be in the eye of the world and *in the chronicle to our posterity!*"

Notwithstanding, these troublesome guests continued to be forced upon the Bishop for several months.

Sir Denis Rowghan had come from Ireland professing to be a convert to the Protestant faith, and to reveal to the queen's Council certain treacheries of her Majesty's officers, and certain rebellious plots, in his native country. For these disclosures "he expected to have been made a bishop, or have been raised to some high place." The Council did not like the aspect of the man, and therefore committed him to custody. But why to the Bishop of London?[1]

It has appeared from the correspondence — cited in this chapter — between the Bishop of London and the Lord Treasurer, and from other facts before stated, that there were men in the Council who were displeased with the prelate's "urging ceremonious points so much and pushing his ecclesiastical officers to such rigor." We mean such men as Burleigh, Walsingham, Leicester, and Knollys. Beal also, the Clerk of the Council, and who had no small influence there,[2] was as stanch a Puritan as Sir Francis Knollys.[3] We know, too, that the Bishop's severe policy was so "odious" to his colleagues in Commission, that — except Doctor Clark, who was Dean of the Arches, and Sir Owen Hopton, the Lieutenant of the Tower — "they were ready to slip away from the work, had not the Bishop acted vigorously and carried them along with him;" so very ready to slip were they, that he was constantly calling upon the Lord Treasurer "a little to touch their slackness," to furnish him with "other able and courageous men to be joined with the Commission."[4]

In view of these antecedents, and of the singular

[1] For this whole account, and more, see Strype's Aylmer, 162–168.

[2] Fuller, Bk. IX. p. 149.

[3] Ibid., 152.

[4] Strype's Aylmer, 92–95.

fact of such a commitment to such custody, we submit to the reader whether it was, or was not, concerted by the Lords of Council for the very purpose of making Bishop Aylmer feel upon his own neck the galling of that yoke which he had so mercilessly laid upon others? Be this as it may, the lesson, we trust, was of use; for we find no instance of his doing so again after this his own experience which took place in 1592, about two years before his death; a death so Christian-like,[1] that in view of it we are fain to ask, who can say *how much* of wrong opinion and human naughtiness the grace of God can dwell with? We deprecate Bishop Aylmer's notions — common, to be sure, to his whole generation — about the rightful power of the State over the Church. We deprecate the real wrongs which these false notions led him to inflict. But we admire the energy of his character; the manhood, the manliness, the clear-headedness, indicated in his racy letters; and, more than all, the peaceful trust and the pure aspirations with which he fell asleep.

[1] I confess myself surprised by the following words of Strype (Life of Aylmer, 183): "When he found he approached nearer unto death, *according to the Order of the Church he made his Confession* to the Preacher his Assistant, and *received absolution.*" There may have been some relics of Popery still lingering at that time in the usages and "orders of the Church," about which I ought to be better informed than I am.

Since this note was in type, I find the following in Izaak Walton's "Life of Richard Hooker."

"About one day before his" — Hooker's — "death, Dr. Saravia, who knew the very secrets of his soul (for they were supposed to be confessors to each other) came to him, and after a conference of the benefit, the necessity, and safety of the Church's absolution, it was resolved the Doctor should give him both that and the Sacrament the day following. To which end, the Doctor came, and after a short retirement and privacy, they two returned to the company; and then the Doctor gave him and some of those friends which were with him, the blessed Sacrament of the body and blood of our Jesus."

CHAPTER X.

THE INITIATION OF PRESBYTERIAN DISCIPLINE.

THE FIRST PRESBYTERIES. — PRESBYTERIANS NOT SEPARATISTS. — "NO-SACRAMENT MINISTERS." — TEMPORARY LENITY TOWARDS THE PURITANS. — THEIR SECRET CONSULTATIONS. — "THE DECREES," OR A SKETCH OF THE PRESBYTERIAN PLAN. — "THE SYNODICAL DISCIPLINE," BY WALTER TRAVERS. — THE UNITY OF THE CHURCH AND SELF-GOVERNMENT THE FUNDAMENTAL PRINCIPLES OF PRESBYTERIANISM. — THE SCALE OF CHURCH ORGANIZATION. — THE SYSTEM TO BE PROSECUTED WITHIN EPISCOPACY. — ULTERIOR DESIGN.

1582, 1583.

THE Presbytery of Wandsworth was not a "Presbyterian church."[1] It was not "a formal separation"[2] from the Ecclesiastical Establishment. It arranged for no worshipping assemblies, for no ministration of sacraments, apart from those sanctioned by the state. It was but a private association of a few clergymen, — *not* "surrendering their professional appointments,"[3] — and of a few laymen for carrying into effect, among themselves and as far as practicable, that form of ecclesiastical discipline which obtained at Geneva.

Nor were the younger members of the Presbyterian sisterhood in England other than "the first-born"[4] in filial sentiment and decorum. They all

[1] Neal, I. 126.

[2] Mackintosh, III. 163, London edit., 1831.

[3] Taylor, II. 70.

[4] Fuller, Bk. IX. p. 103.

clung to the family hearth. They would neither repudiate the Mother nor desert her altars.

Averse as they were to Episcopacy, the Puritans still regarded the Church, which had adopted it, as a very Church. They still revered the old Idea of ecclesiastical oneness; and regarded a departure from the established assemblies and communion as a monstrous abandonment of the household of faith, an unfilial and wicked schism. Except occasionally before the formation of the Wandsworth Presbytery, they all continued within the Church, until a movement took place which we shall bring to notice in our next chapter.[1] Since the date of Presbytery,

[1] I do not forget that Mr. Neal says (I. 131), under date of 1573, that "separate communions were established where the sacrament of the Lord's Supper was administered privately after the manner of the foreign Reformed Churches." I am aware also that Mr. Strype, from whom Mr. Neal evidently derives his statement, speaks under the same date of a "more formal separation," and of an "establishment of private, separate congregations." (Strype's Parker, 434, 436.) But these expressions are based upon a certain Paper without date, "without father, without mother, without pedigree, having neither beginning of days nor end of life," with no voucher, so far as I can ascertain, but a very suspicious "paragraph writ by *Archbishop Parker's* own hand," and added thereto. (Strype's Parker, 435, 436.)

Such a document, of which I find no trace, similitude, or collateral evidence elsewhere, can hardly claim faith as having had Puritan sanction. It is *possible* that something like it may have been drawn up by some of the ephemeral separatists of 1567; but as a Paper expressive of Puritan sentiments and conduct generally in 1573, it has no sufficient authority.

The statement of Mr. Strype, — Life of Parker "[446]," — that in the same year "new churches were set up," is based upon the queen's Proclamation which immediately follows. But that Proclamation *alleges* no other disorder in worship than variations from the prescript forms; and speaks of forsaking the sacraments of the Church and of private assemblies only *hypothetically*. I have, to be sure, in Vol. I. (page 484) adopted Mr. Strype's phrase, "new churches set up;" but have qualified it as designating new *Presbyteries* only, — sometimes mistaken by writers for new churches or communions.

they had indeed varied, as we have seen, the forms of public service from those of the English Liturgy,—some more, some less. They had also their "separate religious meetings;" but these seem to have been for "the private exercise of their *discipline*,"[1] not for divine worship properly so called. In 1576, those who resided in the counties of Northampton and Warwick, indiscreetly attempting to introduce their discipline in their parish churches, had excited opposition in some such way as to create open disturbance,—perhaps, "to the making of *great* Hubbubs and Disturbances."[2] Archbishop Grindal, having received peremptory orders from the Court to attend to these doings, and particularly to look after two Puritan divines, Eusebius Paget and John Oxenbridge, who were represented as "the chief stirrers," gave commandment to the bishops in those counties "to see these things reformed," and, if necessary, to call upon himself or upon the Ecclesiastical Commission for aid. He also wrote to inquire about the two clergymen, and "to cause them to be sent up with expedition;" probably with the same proviso,—"if necessary."[3] It is but an *inference*, however, to say that "they were both carried prisoners to the metropolis."[4] They may have given satisfaction without. The "inquiry" may have shown that there was no sufficient reason for their being "sent up."

Soon after, the Puritan aversion to "ceremonious points" had assumed a new form. Unwilling to administer the sacraments according to the prescript of the Liturgy, or to expose themselves to deprivation

[1] Strype's Grindal, 215.
[2] Ibid.
[3] Ibid., 215, 216.
[4] Brook, II. 254. Neal, I. 140.

by adopting another mode, or to withhold the sacraments from their people, many beneficed clergymen had "applied themselves only to the office of preaching," and had been in the habit of deputing the administration of the sacraments in their parishes to others who were properly qualified. The latter came to be distinguished as "Reading and Ministering Ministers;" the former, as "Preachers and No-Sacrament Ministers."[1] This practice gave offence to the queen, and produced an Order from the Lords of the Council in January, 1579–80, that all Parsons[2] should be compelled to execute both these services of the sacred office; that the bishops should search out such defaulters in their respective dioceses, certify them to the Lords, and send up to them, for dealing, such as should prove intractable.[3] Accordingly, inquisition had been made upon this point; not only, as we have stated, in the diocese of London, but throughout the Province.

Whenever those bishops who had been most officious in persecution had made their appearance at Court, they had encountered such contempts, frowns, and taunts from the Earl of Leicester, that their zeal

[1] Order of Council.

[2] "A Parson—*persona ecclesiæ*—is one that hath full possession of all the rights of a parochial church. He is called parson—*persona*—because by his person the Church, which is an invisible body, is represented; and he is in himself a body corporate, in order to protect and defend the rights of the Church (which he represents) by a perpetual succession. He is sometimes called the rector or governor of the Church; but the appellation of *parson* (however it may be depreciated by familiar, clownish, and indiscriminate use) is the most legal, most beneficial, and most honorable title that a parish priest can enjoy." (Blackstone, I. 384.)

[3] Strype's Grindal, 244. Strype's Aylmer, 65–68, 82.

had been effectually cooled. The queen, also — although still as sensitive as ever touching uniformity, and unable to restrain her anger when any flagrant breach of it was reported to her — had not goaded on her Commissioners, as at that time, since their disgraceful campaign in 1573. This abatement of her rigor had been produced in part by the disgust which the campaign had excited, and partly by the persuasions of the Earl, who took as good care to use his unabated influence with her Majesty to procure lenity towards the Puritans as he did, for the same end, to wither the zeal of the bishops. Thus those preposterous and arbitrary oaths which had been invented under Archbishop Parker, and the illegal enforcing of subscription to *all* the articles of Religion, — both of which had brought odium upon his administration, — seem to have fallen into disuse. Indeed, no subscriptions of any kind seem to have been required in the mean time, except to promises such as have been mentioned in our last chapter.[1] In addition to these things, since the arrival of Campian and Persons, the attention of the Commissioners had been mostly engrossed with the Papists; in whose arrest and prosecution the Puritans were no less zealous than the most rigid of the Precisians. "Some lenity of course" — and perhaps through royal policy[2] — "fell to the share of the non-conformists," or Presbyterians, "who now" — in 1582 — "found so much favor as almost amounted to a connivance at their discipline."[3] This opportunity they improved.

[1] Compare Fuller, Bk. IX. pp. 138, 139, with the "Decrees" of the Presbyterians, p. 140, and with p. 141, paragraph 5.

[2] Carte, III. 578.

[3] Fuller, Bk. IX. p. 135.

On the eighth day of May,[1] sixty clergymen, from the counties of Norfolk, Suffolk, and Cambridge, met by appointment in the county of Suffolk, at Cockfield, where was the cure of John Knewstubbs, B. D., to confer about the Book of Common Prayer, — what parts of it might be used and what ought to be rejected; and to weigh in like manner all questions about apparel, saints-days, holidays, fast-days, and injunctions. The deliberations and acts of this meeting were not matters of record; nor were they communicated to others except by word of mouth, and even in this way only by permission, and to such and such brethren. Those who *wrote* anything about their doings, wrote only in general terms and vaguely.[2]

A like meeting took place at Cambridge on the second day of July, at the time of Commencement,[3] and probably was but an adjournment of the former.[4]

Joining the obscure testimony of a single witness respecting these meetings[5] with the appearance soon after of the Paper which we give below, we infer, with some confidence, that these were consultations to agree upon some plan for the general organization and systematic action of the many *Classes* scattered over the kingdom, "who hitherto had no particular platform of discipline among themselves owned and practised by the whole."[6] Although this Paper —

[1] Fuller, Bk. IX. p. 135.

[2] Ibid.

[3] "In each of these Universities, ... in July, the scholars, ... such as have been called to any Degree in the year precedent do ..... receive the accomplishment of the same, in solemn and sumptuous manner. In Oxford, this solemnity is called an Act, but in Cambridge they use the French word *commensement*." (Harrison in Holingshed, Vol. I. 251.)

[4] Fuller, Bk. IX. p. 135.

[5] Ibid.; letter to Field.

[6] Ibid., p. 139. Heylin's Presbyterians, Bk. VII. Sec. 33. Collier, VII. 3

apparently the result of these consultations — probably was not drafted until 1583, we insert it here, and with Fuller's apology, — "jetting out a little into the next year; no offence (we hope) seeing it makes our history more entire upon this subject."[1] From the title of the Paper it appears that, though called "Decrees," they were only propounded as such, at this time,[2] for the consideration and future suffrages of the different Presbyteries, or *Classes*. It seems to have been the *basis* of certain Articles which were circulated in 1587, and not agreed upon or adopted until 1588.[3]

"These be the things that (do seem) may well stand with the peace of the Church: The Decrees."

"Let no man (though he be an University man) offer himself to the Ministry, nor let any man take upon him an uncertain and vague Ministry" — that is, a Ministry at large, without a specific Cure of souls — "though it be offered unto him.

"But such as be called to the Ministry by some certain church, let them impart it unto that Classis or conference (whereof themselves are), or else to some greater Church-assembly; and if such shall be found fit by them, then let them be commended, by their letters unto the bishop, that they may be ordained ministers by him.

[1] Fuller, Bk. IX. p. 142. Collier, VII. 3, 4.

[2] Fuller, Bk. IX. p. 141, paragraph 2.

[3] Strype's Whitgift, 291. Neal, I. 185.

I think so, because of the similarity of those given in the Life of Whitgift; because the Paper there given, with its dates certified, was "found among the papers of Mr. Wight" when his study was officially sacked in 1590; and because the one which I quote from Fuller was also "under Wight's hand." (Compare Brook, I. 448.)

"Those ceremonies in the Book of Common Prayer which, being taken from Popery, are in controversy, do seem, that they ought to be omitted and given over, if it may be done without danger of being put from the Ministry. But if there be any imminent danger to be deprived, then this matter must be communicated with the Classis in which that church is; that, by the judgment thereof, it may be determined what ought to be done.

"If subscription to the Articles of Religion and to the Book of Common Prayer shall be again urged, it is thought that the Book of Articles may be subscribed unto according to the statute thirteenth Elizabeth, that is, unto such of them only as contain the sum of Christian faith and doctrines of the Sacraments. But for many weighty causes, neither the rest of the Articles in that Book nor the Book of Common Prayer may be allowed"—i. e. approved—by subscription;—"no, though a man should be deprived of his Ministry for it.

"It seemeth that Church-wardens and Collectors for the poor might thus be turned into Elders, and into Deacons, when they are to be chosen. Let the church have warning, fifteen days before, of the time of Election, and of the Ordinance of the Realm; but especially of Christ's Ordinance touching appointing of Watchmen and Overseers in his Church, who are"—whose business it is—"to foresee that none offence or scandal do arise in the Church; and if any shall happen, that by them it may be duly abolished.

"And touching Deacons of both sorts (*videlicet*, men and women) the church shall be monished what is required by the Apostle, and that they are not to choose men of custom and of course, or for their riches, but for their faith, zeal, and integrity; and that the church is to pray (in the mean time) to be so directed, that they may make choice of them that be meet. Let the names of such as are so chosen be published the next Lord's day; and after that, their duties to the church and the church's towards them, shall be declared. Then let them be received into the ministry to which they are chosen, with the general prayers of the whole church.

"The brethren are to be requested to ordain a distribution of all churches according to these rules (in that behalf) that are set down in the Synodical Discipline touching Classical, Provincial, Comitial, or of Commencements, and assemblies for the whole kingdom.

"The Classes are to be required to keep acts of memorable matters, which they shall see delivered to the Comitial assembly;[1] that from thence they may be brought by the Provincial assembly.

"Also they are to deal earnestly with Patrons[2] to

[1] "Assemblies kept in the Universities at Commencements." (Fuller, Bk. IX. p. 142.)

[2] "He who has the right of advowson, that is, of presentation to a church or ecclesiastical benefice, is called the Patron of the Church. When lords of manors first built churches on their own desmenes, and appointed the tithes of those manors to be paid to the officiating ministers which before were given to the clergy in common, the lord who thus built a church, and endowed it with glebe or land, had of common right a power annexed of nominating such minister as he pleased (provided he were canonically qualified) to officiate in that church of which he was the founder, endower, maintainer, or, in one word, the patron." (Blackstone, II. 21.) The property of the advowson pertains to the property of the manor, unless separated from it by legal conveyance; in which case it can never be appendant any more. "The right of advowson, when occasion calls it forth, *entitles* some clerk, whom the patron shall please

present fit men, whensoever any church is fallen void in that Classis.

"The Comitial assemblies are to be monished to make collections for relief of the poor, and of scholars, but especially for relief of such ministers here as are put out for not subscribing to the articles tendered by the bishops; also for relief of Scottish ministers and others; and for other profitable and necessary uses.

"All the Provincial Synods must continually aforehand foresee in due time to appoint the keeping of their next Provincial Synods, and for the sending of chosen persons, with certain instructions, unto the National Synod to be holden whensoever the Parliament for the kingdom shall be called at some certain set time every year."[1]

About the year 1574, a Plan of Presbyterian Discipline, adapted to the meridian of London, had been drawn up and printed in Latin at Geneva, by Mr. Walter Travers,[2] "who (allowing Mr. Cartwright for the head) might be termed the neck of the Presbyterian party, the second in honor and esteem."[3] At this time — 1582 — he was chaplain to the Lord Treasurer Burleigh; another outstanding fact significant of that statesman's good-will to the Puritans. The Book containing this Plan was entitled, "The Holy Discipline of the Church described in the Word of God."[4] It was now in high esteem with the Puri-

to nominate, to enter and receive bodily possession of the lands and tenements of the church. . . . . The patron has a right of presentation to the bishop or ordinary; and, moreover, to *demand* of him to *institute* his clerk, if he finds him canonically qualified." (Ibid., 22.)

[1] Fuller, Bk. IX. p. 140.

[2] Neal, I. 172.

[3] Fuller, Bk. IX. p. 136.

[4] Neal, I. 172.

tans, and seems to have been undergoing revision and correction "by Mr. Cartwright and other learned ministers"[1] when this advisory Paper, in which it is styled "The Synodical Discipline," was issued. The Paper is to some extent an abstract or outline of the Book; and it seems to have been circulated to secure a preparatory organization of the scattered Presbyterians; so that the Book itself, when perfected, might be regularly brought before a National Synod for their approval and adoption. The ecclesiastical principles — in distinction from the details of organization — of the Paper and the Book are the same as those inculcated by Mr. Cartwright in 1570, in his Lectures at the University of Cambridge.[2]

We here see clearly the two great purposes of the English Presbyterian School. The first was to arrange an Ecclesiastical organization after the form which they believed to have been modelled by the primitive Christians and described in the Word of God. The fundamental idea was the Ecclesiastical Unity of the Church; an idea explicitly brought to view in these words of "The Synodical Discipline," to which the Paper refers, — "A General or Œcumenical Council, which is a meeting of the chosen men of every National Synod." In this idea of the Church as a unit was included the principle of self-government in opposition to government by a hierarchy ranged under an earthly Head; the grand point of difference between Presbyterianism and local or national Episcopacy, between Presbyterian Catholicism and Roman Catholicism. Necessarily (in such a case)

[1] Neal, I. 172.

[2] *Ante*, Vol I. pp. 410–412.

growing out of the doctrine of self-government, was a plan of popular representation.

Under this system, each parochial congregation — not itself an individual, but a member — elected its own eldership; and, "by common counsel" or "the most voices"[1] of this eldership or consistory,[2] ordered its domestic affairs in subordination only to the rules of the body catholic. Thus the right of electing its own pastor or pastors — instead of having them thrust upon them by others — was recognized; and all doubtful matters of expediency or of duty, of doctrine or of discipline, arising in any particular congregation, were to be referred for counsel to the conference, or classis, to which it belonged, — this conference consisting of delegates from the elderships of a few neighboring congregations, usually about twelve.[3]

Next in order of ascent was the Provincial Synod, composed of two ministers and two elders from every conference within a province, — each province containing twenty-four conferences. To this body was "to be sent the matters that seemed to the particular conferences more difficult for them to take order in, and such as belong to the churches of the whole province; and by it were to be prepared those things that pertain to the National Synod."

The National Synod was to be composed of "three ministers and three elders, chosen men, of every province within the dominion of the same nation and civil government." This body was "to handle the things pertaining to the churches of the whole

[1] Neal, II. 443. [2] Ibid., 440. [3] Ibid., 444.

nation or kingdom; as the doctrine, discipline, ceremonies, things not decided by inferior meetings, appeals, and such like."

Above the National Synod, the theory embraced a General or Œcumenical Council,—"a meeting of the chosen men of every National Synod."[1]

Such was "The Directory of Church government" now projected by the Puritans, and soon generally adopted by them, "as far as the times would suffer."[2] The members of the several conferences were to subscribe to it in these words,—"Allowing it as a godly discipline and agreeable to the Word of God, ... to be furthered by all *lawful* means; that by public authority of *the magistrate and of our Church*, it may be *established*..... In the mean time, we promise to observe it, *as far as may be lawful* for us so to do by the public laws of this kingdom and by the peace of *Our Church*."[3]

[1] Neal, II. 445.

[2] Ibid., 440. Compare Calvin's project for Presbyterian Catholicity, indicated above, Vol. I. p. 331, note.

[3] Neal, II. 445.

With this unequivocal declaration before us, I ask the reader to revert to note 1, p. 265; and to the statement in the beginning of this chapter, that the Puritans regarded separate religious assemblies with abhorrence.

Fuller, indeed (Bk. IX. p. 102), speaks of such assemblies as existing in 1572; his authority being no better than Bishop Bancroft's "English Scotticizing." Camden (p. 191) says the same as Fuller; and *his* vouchers were probably only the rumors current among the Church Precisians of his time, who mistook the "*Conferences*" of the Presbyterians.

The language of Grindal upon this point, in his letter to Bullinger, dated June 11th, 1568, I consider *retrospective*. (Zurich Letters, p. 314.)

Bishop Horne's letter to Bullinger, August, 1571, describes certain of the disaffected in the Church as "shaping out for themselves their own barks; calling together conventicles; electing their own bishops; holding synods with one another; framing and devising their own laws for themselves; rejecting preaching; despising communion; desirous to have all churches"—places of worship—"destroyed, as having been

Such was the *first* great purpose of the English Presbyterians indicated in the Paper of 1583 which we have transcribed; and given in detail in "The Synodical Discipline" to which that Paper refers.

Their *second* purpose is brought into clear relief in the words of subscription, — to seek, by all lawful means, the *establishment* of the Discipline; and in the mean time to practise it only so far as might consist with the laws of the realm and the peace of the

formerly dedicated to Popery; deriding our ministers, and regarding the office itself as not worth a straw." (Ibid., p. 356.) But this description by no means applies to any class of Puritans of whom we find record; though perhaps, to the congregation of whom Bonham and Crane were the leaders, about the year 1570, and of whom we find no trace afterwards. The language, however, may truly represent Bishop Horne's *opinion* of the meetings of Presbyteries, — he supposing them to have been what were called "conventicles," — and of the discipline and theory of the Presbyterians.

Under date of February 12th, 1571-2, in a letter from Bishop Cox to Gualter we find the following: —

"Some . . . . now obstinately refuse to enter our churches, either to baptize their children, or to partake of the Lord's Supper, or to hear sermons. They are entirely separated from us; . . . . they establish a private religion, and assemble in private houses, and there perform their sacred rites." (Ibid., p. 390.)

If Bishop Cox did not mistake the habits of the Presbyterians and the business of Presbyteries, and if what he represents was indeed the case, it is unaccountable that such persons should not have been discovered, and treated as the Plumbers' Hall congregation had been, and that we should have no record of their prosecution; unaccountable that, in the vigorous action of the Commissioners in 1573, no *such* persons seem to have been dealt with.

It is *possible* indeed — though I find no reliable evidence of it — that those Puritans who were afterwards known as "Independents" may have sustained such separate religious assemblies so early as 1572. But it is important, as I have stated at the close of this chapter, to quit the Presbyterian Puritans of all suspicion of being Separatists either in fact or in wish. They abandoned all thought of such a movement after the disapproval of the foreign divines in 1567.

By the words "Our Church" is not to be understood the Presbyterian Fraternity; but, the *primaria ecclesia*, that is, the "Mother Church." The national Church was so called by way of distinction from any parochial Church. (Blackstone, I. 113.)

Church. In other words; they would make their own elections of pastors, elders, and deacons to *coincide* with the patron's right of presentation, with the bishop's prerogative of ordination and induction, and with the offices, appointed by law, of churchwardens and collectors for the poor; they would thus exercise their own Discipline without interfering with that of the Established Church; they would by no means separate from her, for it would be doing violence to their idea of a Church catholic; they would,— and here we adopt the words of their adversaries,— they would cherish Presbyterian practice, "so as to make no rupture in the Church and to create no eminent danger to themselves;"[1] they would cherish it "under the wing of Episcopacy;"[2] they would "carry on their Discipline and cover themselves from prosecution;"[3] they would "set up a Discipline *in* a Discipline, Presbytery *in* Episcopacy, which (as appears from the preface) they thought 'might well stand with the peace of the Church.'"[4]

"Their chief debate in their assemblies was,— how far this or the other conclusion .... might be moulded into a consistency with Episcopacy."[5] Hence, while "they maintained the choice of the people to be the essential call to the pastoral charge," "they ordained no ministers," but sought it from the hands of the bishops; both because they regarded prelatic ordination as evangelically valid; and because it was necessary — when imposed within the kingdom — "that the minister might be enabled to demand his legal dues from the parish."[6]

[1] Heylin's Presb., Bk. VII. Sec. 33.
[2] Ibid., Sec. 35.
[3] Collier, VII. 4, 5.
[4] Fuller, Bk. IX. p. 142.
[5] Neal, I. 140.
[6] Ibid.

This election of ministers by parishes had been practised so long ago as 1573;[1] and there were cases when the minister, presented to a living who scrupled some of the ceremonies and orders of the Book of Common Prayer, was promised, both by his patron and by his ordinary, that he should not be urged to the precise observation of these things, and was inducted on this condition.[2] There were also cases, so late at least as 1587, when ministers chosen by a popular election were permitted to exercise their functions "without question or exception, and were entertained with *a stipend raised by voluntary contribution.*"[3]

This purpose of the Presbyterian Puritans to adhere to the communion and assemblies of the Established Church, this their evident abhorrence of separation, it is important to keep in view; partly to the right understanding of their complicity in certain Acts of Parliament, and partly to distinguish them from another class of Puritans with whom they were at variance and whom we shall now introduce.

[1] Strype's Parker, 436.

[2] Brook, II. 254.

[3] Strype's Aylmer, 155.

CHAPTER XI.

ROBERT BROWN.

St. Edmond's Bury. — Puritanism in Suffolk County. — Robert Brown previous to 1581. — He establishes separate Congregations in Suffolk, and is committed to Prison. — Lord Burleigh intercedes for him. — He is liberated and sent away. — He returns and "troubles the whole County." — The Magistrates favor the Puritans. — The Bishop's Commissary put under Bonds "for good Behavior." — The Bishop complains of the Justices to the Queen's Council. — He appeals to Burleigh against Brown, who then leaves the County. — Brown in Zealand. — Forms a Church and publishes Books. — He goes to Scotland, and thence to England. — Is summoned before Whitgift in 1585, and is sent to his Father. — His itinerary Mission against the Establishment. — His subsequent History to his Death in 1630. — The Ecclesiastical Principles of the Brownists. — Their Reasons for Secession from the Established Church. — Their Variance with the Presbyterian Puritans. — Copping and Thacker, the first Puritan Martyrs. — The Grounds of their Conviction.

1581-1583.

In the year of our Lord 870, Hinguar, one of the Danish kings, counts, or pirates, made a sudden inroad upon the kingdom of East Anglia, which included the present counties of Norfolk, Suffolk, Cambridge, and the isle of Ely. Slaughtering men, women, and children alike, the invaders burned the city of Thetford, the metropolis of the kingdom, and compelled King Edmond to retreat to his castle of Framlingham, in what is now the county of Suffolk. Finding resistance vain, and hoping to save the lives of his subjects, he surrendered his person to his enemies, then at Hoxon, or Hoxne, a neighboring village. To compel him to renounce the Christian faith, Hinguar ordered him to be beaten with clubs; afterwards, to be scourged. These failing, the victim was bound to a tree on the skirt of a wood hard by,—a mark for the freebooter's archers. One by one they lodged their shafts in his flesh, and at such intervals of time "that he might the better digest one pain before another succeeded." But, like the first Christian martyr, "looking up steadfastly into heaven" and calling upon the name of Jesus, "this holy St. Edmond," the last of the East Anglian kings, "continued constant in the Christian faith" until he fell asleep. The rage of the heathen was not sated until his body was riddled to shreds, and his head cast contemptuously into the forest.

The place of his burial—the same, probably, with that of his martyrdom—was held sacred by the Christians; and some fifty years afterwards, Edward, King of the West Saxons, having expelled the Danes, founded an abbey there in honor of the martyr. The shrine was a place of great resort and veneration; and the abbey became one of the largest and richest in England, having a revenue equivalent to fifty thousand pounds sterling in the present day. Of this luxurious house, the only remains are, part of a tower, a beautiful Norman gate eighty feet high,—a fine specimen of its former grandeur,—and the abbey church with its gate. From this abbey, Bury St. Edmond's,—the House of St. Edmond,—the town in which it was situated, derives its name. It is so remarkable for the salubrity of its air, that it is sometimes called the Montpellier of England.[1] In the times of which we write, it was equally remarkable for its religious atmosphere.

Puritanism had made great advances there in 1581; and not there only, but throughout the county of Suffolk. Five years before, Dr. Deye, the Commissary of the Bishop of Norwich, had committed to the common jail of Bury two ministers of the Gospel for their non-conformity; and during all this time had kept them there without trial. They were Mr. —— Tyler and Mr. John Copping. The latter — reserved for a melancholy fate which we shall note hereafter — was the minister of a neighboring parish.[2] But during these five years, a change had come over the Commissary's jurisdiction. "Fantastical innovations" had prevailed. The buyers and sellers at market-days and fairs were Puritans. The gossips at "The Angel" inn were Puritans. Counsel and client and hangers-on at the Assizes were Puritans. The Precisians said, that the worshipping assemblies of Bury "were for nothing but Geneva Psalms and for sermons;" while the people retorted, that "the Psalms were David's, and other holy fathers' inspired by the Holy Ghost, and that the necessity of sermons was well known by their bishop." [3] There were Puritans all around the Commissary, — Puritan plebeians, Puritan gentry; and, maugre his official zeal and his official terrors, Mr. Hansdon, the curate of St James's [4] stood erect and fearless in the pulpit, and spake Puri-

[1] Stow's Annals, 61, 64, 90, 93. Fuller, Bk. II. p. 115. New Edinburgh Encyclopædia; Article, Bury St. Edmond's. Lavoisne's Atlas, No. 28.

[2] Brook, I. 262. Compare, *seriatim*, Strype's Annals, V. 28; VI. 172; and IV. 186.

[3] Strype's Annals, V. 28; VI. 174.

[4] Strype's Parker, 452.

tan doctrines to his face. Mr. Hill, the curate of St. Mary's, was no better.[1] Yet to check all this, and even to punish deviations from the orders of the Church, the Commissary was impotent. "Of a truth," said he, "I confess I dare scarcely do anything touching my office for fear of violence, I do see the lewd sort so animated against me." Yet, with an inconsistency which should have made him blush, he added in the same breath, "I thank my God, I care not what man can do unto me!"[2] His occupation was gone. His cries to the bishop, his master, for help, were piteous. How this "ill state of affairs" was brought about we shall explain.

The two Puritan curates of Bury labored more to preach Christ than they did to preach the Church; more to show that the handwriting of ordinances was nailed with Christ to his cross, than to exalt the injunctions of her Majesty or the rites of the Common Prayer. Thus, as there was much more which was befitting the people's spiritual wants in a Sacrifice for sin, than in signing the cross with the finger, or in receiving a singing-cake on the knees, or in making a prescript response, forms fell into disrepute with them, and they clave rather to the Truth which their consciences commended. By natural consequence came the convictions, that "the High-Priest who put away sin by the sacrifice of himself" was the only rightful Head and Lawgiver of his redeemed; that the commandments and traditions of men were out of place within the precincts of his Church; and that any but the rule of brotherhood was equally so, among those whom "he is not ashamed to call

[1] Brook, I. 174. [2] Strype's Annals, V. 25.

brethren." It is no wonder that a field thus cultivated was susceptible of further improvement — for the people of Bury and Suffolk "had not already attained" — or that it was selected for the opening of a new act in the drama of religious progress.

In the winter and spring of 1580–1, the "fantastical innovations" upon the prescribed religious forms "in the town of Bury and the country thereabouts," had become notorious. The "disorders," so called, were "great as well in the clergy as the laity." Many of the people were undisguised in their dislike of "the worship and service of God prescribed and used in the Common Prayer." In the town of Bury itself, the curate of St. James was esteemed "the only man that blew the coals whereof this fire was kindled."[1] But in the neighborhood, he had a vigorous coworker in Robert Brown. He, too, greatly cherished the popular dislike to the ritual and government of the Church.

Robert Brown was about thirty-one years of age, having been born in Rutlandshire, — a very Rhode Island among the counties of England, — just about the time when Hooper made his memorable appearance before King Edward and his Council.[2] He was of "right worshipful extraction;" *for* his grandfather had received a charter from Henry VIII. and his Parliament, "giving him leave to put on his cap in the presence of the king or his heirs, or any lord spiritual or temporal in the land, and not to put it off but for his own ease and pleasure."[3] The grandson Robert

[1] Edmund Freke, Bishop of Norwich, to Lord Burleigh; Strype's Annals, V. 21. Hanbury, I. 19.

[2] "Above eighty years of age in 1630," says Fuller, Bk. IX. pp. 168, 169.

[3] Ibid., p. 167.

was near kinsman to the Lord Burleigh.[1] He studied divinity at Cambridge; where, "though he was not known to take any degree, he would many times venture into the pulpit" of Benet church in Corpus Christi College. Dr. Still, afterwards Master of Trinity College, used to hear him, and sagaciously detected something in him which might some day make disturbance in the Church, — "a vehemence of utterance which passed for zeal among the common people, and made the vulgar to admire, the wise to suspect him."[2] He was afterwards Master of the Free School at St. Olave's in Southwark;[3] then, a lecturer at Islington.[4] In 1571, when but twenty-one years of age, and while employed as chaplain in the household of the Duke of Norfolk, he was cited to appear before the High Commission, together with Goodman, Lever, Sampson, Deering, and Whittingham. The Duke made an attempt to shield him, which was resented by the Commissioners.[5] He seems to have escaped discipline; and, it has been conjectured, through the interference and influence of "his high connections."[6] From that time, we find no trace of him until his appearance in the county of Suffolk. His preaching was characterized by the marvellous boldness with which he reproved the Precisianism of the Establishment, its corrupt ceremonies, and its lordly pretensions. He was a favorite with the common people, "whom he exhorted by no means to comply with the discipline and ceremonies of the

[1] Burleigh to Freke; Fuller, Bk. IX. p. 166.

[2] Ibid. Heylin's Presb., Bk. VII. Sec. 29.

[3] Hanbury, I. 18.

[4] Neal, I. 149.

[5] Strype's Parker, 325 – 327.

[6] Hanbury, I. 18.

Church."[1] His ascendency over them was sufficient to prevail upon many to assemble, much to their jeopardy,[2] in private houses for the free and independent worship of God. In these assemblies, he himself preached.[3]

Thus were separate congregations once more established. But we do not discover here any church organization, any ecclesiastical separation from the national communion; nor, however "satirical" he may afterwards have been "against the Church of England," have we any authority for supposing that, at this time, Brown denounced her "as no true Church of Christ, or her Liturgy as a mixture of Popery and Paganism, or her clergy as no better than Baal's priests."[4] The complaint of the Precisian preachers in the county was — in general terms — only "that he delivered unto the people corrupt and contentious doctrine."[5] The specific "articles ministered against him, and his personal answers thereunto," would enlighten us upon this point; but they seem to have been lost.

The bruit of these disorders at length reached the ears of the High Commissioners at London,[6] who immediately required the Bishop of Norwich, one of their associates,[7] to move in the matter. Accordingly

[1] Neal, I. 149.

[2] "Not without danger of some *evil event*," according to Strype's version of the Bishop's letter. "Not without danger of some *thereabout*," according to Hanbury's, from the Lansdowne MSS.

[3] Bishop Freke to Lord Treasurer Burleigh; Strype's Annals, V. 22. Hanbury's Memorials, Vol. I. p. 19, note.

[4] Collier, VII. 1. Biographia Britannica.

[5] Freke to Burleigh.

[6] "London," says the Bishop's letter in Strype. "Bury," says the same in Hanbury. London was the head-quarters of the High Commission; and orders to rural members would doubtless emanate only thence.

[7] Strype's Grindal, Append. p. 65.

he visited St. Edmond's Bury in the month of April, with others of his associates in Commission ecclesiastical. This Court — any three of the Commissioners, one of the three being a bishop, were empowered to act[1] — upon investigating affairs, required "the blower of the coals" in Bury "to enter into bond, to her Majesty's use, hereafter to teach and preach the Word sincerely and purely, without impugning or inveighing against the Communion Book, the order of government and laws of the realm now established." This he refused to do. Whereupon he was suspended from preaching.[2] Mr. Hill, the curate of St. Mary's, seems to have escaped censure for the present.

"The blower of the coals" *outside* of Bury was committed to the prison in Norfolk; it being "feared lest, if he were at liberty, he would seduce the vulgar sort of people."[3]

The Bishop immediately gave an account of these men, and of the proceedings of the Commissioners against them, in a letter to Lord Burleigh, dated April 19th, from which we have drawn our account. But before this letter could have been received, his lordship had heard of the imprisonment of his kinsman and, on the 21st, wrote to the Bishop as follows: —

"After my very hearty commendations to your lordship: Whereas I understand that one Brown, a Preacher, is by your lordship and others of the Ecclesiastical Commission committed to the custody

[1] Strype's Grindal, Append. p. 65.
[2] Freke to Burleigh, April 19th.
[3] Freke to Burleigh; Strype's Annals, V. 22. Burleigh to Freke, April 21st; Fuller, Bk. IX. p. 166.

of the Sheriff of Norfolk, where he remains a prisoner, for some matters of offence uttered by him by way of preaching, wherein I perceive by sight of some letters written by certain godly preachers in your lordship's diocese, he hath been dealt with, and by them dissuaded from that course he hath taken. Forasmuch as he is my kinsman, if he be son to him whom I take him to be, and that his error seemeth to proceed of zeal rather than of malice, I do therefore wish he were charitably conferred with and reformed. Which course I pray your lordship may be taken with him, either by your lordship or such as your lordship shall assign for that purpose. And in case there shall not follow thereof such success as may be to your liking, that then you would be content to permit him to repair hither to London, to be further dealt with as I shall take order for upon his coming. For which purpose I have written a letter to the Sheriff, if your lordship shall like thereof. And so I bid your lordship right heartily farewell. From the Court at Westminster, this 21 of April, 1581. Your lordship's very loving friend,

"W. BURLEIGH."

Thus, if the letters of "certain godly preachers" were correct, Brown had given signs of repentance for his erratic "course." Because of this, or out of consideration to the Lord Treasurer, he was soon set at liberty, but ordered to leave the diocese of Norwich.[1] Yet by the Act 1 Elizabeth, Cap. II. Sec. II., being not beneficed, he should have been imprisoned "one whole year without bail or mainprize."[2]

[1] Strype's Annals, V. 22.

[2] That Brown was liberated and

The diocese, however, was by no means purged of the new leaven. The Bishop's visitation had accomplished but little. Brown had not only the good-will of "the vulgar sort of people," but was countenanced and supported by many of the gentry of Suffolk. He was, therefore, bold enough and zealous enough soon to venture back again.[1] As he happened at Bury, Sir Robert Jermin, one of the justices, sent for him and cautioned him lest, with "his young years and experience," his zeal should carry him too far. Sir Robert, if not an avowed Puritan, was a stanch friend and protector of the Puritans, and had a great regard for Brown as "a man very able to yield the Church his profitable service." But he had discovered in him a disposition to venture farther than the Puritans from the established order; a disposition to persist in separate worship and wholly to discard all rituals. He therefore told him, that "his course seemed dangerous in the opinion of many honest and godly men;" and that the Papists would be apt to slander and discredit the Protestant communion, "if his singular conceits might not be warranted by the Word of God and Christian policy." In Sir Robert's opinion, there were many things in Brown's answer godly, reasonable, to be wished, and to be prayed for. At the same time, his young friend threw out some strange notions about setting up a new Discipline, and about overthrowing episcopal government, and about the means for putting these things into execution, which startled his Worship as opinions over

dismissed, shows conclusively that he was not at *this* time sent to London to be dealt with, as Fuller supposes he was. Other writers have followed him in his mistake.

[1] Strype's Annals, V. 22.

dangerous, and as means which exceeded the proper functions of either a justice or a minister.[1] From this it would seem that Brown proposed some scheme against the Establishment and for a new Discipline which Sir Robert and himself should initiate, but which, to the mind of the former, seemed too much like a defiance of constituted authority; and so their interview ended.

The daring young man went his way, and went to his work alone. "He taught strange and dangerous doctrine in all disordered manner. He greatly troubled the whole county. He brought many to great disobedience of all law and magistrates." So said Bishop Freke. The Lord Chief Justice and Master Justice Anderson had greatly frightened the people and bridled the disaffected among the gentry, by threatening the punishment due for breach of the orders of the Church. But now Brown inspired them with new courage; so that the disorders continued, and he held "private meetings in such close and secret manner, that the Bishop knew not possibly how to suppress them."[2]

Nor was this all. The suspension of Mr. Handson did not free the pulpit of St. James from Puritan preaching. Dr. Deye, as he sat beneath it, was even more annoyed than before. "Do you, sir," said one who years before had been scourged in the name of Law,—and he said it when preaching,—"do you, sir, assume to punish God's people who come not to church! Yet you absent yourself for the sake of

[1] Sir Robert Jermin to Lord Burleigh; Strype's Annals, V. 30, 31.

[2] Strype's Annals, V. 22, 23; Hanbury, I. 20, note,—Freke to Burleigh.

a dinner, and license another to be absent that he may be your guest! Ay, sir, you and your fellows do mightily urge orders; but only so long as orders do maintain superstition. With you and with them, all other orders be no orders. Know you not that it is concluded by the first of the Acts of the Apostles, that no one may appoint ministers but the disciples in every parish, and none other? And for the matter of inducting one who is utterly unable to discharge the place, know, sir, that none may be suffered in the Church but preachers only; neither ought any in government of the Church to be urged other than God in his Word commandeth."[1]

To such a pass had things now come in Bury, that even a prelatic officer could not resent the rebuke, nor punish the doctrine, of a Puritan preacher; for the magistrates were Puritans and stood firm to shield their clergy from any prosecution the process of which did not strictly tally with the letter of the law. They went further. They were quick to punish attempts adverse to Puritan interests when such attempts were illegal or even indecorous. Thus — with one exception, Mr. Justice Andrews — there was war between the Bishop's commissary and the justices in commission.

"That the old preachers should be troubled, or be made less able to live, and by that means the ministry of the Word be beaten quite out of town," the few Precisian partisans there sought to instate as a preacher in St. James's parish[2] one Wood, or

[1] Strype's Annals, V. 26; Deye's account to the Bishop of Norwich. Ibid, VI. 174.

[2] In this parish, I suppose; for, if I have not been misled, Mr. Hill was the incumbent in St. Mary's,

Wodde, "a very simple young man." As a countermove, the justices called together all the inhabitants of the parish; in accordance with "the usage or custom that the people of Bury, ever sithence the suppression of the abbey, used to choose their ministers." Upon trial — to which Wood was elected — he was found incompetent, "because he could only read;" and was thereupon advised by Mr. Justice Badby, "not to intrude himself into that charge without the good-liking and approbation of the people, another person being then prepared to serve." Wood, at the instigation of the Bishop and Mr. Justice Andrews, retaliated by causing Mr. Justice Badby to be indicted as a disturber.[1]

At the instance of Dr. Deye, a minister of the Precise school "made a sermon at Bury, wherein, for the most part, he was occupied in depraving the godly preachers of the town and county; comparing them to unbridled colts rushing through the whole hedge; and yet not so contented, called them vipers, serpents, stingers, and insatiable beasts." Whereupon the justices bound him for his appearance at the next Sessions; and, at the Sessions, the whole Bench, Lord North himself being present, "thought good to bind him further to his *good behavior*."[2]

Nor was Dr. Deye exempt from justiciary discipline. He also was put under bonds "for his forthcoming at the next Sessions holden at Bury, and in

and there were but two parishes in Bury. (Strype's Annals, V. 25.) Yet I cannot understand how a new minister could be collated to the living, — as is implied in Strype's Annals (V. 28, 29, VI. 175), — while Mr. Hansdon was as yet suspended only, not deprived. I have therefore written, "instate as a preacher."

[1] Strype's Annals, V. 28; VI. 174.

[2] Ibid., V. 24; VI. 177 – 179.

the mean time to be of good behavior;" for contrary to the remonstrances of the justices, contrary to his promise, and contrary to law, he had taken a step "on purpose to annoy the preachers, ministers, and honestest sort of the town with continual presentments" for deviations from the Statute of Uniformity.[1]

Philips the railing preacher, and Deye the aggrieved commissary, complained to Edmond, Bishop of Norwich.[2] The Bishop, "finding himself not strong enough to encounter these gentlemen and justices, who carried all before them in their countenancing of persons disaffected to the orders and discipline of the Church," sent to the Lord Treasurer twelve articles of accusation against the justices, and appealed to the queen's Council. The accused were cited to London; appeared; answered by a statement of facts; and demanded an honorable dismissal, which was granted.[3]

Such were the disturbances in Bury in the summer of 1581. The Bishop — who may be supposed to have known — attributed them to Brown; for, in a letter to Lord Burleigh dated August 2d, he said expressly, that "had not Brown returned again and greatly prejudiced the good proceedings of the Lord Chief Justice and Mr. Justice Anderson, he verily hoped of much good and quietness to have ensued thereof."[4]

Mr. Handson continued under suspension, notwithstanding the urgent and repeated efforts of the Lord

[1] Strype's Annals, V. 25; VI. 176, 177.

[2] Ibid., V. 24-27.

[3] Ibid., V. 28, 29; VI. Append., No. III. pp. 172-180. Neal, I. 150.

[4] Strype's Annals, V. 23.

Treasurer, the Lord North, Sir Robert Jermin, and others, that "he might be restored to his preaching." The Bishop roundly declared that, "unless he would publicly confess his fault and be bound to follow another course, he would not set him free."[1] There was some apology for this. His lordship was in great tribulation. He was extremely apprehensive for his diocese; lest "all religion should be overthrown there by the action of Brown and his fellows, and by the strange dealings of gentlemen in Suffolk about Bury, who winked at the disordered, if they did not incite them." "And therefore," he wrote to Lord Burleigh in August, "the careful duty I ought to have to my charge enforceth me to crave most earnestly your lordship's help in suppressing Brown especially."[2]

From the date of this appeal, we lose sight of Brown upon this field of his operations; from which we conjecture that Lord Burleigh's "help" was granted in the form of urgent advice to Brown that he should depart. How far he had matured, and how far he had propounded, the scheme (which he had darkly hinted to Sir Robert Jermin) for erecting a new Discipline, it is impossible from our data to determine. Yet it is not probable that the ecclesiastical principles for which he soon after became obnoxious were *openly* avowed by him in Suffolk; for he retained to the last the countenance and friendship of Puritan gentry there, by whom the known abettor of such principles and schemes would have been held in abhorrence.[3]

[1] Strype's Annals, V. 30.

[2] Hanbury, I. 20, note. Strype's Annals, V. 23.

[3] Witness, Sir Robert Jermin's letter to Burleigh; quoted above, from Strype's Annals, V. 30, 31.

The next year — 1582 — he was in Walcheren, the most important of those islands, in the German sea at the mouth of the Scheldt, which constituted almost the entire state of Zealand. In Middleburgh, the capital of Zealand, and situated upon this island, he organized a church, composed in part of several friends who accompanied him from England; himself being their pastor. Here the press was free. He therefore availed himself of the opportunity to digest and publish two books, for the doctrines of which he became distinguished as the founder of a sect; the one entitled, "A Book which showeth the Life and Manners of all true Christians;" the other, "A Treatise of Reformation without tarrying for any, and of the wickedness of those who will not reform themselves and their charge because they will tarry till the Magistrate command and compel them." Both these books appeared in 1582.[1] They were assiduously distributed in England.[2] Their peculiar tenets we shall soon recite.

In about two years there was strife between the pastor and his church at Middleburgh; and their connection was terminated by his departure for Scotland early in the summer of 1584, accompanied by a few of his friends.[3] Considering that his temper was notably imperious, irritable to the last degree, inflamed by the least question of his opinion upon the most trivial points,[4] and that the platform of his

[1] Another fact conclusive of Fuller's mistake (Bk. IX. p. 167), in seeming to represent Brown as detained in London from August, 1581, to October, 1585.

[2] Hanbury, I. 19, 20, note *a*; 23, note *b*. Collier, VII. 2.

[3] Hanbury, I. 22.

[4] Fuller's testimony on this point is decisive. "For my own part

church was purely democratic,—we can only wonder that their connection continued so long.

After declaiming against the Presbyterian clergy of Scotland and challenging their ecclesiastical authority, for which he was imprisoned, he ventured into England.[1] In September (probably), 1585, he was summoned before Whitgift, then Archbishop of Canterbury, "to answer for a book made by him." Burleigh again interfered, by whom his Grace was induced to Brown's discharge; and the more, because "no proof was found that he had been accessary to the dispersion of his book in England;[2] and also because he had "yielded unto his Grace further contentment,"[3]—*conjectured* to mean, that "he was brought to some tolerable compliance with the Church of England."[4] Upon his discharge, he was sent by Lord Burleigh to his father, with the advice that he should receive kind and temperate usage.[5] But the

(whose nativity Providence placed within a mile of this Brown his pastoral charge) I have, when a youth, often beheld him. He was of an imperious nature, offended if what he affirmed but in common discourse were not instantly received as an oracle." (Bk. IX. p. 168.) "Imperiousness" and "Independency" are antagonistic. *Such* a man was but a Balaam blessing Israel. His proper sphere was Episcopacy; and he found it so, at last.

[1] Hanbury (I. 22, note) says that Brown was in, or about, London June 17th, 1584. This is a mistake; and has been adopted by others. The letter from Lord Burleigh, which Hanbury quotes, was about one *Brayne*, whose case will come under our notice hereafter. The error occurs (perhaps, the printer's) in Fuller (Bk. IX. p. 159); and is corrected by Mr. Strype in his Life of Whitgift, p. 160. See the history of Brayne's case, Chap. XV., *infra*.

[2] Hanbury, I. 23.

Nevertheless, the want of such proof was no legal ground for discharge, according to the construction, to be hereafter noted of the Act 23 Elizabeth, Cap. II. Sect. IV. The penalty of death is there prescribed for "devising and writing, either within this realm, or in *any other* place."

[3] Burleigh to Brown's father, October 8th, 1585; Fuller, Bk. IX. p. 167.

[4] Fuller, ibid. Collier, VII. 3.

[5] I transcribe this letter of Lord Burleigh:—

son remaining incorrigible, the father, a Precisian of the Precisians,[1] prayed to be rid of his custody; which was granted after he had labored with him a little more than four months.[2]

After some incipient proselyting among certain Dutch immigrants who had a large congregation in the diocese of Norwich,[3] Brown ranged the country

"After my very hearty commendations: Understanding that your son Robert Brown had been sent for up by my Lord Bishop of Canterbury to answer to such matters as he was charged withal, contained in a book made by him, and published in print (as it was thought) by his means; I thought good, considering he was your son and of my blood, to send unto my Lord of Canterbury in his behalf, that he might find what reasonable favor he could show him. Before whom I perceive he hath answered in some good sort; and although I think he will not deny the making of the book, yet by no means will he confess to be acquainted with the publishing or printing of it. He hath besides yielded unto his lordship such further contentment, as he is contented (the rather at my motion) to discharge him; and therefore, for that he purposeth to repair unto you, I have thought good to accompany him with these my letters, and to pray you for this cause, or any of his former dealings, not to withdraw from him your fatherly love and affection; not doubting but with time he will be fully recovered, and withdrawn from the Reliques of some fond opinions of his; which will be the better done, if he be dealt withal in some kind and temperate manner. And so I bid you very heartily farewell. From my house near the Savoy, this eighth of October, 1585. Your loving friend and cousin, WM. BURLEIGH."

[1] Fuller, Bk. IX. p. 167.

[2] Neal says "four years."

The application of Brown's father, that his son might be removed from his house, was thus answered by Lord Burleigh. Its date, compared with that of the letter above, shows how long the father and son were together.

"After my very hearty commendations: I perceive by your letter, that you have little or no hopes of your son's conformity, as you had when you received him into your house; and therefore you seem desirous that you may have liberty to remove him farther off from you, as either to Stamford, or some other place, which I know no cause but you may very well and lawfully do, where I wish he might better be persuaded to conform himself for his own good; and yours and his friend's comfort. And so I very heartily bid you farewell. From the Court this seventeenth of February, 1585," — i. e. 1585–6. Your very loving friend and cousin,

"WILLIAM BURLEIGH."

[3] Collier, VII. 2 Hanbury, I. 19.

inveighing against bishops, ecclesiastical courts, ceremonies, and episcopal ordination; boldly teaching that the Church of England was no true Church of Christ, with but little of Christ's institution in her public ministrations; exhorting all good Christians to the solemn duty of separating from her worship and sacraments; and forming separately organized churches accordingly. This was the first gathering of churches, the first systematic defection, from the Reformed Church of England; "not as before among the Presbyterians from some offices in it;" and not as the Plumbers' Hall worshippers in 1567, who were a separate *assembly* merely.[1]

While performing this roving mission, Brown's fortitude was no less apparent than his intrepidity; for he was afterwards able "to boast, that he had been committed to thirty-two prisons, in some of which he

[1] Fuller, Bk. IX. p. 168. Heylin's Presb., Bk. VII. Sec. 30. Collier, VII. 2.

"Our controversy concerning the habits . . . . broke out again last winter. . . . . Some London citizens of the lowest order, together with four or five ministers, remarkable neither for their judgment nor learning, were openly separated from us, ... have held their meetings, and administered the sacraments. Besides this, they have *ordained* ministers, elders, and deacons, after their own way, and have even excommunicated some who had seceded from their Church." (Bishop Grindal to H. Bullinger, June 11th, 1568; Zurich Letters, cxxxv.)

This was a distinct church organization. But the reader is reminded that, during "*the last winter*," the Plumbers' Hall convicts were *in prison;* having been committed in June, 1567, and not liberated until May, 1568. (*Ante*, Vol. I. pp. 306, 317.) Thus Bishop Grindal, in the letter quoted above, does not refer to *them;* but to a more radical sect of whom Bonham and Crane were leaders, and to whom I have before alluded. *These* men seem to have been deficient in common integrity (see Strype's Grindal); and their sect, to have had but an ephemeral existence. I direct attention to them thus particularly, because the followers of Bonham and Crane are *uniformly* (I think) confounded by historians with the followers of Coleman, Benson, Rowland, and Hawkins, — of the assembly at the Plumbers' Hall.

could not see his hand at noonday."[1] At last he was cited to appear before Lindsell, Bishop of Peterborough; refused; was excommunicated for contempt; was overawed by such a censure; submitted; and was restored.[2] From the following letter, it would appear that this submission and reconciliation must have occurred before the close of 1588,—*our* reckoning:—

"To the Reverend Father in God, my very good Lord the Bishop of Peterborough, after my very good commendations to your lordship: Although it might seem somewhat strange that I should write to your lordship in favor of this bearer, Robert Brown, who hath been so notably misliked in the world for his strange manner of writing and opinions held by him; yet seeing he hath now *a good time* forsaken the same, and submitted himself to the order and government established in the Church, I have been the rather moved to recommend him to your lordship's favor, and to pray you, if haply any conceit may be in you that there should remain any relics in him of his former erroneous opinions, your lordship would confer with him, and, finding him dutiful and conformable, as I hope you shall, to receive him again into the ministry, and to give him your best means and help for some ecclesiastical preferment. Wherein I am the more willing to do him good, and am not a little glad at the reclaiming of him, being of kindred to me, as your lordship, I think, knows. And so I very heartily bid your lordship farewell. From my house near the Savoy, the

[1] Fuller, Bk. IX. p. 168.

[2] Collier, VII. 3.

20th of June, 1589. Your lordship's very loving friend,

"W. BURLEIGH." [1]

Thus Brown, having deserted his followers, was received into Court favor. He not only evaded, for many years, his thirty-third prison, but in 1591 bartered his manhood for a mess of pottage,—"a benefice called Achurch, or Aychurch, in Northamptonshire;" and then he used to say, in his intervals of miserable merriment, that "there was no Church in England but his, and *that* was A Church.[2] No one, however, supposed that he had changed his principles about ecclesiastical government or the constitution of the Church;[3] nor is there reason to believe that "he ever formally recanted his opinions either by word or writing."[4] On the contrary, so evident was it that he was unchanged, that a controversialist Churchman of the day did not hesitate to declare from the press, "Brown cunningly *counterfeiteth* conformity, and dissembleth with his own soul, for" (the sake of) "liberty."[5] He was but a nominal curate; his benefice a sinecure to himself with a good salary, and its duties discharged by a hired vicar; while he himself never more preached.[6] He used to beat his wife—till they separated,—shrewdly "*distinguishing* that he did not beat her as his wife, but as a curst old woman." He beat the constable of his parish, too, who was his godson; for which he was summoned to

[1] Strype's Whitgift, 323. Hanbury, I. 24, note.

[2] Paule's Life of Whitgift, p. 53. Wood's Athenæ, II. 17. Hanbury, I. 24.

[3] Strype's Whitgift, 323.

[4] Fuller, Bk. IX. p. 168.

[5] Hanbury, I. 23, note *b*.

[6] Fuller, Bk. IX. 168.

answer. For his insolence to the justice, he was committed to his *last* prison, the jail of Northampton; carried there in a cart; sickened there and died there, somewhat more than eighty years of age. This was in 1630.[1]

Robert Brown was but a Jehu in Israel, boastful of his zeal against Baal, who yet "departed not from the golden calves." He was only the chief declaimer of a school. There were others, less daring, less noisy, less notorious, less gifted in popular harangue, than he, but equally devoted to the same reform, and more efficient. Two of these — if we mistake not — were already in the toils of the hunters when he appeared in Suffolk, and soon yielded their lives where he yielded his conscience. Derisive as it is, the testimony of one then living is decisive, that he was but one among many, — *primus inter pares,* — and that his conspicuous position and historical notoriety were fortuitous. "Although sundry among them, from time to time, have labored to be leaders, and so upon the spur of emulation have galloped as hard as they could; yet without all question, there is none among them that can justly take the garland from Robert Brown. His writings do forejudge the cause against all competitors."[2] While he did run, he was the nimblest on the course. That was all; except —

[1] Fuller, Bk. IX. p. 168. Hanbury, I. 24, note *e*.

In the narratives before me of Brown's movements from 1581 to 1585, there is no chronological order whatever. Strype, in his Annals, furnishes us with clear and documentary data so far as he follows Brown; and so far, I have followed Strype. But the order of events, as given by Fuller, Collier, and Neal, is no order; and is utterly irreconcilable with the times of Brown's appearance in Suffolk and in Zealand. My own narrative, therefore, has no consecutive agreement with either of these three.

[2] Hanbury, I. 23, note *b*.

when the hare takes her nap, the turtle wins the race. Hence it was, that after Brown's disappearance from Suffolk, "the course of things went on at Bury for some years," until "the Bishop, quite weary of living there, got a remove."[1] And hence it was, that Brown's subsidence into the lap of the Church did not affect the vitality or the progress of the new reform.

The Brownists (so called) propounded no *theological* opinions, either old or new, which were offensive to the English Church. They were singular and offensive, only for opinions about ecclesiastical organization and government which brought them into direct collision, not only with the Establishment, but with the party who were seeking its adoption of the Genevan constitution. Their most prominent tenets were, —

That every congregation gathered in the name of Christ, worshipping him aright, and covenanting with him and with one another to observe his commands, constitutes a distinct church, or Christian body politic:[2]

That every church has a right to regulate its own religious affairs, to elect, inaugurate, and depose its own functionaries, to arrange its own mode of public worship and of administering the sacraments, to preserve its own peace and purity by discipline and excommunication; and that, in the exercise of these several rights, each member has an equal voice, — responsible throughout to the Great Head of the Church alone:[3]

1 Strype's Annals, V. 31.

2 Hanbury, I. 21, 28, 81. Neal, I. 150.

3 Hanbury, I. 32, 33, 41. Neal, I. 150.

That the proper officers of each are, — the *Pastor*, to preach and minister the sacraments, but *particularly*, by personal intercourse, to watch over, to exhort, to cherish, according to the Gospel, the individual members of his flock; the *Teacher*, or Doctor, also to minister the Word and sacraments, but *particularly* to instruct his people plainly, simply, and purely in the doctrines of the Word, and to expose and bar out false doctrines; the *Elder*, to preserve together with the Pastor and Teacher the peace and the rights of all, to see that the ordinances are duly taught and observed, and that things amiss are redressed; the *Deacon*, to collect the benevolences of the church and to distribute them among their poor in proportion to the necessities of each; the *Widow*, to minister personal attendance to the sick, the lame, the weary, and the afflicted. This office seems not to have been recognized after a short time.[1] The word "Elders" seems sometimes used to include the Pastor and Teacher as well as the Elders strictly so called:[2]

That all these officers ought to be called to their several offices only by the suffrages of the church in which they are to officiate:[3]

That *Ordination*, by prayer and the laying on of hands, should be performed by the Elders of the church, or, in default of these, by the Elders of some other faithful church, or, in default of both, by "the forwardest and wisest of their own number;" but that "this action belongs to the Elders, not as over and

[1] See Hanbury, I. 41, where Barrow ignores it.

[2] Hanbury, I. 41. For the functions of these several officers, see ibid., 21, 30, 31, 41.

[3] Ibid., 22, 57.

above, but as *the most fit members* and instruments of the church:"[1]

That this action of ordination does not impart power, confer indelible character, or create a distinct order of men in the church; but is "only a publishing of a formal contract and agreement betwixt the whole church and these elect"[2]—"a pronouncing them . . . . that they are called, and authorized of God, and received of their charge to that calling:"[3]

That the relation of different churches is that of a sisterhood only; a relation involving the privilege of inter-communion, the obligation to help one another, the right to seek and render counsel, to admonish, and, for disorder or corrupt doctrine, to withdraw fellowship,—but not the right, in any case, to exercise authority or jurisdiction:[4]

That no authority is found in Scripture, or in the usage of the primitive churches, for forms of public prayer; that, therefore, it is high presumption to impose them upon the Church;[5] and that, whether enjoined or not enjoined by men, they are unfit for "the spiritual temple of God where the offerings are spiritual," and where "God hath given graces unto his servants of the ministry," so that "the Church may use them as their mouth unto the Lord."[6]

No society could stand upon this platform, but brotherhood; no government, but Democracy; no laws, but Christ's; no Priest; no Lord Bishop; no

[1] Hanbury, I. 22, 57, 58.
[2] Barrow; Hanbury, I. 58.
[3] Brown; Hanbury, I. 22.
[4] Hanbury, I. 57. Neal, I. 150.
[5] Barrow to the High Commission; Harleian Miscellany, IV. 332.
[6] Barrow's "Brief Discovery;" Hanbury, I. 43, 44. Neal, I. 150.

Archbishop;[1] no ecclesiastical Court; no Convocation; no Presbytery, or Synod; no Magistrate.

The prince was acknowledged and reverenced, but not *here;* "to rule the Commonwealth in all outward justice," but not the Church; "to maintain the right, welfare, and honor of the state, with outward power, bodily punishments, and the civil" — but not religious — "forcing of men."[2] The queen was freely acknowledged "to be Supreme Governor of the whole land, and over the Church's bodies and goods; but not to make any other laws for the Church of Christ than he hath left in his Word;"[3] and not "to *compel* any to be a member of the Church, or the Church to receive . . . . or to retain any."[4]

So much for lordship in the Church of Christ! So much for Prelatic oppression! "Out of the eater came forth meat; and out of the strong came forth sweetness!" Under the strait Precisianism of the

[1] Penry; Hanbury, I. 79.

[2] Brown's "Points and Parts of True Divinity," Def. 117; Hanbury, I. 21, 22.

[3] Barrow to the High Commissioners; Harleian Miscellany, IV. 333.

[4] Barrow and Greenwood; Hanbury, I. 52, 53.

Yet we find the following opinions, which show that the ideas of this school respecting the relation of the Church to the State were not yet clear, and that their system was by no means perfected.

"Her Majesty hath full authority from the Lord to establish and enact all laws, both ecclesiastical and civil, among her subjects: in making whereof the Lord requireth that her ecclesiastical, be warranted by his written Word, ... and her civil, to be grounded on the rules of common justice and equity." (Penry; Hanbury, I. 79.)

"If her Majesty and this High Court require of us that we resort unto the public assemblies of the land, and so to enter . . . . into the tents of the anti-Christian band and to continue therein . . . . this is against the written Word of God, and therefore her Majesty hath no power, no authority, from the Lord to require this at our hands." (Penry; Hanbury, I. 82.)

"The prince may command and compel subjects to the hearing of the public doctrine and prayer of the Church." (Greenwood; Hanbury, I. 52, 68.)

English Establishment, the preposterous pretensions of the hierarchy, and the galling domination of statutes, the idea of pure religious liberty, dormant for ages in the dungeons of giant Power, was at last evolved, — a light to men sitting in darkness and in the region of the shadow of death. Once guided thereby to the threshold of their prison, the Independents of the sixteenth century, outstripping their teachers of the Presbyterian school, lingered not to admire its massive and hoary structure, did no reverence to the watchmen on its walls or the wardens at its gates, but shook off the gyves of old traditions, — such as the political Unity and the civil government of the Church, — and hasted to realize this resuscitated idea; to embody, in *one* form, that democratic liberty to which nature and Christianity had given them a right. With no thought beyond the simple affairs of religious fraternity in a worshipping congregation, and loyal to the institutions of Monarchy, they had rallied around a principle adverse to Monarchy as it then was, and had taken a large step towards *political* freedom. So unconsciously do men sometimes initiate the high purposes of God.

These were not men of station. They were ignoble and despised. Some of them "had stocks in their hands," — merchandise; some "had likely trades to live by;" some were "poor ones who had no such means."[1] Not a titled name stood upon their rolls. Not a man in power stood their friend, and not a member of the Parliament-House. But they were men of mark. Lowly and friendless, they were fearless; daring to do what the Reformed Church of

[1] Penry's farewell letter; Hanbury, I. 77.

England had never done and never dared, — to pluck Antiquity by the beard and brave the power of the state.

To justify secession and promote reform, it was necessary to expose and denounce the corruptions of the National Church, — nor did they cower at the peril involved in doing so. They acted their part boldly, vehemently, unsparingly; as men always do things when standing at bay and selling their lives for a Truth.

"That a Christian prince may forthwith make all in his realm a Church to whom belong a holy ministry and sacraments, is a doctrine most false, corrupt, unclean, dangerous, and pernicious; breaking down all Christian order, corrupting all Christian communion, poisoning all Christian fellowship, and sacrilegiously profaning the holy things of God. Whom the Lord calleth, he calleth to depart from all iniquity, to lay hold on Christ as alone their Saviour, to honor and obey him as their King, Priest, and Prophet, vowing faithful obedience to his most holy Word as it shall be made plain unto them. *Thus* it is, that every member of Christ *entereth into and standeth in* the Church.[1] But that which you call your Church is constituted, not by the calling of God, but by the edict of the prince; not by a profession of faith, but by an act of Parliament; not by a voluntary covenant of obedience, but by a compulsion of the flesh. There are many excellent Christians in it, many precious and elect vessels of the Lord;[2] but it

[1] Hanbury, I. 40, 41.

[2] Barrow to the High Commissioners; Harleian Miscellany, IV. 332.

openly alloweth and compelleth to the same fraternity, fellowship, and most holy sacraments, the undevout and the unbeliever, the profane and the licentious.

"Such a society 'is not the true established Church of Christ; and the people, as they now stand in this disorder and confusion, are not to be held the true and faithful people of Christ.'[1] Therefore it is that we 'will not go to your parish assemblies, which you call churches, nor commune with you either in prayer or sacraments,' 'nor hold fellowship with any congregation or member.'[2]

"If this suffice not as a reason for our separation, then we add thereto: 'The sacraments, as ministered in these your public assemblies, are not true sacraments. Many of the laws, decrees, and canons of your Church are unlawful and unchristian; as also are all your ecclesiastical courts and governors.'[3] 'Your ecclesiastical Discipline is corrupt, unlawful,

[1] Barrow, as above. Strype's Annals, Vol. VII. 202.

[2] Ibid. Hanbury I. 41.

Mr. Neal is severe upon the Brownists; charging it upon them as "a crime, that they renounced communion, not only with the Church of England, but with all foreign Reformed Churches, which, though less pure, ought certainly to be owned as the Churches of Christ." (I. 150.) But it should be remembered that the paramount reason with these men for breaking off communion with the English Church, was, — that it was constituted by *compulsion of the civil magistrate*, and embraced alike the believing and the unbelieving. There were "churches abroad, where the people, with direction of their godly ministers, had, even against the will of the magistrate, brought in the doctrine and discipline of Christ." (Hooker's Preface, 146.) We have yet to learn that the Brownists did withhold communion with such. But the same grand impediment to Christian fellowship was found as much in the Reformed Churches abroad indiscriminately gathered by civil coercion, as was found in the Church at home; and of each it might be said with equal truth, that they were political societies, not Christian churches.

[3] Barrow, as above. Strype's Annals, VII. 202.

popish;[1] for it lieth wholly with your bishops to command, to restrain, to execute upon, all persons; and they themselves be subject to no reproof, liable to no censure.'[2] Your clergy are not rightly ordained; are a false and antichristian ministry; are thrust and imposed upon your assemblies, not freely chosen by the Lord's people according to his ordinance; are but 'herds to the Lord's goats and swine, blessing them with the blessing of the Faithful' One, 'and delivering to them the holy sacraments of God.'[3] Your whole public worship is superstitious and idolatrous; devised by men after the prescript of a rotten popish liturgy.[4]

"Hath God left his ministers so destitute of his grace, that they cannot find words to express their thoughts and desires, but need to be taught line upon line what and when to say, how much to say, and when to make an end? Can any read, prescript, stinted liturgy, penned many years before, be called *prayer*, — a pouring forth of the heart unto the Lord? Is this old, rotten liturgy your new song you sing unto the Lord with, and for, his graces? May such apocrypha trumpery be brought into the Church of God, and there read, reverenced, and received as the sacred Word of God is? thrust upon men's consciences, yea, upon God himself? Is it not utterly to quench the Spirit of God, both in the ministry

[1] Strype's Annals, VII. 202. Hanbury, I. 53.

[2] Hanbury, I. 56.

[3] Ibid., I. 53, 54. Strype's Annals, VII. 202.

[4] Hanbury, I. 53, 60. Strype, ibid.

The reader who is curious to know minutely for what the Brownist considered "the whole public worship of the Established Church superstitious and idolatrous," will find particulars in Hanbury, I. 60, 61.

and people, while you tie both them and him to your stinted, numbered prayers? Is this the unity and uniformity that ought to be in all churches, — and is, amongst all Christ's servants, — to make them agree in a stinking, patchery-devised, apocrypha liturgy; good for nothing but for cushions and pillows for idle priests, and profane carnal atheists, to rock them asleep withal, and to keep them in security?"[1]

Nor is this all. "We find this Book to be the very groundwork of your faith, church, and ministry; in place, to you, of the Word of God, as whence you fetch all your directions for all things! Yea, the Word of God may not be taught but where this Book hath first been read and hath the pre-eminence! In your churches, it may not be gainsayed or controlled. The priest who will not be conformable to it, must be deprived of his priestdom. If he be found stout or contumacious, then is he cast into prison to cool him, until his stomach come down that he make suit unto his 'Grace,' or some other Lord Bishop, and enter bond to be conformable or silent. Moreover, this Book, in that it standeth a public prescript continued liturgy, in this place and use being brought into the church, yea, or into any private house, becometh a detestable idol, standing for that it is not in the Church of God and consciences of men, namely, for holy, spiritual, and faithful prayer; it being nothing less, but rather[2] abominable and loathsome sacrifice in the sight of God, even as a dead dog."[3] Or, to say the least, — "as it is publicly enjoined and received in the assemblies of this land,

[1] Hanbury, I. 44, 45. [2] *Sic.* [3] Hanbury, I. 43.

it is *well-nigh* altogether idolatrous, superstitious, and popish."[1]

"For their idolatry, confusion, sacrilege, false and antichristian ministry and government; for their obstinacy in all these sins; for their hatred of the truth; and for their persecution of Christ's servants, — we have proved the Church of England not to be the true, but the malignant church. We but discover their sins, and show them their estate, by the Word of God; refraining from, and witnessing against their abominations and their popish parish assemblies as we are commanded by that voice from heaven, — 'Go out of her, my people, that ye communicate not in her sins and that ye receive not of her plagues.' Let the wise that are warned and see the evil, fear and depart from the same."[2]

Such was the theory of Brown and his disciples respecting the proper organization of the Christian Church; such were their reasons for separation; and such, their bold, severe, and public denunciations of the polity and formalism of the Establishment. Nearly all which we have quoted — in a condensed form — was written and published when the authors were in prison; or uttered by them when face to face with their inquisitors, when their executioners were standing, as it were, at the door, and when concession or even neutrality would have saved them from the gallows. We can estimate, therefore, the heroic daring of their controversy, and their single-hearted devotion to the spiritual worship of God, to religious liberty, and ecclesiastical independence.

[1] Barrow to the High Commissioners; Harleian Miscellany, IV. 332; Strype's Annals, VII. 202.

[2] Hanbury, I. 66.

On the other hand, and in the light of the records which we have quoted above, we commend these words from an oracle of English Law, "The dissenters divided from the Church *for no reason at all;*"[1] and in charity conclude, that a libel so flagrant has been inscribed, and dispersed, not wilfully and in malice, but through a religious obtuseness, or a historical lack, perfectly consistent with legal acumen and professional eminence.

Nor were the differences less irreconcilable, though less numerous, between this class of dissenters and that who still adhered to the Church. The latter were as earnest for a National Church, to be established by law, to be defended by the prince, to be upheld by pains and penalties, as were the Prelatists.[2] The former, as we have seen, would have limited the Church to the disciples of Christ, and would have placed it beyond the reach of all civil interference. "The false brethren" — the Brownists used hard names — and "the poor brethren" — so did the Genevans — held many opinions in common against the Church of England; that "her public service of God was laden with intolerable pollutions borrowed from the shop of antichrist; that her government by bishops and archbishops was antichristian; that her sacraments were desecrated by notorious badges of antichristian recognizance." Yet, though "some time the companions, the guides, and familiars" of the new sect, the Presbyterian Puritans "were their professed adversaries, because they" — the advocates of

[1] Blackstone, IV. 52.

[2] Strype's Annals, VII. 198. Cartwright, as quoted by Hallam, 114; and Neal, as quoted by Hallam, 129, note.

Independency — "thought the statute-congregations in England to be no true Christian churches; because they severed themselves from them; and because, without leave or license from those in civil authority, they secretly framed churches on another platform."[1] The Puritans "abhorred"[2] separation; the Brownist, all complicity with ecclesiastical lordship and corruption, and all "servile subjection to the government of antichrist."[3] The former taught that Presbytery should be established by law; the latter, that it was but a mockery of the rights of the people; or, in other words, that "Presbyter was but old priest writ large;" and they used the same plainness and vehemence of speech against the Genevan system as against the Anglican.

"Your learned preachers," said they," "your *good* men that sigh and groan for reformation, would raise up a second error even as a second 'Beast;' by so much more dangerous, by how much it hath more show of truth. These men would bring in a new, adulterate, forged government, in show, or rather in despite of, Christ's government, which they most miserably innovate, corrupt, and pervert. Their false manner of exercising this their pretended Discipline, may partly appear by the weak and fearful practice of some of their forward men; who, that they might make a fair show amongst their rude, ignorant parishioners, instead of Christ's government, set up their counterfeit 'Discipline' in and over all the parish, making the *popish churchwardens, and perjured questmen*, Elders. And for Mr. Parson himself,

[1] Hooker's Preface, pp. 144, 145.
[2] Strype's Annals, V. 266.
[3] Hanbury, I. 59.

he taketh unto him the instrument of that 'foolish shepherd,'—his pastoral staff, or wooden dagger, of suspension; wherewith he keepeth such a flourishing as the flies can have no rest; yea, by your leave, if any poor man in any parish offend him, he may, peradventure, go without his bread and wine for that day.

"Their permanent synods and councils also, which they would erect, should only consist of priests, or ministers as they term them:[1] people of the churches be shut out, and neither be made acquainted with the matters debated there, neither have free voice in those synods and councils, but must receive and obey, without contradiction, whatsoever those learned priests shall decree. These synods' and councils' decrees are most holy, without controlment, unless it be by the prince or the High Court of Parliament. These Reformists, howsoever, for fashion sake, they give the people a little liberty, to sweeten their mouths and make them believe that they should choose their own ministers, yet even in this their pretended choice, they do cozen and beguile them also; leaving them nothing but the smoky, windy title of election only,—enjoining them to choose some University clerk, one of these college-birds of their own

[1] The Presbyterian system in England, so far as matured at the time (1591), did not constitute its synods and councils of the clergy only, but of the clergy and elders; the latter appearing as representatives of the laity. This system, however, was but imperfectly known except by those who had subscribed to the Book of Discipline. I therefore think that Barrow must have had in mind Presbytery as it then existed openly in Scotland, where the Assembly consisted of *ecclesiastical* persons only. (Hanbury, I. 6.)

In Geneva, the Assembly, or standing ecclesiastical Court, consisted of the ministers, who were members perpetually, and of two laymen to each minister; the laymen chosen annually. (Hooker's Preface, 112.)

brood; or else comes a synod in the neck of them and annihilates the election, whatsoever it be! They have also a trick to stop it before it come so far, — namely, in the ordination, which must, forsooth, needs be done by other priests; for the church that chooseth him hath no power to ordain him! And this makes the mother-church of Geneva and the Dutch classis — I dare not say the secret classis in England — to make ministers for us in England."[1]

The Presbyterian Puritans, stung by such reproaches, replied with no more courtesy, and with no less acrimony. Thus there was not only controversy, but "unappeasable animosity" between the two parties who sought ecclesiastical reform.

We return to our narrative of events in the county of Suffolk.

Variations from the Act of Uniformity, and disturbances occasioned thereby, continued in Bury — as we have already stated — after Brown's departure; "and all this in great measure by favor of some of the justices."[2] In addition to these troubles — strictly of a *Puritan* stamp — practical Brownism had obtained a footing; for "no small numbers brake off all communion with the Church."[3] In 1582–3, Brown's books, which "condemned the Book of Common Prayer and the whole constitution of the Church,"[4] had made their appearance there. John Copping, "a zealous Puritan of the Brownist persuasion,"[5] was still a prisoner in the jail at Bury, and had zealously dispersed them.

[1] Barrow; Hanbury, I. 46, 47.
[2] Strype's Annals, V. 31.
[3] Ibid., 269.
[4] Ibid., 28.
[5] Brook, I. 262.

As we have stated before, he and Mr. —— Tyler had been committed by the Bishop's Commissary so long ago as 1576; and now in 1583 were still in ward. It is said that they "were imprisoned for spreading Brown's books;"[1] which were not printed, however, till six years afterwards.[2] The offence for which Copping was committed is stated in very general terms,—"disobedience to the ecclesiastical laws of the realm."[3] "At sundry times, many godly and learned preachers had in vain exhorted him to conformity; for, in their opinion, he held *many fantastical* opinions whereby he did *much hurt* there in Bury, so that they wished him removed."[4] At first, Sir Robert Jermin and his Puritan associates had interceded with the judges for his freedom and for Tyler's; but when they found all efforts "to do good unto them by Christian persuasion and counsel could not prevail," these *Puritan* justices "gave them up"—we use their own words—"to their froward wills, and became earnest suitors, both to the bishop and judges, that the prisoners might be removed out of that prison to the prison at Norwich *for fear of infecting others*."[5]

[1] Strype's Annals, V. 28.

[2] Mr. Strype does indeed state incidentally, under date of 1582, that one Gibson, a bookbinder in Bury, "*had* printed Brown's books." (Annals, V. 177.) This is the only intimation which I find that Brown had at that time published any books in England. Yet the words do not necessarily imply this; for Gibson may have gone to Middleburgh, printed the books *there*, and returned.

[3] Strype's Annals, IV. 186.

[4] Ibid.

[5] I am surprised at Mr. Neal's whole statement of this affair (I. 150); particularly at his words,—the justices "very justly tax his lordship with cruelty in keeping men so many years in prison without bringing them to trial according to law. I find nothing like this in the Paper to which he refers. (Strype's Annals, VI. 172–180.) The words of the justices, which I have given in the text, show that they themselves thought, when the Bishop's "Articles" were penned, that Copping and Tyler

But the Bishop — the justices thought — chose to keep them *there* "for decoys to catch and endanger men with."[1] Collating all these facts, and remembering how Sir Robert — nine tenths, if not wholly, a Puritan — shrank from Brown's hint of his *ultra* purposes of reform, we find strong indications that the overt acts called "disobedience to the ecclesiastical laws," and the "many fantastical opinions," were something *more* than pertained to Puritans; something offensive to them. Were not these acts and fantasies like those of Brown? and did not these two men *precede* him as denouncers of the Church and as *preachers* of separation, by at least six years? If they were not *more* than Puritans, and that too in 1581, before Brown had avowed his ultra opinions, the conduct and language of the Puritan justices are unaccountable.[2]

But, however this may have been, Copping set in motion Brown's books; and so did Elias Thacker, another minister of the same "persuasion," who in 1583 was his fellow-prisoner.[3] For this, both were indicted at one Assizes held at Bury in June of that year; Sir Christopher Wray, Lord Chief Justice of England, presiding. They were tried and convicted

ought to be kept in prison, though not at Bury. I am the more particular to note Mr. Neal's disagreement with the document whence we both derive our facts, because his statement materially affects my supposition — which is of some interest and perhaps importance — that the prisoners had preached "Independency" before Brown appeared upon the field.

[1] Strype's Annals, V. 28; VI. 172, 173.

[2] Mr. Hallam (p. 129, note) is the only writer, I think, who designates these men as "Anabaptists." His authority I cannot conjecture. He cites the very page of Strype now before me; where they are expressly and only called "Brownists." Holingshed (IV. 505) has it that Thacker was a tailor; and Copping, a shoemaker!

[3] Strype's Annals, V. 269. Brook, I. 263.

on the statute 23 Elizabeth Cap. II., entitled "An Act against seditious words and rumors."

The Archbishop's chaplain and others bootlessly "travailed with them" for their conversion; but the hankering zeal of the judges could not brook delay. The two convicts were hurried to the gallows; Thacker, on the fourth day of the month; Copping, on the fifth or sixth. In mockery of their opinions, as many of Brown's books as could be collected were burned before them as they stood haltered upon the scaffold; and, while the smoke was going up, a witness against the "sleight of men," they went to the one brotherhood of the redeemed, where is but *one* Bishop and *one* "Priest forever."[1] The Church, prostituted to the State, went her way as before; like the adulterous woman, "wiping her mouth, and saying, 'I have done no wickedness.'"[2]

[1] Stow's Annals, 697. Fuller, Bk. IX. p. 169. Sir Christopher's letter to Burleigh; Strype's Annals, V. 269.

[2] Mr. Neal says (I. 154), "It seemed a little hard to hang men for spreading a seditious book, *at a time when* the author of that very book was pardoned and set at liberty."

Upon this, Bishop Warburton, in his breakfast-table notes, makes the following comment: "That is, it is hard that the dispensers of a poison should be hanged for going on obstinately in mischief, because he who compounded the poison was on his repentance pardoned." (Vol. XII. pp. 381, 382. London edit. 1811.)

The reader will perceive that neither of these strictures is in point, because, when Thacker and Copping were executed — 1583 — Brown was not within the realm; and had neither been arrested nor pardoned *for publishing his book*, — i. e. compounding the poison which others had dispensed. Afterwards, when he *was* arrested to answer for his book, he was discharged, not because he did not make it; not because the making it out of the realm was not (according to the construction of the Court who sentenced Copping and Thacker) a hanging offence; not because he had either repented or conformed (witness Lord Burleigh's letters to Brown's father); not because he had answered to the book "in some good sort;" and not because he had

Thus was the crude Congregationalism of the day scotched — but only scotched — in its cradle. Rather, such was its infant baptism; a baptism which only invigorated for a stouter manhood what it was intended to drown.

Sir Christopher Wray was at his wit's end. That the men were to die by the hangman was a point settled, — a thing not unusual in Elizabeth's day.[1] To save appearances, to make it look as though the queen would not force *consciences,* the statute must be artistically noosed to execute, as felons, good ministers of Christ and loyal subjects of her Majesty. The law-craft was on this wise.

'The prisoners at the bar have distributed Brown's books. Now the statute 23 Elizabeth, Cap. II., was *intended,* as is well known, to prevent the circulation of "naughty *papistical* books," which incited to rebellion in favor of the Queen of Scots.[2] But never mind the intent. Let us look at the letter. Now Section IV. of the act says nothing specially about *papistical* books; but simply, "*Any* manner of book containing .... *seditious* .... matter to the defamation of the Queen's Majesty." Examine these books of Robert Brown. Do they contain seditious matter to the defamation of the Queen's Majesty? Unquestionably. But how so? Do they not allow her Majesty's

"yielded the Archbishop further contentment;" but "the rather at the motion" of his kinsman, the Lord High Treasurer of England.

It was not the statute, but an infamous construction of the statute, which hung Thacker and Copping. When Brown was apprehended, his "high connection" took care that the construction should sleep. It had answered the special purpose for which it had been incanted; and, I think, was never revived.

[1] Hallam, 138, 139.

[2] See *ante,* Chapter VII.

civil supremacy? Most certainly. But they deny her ecclesiastical supremacy. Surely this is seditious; for it alloweth ecclesiastical *contradiction* to her Highness. Again: it is "to the defamation of the Queen's Majesty;" for she *is* supreme in the Church; and to assert that she is not what she is, is to defame. The factors of these books have, therefore, circulated seditious matter to the defamation of the Queen's Majesty. Which is demonstrated. Therefore, gentlemen of the jury, your duty in the light of the statute is plain,—a verdict of guilty.' Thus sophistically, thus tortuously, thus by ignoring the intent, and torturing the words of the statute, the tragical fate of good Christians and good citizens was brought about under color of law.[1]

'Denying the ecclesiastical supremacy of the queen!' There was not a Papist in the realm but denied it. There was not a disciple of Cartwright and Travers but denied it.[2] The hottest Precisians among Elizabeth's first bishops had denied it,—in effect and in intent, if not in the letter;[3] and in like manner had the present Primate, Grindal, in his stinging letter to the queen. So, according to the Court's construction of the statute, its *third* section would have required a vast holocaust to have appeased, avenged, and vindicated this dishonored supremacy.[4]

'Denying the ecclesiastical supremacy of the queen seditious!' Why, the same books and the

[1] Hallam, 129, note. Lingard, VIII. 146, 147.

[2] See *ante*, Vol. I. Chapter XVIII. note 8. Strype's Annals, VII. 198. Hallam, 114, 126.

[3] See *ante*, Chapter II.

[4] See the section, *ante*, Chapter VII. p. 189.

same men declared right loyally her *civil* supremacy; and what was this but a *denunciation* of sedition?

Had the Puritan House of Commons, in framing this act, consented to the sly suggestion of the Lords to leave in force the Act 1 and 2 Philip and Mary, Cap. III. Sec. I.,[1] Sir Christopher would have found it but a straightforward matter to have convicted Thacker and Copping for "slanderous words against the *Lords and Clergy;*" and would have been spared the polluting his own soul by such atrocious chicanery.

Common sense disposes of this whole matter at once. It was determined to consign these men to the gibbet, for a terror to all upstart Brownists. Thus Sir Christopher gave them over to the hangman, not as *Brownists,* for their religion,—by no means!—but as *felons,* for sedition. So Brown himself "distinguished." He did not beat his wife *as* his wife, but *as that curst old woman.*

[1] See *ante,* Chap. VII. p. 194, note 7.

CHAPTER XII.

EDMUND, ARCHBISHOP OF CANTERBURY.

Thomas Radcliffe, Earl of Sussex; his Death and Character. — Archbishop Grindal "under a Cloud." — The Convocation intercede for him. — He becomes Blind, and tenders his Resignation, which the Queen refuses. — The Queen requires his Resignation; but abandons her Purpose. — Grindal's Death. — Thomas Sampson's Letter to him in 1574. — Grindal a Conforming Puritan; and in what Sense such. — His Charitable Spirit and Deportment towards Non-conformists. — His Opinions respecting Cartwright. — The Character of his Controversy with the Queen.

1583.

The thief and his Redeemer met on the same day in Paradise. On one and the same day — almost — the felon and the courtier, the convict Brownist and the Metropolitan, met there also; without difference and "without fault before the Throne, redeemed from among men unto God and the Lamb."[1]

The law of Elizabeth had but just martyred men of her own faith, when the law of Retribution took from her nobility its brightest star, and from her Establishment its most apostolic Primate, — Thomas, the second Earl of Sussex, and Edmund, the queen's second Archbishop of Canterbury. The gibbet had profited her nothing.

Sussex has been incidentally mentioned in our nar-

[1] Rev. xiv. 4, 5.

rative. Though chivalrously devoted when his services were needed as a soldier, yet he had "that swell in his stomach" which he could not suppress when suffering indignity from his queen; a swell which made him prefer "leaving to serve" her rather than "lose his honor." [1] He was not only a rival of Leicester at Court, but was open in his detestation of the favorite's craft, licentiousness, and hypocrisy. Thus they were at constant feud; restrained from open strife only by the authority and address of their mistress.[2] Yet when the man whom he most detested was in disgrace and confinement, Sussex was his intercessor for the queen's forgiveness.[3] His antipathy, however, was perpetual. "Beware of him," he said to his friends on his dying bed; "beware of the gipsy, for he will be too hard for you all. You know not the Beast so well as I do." [4]

It is, however, as a peacemaker, that we most admire him; making peace between his sovereign and the man he loathed; making peace also between others. It seems to have been his habit; so that, upon the authority of our Saviour, we have a right

[1] *Ante*, Vol. I. p. 361, note 4.

[2] "Thomas Radcliffe, Earl of Sussex, ... less cunning and dexterous than Leicester, and much the honester man..... There was such an antipathy in his nature to that of Leicester's, that being together in Court, and both in high employments, they grew to a direct frowardness, and were in continual opposition; the one setting the watch, the other the sentinel, each on the other's actions and motions. For my Lord of Sussex was of a great spirit; which, backed with the queen's special favor, and supported by a great and ancient inheritance, could not brook the other's empire: Insomuch as the queen upon sundry occasions had somewhat to do to appease and attain them, till death parted the competition, and left the place to Leicester, who was not long alone without his rival in grace and command." (Naunton's Fragmenta Regalia, in the Phœnix, p. 194.)

[3] See *ante*, Chap. VI.

[4] Naunton; Frag. Regalia, in the Phœnix, p. 194.

to "call" him one of "the children of God." The earnestness and touching eloquence with which he prosecuted this vocation in 1569, when volunteering as a days-man between Cecil and the Duke of Norfolk, are radiant with the spirit of Christ. It is gratifying to know that, with such a spirit, he prevailed.[1]

[1] I transcribe Sussex's letters; not only as sustaining the text, but as being of interest to every lover of Christian nobility.

"The Earl of Sussex to Sir William Cecil."

"Good Mr. Secretary: I am sorry from the bottom of my heart to conceive, by the end of your letter which I received this morning, that my Lord of Norfolk and you should stand in worse terms of amity than ye in foretimes did; or that any of you, either clearly without cause, or upon suspect of some cause, should forbear towards the other that good opinion that hath so long time been conceived on either side. I have been well acquainted with the faithful good-will that either of you hath borne to the other, grounded upon both your steadfast zeals to the service of the queen and the realm; whereby, in all wise men's opinions, great good hath ensued, and therefore the grief is the greater to me to suspect the quailing of your friendships, whereby the one of you might fail to the other (in that I never thought any of you would have failed to any), and the whole realm thereby fare the worse. This is the first time I have heard hereof, and truly it is the worst thing to my grief, that of long time I have heard of; but such be the plagues in this wretched world by the permission of God for the punishment of our sins.

"What should be the ground hereof I cannot guess; and then not knowing the sore, I can hardly devise of any special salve. This only I crave of you, as a general medicine for many such diseases in this time; that if seditious tongues have sowed cockle in any of you, ye will both of you remember what good ground ye be, and what seed ye have both heretofore brought forth; and with the touchstone of old and pure faithfulness that was wont to be between you, ye will try both the sower and the cockle, and cast them both away, and so return to yield your former fruits; whereby God, the queen, and the realm shall be better served, and every of yourselves, in your own particular, the more honored, loved, and esteemed. When I remember what ye both be, I cannot conceive that by any possibility the one of you would willingly do any fact whereby the other might have just cause to conceive offence: and then I certainly think the mistrust, on either side, must grow by sinister reports; wherein there is no remedy so good as to discover the untruth in the beginning. Therefore, good Mr. Secretary, seeing God hath dealt so liberally to you his gifts of patience, wisdom, and other

Mr. Lodge's beautiful tribute to his memory comprises an admirable list of modest virtues: "Thomas, second Earl of Sussex, ... united all the splendid qualities of those eminent persons who jointly rendered Elizabeth's Court an object of admiration to Europe, and was perfectly free from their faults.

virtues, I exhort you in the bowels of our Lord Jesus Christ, that ye will plainly and fully rip up this matter from the bottom with the Duke himself, in whom you know you shall find honor, truth, wisdom, and plainness; and as I trust by this dealing there shall need no third person to interpone, so if I know a need thereof, I would leave all other matters, and, upon some feigned cause, ride post to London, yea, to Jerusalem, to do the good I desire therein; and surely I think it presently to be one of my greatest misfortunes to be absent in such a time; and so I end, and wish unto you as to myself. From York, the xvth of May, 1569. Yours assuredly, T. SUSSEX."

"I am heartily glad, good Mr. Secretary, to perceive by your letters of the xxxth of last, and by my Lord of Norfolk's of the xxxist, the good and hearty reconcilement between you, which I trust shall long continue; and your faithful promises of love and trust, made on both sides, shall I hope remain so sure as no practisers by evil offices shall undermine any of you. His Grace writeth very frankly of the assured trust and confidence he reposeth in your good-will; and surely I was very glad to receive the knowledge thereof, not only in respect of you both, whom I protest I have loved, do love, and will love, better than any other two subjects in the realm, but also and principally for the service of our good queen, whose surety and honor I weigh above all other things in the world, and hath been, is, and must be, chiefly supported by you two, whom the world hath always judged to be void of private motives, and to respect only her, and the realm, in all your actions. In respect whereof a great number of honorable and wise, in all parts of the realm, will gladly, and of good conscience, aid, assist, and set forth all your intents and doings, by all the good means they may, for the more honor and surety, and the better service of her Majesty. And if the ground whereupon they build their actions (which is your amities and knitting together in the true service of her Majesty and the realm) should fail, although their zeals should remain good, yet their exertions, for lack of such maintenance, should take small effect; and therefore I will end this matter with the old proverb, *valeant qui inter vos dissidium velint;* and betake you to the Almighty, who guide you with the same spirit that he hath ever done. From Cawood, the ixth of June, 1569. Yours assuredly, T. SUSSEX." (Lodge, II. pp. 15–18.)

Wise and loyal as Burleigh, without his blind attachment to the monarch; vigilant as Walsingham, but disdaining his low cunning; magnificent as Leicester, but incapable of hypocrisy; and brave as Raleigh, with the piety of a primitive Christian; he seemed above the common objects of human ambition, and wanted — if the expression may be allowed — those dark shades of character which make men the heroes of history. Hence it is, probably, that our writers have bestowed so little attention on this admirable person, who is but slightly mentioned in our historical collections, unless with regard to his disputes with Leicester, whom he hated almost to a fault. . . . . He died at his house at Bermondsey, June 9th, 1583."[1]

During nearly six years, the Archbishop of Canterbury, stripped of all the dignity of his high office, called to exercise some of its minor functions only and upon few occasions, had lived to no better purpose than to serve as a conspicuous monument of the queen's withering wrath, a warning to other prelates, and a silent example of meekness and fortitude. Himself as it were under wardship, his Primacy reduced to a Vicarage, he was treated as if an imbecile whose affairs must be administered by others.

To some orders of discipline against recusants and against "no-sacrament ministers," we find his signature "Edmund Cantuar:"; and to some other Papers, — now to hush a college strife, and now to levy alms for a penitent Jesuit.[2] Upon two occasions, we find

[1] Lodge, I. 367, 368. [2] Strype's Grindal, 231, 245, 249–253, 263.

him officiating in the consecration of bishops.[1] But when commissions were issued for metropolitan visitations,[2] and when "the noted preachers and other ecclesiastical persons" needed special exhortation,[3] the necessary Papers were signed by the Vicar-General in behalf of "My Lord's Grace of Canterbury;" or, "*in tempore Reverendi Patris D. Edmundi Grindal.*"[4]

When the Convocation of 1580–1 met, as usual in connection with the meeting of Parliament, it "appeared rather a trunk than a body, because Edmund Grindal, Archbishop of Canterbury, groaning under the queen's displeasure, was forbidden access to the Convocation. Whereupon it began sadly (not to say sullenly) without the solemnity of a sermon, abruptly entering upon the small business they had to do. Some hotspurs therein motioned that they should refuse to meet together till their company were completed and the Archbishop restored unto them. But the gravity of the rest soon retrenched this distemper."[5] By virtue of "an instrument of substitution

[1] Strype's Grindal, 256.

[2] Ibid., 256, 267.

[3] Ibid., 243. "Remains of Grindal," P. Soc.'s edit., 409.

[4] Strype's Grindal, 271.

Most writers suppose that Grindal was restored to the exercise of his ecclesiastical jurisdiction in 1582. This opinion seems to be derived from Strype (Life of Grindal, p. 271), who says, "Soon after in this year, 1582, Aubrey had the sole jurisdiction and office of Vicar-General; the Writs and Instruments from this time running all along in his name, and no name of Clark henceforward mentioned."

From this fact Strype "is apt to think, that from henceforth our Archbishop . . . . was restored to the exercise of his ecclesiastical jurisdiction." From the same fact, I am apt to think only, that henceforth Aubrey, *without Clark*, had "the *sole* jurisdiction;" that the writs and instruments from this time ran all along in *Aubrey's* name, not Grindal's. If so, Grindal was not restored.

[5] Fuller, Bk. IX. p. 119.

from the Archbishop," Aylmer, Bishop of London, presided as his Deputy.[1]

At their first meeting, the Convocation drew up a Petition to the queen; representing "their grief that the Reverend Father whose life had been without reproach and without suspicion, who had suffered persecution and exile for the cause of the Gospel, who had kept clear of Popery on the one hand, and of schism on the other, should have given so grave and lasting offence to her Majesty; and that, not so much through perverseness as through conscience; and praying her not only to lift up the Archbishop broken and feeble through grief, but to restore the Church to him, and him to the Church, to her subjects, to his brethren, to foreign nations, and—in a word—to the world."[2] But the Earl of Leicester was at hand to prosecute Julio's revenge and his own; urging artfully upon her Majesty, that a patron of prophesyings was no better than a patron of that which "would prove the bane of the Church and Commonwealth." He prevailed; first, for delays, and then for a denial of the Petition.[3]

Soon after the Convocation had been adjourned,[4] the Archbishop's sight began to fail; and, though for some time he clung to the hope of recovery, his malady increased to complete blindness. Had Julio "touched" him? In the mean time, unwilling to retain an office in which he was crippled, partly by the dispensation of God and partly by the displeasure of his sovereign, he had desired her to accept his

[1] Strype's Grindal, 257.

[2] Fuller, Bk. IX. pp. 120, 121. Strype's Grindal, 257.

[3] Fuller, Bk. IX. pp. 121, 130.

[4] Holingshed, IV. 505, 772.

resignation,[1] — "having made great suit to be removed,"[2] — which she had refused to do. But in January, 1582–3, she not only saw fit to require it,[3] but also to require that it should take place as soon as the twenty-fifth day of March, disregarding the special reasons which he had urged for its delay until September. "To this her order he humbly submitted, and withal thanked her that, of her gracious goodness, she had offered him an honorable pension for the few and evil days which he had yet to live."[4] But he asked "his constant friend the Lord Treasurer Burleigh," to intercede with her Majesty to grant him Croyden House with some small adjoining grounds, because it was near to London and pertained to his See; he "having not at that hour any house of his own to put his head in after he should remove from Lambeth."[5]

But, although "the Archbishop was now ready to resign his bishopric" at the time appointed,[6] yet "the going through with the resignation was not then compassed."[7] An unexpected obstacle had intervened. Her Highness had desired the Bishop of Worcester to fill the Archiepiscopal chair as soon as it should be vacated; and Grindal, who had a high esteem of his lordship's capacity, had seconded her Majesty's desire. But Whitgift had utterly refused; and in person had implored the royal pardon for so doing, at the same time iterating that no condition or consideration could induce him to accede to her

1 "Remains," 397.
2 Birch, I. 35; Faunt to Bacon.
3 Strype's Grindal, 277.
4 Ibid., 277, 284. "Remains," 397, 398.
5 Strype's Grindal, 284. "Remains," 399.
6 Strype's Grindal, 285.
7 Ibid., 286.

Majesty's proposition while Grindal should still be living. Whereupon she abandoned her purpose; making a virtue of necessity by declaring that, "as she had made the good old man an archbishop, an archbishop he should die."[1]

But it was not the whole of the Archbishop's infirmity, that "the sun and the light, the moon and the stars were darkened." He now perceived that "the silver cord was about to be loosed, and the golden bowl to be broken;" and, after having set his house in order, he expired in his humble retreat at Croyden,[2] on the sixth day of July, 1583, in the sixty-fourth year of his age. In his will, which was made about two months before his death, he "bequeathed his soul into the hand of his Heavenly Father," in the name of Christ; "his body to be buried in the choir of Croyden church;" and his "New Testament of Jesus Christ, in Greek of Steven's impression"—"one of the finest and correctest editions that ever was"—"to her Majesty, humbly beseeching her the same to accept at his hands as an argument of his dutiful and loving heart towards her Highness."[3] He was never married; but made "his book his bride, and his study his bridechamber."[4]

Thus—at peace with the world, at peace with her who had consigned him to unmerited disgrace—Edmund Grindal rendered back his soul; "his loss bewailed by the great body of the people; his name—long fragrant to those who knew him—embalmed

[1] Sir George Paule's Life of Whitgift, Sec. 50. Fuller, Bk. IX. p. 163. Strype's Whitgift, 111.

[2] Holingshed, IV. 773. Stow, 697. Birch, I. 35, note.

[3] Strype's Grindal, 287.

[4] Holingshed, IV. 505.

in the memory of the poor; and himself honored by the sweetest poet of the day as the model of a meek and lowly pastor."[1] "The good name which he left behind him was a monument perpetual, because virtue was the founder of the same."[2]

"Your loving letters, dated 20 October, written frankly and cordially,[3] have so thoroughly satisfied me touching that rude report of which you do solemnly protest yourself to be clear, that now I do know what to say in your behalf at all times when I do hear any report thereof.

"You say, also, that you are not lordly; that you do not set by that lordly state. I did not charge you with it: But since you say so of yourself, I will add this, that I trust you have learned a better lesson than the common sort of men have. For as the manner is now, the proud man will say that he is not proud; and the covetous man will say that he setteth not by money. I hope you do say of yourself as you are, and that you are as you do say. And I say further of you, that to be in the fire and not to burn, to touch pitch and not to be defiled therewith, to walk among thorns and not to be pricked with them, argueth a special and divine preservation; nor is it granted to every one. And if you, whom Policy hath made a great lord, be not lordly, but do keep your humble and strait course of a loving brother and minister of Christ's Gospel, shall I say that you are a Phœnix? I will say, that you are most happily, by God's special grace, preserved and directed.

1 "Remains," Biographical notice, p. xiii. note 7.

2 Holingshed, IV. 506.

3 "Sine fuco aut fastu."

"You do speak, I think, of your affection and of the disposition of your heart,—that it is not lordly nor liketh lordly state. Truly, for my part, I do love you so well that I can both easily think that it is true which you do write of yourself, and also wish that it be so with all my heart. But yet your state, your port, your train of men waiting on you in the streets, your gentleman-usher going before you with bare head, your family full of idle serving men, and so the rest of your *apparatus*, in the world and sight of men, is very lordly. . . . . It may be that the same Policy which makes you a great lord, doth also lay on you the charge of this lordly port and state.[1] But doth the Lord Jesus, whose minister you do rejoice to be, charge you as his minister with it? I think, nay. If then it be Policy only which doth it, I suppose that, besides your own misliking of that state, this one thing might make your *nay* of it, and stir you up to pray and sue that you may be discharged of that *stately* charge. . . . . But if, without the charge[2] of Policy, you be contented of yourself to take this charge and state upon you, your fault is the greater, and it doth bewray in you a desire and liking of lordly state: Which is one of the great stains which Popery hath left behind in this Church of England.

"Be you indeed, as you say you are, not lordly.

[1] Sampson does not here express a *doubt*, but admits a known fact. At the opening of Elizabeth's reign, he wrote to his friend and "father" Peter Martyr, that "in the case of bishops so much expense *must* always be incurred for their *equipages, retainers, and attendance at Court*, that a very small portion of their revenue is left for . . . . the support of learned men, the relief of the poor," &c., &c. (Zurich Letters, p. 2.)

[2] That is, the burden imposed.

Lay abroad your gifts in labor; and dispose that which is committed to you, in maintaining of laborers and laboring in the harvest of the Lord Jesus. So shall you indeed show yourself to be a brother, yea, a father, a feeder and cherisher of Christ's poor servants and people; a laborer yourself and a cherisher of laborers, and a faithful disposer of that Patrimony of Christ which is committed to you. . . . .

"I do not well understand what you do mean by those Puritans; because you do use a dark phrase noting them to hold a *pure* superstition. Till I be further instructed in this, I say, that if Puritans now be noted to be such as do revive the old rotten heresy of Novatus, from whom the old καθαροί did spring, I do not know any in England which do hold that desperate doctrine. But if that be true which a German writer hath published,—'The Novatians, Hieronymo being witness, alway dissembled[1] penitence, claimed the faculty of teaching in the Church, wished that the ceremonies should be observed, but yet hated the custom of the primitive Church,'—if this authority be true, and you do call this kind of men Puritans, indeed the Church of England is full of them. Neither is there any state or degree of office in this Church, in which there are not some of these. These do swarm in great numbers, as bees in fair weather; so are they cherished. The Lord reform them, and either make them more profitable workmen, or turn them out and put better in their places. Justly, by this authority, may a number of our Churchmen be called Puritans. The Lord purge them, and make them more pure. But

[1] Affected.

unjustly to impose this name on brethren, with whose doctrine and life no man can justly find fault, is to rend the seamless coat of Christ, and to make a schism incurable in the Church, and to lay a stumbling-block to the course of the Gospel. And woe unto the man by whom an offence cometh! . . . .

"I never heard you accused for surprising any press or print. But that, if some prints had been suppressed, it had made much more for the edifying of the Church in godly quietness and sincerity, than the publishing of them hath done.

"You do say, that you do love some godly brethren which do wish that such things as are amiss were reformed. As you are in credit, place, and calling, above them, so go before them in procuring the orderly way of Reformation. So shall your inferiors by your example be encouraged, and in well-doing join with you.

"Thus occasioned by your loving letters, I have answered some points of them with old, familiar simplicity, trusting that you will not mislike my simple dealing. Assuredly, I do wish as well to you as he that wisheth the best. The Lord Jesus direct you by his Spirit to think and do that which is pleasing in his sight; and that whereof you may have comfort in that day. Leicester, 9 November, 1574. Yours in Christ,

"THO. SAMPSON."[1]

This letter, no less interesting for its exhibition of certain Puritan sentiments, than remarkable for its

[1] Strype's Parker, Append., No. XCIV. Compare also Strype's Grindal, 301, and Strype's Parker, 468.

plain-speaking and for its brotherly spirit, was addressed to Grindal when Archbishop of York. It indicates the tenor and spirit of letters preceding it, which we cannot but regret are wanting in our collections. Sampson, as has been mentioned under the proper date, had been deprived for his non-conformity, and was now in comparative obscurity as the humble Master of Leicester Hospital. Yet, but for his non-conformity — for he had no sympathy with Cartwright's scheme of Presbytery[1] — he might have enjoyed the queen's favor.[2] He was highly esteemed by Grindal "as a man whose learning was equal to his piety."[3]

The mildness and gentleness of the Archbishop — to whom such letters might be freely addressed without offence, and who could reply as is indicated in the one which we have given — are here no less evident than his urbanity and his esteem for his dissenting brethren. We measure the nobleness of his spirit and bearing, under what to most men would seem to justify resentment, by the standard of a primitive Apostle: "For what glory is it, if, when ye are buffeted for your faults, ye take it patiently? but if, when ye do well, ye take it patiently, this is acceptable with God."[4] The same Christ-like spirit, Grindal signally manifested by his dignified, unmurmuring, and placid submission to royal chastisement.

Grindal, in an important but qualified sense, was a Puritan; a *conforming* Puritan, like Parkhurst, Bishop

[1] Zurich Letters, No. CLXXXII. p. 435; Grindal to Bullinger.

[2] Ibid., No. CXI. p. 243; Grindal to Bullinger.

[3] Ibid., No. CXXI. p. 273.

[4] 1 Peter ii. 20.

of Norwich, and Pilkington, Bishop of Durham; both, at this time, in their graves. When first elected to the See of London, he had a serious struggle with himself whether he could accept an office in which he would be required to adopt "the appearances and shadows of Popery in the use of the Habits and some other rites."[1] At length he concluded to enter upon the bishopric and to conform obediently to what he disliked; reasoning that neither himself nor his brethren ought—for the sake of a few ceremonials not in themselves unlawful—to desert a Church whose constitution and ritual were already fixed by law; especially as their places would otherwise "verily" be filled by "a papistical, or at least a Lutherano-papistical ministry, or none at all;"[2] and again especially, as "the habits were proposed as a matter of indifference, and enjoined only for the sake of order and due obedience to the laws;"[3] and still more especially, as "the pure doctrine of the Gospel remained in all its integrity and freedom."[4] His true position was distinctly and publicly avowed in his own Court in 1567: "I had *rather* minister without the cope and surplice, but for order's sake and *obedience to my prince*."[5] It was also declared about the same time, and with the utmost solemnity, in his letters to foreign divines: "We who are now bishops, on our first return, and before we entered on our ministry, contended long and earnestly for the removal of those things,"—the vestments and certain ceremo-

[1] Strype's Grindal, 28, 295.

[2] Zurich Letters, No. CXI. pp. 243, 244. No. CXXI. p. 275; Grindal to Bullinger.

[3] Ibid., 274.

[4] Ibid., 243.

[5] "Remains," p. 211. *Ante*, Vol. I. p. 315.

nies;[1] "and we call Almighty God to witness that . . . . it is not owing to us that vestments of this kind have not been altogether done away with: so far from it, that we most solemnly make oath, that we have *hitherto*" — 1567 — "labored with all earnestness, fidelity, and diligence to effect what our brethren" — the Puritans — "require, and what we ourselves" — Grindal and Horn — "wish. But now we are brought into such straits, what is to be done, but that, since we cannot do what we would, we should do in the Lord what we can?[2] We receive, it is true, — or rather *tolerate* until the Lord shall give us better times, — the interrogations to infants, and the sign of the cross in baptism, and kneeling at the Lord's Supper."[3]

But while many of the bishops — as has been narrated — fearfully persecuted the Puritans for their non-conformity, we have yet to find a single instance in which Grindal, of himself, deposed from the ministry or consigned to prison any person for this reason alone. While Horn, Bishop of Winchester, continued to regard the bishops as "*badly habited*," he could rail at those who scrupled the habits, styling them men "deficient both in sagacity and sense;"[4] and while Cox, Bishop of Ely, could say, "equally with themselves," — the Puritans, — "we seriously reject and condemn the popish dress," he could also say, that they who were offended at those things which have been sanctioned by the laws were "neither good pastors nor pious laymen."[5]

[1] Zurich Letters, p. 243; Grindal to Bullinger, in 1566.

[2] Ibid., 275.

[3] Ibid., 277.

[4] Ibid., No. CLV. pp. 355, 356; Horn to Bullinger, Aug., 1571.

[5] Ibid., No. CLXI. p. 389; Cox to Gaulter in 1572.

Not so with Grindal. We do not find him using words of contempt or invective towards those who, like Coverdale, Fox, and Sampson, refused to conform to the vestiarian laws. On the contrary, he could honestly express his affection for dissenters as godly brethren, and was "never accused for surprising any press or print." In his official capacity as an associate minister of the law, he was obliged to be privy to the deprivation of some, yet not without pleading with them even to "tears."[1] In one instance, but in the same official capacity, he submitted to the command of his sovereign, by sending to prison men and women who had transgressed the Statute of Uniformity; but it was for more than non-conformity. It was "not only for absenting themselves from their parish churches, ... but also because they had gathered together and made assemblies, using prayers and preachings, yea, and ministering the sacraments among themselves."[2] At the same time he decreed the like sentence upon *others*, — apparently Bonham and Crane,[3] — who, "besides this, had ordained ministers, elders, and deacons, after their own way."[4] Such things — but particularly the conduct of the last-named party — were repugnant to all his ideas of Christian propriety, and a violation of that unity of the National Church which he, in common with almost all others, held as sacred. But even these parties he treated fraternally; striving to convince them, and to win them to obedience of the laws. To his judicial sentence against Separatists, he "thought

[1] *Ante*, Vol. I. p. 234.

[2] "Remains," 202. *Ante*, Vol. I. p. 307.

[3] Strype's Grindal, 153 – 156.

[4] Zurich Letters, No. CXXXV. p. 314; Grindal to Bullinger.

himself bound as a faithful and careful overseer of the Church;" and, as overseer and *magistrate*, he certainly was.[1] Unlike many other bishops whose severities we have described, he did not *exceed* the law.

So reluctant was he to annoy his Puritan brethren about gowns and caps, that Archbishop Parker thought him unfit for the diocese of London, where non-conformity was rife, and was therefore glad of his translation to York;[2] so reluctant, that even "the Puritan party"—Presbyterianism had not then been propounded—"confided much in him, and gave out that my Lord of London was their own, and that all he did was upon a force, and unwillingly;"[3] so reluctant, that Archbishop Parker complained that he himself was obliged to enforce discipline in the diocese of London, "another man's charge;"[4] so reluctant, that "he would not run of himself; yea, would *hardly answer the spur* in pressing conformity."[5]

In the light of all these things, we see that, so far as the vestiarian controversy, interrogations to infants at baptism, the sign of the cross in baptism, and kneeling at the Lord's Supper were concerned, Grindal, in his opinions and sympathies, was a Puritan; yet a reluctant though obedient conformist.[6] But with

[1] Strype's Grindal, 295, 302.

[2] Ibid., 158, 161.

[3] Ibid., 105.

[4] Ibid.

[5] Fuller, Bk. IX. p. 81.

[6] *Ante*, Vol. I. pp. 332, 333.

On this point, I may be met by a letter long ascribed to Grindal, to show that, so far from having respect and sympathy for the Puritans, he was most bitter against them. The superscription to the letter is as it stands in Murdin, p. 275. From the letter, I select only what is in point.

"From the Bishop of London (Ed. Grindall) to the Lord Treasurer, June 26, 1574."

"My good Lord: .... Your lordship's last speech unto me hath so troubled me, that I could not have endured thus long, if the testimony of a good conscience had not greatly relieved me. My Lord, no man sus-

other matters afterwards agitated — the doctrines of Cartwright and the scheme of a Presbyterian Establishment — he had no sympathy; nor had Humphrey or Sampson, Pilkington or Parkhurst. He was satisfied with the prelatic constitution of the Church, though not with the ecclesiastical autocracy of the prince.

Cartwright, at the outset of his career, he thought worthy of strict discipline. "I am credibly informed," said he in a letter to Cecil, who was Chancellor of the

taineth more wrongs than I do. I well hoped that no devil had been so impudent to have charged me with so great and manifest an untruth. Yet some incarnate, sleepless devil hath wrought me this wrong. . . . . I claim . . . . to be heard, the accuser to be brought forth, and that I may be lawfully tried, and so will I stand to justice, and refuse all mercy. If I should openly preach, write, and publicly proceed against these innovators, disturbers of the State, and notwithstanding privily consent with them, maintain them, and aid them, truly no punishment were too hard for me; for I would think myself unworthy to live in any commonwealth. But being most untruly charged herewithal, while I remain unpurged, I remain blotted and defaced, my office is slandered, and the Gospel which I preach *male audit.* My Lord, if ever you favored me, if you be a friend to equity, or love the Gospel of God, I require it, I crave it at your hands, that you will be a means unto her Majesty, that I may come to my trial, and be indifferently heard. . . . . Thus hoping that by your good means my grieved mind shall shortly be eased, I humbly take my leave. . . . . Your lordship's at command,

"Ed. London."

"From my house at Fulham, this June 26, 1574.

"To the right Honorable my singular good Lord, the Lord Treasurer of England."

Our historians have naturally been misled by the name "Grindall" *over* this letter (an error of the editor or of the printer), and by the signature "Ed. London," so similar to "Edm. London," Grindal's signature when occupying that See. With these two corresponding indices, it is not a matter of surprise that the *date* of the letter — sufficient to denote the typographical error — should have been overlooked. Murdin has, indeed, corrected it, at the end of his volume; but few persons look at *errata.*

It is therefore an unfortunate, because unjust, inference which Sir James Mackintosh has made from the letter, — "Grindal's toleration, therefore, may be imputed to *imbecility.*" (Vol. III. Chap. V. p. 288. London edit., 1831.)

University of Cambridge, "that he maketh in his lectures daily invectives against the extern policy and distinction of states" — inequality of the clergy — "in the ecclesiastical government of this realm. . . . . For reforming whereof, if it please you to know my opinion, I wish you wrote your letters to the Vice-Chancellor with expedition, willing him to command the said Cartwright and all his adherents to silence, both in schools and pulpits; and afterward, upon examining and hearing the matters past, ... either to reduce the offenders to conformity, or to proceed to their punishment by expulsion out of their colleges, or out of the University, as the cause shall require. And also, that the Vice-Chancellor do not suffer the said Cartwright to proceed Doctor of Divinity at this Commencement, which he now sueth for. For, besides the singularity above rehearsed, the said Cartwright is not conformable in his apparel; contemning also many other laudable orders of the University. Thus I cease to trouble you, and commend you heartily to the grace of God. St. Paul's, June 24, 1570."[1]

[1] Strype's Grindal, 162.

It is said indeed, that, as "an opponent of Cartwright," Grindal went much further; styling his followers "a fanatical and incurable faction, who should be with all expedition severely punished," and recommending to the Lords of the Council, that "it were not amiss that six of the most desperate of them should be sent to the common jail of Cambridge, and six likewise to Oxford, and some others of them to other jails, as to your wisdoms shall be thought expedient." (Marsden's "Early Puritans," p. 73.)

These are indeed Grindal's words; but the letter from which they are taken, and which is thus applied, had no more reference to Cartwright and his followers than to Lucifer and his; but to certain violent, extreme, and apparently dishonest *Separatists*, of whom Bonham and Crane were the leaders (*ante*, p. 298, note), whom his lordship had committed and liberated about the same time that he did the

Nor was Grindal averse, in all cases, to the punishment of deprivation. He was indeed *willing* that some who held livings should be deprived of them. These were indeed non-conformists; but they were not peaceable non-conformists. They were incumbents who denounced the Church as no Church, and who performed no ecclesiastical duties, — or, at least, those whom he believed to be such. He thought them out of place; affirming rightly enough,[1] — and his words were as applicable to the *boys* who held benefices as to the men,[2] — "The benefice is given for the office. If they will do no office, let them enjoy no benefit."

Only in one other instance do we find Grindal recommending severity; in the case of certain Anabaptists, and in the very letter in which he was pleading for their lives.[3] In this instance he urged banishment from the realm; and death, if the convicts should return. But, it should be remembered, these men were not only religious, but *political* here-

Plumbers' Hall offenders, but who afterwards *seem* to have broken the promises on condition of which they had been enlarged. Their original offence had been committed, and this letter written, before Cartwright's offensive lectures had been commenced. Besides, Cartwright was no leader of *such* men; for they not only separated from the communion of the Church, — a step which Cartwright never allowed, — but organized a church, or churches, and even ordained their clergy, and excommunicated their offending members. These points clearly show Mr. Marsden's mistake; and are sufficiently verified by the authority which he cites, — Grindal's letter in the "Remains of Grindal," by the Parker Society, p. 319, — also by Strype's Grindal, 153 - 156, compared with the "Zurich Letters," second edition, p. 314, Grindal to Bullinger.

J. B. Marsden, M. A., Vicar of Great Missenden, England. His volumes — "The History of the Early Puritans," London, 1850, and "The History of the Later Puritans," London, 1853 — will be read with pleasure and profit.

[1] Strype's Parker, 414. Strype's Grindal, 302.

[2] Zurich Letters, 247, 271.

[3] Chap. I. of this volume.

tics, dangerous to the Commonwealth. How much farther was this from Puritanism, than the like policy towards political disorganizers which obtained in the Colony of Massachusetts Bay?

That this prelate, whose whole life was an example of "the greatest" of Christian virtues, could sink so low in the scale of humanity as to advise torture for the sake of "a good mass of money," few will be credulous enough to believe. Yet we find it slyly inserted in a corner, by a standard though a partisan historian.[1] The select language in which it is couched, does not escape our notice; neither do we fail to see that it yet contains, not an insinuation, but a charge; and that by most readers it would be naturally taken as such and as sustained by the best possible evidence, — Grindal's own. It must have been ungenerously intended to be so taken; unless, indeed, the writer failed to understand a plain English letter. To exonerate Grindal from a charge so atrocious, we simply deny it, and challenge in proof his own letter, — the document whence it has been too inconsiderately if not too culpably derived.[2]

[1] Lingard, VIII. 148, note.

[2] The letter is as follows; and is preserved in Haynes's State Papers, p. 395: —

"Please it your Honors to understand, that, whereas we labored the 10th of this month to examine the Sayer and Hearers of the Mass at my Lady Carew's house, ... so it is we can come to no knowledge of any more matter. . . . . Some think that if this priest *haverd* might be put to some kind of torment, and so driven to confess what he knoweth, he might gain the Queen's Majesty a good mass of money by the Masses that he hath said: But this we refer to your lordships' wisdom, and so commit the same to Almighty God. 13 Septembris, 1562. Your honorable lordships at commandment.

"EDM. LONDON,
RICHARDE ELY.

"To the Right Honorable and our very good Lords, the Lords of the Queen's Majesty's most honorable Privy Council."

Dr. Lingard's words are: "In

We linger upon the instructive controversy between Archbishop Grindal and the queen. Viewed only as a passage-at-arms between two resolute wills; or, in its more imposing aspect, as a strife between the highest Dignitary of the State and the highest Dignitary of the Church about their respective prerogatives, it is of little interest. They were at issue on a graver question, — a question involving the spiritual wealth or poverty, fulness or famine, of a whole people; and, by consequence, their morality, their peace, their civil prosperity. It was the question whether the clergy — at that time almost the only educators of the public mind — should be ignorant or enlightened; whether the pulpit should be dumb or eloquent; whether God's grand ordinance for purifying the lives and saving the souls of men should be cherished or crushed. Elizabeth feared that God's Establishment would undermine hers; that the clergy, knowing too much and preaching too much, would spoil an unquestioning and obsequious people. Archbishop Grindal knew that men could not preach except they understood the Oracles of God; that a well-taught clergy, proclaiming the glad tidings of the Gospel and expounding its broad

Haynes is a singular letter to the Council from the Bishops of London and Ely; who, having examined the persons taken at Mass at Lady Carew's, suggested that the priest should be tortured to make him confess the names of those who had attended on other occasions." (Lingard, VIII. 148, note.)

I submit to the candid reader whether the letter of Cox and Grindal does, or does not, "suggest that the priest *should be* tortured;" whether, upon a fair and natural construction of its language, it contains, or does not contain, anything more than the statement of *a fact*, — which, as the servants of the Crown, the bishops were in duty bound to make; the statement that *some people thought* so and so; in other words, that probably *a great many* masses had been said by only this one priest.

and heavenly morality, were essential as the Pillars of the Church and the Conservators of the State. Above all, he knew that the ordinance of preaching was sacred as the ark of God, and should not be touched. She would not abandon her doctrine. He could not yield such convictions.

In no one act did Elizabeth ever appear to such disadvantage in the eyes of her subjects. The popular voice was against her, and arrested her purpose of deposition, although she did not recede from the ground she had taken. Yet, while the Monarch could not coerce the Christian, she was deplorably triumphant in sustaining her unchristian policy,— for there was no *other* Grindal in her hierarchy,— a policy which wrought shame and ineffable woe to the Church, and which erelong humbled the Crown in the dust. History has justified the Prelate. Instead of "Contumacy," her verdict is, "Christian heroism." Posterity accepts it, and reveres his name.

Edmund Grindal took his stand for God. Elizabeth took hers for herself. His action was a towering, manly *fact;* mutely rebuking before the Christian world the monstrous pretensions of his sovereign. Hers was a petulant struggle, which exposed, as widely, her weakness. He stood, a champion for his Lord the Christ; she, a potentate powerless to wring submission from a meek and lowly priest.

CHAPTER XIII.

WHITGIFT'S THREE ARTICLES.

The Puritans, repressed by the Severities of 1574, recover Courage and Preferments. — Whitgift's Affection towards Puritanism is stimulated by the Queen's special Charge. — The Things which "were out of Square." — The Archbishop's Three Articles. — His railing Sermon at Paul's Cross. — The Articles sent forth. — The Resistance of the Puritan Clergy. — The Archbishop in Discussion with Underdown and others. — The Archbishop in Person resisted on Legal Grounds. — Cooper, Bishop of Winchester, in Argument to enforce Subscription. — Remonstrances against enforcing the Three Articles. — The Archbishop himself suspends Fourteen Ministers of Kent. — His Conference with those who interceded for their Restoration. — The Prayer of the People and Clergy of Kent to the Archbishop for Mr. Stroud. — The Prayer of the suspended Ministers of Kent to the Privy Council. — Like Supplications to the Council from other Counties. — The Archbishop and the Council. — The real Question now at Issue. — The Puritans take their Stand upon the Law.

1583.

"Our Puritan brethren, the innovators who have been striving to strike out for us a new form of a Church, are lying in concealment; partly silenced by a most able Treatise,[1] and partly terrified by the authority of our queen, — a sincere lover of truth and peace, — who attacks them with the severity of the law. For our government is apprehensive that danger may arise from frivolous and unnecessary innovations. They have grown wonderfully cool, and are not doing us much harm; except that from time to time they vomit forth the venom of spite in

[1] Whitgift's "Reply."

secret. Indeed, these contentious, or, if you choose, vainglorious and certainly mischievous men, who, by their ungovernable zeal for discord, were retarding the free progress of the Gospel among us, drawing away the people and alluring the nobility into their net, — into what they call *purity,* — are now silenced, skulk about, and are become of no importance. Meanwhile we know not *what monstrosities they are hatching in secret.*"[1] Such was the condition of the Puritans in 1574 and 1576.

Thus the campaign of the Queen's Commissioners in the winter of 1573–4, which immediately followed her order for Cartwright's arrest, had had its *first* natural effect upon the Puritans, — to stun and bewilder them. Yet before the death of Archbishop Parker, illegal severities had produced a reaction in their favor;[2] and when public attention was occupied by the Jesuit mission of 1580–1, they had "found so much favor as almost amounted to a connivance."[3] Notwithstanding these more favorable circumstances, their *open* zeal seems to have been repressed, partly from prudential considerations; partly, perhaps, through an apprehension awakened by the movements of the Separatists.[4] At the same time they had regained strength, position, and Church prefer-

[1] Zurich Letters, Nos. CXCIX. p. 475; CCII. p. 478; CCIII. p. 478; CCVI. p. 482; CCVIII. p. 486; CCIX. p. 487; CCXV. p. 499.

I have constructed this paragraph from the letters of Bishops Sandys, Cox, and Horn, written at different times from July, 1574, to August, 1576; as indicated by the references. I have done this merely for the sake of brevity, and without having changed the purport of words or clauses by the collocation.

[2] *Ante*, Vol. I. Chapters XVII., XVIII., XIX.; and Vol. II. Chapter X.

[3] Fuller, Bk. IX. p. 135.

[4] Hooker's "Preface," p. 144.

ments, in a quiet way, through their friends and patrons at Court.[1] Such was their condition, when Whitgift was inducted to the Primacy on the twenty-third day of September, 1583.[2]

By his noted controversy with Cartwright, Whitgift had pledged himself to the extreme of Prelacy, and to the straitest and most unsparing Precisianism. By the same process, his idea of the Puritans — like the Bishop of Ely's — had come to be that of men "hatching monstrosities;"[3] cousins-german to Milton's "Sin." In these qualifications, doubtless, we find the reasons which determined her Majesty's selection of him as her next Primate of Canterbury. "There could be no danger of *his* Grindalizing, by winking at the plots and practices of the Puritan faction."[4] Yet, to stimulate his zeal, her Majesty "straitly" gave him a formal charge "to be vigilant and careful for the reducing of.... all ministers.... to the settled orders and government;"[5] "to restore the Discipline of the Church and the Uniformity in the Service of God established by Parliament, which, through the connivance of the Prelates, the obstinacy of the Puritans, and the power of some Noblemen, was run out of square."[6] In other words, "she referred all ecclesiastical business wholly to Whitgift's management;"[7] constituting him her Vicar-General, her Plenipotentiary, her "other self," to whom were delegated the powers of her ecclesiastical supremacy.

1 Strype's Whitgift, 114.

2 Ibid., 113. Sir Geo. Paule's Life of Whitgift, Sec. 51, p. 28. Stow, 697.

3 Zurich Letters, p. 475.

4 Heylin's Presb., Bk. VII. Sec. 36.

5 Paule's Whitgift, Sec. 54, p. 30.

6 Camden, 288.

7 Collier, VII. 6.

There were ministers who questioned this supremacy; there were "No-Sacrament ministers;" there were anti-prelatic ministers; there were Separatists; and there were private meetings held on pretence only — it was believed — of reading the Bible and other good books, of catechising and instructing youth, and of praying and conferring together; which last sort of assemblies, particularly, were thought "dangerous to the Church." Besides, some preachers, it was thought, had not been ordained, and some had been "ordained differently from the English Book of conferring Holy Orders." These were the things that were "run out of square."[1]

The Church — partly on account of these things — "was evidently now but in a tottering condition."[2] To meet the emergency, the new Archbishop girded up his loins, and "fell to a flat argument from authority."[3] Certain Articles were drawn up, signed (as orders) by himself and other bishops, and sanctioned by the private connivance of the queen, before the month of September had expired. The most prominent of these were the three which were called, by way of distinction, "Whitgift's Articles."

The first was a declaration, that her Majesty hath the sole sovereignty over all her born subjects, "of what estate ecclesiastical or temporal soever they be."

The second, a declaration that the Book of Common Prayer and of Ordering[4] bishops, priests, and

[1] Camden, 288. Strype's Whitgift, 115, and margin.

[2] Strype's Whitgift, 115.

[3] Fuller, Bk. IX. p. 170.

[4] "And *another* Book of Ordaining," &c., says Camden, more explicitly. This *other* Book, I suppose to have been that contained in Sparrow's Collection, pp. 135 – 164. It appears there without date; but Sparrow, in his table of Contents, gives it the date of 1559. It is

deacons, containeth nothing contrary to the Word of God; that the same may be lawfully used; and that the subscriber himself will use the prescribed Form of Prayer and administering the sacraments, and none other.

The third, an approval of the Articles of the synod in the year 1562, set forth by the queen's authority; and a declaration that all those Articles are agreeable to the Word of God.

By other Articles, it was forbidden that any person should exercise any ecclesiastical function, unless he did first consent to, and subscribe, all the above declarations; and unless he had been admitted to holy Orders according to the manner of the Church of England. It was also ordered, in the same missive, that all religious exercises in private places and in families — others than the families being present — should be utterly suppressed; "seeing the same was *never permitted as lawful* under any Christian magistrate, but is a manifest sign of schism and a cause of contention in the Church"! All persons in ecclesiastical Orders were also peremptorily required always to wear the vestments prescribed.

In the month of October, his Grace of Canterbury issued orders throughout his Province for enforcing all the above Articles, and some others of minor importance.[1]

probably the same which was authorized by the Act 5 and 6 Edw. VI. Cap. II. Sec. IV.; there described as being appended to the Act, but which is not to be found on the Roll or in the Parliament Office. The date of this Book must have been — that of the Act — 1551–2; not 1559. This same Book was "declared and enacted to be used and observed" by the Act 8 Eliz. Cap. I.; A. D. 1566.

[1] Strype's Whitgift, 114 – 117. Camden, 288. Fuller, Bk. IX. p. 170.

Except the requisition of episcopal ordination, there was nothing new in these demands upon the clergy. They were substantially the same as those to which subscription had been imposed in 1571 and in 1573–4. The oath of Supremacy was required by the Act 1 Elizabeth Cap. I. Sec. IX., as a condition of ecclesiastical office; and the Puritans had largely, and without scruple, accepted it as modified by the queen in her injunctions and by her second Parliament;[1] a modification expressed in the first of Whitgift's Articles. His third Article required an approval of *all* "The Thirty-Nine Articles," and of *all* as being agreeable to the Word of God; whereas the statute[2] required only a declaration of assent, and subscription, to "all the Articles of Religion which *only* concern the confession of the true Christian faith and the doctrine of the sacraments." *No part* of his second Article was required by any law; for the Act of Uniformity enjoined only the *using* — not a *promise* to use — the forms prescribed. The Article requiring ordination according to the English form was in direct conflict with the statute which expressly recognized "*any other* form of Consecration or Ordering." It was a new shaft; expressly fitted against Cartwright and others who had received ordination in foreign Reformed Churches.

For publishing and enforcing these, the Archbishop had derived no authority from the queen, for she could not delegate what she did not possess, and she did not possess authority to make laws for the Church which were contrary to those of the realm; nor could she legally delegate any powers which she did

[1] 5 Eliz. Cap. XII. Sec. XI. [2] 13 Eliz. Cap. XII. Sec. I.

possess, except by Letters Patent under the Great Seal of England,[1] — which Letters the Archbishop had not. Therefore, in this instance, he did not act as an officer of the Crown, but on his own authority, — an authority derogatory to the laws, derogatory to the queen's prerogative. Had her interest or her whim required it, she could have crushed him under the terrible penalties of a Præmunire, as her father had crushed Wolsey, — and for the same cause. In this respect, there was a wide difference between Whitgift's action and that of the Commissioners in 1573–4, who made like impositions; for *they* were the queen's officers acting under the broad Seal.[2] Yet even this fact did not legally justify their exactions.

Hence it was, that the Puritans — willing to be governed by the queen and her laws, and acquiescing in any legal infliction which they conscientiously incurred — stoutly challenged the autocracy and decrees of the Primate; denied his pretensions as their Lawgiver; and took their stand, not against the statutes, but upon that *modicum of Liberty* which the statutes still allowed. Hence it was, that, more loudly than ever before, they protested — in harmony with the queen's ecclesiastical Supremacy — that "*No one man*, either Archbishop or Lord Bishop, should take upon him to control or have dominion over others that are their fellow-ministers."[3]

[1] 1 Eliz. Cap. I. Sec. VIII.

[2] But the subscription required under the canons of the synod of 1571 was equally illegal with that required by Archbishop Whitgift; because those canons lacked *vigorem legis*, not having been ratified by the royal assent and signature. In Grindal's opinion, the bishops who enforced that subscription were exposed to a Præmunire; and doubtless they were. (Strype's Parker, 322.)

[3] Strype's Whitgift, 124.

The professed object of these Articles was, to secure uniformity. Their real object, to bring Puritanism to its grave. Nor do we say this unadvisedly. We say it — because the Act 1 Elizabeth Cap. II., if enforced, was as sufficient as anything could be to secure uniformity; because subscription to these Articles could not be more potent than the law to insure obedience; because her Majesty, who was *Semper Eadem*, had avowed it as her fixed policy "*to root out* Puritanism and the favorers thereof;"[1] and because, under this Primacy, the prosecutions of the Puritans were pursued with a pertinacity, zest, and — in many instances — barbarity, so far beyond what was necessary merely to secure uniformity, as to denote nothing less than a purpose of extirmination.

In honor of "Queen's-day," — the anniversary of her Majesty's Accession, — and also as a preparatory to the severe regimen about to be installed, his Grace preached at Paul's Cross on the seventeenth day of November, before a courtly auditory. "His sermon," said one who wrote at the time, "was only an invective against the best professors, whom he termed *wayward fellows.* His text was of obedience; that there were three enemies thereof, viz. *papists, anabaptists,* and *wayward persons,* meaning such as lacked reformation. Against these last was his whole bitterness and vehemency. . . . . The choice of that man at this time to be Archbishop maketh me to think, that the Lord is determined to scourge his Church for their unthankfulness."[2]

[1] Strype's Annals, IV. 242.

[2] Birch, I. 42; Faunt to Bacon.

That this description, given by a Puritan connected with the Court, is truthful, will appear by a few extracts from the outline of the sermon as given by Strype in his Life of Whitgift, Append. pp. 42–48:—

This public note of warning had hardly been given, when the cry of the sufferers began to be heard. Hundreds of ministers were suspended from preaching, — a time for repentance being allowed before deprivation; but some scores were deprived at once. Most of them were graduates from the universities; the best ministers of the most laborious preachers in the realm;[1] nor should we fail to notice that this action was but in harmony with her Majesty's plan, — "two or three preachers to a county." And, be it had in remembrance, that this was done when, it is acknowledged, "there was great need of this sort of

"*Thirdly.* Three sorts of persons especially are disobedient: Papists, Anabaptists, and *our* wayward and conceited persons. . . . . These wayward and conceited fellows do not *condemn* magistrates, but *contemn* and despise them. These men will obey, but it is what they list, whom they list, and wherein they list themselves. And all because they cannot be governors themselves. . . . . Paul notes them to be lovers of themselves; to have an outward show of godliness; and to go from house to house, and from table to table; especially to the houses of widows and simple women. It is most truly verified of them, that Augustin said of such kind of men in his time, "What we will is holy, and when, and as long as we will." . . . . The Apostle sets down two special marks of them, viz. that they are evil-speakers and contentious. . . . . Men are naturally prone to speak ill of two kinds of persons, viz. of bishops and magistrates. The original cause is, the Devil. . . . . This hath been always in all ages the lot of bishops, to be evil-spoken of. Christ was called a Samaritan, and that he had a devil. . . . . I myself may be counted a partial judge in this cause. And therefore *I appeal to Him* that knows the justice of my complaint. And I SUMMON, in behalf of myself and my brethren, *those blasphemous* tongues to answer *before the judgment-seat of God,* where they shall receive a just reward of their blasphemous speeches, if they repent not. . . . . Although a man hold all the Articles of Religion and break the unity of the Church, he is not of the Church. Yea, albeit he have never so great a multitude of hearers at his sermons. To divide the Church is as great a fault as to fall into heresy, saith Chrysostom. And yet these men color their contention by the names of Religion, Faith, and Perfection. . . . . These be they of whom Christ speaketh, 'They strain at a gnat and swallow a camel.'"

[1] Neal, I. 157. Brook, I. 47.

ministers in the Church, most of those in Orders not having abilities to preach the Gospel to the ignorant, but only to read the Common Prayer and Homilies;"[1] when the traitorous practices of the Papists had just been discovered in two distinct plots against her Majesty's estate and person;[2] when profane swearing, drunkenness, revelling, gaming, and profanation of the Lord's day, were fashionable vices, cherished in the royal palace and unchecked by the spiritual Courts.[3] "The holy religion reformed and established was judged now to be in imminent danger of being overthrown;" not so much because of rank immorality, not so much because of popish propagandists and popish plots, as by "preachers hotly bent upon a new ecclesiastical discipline," although they had hitherto sought for it only by lawful and dutiful means.[4]

The Puritan clergy were willing to subscribe to the Article respecting her Majesty's authority; and to that concerning the Articles of Religion, *so far as by law* required; but they prayed to be freed from all subscription which, "as they verily thought, the estates of the realm *had not* required." As for the Book of Common Prayer, they were willing to use it, and did use it; they were willing to withhold all censure of it in their public ministry; they were willing to walk in all quiet and Christian behavior towards those who used it in some things more strictly than they did; they were willing to *pledge* themselves to all these things;[5] but they refused to declare that

[1] Strype's Whitgift, 121.
[2] Birch, I. 41.
[3] Neal, I. 154. Birch, I. 39.
[4] Strype's Whitgift, 121, 122.
[5] Brook, I. 289; II. 309.

the Book "contained *nothing* contrary to the Word of God," and to pledge themselves to use unreservedly its forms of prayer and administering of the sacraments. In justifying this refusal, they were sometimes, at least, too stout for the bishops; and even for his Grace of Canterbury, although he "protested that he was ready by learning to defend his 'Three Articles' in manner and form as they were set down, against all mislikers thereof in England or elsewhere."[1]

"To *what* Book of Common Prayer," said one to his Grace, "would your lordship have us subscribe? There be many copies which *differ in many points of weight;* and those which have been printed last have *most declined* to superstition."

The querist was Mr. Underdown, who, with some half-score of his brethren belonging to the diocese of Chichester, had come to Lambeth as suitors to his lordship, that they might be released from subscription to his Articles.

"I mean the Book now used for divine service and administering of the sacraments in the Church of England."

"That is not the Book *established by law* according to the first of Elizabeth; but differeth in more points from the Book of the fifth of Edward the Sixth than the *law of the land* alloweth."

"What is the difference?"

"The calendars are not the same. In many popish particulars, the present exceedeth the former. Among other things, the Book now in use omitteth the advertisement (after the communion) to avoid

[1] Fuller, Bk. IX. p. 148.

the popish adoration in kneeling at the sacrament."

"The calendars are not of the substance of the Book."

"They form a principal part, and the statute calleth it a part."

"What other doubts have you?"

"The Book prescribeth certain parts of the apocrypha to be read in public worship which contain gross errors."

"What errors?"

"The Devil is said to have loved Sara; which is fabulous."

"Is it strange to you that the Devil should love men and women? Do you think the Devil doth not love? . . . . Is there any other reason why you will not subscribe to the Book of Common Prayer?"

"Yes, my lord. If we subscribe to the Book, we must subscribe to the massing apparel."

"Whatever you are discharged from, by any article or injunction, you are not required to subscribe unto it in the Book."

"Who then shall interpret how far our subscription shall extend?"

"Myself and the other bishops. *We know best* what the Book and subscription meaneth."

"But, my lord, we dare not subscribe without protestation."

Some were willing to subscribe the Articles with this protestation in open court, "as far as they are agreeable to the Word of God."[1]

"I will have no protestation. You are not called

[1] Neal, I. 157.

to rule in this Church of England; and you shall not rule, but obey. And unless you subscribe, you shall have no place in the ministry. . . . . You seem to be sober and discreet men. I would not have you depend on any vain fancies; but be ruled and enjoy your places, which, without this subscription, you shall not hold."

"We desire to keep our places, if it may be done with peace of conscience."

With a few words more, the conference was suspended; but the next day resumed,—other bishops being present,—after the Archbishop had rehearsed the substance of the previous conversation, "with some enlargement upon the Devil's loving women." Upon this, the Bishop of London remarked:—

"If you had read either *divinity* or *philosophy*, it would not be strange to you that the Devil should love women."

"My lord," replied Mr. Underdown, gravely, "we have *not* learned any *such* divinity."

"You must subscribe," said the Archbishop. "It will be *much to your advantage;*" an artful inducement which prevailed with some, who, nevertheless, were neglected, forgotten, and troubled in the Courts of the Commissaries as much as before.[1]

"We cannot subscribe, my lord, without protestation," said Mr. Hopkinson, another of the ministers. "There are many things in the Book which belong not to us, or to our ministry. Therefore we desire favor in this subscription."

"You shall subscribe, or you shall enjoy no place in the ministry. And because you are the first who

[1] Neal, I. 157.

have been thus far proceeded against in this case," — they had been suspended, — "you shall be made an example to all others. . . . . You of Sussex have been accounted very disorderly and contentious; . . . . and I mean to proceed strictly with you."

"My lord," replied Mr. Underdown, "the ministers of Sussex have been as well ordered as any in the kingdom, until certain points of popery and heresy were broached among them."

"It would have been a wonder if you had not been quiet" — did his Grace retract? — "seeing you have all done as you pleased, without the least control. *The Devil will be quiet so long.* . . . . If you have any more doubts, propose them now, seeing there are so many bishops to answer them."

"In the rubric before confirmation," said Mr. Hopkinson, "salvation is ascribed to baptism. For whosoever is *baptized is said to be undoubtedly saved.*"

"*Is there* any such thing in the Book?" — a marvellous question from a Primate of the Church.

"Yes, my lord, those are the words."

"Let us see the Book."

Whereupon his Grace, taking lessons of "boys," read as follows: —

"'And that no man shall think that any detriment shall come to children by deferring of their confirmation, he shall know for truth, that it is *certain by God's Word,* that children being baptized have all things necessary to their salvation, and *be undoubtedly saved.*'" [1]

"We would know, my lord," said Mr. Hartwell, another of the suitors, "whether by those last words

[1] Strype's Whitgift, 129.

of the rubric the Book confirmeth this opinion, that the sacrament doth of itself confer grace, *tanquam ex opere operato;* that is, that whosoever is baptized must of necessity be saved *ex opere operato,* though otherwise a hypocrite or infidel."[1]

"The meaning is," replied the Archbishop, "to exclude the popish opinion of confirmation as if it were as necessary as baptism. Therefore, those who have been baptized have all outward things necessary to salvation, even without confirmation. In other words, the Book hath no such meaning as you describe. The words only dissuade from the opinion which the Papists have of their confirmation called *Bishoping,* which they believe to be necessary to salvation and do think that children are not perfectly baptized till they be also bishoped. And therefore they make confirmation a sacrament; and bring their children thereunto being infants. Whereas this Church of England hath no such opinion thereof, but doth use it to this end especially, that children may know what their godfathers promised for them in baptism, and also learn to perform the same. And likewise that it may be known whether the godfathers have performed their promise in seeing these children instructed, as the Book requireth. And *therefore,* that rubric containeth nothing contrary to the Word of God, or to the substance of religion now professed by this Church of England."[2]

[1] Strype's Whitgift, 129.

[2] Ibid.

The first two sentences in this answer of the Archbishop are the whole of the answer as contained in Brook. I have been slow to insert the rest, which is from Strype; for I can see neither answer to the question proposed, nor meaning of any sort, in all this tissue of words. I have, however, made the addition because I would not seem to slight

"But," said Mr. Hartwell, "the words *may* be taken in *another* sense, — to mean what they say, — and therefore may not be subscribed without some deliberation."

"I wonder," said the Dean of Westminster, "you do not subscribe; seeing there is nothing in this second Article" — the one about the Book of Common Prayer — "which is not in the third; and you are willing to subscribe to the third."

"We have subscribed to the third already," answered Mr. Underdown; "and if *all things in the second are in the third*, we desire you to be satisfied with *that* subscription."

"Not so," said one of the bishops; and, if he referred to the Dean's incautious admission, no wonder that he said it.

Mr. Norden, another of the ministers, then asked, "How do your lordships understand these words, 'Receive the Holy Ghost,' for the office of a priest?"

"Not imperatively," replied the Archbishop, "but optatively."

"We cannot give you the Holy Ghost," added the Bishop of London.

"Do you not think," said the Bishop of Rochester, "that when we use these words we do communicate something?"

"I think not, my lord," said Mr. Underdown, rather severely; "for persons return from you no better furnished than when they came unto you; if we may form our opinion from their practice."

Strype's version. He adds to it, that "with this answer these ministers were *satisfied*"! which I may believe whenever I may be enlightened respecting its meaning.

"We hope you are now resolved and will now subscribe," said his Grace. "You are *unlearned*, and only *boys*, in comparison of us who studied divinity before most of you were born."

"We acknowledge our youth, my lord, and have no high opinion of our learning," replied Mr. Underdown. "Yet we hold ourselves sufficiently learned to know and to teach Jesus Christ as the way of salvation."

"If we subscribe under such interpretations as you have given us," said Mr. Hopkinson, "our subscription may become dangerous to us hereafter, when no interpretation may be allowed. Therefore we desire some protestation."

"I will admit no protestation," said his Grace.

"Come, Mr. Hopkinson, subscribe," interposed the Dean, coaxingly. "My lord will favor you, and help you against your adversaries."

"We must be better advised, Mr. Dean."

"Go into the garden; go into the garden, or somewhere else," interrupted the Archbishop. "Think this matter over, and then return."

In the end the ministers consented to subscribe, on the conditions that their subscription should not be required to anything against the Word of God, or contrary to the analogy of faith, and that it should not be extended to anything *not already* contained in the Book of Common Prayer; and with the protest, that the Book of Consecration did not belong to them, and that they could not subscribe to it. To these conditions the Archbishop and the bishops agreed! The ministers accordingly subscribed, and their suspensions were taken off.[1]

[1] Brook, I. 264 – 272. Strype's Whitgift, 128 – 130.

The bishops had certainly failed. Except upon the amatory capacities of the Devil, they had conveyed no instruction. They had not manfully met, much less had they answered, a single objection of the ministers. On the other hand, we find the highest prelate of the realm staggered by "unlearned boys;" forced to interpret language contrary to its rules and contrary to common sense; betraying that he knew less than they of the very text-book of the Church; perplexed by the stern fact, that the Book, on the accuracy of which the whole discussion hinged, was *not the Book established by law;* meeting grave difficulties with evasions, or with contemptuous, lordly, wheedling words; and finally accepting a compromise, which, again and again, he had most positively refused. All this was but poorly sustaining his vaunt, that "he would by learning defend his Articles against all mislikes thereof." Nor was the following, which shows the controversy in another aspect.

"Your subscription is required by the statute of the thirteenth of Elizabeth," said his Grace to another minister, who had been suspended, and whom he was urging to subscribe.

"My lord, that statute extendeth no further than the confession of the Christian faith and the doctrine of the sacraments."

"There is a provision in the statute of the first of Elizabeth, that the queen, with her Commissioners or the Archbishop, may take further order."

"The proviso of the first of Elizabeth can have no relation to the statute of the thirteenth of Elizabeth, which was some years after. And the proviso expresseth how far it is to be extended, — to the taking away and establishing *ceremonies* only." [1]

"But so much of the *canon* law is still in force as is not contrary to God's Word; and you have promised canonical obedience."

"But the question is, whether the things required *be* agreeable to God's Word? And not only so, — there is no canon which requires us to subscribe to the *judgment of our Ordinary*."

"That I allow. But the law hath charged the bishop to see that all things for the ministry be duly observed, as by law established; and I take this order" — of subscription — "for the more effectual execution of things already established."

"My lord, your care and diligence in the execution of laws must be *according* to law, and not *contrary* to law; that is, by admonition, by suspension, by sequestration, or by deprivation, as each particular case may require.[2] But these proceedings are *not* according to law; but an inquisition into our hearts and consciences" — to find out what *we think* on the points in your lordship's Articles — "for which there is no law."

"I make this a decree and order for the whole of my province; and therefore it is to be observed as if it had been made before." [3]

"No *one* person, nor *any number* of persons, *hath*

[1] In Brook, this reads: "The proviso of 7 Elizabeth can have no relation, &c. The proviso expresseth how far it is to be extended; *not* to the taking away," &c. There were no statutes enacted in the *seventh* year of Elizabeth, for there was no session of Parliament in that year. I do not doubt that the misprint should read "1 Elizabeth;" or that the word "not" is also an error of print. I have framed the text accordingly.

[2] 1 Eliz. Cap. II. Sec. IV.

[3] *Qu.* before the law?

authority to make decrees or constitutions, except in Convocation; which assembly must be called together by the queen's writ."

"I have the queen's consent."

"But that consent was not according to law provided in this behalf. Nor was it done in Convocation."

"I have the consent of my brethren and some others."

"That was not according to the order of Convocation, wherein we"—the inferior clergy—"are to have our free choice of clergy in the Lower House."[1]

This is all we have of this conversation. How well—we ask again—did the Archbishop redeem his pledge to defend his Articles? The reader can judge whether, when the *legality* of his proceedings was in debate, he was not fairly driven from the Statute law to the Canon law; and from the Canon law to—nothing.

We produce one case more; in which Thomas Cooper—whom we have mentioned before as having been puzzled by a Puritan letter—was the bishop demanding subscription; lately translated from the See of Lincoln to that of Winchester.[2]

"Have you not subscribed?"

"No, my lord."

"Why not?"

"My lord, I perceive that you wish me to signify my allowance of the Book of Common Prayer. There is no cause why I should be called in question for this matter; *for* I use the Book; do not refuse it;

[1] Brook, I. 445, 446.

[2] Strype's Whitgift, 132.

and speak not against it. These are manifest proofs that I allow of it."

"Many of you who say so will not confess what you have done, neither what you will do. Therefore you must subscribe."

"I consider it a greater allowance to *use* a thing than to *subscribe* unto it."

"So you think and say, that it is unreasonable and unlawful to require you to subscribe."

"Do you gather this, my lord, from what I have said?"

"No."

"Then all is well."

"But you must subscribe, or show some cause why you will not."

"My lord, if no excuse will serve, but I must subscribe or show some cause why I refuse, I will show your lordship three reasons: As, there are some things in the Book of Common Prayer *against* the Word of God, and therefore *repugnant* to it. Again — "

"Nay, stop. Let us talk of the first."

"I like your order well, my lord. And to prove what I have said, I refer you to the words of the rubric, before the office of confirmation, where it is said, 'That no man shall think any detriment will come to children by deferring their confirmation, he shall know for *truth* that it is *certain by God's Word* that children being baptized have *all things necessary to salvation*, and be *undoubtedly* saved.'"

"You must not take it as the words import."

"No! my lord? Is it not your pleasure that we should subscribe to the things in the Book? Or, is it your pleasure that we should subscribe to your interpretation of those things?"

"You must subscribe to *the sense* of what is contained in the Book."

"If we must subscribe to the sense, then you must amend your Article. For your Article, to which you require us to subscribe, saith that there is nothing in the Book of Common Prayer repugnant to the Word of God."

"If you were to subscribe to the Gospel, would you subscribe to the words, or to the sense?"

"I would subscribe to the words —"

"YOU LIE!"

"My lord, I beseech you let us have good words! I say again, we must subscribe both to the words *and* to the sense."

A little more passed, when the Bishop conceded.

"I confess we must subscribe both to the sense and the words."

"Then in this we are agreed."

"In the place you cited from the Book, the meaning is, that those who are baptized, *and therewith receive the grace* of that sacrament, being of the number of the elect, are undoubtedly saved:" an exposition of the dogma of baptismal regeneration more intelligible certainly than that of Archbishop Whitgift; and, by the help of the interpolation, much more orthodox than the rubric.

"I beseech your lordship to read the words of the Book, and let it be seen how you *can* give it that interpretation. But I wish to mention a second reason; and that is, the administration of the communion to an individual person in private. How doth this agree with the Word of God, and with the word *communion?*"

"The doctrine contained in the sacrament belongeth to wise and learned men to determine. *You* had best exercise yourself in catechising, and let this alone."

"My lord, you must bear with me. For I think God requireth it at our hands, that we learn and teach all things revealed in his Holy Word."

"The communion in private is a *single* communion."

"How can the words *single* and *communion* be made to agree?"

"I do not say they can."

"Why, then, do you join them together?"

"In the time of Justin Martyr, being two hundred years after Christ, the sacrament, in time of persecution, was carried from house to house, because the people dared not come together."

"But, my lord, the example of primitive Christians is not in point. Our question is, whether the Book of Common Prayer containeth anything repugnant to the Word of God? And, my lord, I think no good man will deny, that the two places I have mentioned *are* repugnant to the Word of God."

"What! do you condemn all who have subscribed! Do you say they have all acted wickedly!"

"You misunderstand my words. What I speak, I speak with consideration, and I know what I say."

"What o'clock is it?"

"We have not yet done. I told you I had three reasons."

"I have had more ado with you than with all the rest."

"You have not yet finished with me. As I said, I have three reasons; and I trust you will hear them before you proceed against me."

"What are your other reasons?"

"If you will promise that we shall examine them, I will mention them. But if not, it is unnecessary."

"I had rather persuade many learned men than you."

"I speak not of learning, but of conscience; and my conscience, without persuasion, will not yield. Hitherto in my ministry, I have enjoyed a good conscience, founded upon the Word of God; and, my lord, with as good a conscience, by God's help, will I be removed from it, or I will not be removed."

Here the conversation ended.[1] It needs no comment.

These specimen interviews between the Puritan clergy and their lords give a pretty clear idea of the points upon which they were at issue. In substance, the prelates claimed that every word, ceremony, and article written in the Book of Common Prayer, and in the Book of Ordination, was as faultless and as binding as the Book of God, and must be acknowledged as such. The Puritans dared not say it. The prelates claimed to themselves — or, more modestly, to the Church which they personified — an infallibility of judgment in *all* things pertaining to religion. The Puritans denied the claim. The prelates claimed obedience; the Puritans, manhood; the prelates, spiritual lordship; the Puritans, Christian liberty. Such was the difference, in theory, between the two. The difference in spirit, in reasoning, in discernment, in Christian courtesy, in manly honesty, is better shown, we think, by the words which passed, than by analysis or rhetoric.

[1] Brook, I. 285 – 288.

Although from some ministers — as those of Sussex — a qualified subscription to the "Three Articles" was reluctantly accepted; and although some others, under the influence of specious promises of indulgence, yielded their names to an unqualified assent; yet the arbitrary course of the Archbishop made many a strong man weep in secret places, and stayed many a fountain where the people were athirst.

Expostulations, remonstrances, entreaties, came in from all quarters, — from the stricken and imperilled shepherds, from the bereaved and trembling flocks, from the Lords of the Privy Council.

Fourteen ministers of Kent,[1] bound over to answer at law for *contumacy* in refusing to subscribe the "Three Articles," presented themselves before the Archbishop at Lambeth to plead for some indulgence to their consciences. His Grace was alarmed. So many "contentious fellows!" They might make uproar, perchance do violence, in his very palace![2] But when he saw that they seemed disposed to no such things, but behaved peaceably and decorously, he listened to them at times for two or three days; but then suspended them from the ministry. As he pronounced their sentence he told them, that — refusing subscription — they did *thereby* disobey her Majesty's authority, condemn the right service of God and the ministry established, and did *separate* themselves from the Church.[3] So they departed; not only under censure, but under brand and libel.

"We have come to pray your lordship's favor for our suspended ministers, that they may be restored," said several of the gentry of the same county, who

[1] Strype's Whitgift, 123. [2] Ibid., 127. [3] Ibid., 125.

afterwards went to Lambeth expressly for the purpose.

"Why, sirs! it be a thing intolerable, that a few men like them — for the most part young and of very small reading and study, and some of them utterly unlearned — should oppose themselves to what hath of so long time been allowed and confirmed by the most notable and famous men in learning; the same also being by law established. Albeit, let them be content to yield and submit themselves to the order by law established, then shall they be restored; otherwise, not. But this impugning of the Book hindereth religion, balketh the peace of the Church, and shall not be borne with."

"But we assure your lordship, that these our ministers have never so much as spoken against the Book in their sermons. Moreover, they *do use* it in their ministry."

"Troth! Then there be no cause why they should refuse to subscribe. Surely it is *less* to subscribe than to use. But I know your men. They say, and do not. They *say*, they observe the Book. They observe it *in part*, as it pleaseth them; not *wholly*, as they ought."

"It seemeth to us very hard to deal in this manner against preachers as do in all points of doctrine and substance agree with your lordship and the other lords spiritual; differing only in rites and ceremonies."

"They *do* differ from us in some points of substance; and, if they did not, they are not to be suffered unless they do conform. Ye may not think so basely of this realm of England that therein schisms and sectaries shall be tolerated, and every man do what he list."

"But our ministers be not heretics nor schismatics."

"They avoid the name of heresy, mayhap; but I say they be schismatics. Whoso consenteth with the Church in all articles of salvation and substance, yet nevertheless varieth from the Church in orders and ceremonies, know ye not, sirs, that he is a schismatic?"

"We pray your lordship's Grace to consider that we be faint for lack of the preached Word. An your Grace restore not these men, who be of an upright and holy conversation, and withal diligent preachers of the Word of God, what shall we do? Verily our souls, and the souls of our families, be in danger; for who but these our loving pastors will so care for us as to break to us the bread of life, for livings of so small a value?"

"In good sooth, ye have no cause to find fault for lack of preaching, or to faint, or to talk about the peril of souls; for there be in this my diocese of Kent fourscore preachers, all which have subscribed and do preach, five or seven, or ten at the most, excepted. Besides, the more part of you do dwell in the Inns of the Court, or elsewhere, where preaching is plentiful. Moreover, the profit of preaching consisteth not in many sermons or much talking, but in learned, material, and effectual sermons; and some of your suspended ministers be so unlearned, that I would be loath to give them license to preach, though they should subscribe. But, to quiet you about preaching, I do now offer unto you, that wheresoever I have displaced any preacher or minister, I will place as good or better in his room, if so be I may have the disposition thereof."[1]

In short, his Grace rejected their petition. At their departure, they told him that they should appeal unto her Majesty, or to the Lords of her Highness's most Honorable Privy Council; some of them also "*after a sort*," as his lordship thought, "threatening otherwise than they durst have done in times past to men of his calling."[2]

But there came another cry from Kent. "Bereave us not of so excellent a laborer in the Lord's harvest, lest the enemies of God's truth, the Papists, have cause of joy and triumph. He hath ofttimes been beaten and whipped with untrue reports; he preacheth Christ truly; rebuketh sin boldly; applieth himself to his calling faithfully; liveth peaceably; and *controverteth not the discipline* of the Church. We therefore most humbly beseech your Grace, for the poor man's sake, for your own sake, for God's sake, take *judicial* knowledge of his cause,—now deprived and ordered away from us without having been examined,—and of your wisdom and goodness restore him to his liberty of preaching the Gospel here. So shall we heartily thank God and shall continually pray for you."

So prayed the people of Kent in behalf of John Stroud, the minister late at Cranbrook. And thirty-five ministers, and the parishioners of the thirty-five, wrote "Amen." But could it be expected that *he* would be restored? He had published Cartwright's "*Reply to Whitgift;*" and, in 1573, had been ar-

[1] Strype's Whitgift, 137 – 139. Neal, I. 159.

[2] Whitgift to Hatton; Life of Hatton, 372.

raigned for the offence before the High Commissioners![1]

The suspended ministers of the same county appealed to the Privy Council; complaining that, because they had refused subscription, they had been defamed by his Grace of Canterbury, and in public sermons, as *Separaters* from the Church. "So we think it our bound duties, most humbly on our knees to make manifest to her Majesty, that we in all reverence judge of the authority which is established; . . . . and that we so esteem of the Book of Common Prayer, and the Book of the Ordering of bishops, priests, and deacons, that there is nothing in them to cause us to separate ourselves from the Unity of the Church . . . . ; and that we count the ministry of the Word and the administration of the sacraments exercised in this land according to authority, as touching the substance thereof, lawful and greatly blessed of God." They concluded by praying that they might be heard and judged upon their own refusal to subscribe, upon their own hard condition under suspension, and upon the lamentable state of the churches to which they belonged.[2]

Supplications were also forwarded to the Lords of the Council from the ministers of Norfolk; from the ministers of Lincolnshire; from the ministers of Essex; from the ministers of Oxfordshire; from those in the diocese of Ely and Cambridgeshire; and from the London ministers; in all of which the petitioners pledged themselves to the statute 13 Elizabeth, Cap. XII., and to the Articles of Religion *not* required by

[1] Brook, I. 298 – 301.

[2] Fuller, Bk. IX. p. 144. Strype's Whitgift, 125, 126.

that statute, "so far as they were not repugnant to the Word of God," and also to make no disturbance and no separation if such their subscription might be accepted. To these peaceful and reasonable overtures, they added a touching appeal to parental instinct and Christian principle. "We commend to your Honors' compassion our poor families; but *much more* do we commend our doubtful, fearful, and distressed consciences, together with the cries of our poor people who are hungering after the Word, and are now as sheep having no shepherd. We have applied to the Archbishop, but can get no relief. We therefore humbly beg it at your Honors' hands."[1]

The ministers of Suffolk also petitioned the Council for relief, and at the same time entered a bill of complaint against the Bishop of Norwich. These two Papers, and that from the ministers of Kent, the Lords of the Council sent to the Archbishop, with a request that he would appear before them touching the matters therein contained.[2] His Grace declined

[1] Neal, I. 158.

[2] Two remarkable Papers of the time I have not used. They are without date, so that I could not determine where they belonged. Neal, who is by no means strictly chronological, gives them as written before Archbishop Grindal's death. Strype gives them immediately *after* a Paper which was dated "Feb. 19, 1583," i. e. 1583-4. True, this sequence determines nothing; for immediately after, Strype records the execution of Thacker and Copping, which took place in June, 1583. But the Papers I cannot neglect; and I give them in this connection, because one of them shows the temper of the Privy Council about the prosecutions of the Puritans. Certain ministers of Suffolk — Brown's first theatre of action — had been "indicted and arraigned for the non-observing of ceremonies." Certain "gentlemen and justices of the peace" complained of this to the Privy Council as follows: —

"The painful" — laborious — "pastors and ministers of the Word are marshalled with the worst malefactors; presented, indicted, arraigned, and condemned for matters, as we presume, of very slender moment. . . . . If these weak cere-

the honor, but wrote an elaborate letter to the Council, alleging that the Suffolk men were contentious, schismatic, mislikers of her Majesty's laws and government *in causes* ecclesiastical, — substituting the words "in causes" for the words "over persons," as in her Majesty's explication of the oath of Supremacy, — and dissuaded others therefrom; that the Kentish ministers amazed him, in that, unlearned and young

monies be so indifferent as their use or not use may be left to the discretion of the ministers, we think it very hard to have them undergo so hard handling. . . . . We serve her Majesty and the country, not according to our fantasies, as the world falsely bears us in hand, but according to the law and the statutes of England.,. . . . By law we proceed against all offenders. We touch none that the law spareth; we spare none that the law toucheth. . . . . We allow not of the Papists. We allow not of the Family of Love, an egg of the same nest. We allow not of the Anabaptists. We allow not of Brown, the overthrower of Church and Commonwealth. We *abhor* all these. No, *we punish* all these.

"But now, humbly upon our knees, we pray your good lordships give us leave to advertise you how the adversary very cunningly hath christened us with an odious name. . . . . It is the name of *Puritanism*. We detest both the name and the heresy. It is a term compounded of all other heresies aforesaid. The Papist is *pure* and immaculate: he hath store of goodness for himself and plenty for others. The Family cannot sin: they be so *pure*, that God is *hominified* in them, and they *deified* in God. But we do cry in the bitterness of our souls, 'We have sinned, with our fathers.' . . . . Yet before the world we labor to keep ourselves and our profession unblamable. This is our *Puritanism*. It pleaseth them to use this name to ministers, to magistrates, and to others. . . . . And the name being odious many times with the ignorant sort, it maketh the person odious. A shrewd device; and herewith somewhat dangerous. . . . . So most humbly recommending ourselves . . . . do we take our leave." (Strype's Annals, V. 264 – 267.)

This letter seems to confirm my conjecture that Thacker and Copping, *against* whom these same justices were set, were something more than Puritans, — whom the justices defended; and that they had promulged the same doctrine of Separation for which Brown was noted. It also shows how Puritans regarded Brownists; and throws light upon Sampson's letter in which he objects to the *name* of Puritan.

Upon the phrase "we punish all these," Mr. Marsden remarks ("Early Puritans," p. 137): "It would be difficult to say in what respects some of these seceders were

as they were, they should dare bring his doings in question, seeing he had only done his duty to God, the law, and her Majesty, yet had dealt with them, not as an archbishop with the inferior clergy, not as a master of a college with his fellows, not as a magistrate with inferiors, but as a friend and brother. "They came to me unsent for in a multitude; which I reproved, because it *imported a conspiracy* and had

more deserving of punishment than the most harmless of the Church Puritans themselves." Perhaps so. Yet in their opinion, and according to the prevailing views of the day in regard to Church *unity*, all Seceders were guilty of *a crime* of which even the hottest "*Church* Puritans" were innocent. I cannot, therefore, see the pertinence of Mr. Marsden's remark, that "the magistrates of Suffolk justified the persecution of which they complained, by their own example." It was not *deviation* from the Church orders which they would have punished, but *Separation*. They were consistent.

This letter of the gentry and justices produced a missive from the Council to the Judges of Assize.

"After our very hearty commendations. Whereas we are informed that, at the Assizes in your circuit, divers good preachers, and other godly disposed, have been indicted (under color of law) for things not so much against the *matter and very meaning* of the law, as in some show swerving from *the letter* thereof,— viz. for not using the surplice; resorting to sermons in other parishes *for want* at home; leaving out some collects on the days of preaching; using *private prayers* in their houses, and such like. . . . . These are therefore to desire you, and heartily to pray you, that in every sitting of your circuit you sift and examine the affection of *informers* touching religion. As also to have a special regard, that the inquest at large may be religious, wise, and honest. And if, notwithstanding, such juries creep in as molest good men, that yet your speech and whole proceedings against them may be according to their quality; not *matching them at the bar, or in judgment*, with rogues, felons, or Papists; but rather giving appearance in the face of the country, what difference you hold between Papists . . . . and these other men, which, making some conscience in these ceremonies, do yet diligently and soundly preach the true religion and obedience to her Majesty. . . . . So shall the country learn thereby, at the Assizes, better to reverence the Gospel and love the ministers and professors thereof." (Strype's Annals, V. 268, 269.)

Had the Privy Council managed ecclesiastical discipline according to their own minds, there would have been less Precisianism in the Church, more leniency, and more peace, if not toleration.

the *show of a tumult*, or unlawful assembly. Notwithstanding, I was content to hear their complaint and their reasons; whereof some were frivolous and childish; some, irreligious; and all, such as gave me occasion to think they rather sought quarrel against the Book than to be satisfied, — which is indeed true, as appeareth by some of their own confessions. . . . . Whereas they say" — in their supplication to your lordships — "that the public administration of the sacraments in this land, as touching the substance of it, is lawful, &c. they say no more than the Papists do. . . . . It is not for me to sit in this place, if every curate within my diocese or province may be permitted so to use me; neither is it possible for me to perform the duty which her Majesty looketh for at my hands, if I may not without interruption proceed in the execution of that which her Highness hath especially committed to me. . . . . This disordered flocking together of them at this time from divers places, and gadding from one to another, *argueth a conspiracy* amongst them. . . . . And here I do protest unto your lordships, that the 'Three Articles' are such as I am ready by learning to defend," &c., &c.[1]

That the Archbishop — when in popular parlance "Separation" was almost a synonyme of "Treason" and "Heresy" — should have stigmatized as Separatists men who held Separation in abhorrence, excites our surprise. Giving honest men bad names is a trick unbecoming to any *man;* more so, to the highest functionary of a National Church; and still more so,

[1] Fuller, Bk. IX. pp. 145 – 148. Strype's Whitgift, 126 – 128.

to one whose position, so conspicuous, was that of a disciple of Him who "spake as never man spake." This, however, was but an incident. We turn to the matter in hand.

The edict of subscription, — this it is which absorbs us now, and upon which we have endeavored to throw light. By this, the whole controversy between the hierarchy and the Puritans was changed. The Prayer-Book and the Book of Ordination were now openly exalted to a level with the Word of God; and, on the presumed equality of these three, the subscription required was made a condition of office and benefits in the Established Church. The condition was no longer merely conformity to the ritual, — a condition, as we have admitted, technically justifiable by ecclesiastical usage and by the law of the realm, — but a conformity of *opinion*; and not a conformity of opinion in the articles "which *only* concerned the true Christian faith," but a conformity to each and singular the opinions drafted by the Primate in his "Three Articles." The *test* of this conformity was subscription.

This test was *now* the ground for demurrer and disobedience, on the one hand; for denunciation and deposition, on the other, — a fact not to be overlooked in canvassing the religious history of the time.

In observing this posture of affairs, we do not stop to canvass the enormous pretensions made for the two Books of the Church; nor to inquire in what particulars they may, or may not, have been in conflict with the Word of God; nor wherein the edition of the Prayer-Book then in use varied from that specified in the Act of Uniformity.[1] All these were but collateral matters; claiming grave consideration, to be sure, but made use of by the ministers chiefly as *auxiliary* to their own justification. In its great essential qualities, the case would not have been altered had the Book of Prayer then in use been word for word, syllable for syllable, comma for comma, — punctuation was *very* scant in those days, — the same with that ordained by the statute. Nor would it have been in essence changed, had every minister in the land *believed* the Book to have been faultless in every sentiment it contained and in every rite it prescribed. The grand position in which the Puritans upon this occasion fortified themselves, and which they defended by challenging the infallibility of the standards, was not that of *Christian* liberty which they had taken before, but that of *Civil* liberty; the liberty which was their property and birthright as Englishmen under English law. They claimed that the law only required the *use* of the Book of Common Prayer, not a *promise* to use it, — as the second of the "Three Articles" did; and in this they were right. They

[1] In April, 1584, Robert Beal, Clerk of the queen's Council, stated as follows, in a letter to the Archbishop: —

"Seeing the statute 1 Eliz. is penal, and therefore to be literally and strictly understood (and it alloweth but of a Book with three additions, and not otherwise), — If there be no first Book, nor ever was, *with such three additions*, and not otherwise, then there is no allowance or confirmation of any law. And, forasmuch as *this Book which we have*, hath *more* additions, it is another Book and divers from that which the law requireth and confirmed. And so, hitherto there hath been no Book published according to law at all." (Strype's Whitgift, 144.)

It is noticeable and very significant, that the Archbishop, in his written "animadversions" upon Beal's letter, *takes no notice whatever* of this remarkable statement. (Strype's Whitgift, Append., Bk. III. No. V.)

contended also that *no* statute required subscription; and in this they were right. "Show me," said one of them in open court, — "show me a single statute now in force in England which requires me to subscribe to the Book of Common Prayer, to the Book of making bishops and ministers, or to the whole Book of the Articles," — the Thirty-Nine Articles, — "and I promise, before you and these people, that I will subscribe. But if I offer my hand to subscribe *as far as any statute* doth require, why is the offer not admitted? or *by what law* can it be rejected?"[1] And, finally, they contended that no canon of Convocation, and no legitimate authority whatever, required their subscription; and in this also they were right. Under the like requisitions in 1573–4, they had learned wisdom. Bewildered, scattered, peeled, impoverished and imprisoned, by the lawless proceedings of the Commissioners then, they had *studied* those proceedings in their penury and prisons; had grown wiser by the study; and, in 1583, met the like demands, not by meek and mute submission, but by a manly protest *in the name of English Law.* For this, this year of their annals is memorable; for not until now do we find them sufficiently educated, by adversity to plant themselves, as *religious* men, upon their obvious and sacred rights as *English* men.

"I, JOHN WHITGIFT, make this a *decree and order* for the whole of my Province."[2]

"NO ONE MAN, either Archbishop or Lord Bishop, may take upon him to control or have dominion over others."[3]

[1] Brook, I. 352.

[2] See *ante*, p. 364.

[3] See *ante*, p. 352.

Such was now the strife. It wrought the long-cherished wish of the queen,—"three or four preachers to a county";[1] and went far towards her purpose to "*root out* Puritanism." But her Highness was chary of her popularity. She left the odium of the contest to her Primate; its posthumous, but everlasting honor, to the Puritans.

[1] *Ante*, Chap. II. p. 54.

CHAPTER XIV.

THE COURT OF HIGH COMMISSION.

CIVIL LAW AND CANON LAW. — ECCLESIASTICAL COURTS. — THE ACT FOR A REVIEW OF THE CANON LAW. — THE ROMAN CODES ONLY PERMITTED, AND WITH RESTRICTIONS, IN THE ECCLESIASTICAL COURTS UNDER ELIZABETH. — DISPOSITION OF THE CLERGY TO EXALT THE ROMAN CODES. — THE HIGH COURT OF COMMISSION, — ITS PECULIARITIES. — A NEW COMMISSION ISSUED. — THE POWERS ASSUMED TO BE CONFERRED BY IT. — THE SAME AS PREVIOUS COMMISSIONS. — THE LEGALITY OF ITS FUNCTIONS CONSIDERED; PARTICULARLY, ENFORCING BY VIRTUE OF "OFFICE MERELY" (OR AT WILL) AN INQUISITION BY CORPORAL OATH. — JOHN CALVIN AND THE OATH EX OFFICIO MERO. — THE ARCHBISHOP'S SCHEDULE OF INQUISITION. — ITS FLAGRANT VIOLATION OF FUNDAMENTAL LAW.

1583, 1584.

UNDER the Saxon kings of England the distinction of ecclesiastical and municipal courts was unknown. The clergy almost monopolized learning, and were peculiarly versed in the knowledge of law. The bishop and the alderman (in his absence, the sheriff) sat upon the same Bench, and took like cognizance of temporal and of spiritual causes.

The foreign priests, however, "the bishops and clergy" who followed in the train of the Norman Conqueror, soon embroiled themselves with the nobility and laity" in a contest for the ascendency of the civil law — the Roman code of Justinian — and the canon law, over the common law of the realm. But when it was declared by Parliament, that "they would not change the laws of England," that, "the realm had never been, and never should be, ruled by the civil law," the clergy began to withdraw themselves from the temporal courts. Still they had their separate ecclesiastical tribunals, to which, only, themselves were amenable, and to which, only, all ecclesiastical causes were submitted.

The proceedings of these courts were governed only by the civil and the canon laws; while the temporal courts adhered exclusively to the laws of England. By the Act 25 Henry VIII. it was enacted that the canon laws should be reviewed and rectified; and that, until that work should be effected, such existing canons should still be used and executed as were *not repugnant to the law of the land or the king's prerogative.*[1] But as this review had never been completed, the radical restriction imposed by this statute upon the canon laws continued in force in the reign of Elizabeth. But these, and also the civil laws, were only *permitted* in the ecclesiastical courts as *leges sub graviori lege*, having life only because admitted and received by immemorial use and custom, and only so far as the courts of common law should judge them to agree with the prerogative of the Crown, with the common laws, and with the statutes and customs of the realm.[2] Thus, although the clergy had always

[1] 25 Henry VIII. Cap. XIX. Sec. VII.

[2] This had been clearly expressed by Parliament in the following memorable words:—

"This is your Grace's realm; recognizing no superior under God but only your Grace; hath been and is free from subjection to any man's laws, but only to such as have been devised, made, and ordained, *within* this Realm for the wealth of the same; or to such other as, by the *sufferance* of your Grace and your progenitors, the people of this realm have taken at their free liberty, by their own consent, to be used among them, and have bound

had a judicial prominence in England, their courts had at length been brought under the superintendence of the ordinary courts of the realm. But the old priestly disposition to encroach upon the province and the principles of the municipal law had been transmitted; which appears alike in the history of the clergy generally, and in the Act 25 Henry VIII. particularly. We have already seen this disposition manifested. We shall see more of it as we proceed.[1]

In Elizabeth's third Primate, it was largely stimulated by his antipathy to the Puritans; and naturally excited in him a strong and peculiar desire for a new ecclesiastical commission from the queen. The ordinary courts of the bishops could only touch cases within their respective dioceses, and were constantly exposed to the corrective and even punitive interference of the municipal courts, whenever they exceeded the limits of the common law.[2] Besides, the cases with which they might deal in the way of *discipline* were chiefly such as were obnoxious to the Act of *Uniformity*, and defined therein. The High Court of Commission, on the contrary, had jurisdiction over all the queen's dominions, during the term of their commission; and could find infinite latitude for prosecutions, persecutions, and judgments, under the vague generalities of "errors, schisms, heresies, abuses,

themselves by long use and custom to the observance of the same; not as to the observance of the laws of any foreign prince, potentate, or prelate, but as to the *customed* and ancient laws of this realm originally established as laws of the same by the said sufferance, consents, and custom; and none otherwise." (25 Henry VIII. Cap. XXI.)

[1] Blackstone, I. 17, 19, 20, 80, 83, 84; III. 60 – 64, 87, 100. Coke's Reports, Part XII. p. 29; Part XIII. p. 47.

[2] Blackstone, III. 87.

offences, contempts, and enormities," consigned to them by the Act of *Supremacy*. In addition to this, their commission itself charged the commissioners with peculiar and specified duties, and conferred — or assumed to confer — very indefinite powers both inquisitorial and punitive. A court emanating thus directly from the person of the sovereign, acting under the ægis of her broad seal, and wearing on its front the insignia of regality, had naturally overawed the temporal courts; for, however illegal its proceedings, to inhibit them in any case of wrong would seem like arraigning the sovereign and her supremacy. Who had the hardihood for this? Although it *had* been done, in the tenth and eighteenth years of Elizabeth's reign, it had been effectually repressed as a presumptuous interference, by a sovereign peculiarly jealous of her prerogative.

The renewal of this court, with "its rigors and unjust proceedings, especially to the ministers and preachers of the Gospel," was dreaded by the Puritans, who well knew the temper and proclivities of the new Primate. They therefore took measures at court to have a new Commission stayed; at least for a while. But the Archbishop was on the alert; and, five weeks after his confirmation, sent to the Lord Treasurer, who was the queen's ear, "divers arguments or reasons for such a Commission."[1] In this Paper, the chief and true aim — to reduce the number of preachers and to "*root out* Puritanism" by means which "the Laws of the Weal Public" did not permit — was only shadowed forth in the following words: "The Realm will swarm with disordered

[1] Strype's Whitgift, 134.

persons (commonly called Puritans) who contemn the Censures Ecclesiastical, if they be not met withal by the Commission."[1] An appeal so consonant with Elizabeth's plans and jealousies was only a matter of form, to precede the boon resolved upon.

On the ninth day of December,[2] a Commission for Ecclesiastical Causes was granted by her Majesty,—"To the Most Reverend Father in God, our Right Trusty and Right Well-beloved John, Archbishop of Canterbury, Primate of all England, and Metropolitan, to our Right Trusty and Well-beloved the Bishops of London," and to eleven other prelates, certain Privy Councillors, lawyers, and officers of state, in all forty-four persons; constituting them her High Commissioners for Ecclesiastical Causes. After designating the Act of Supremacy, the Act of Uniformity, the Act[3] for the Assurance of the Queen's Royal Power, and the Act[4] for Reforming Disorders touching Ministers, the instrument proceeds:—

"We.... do give full authority to you, or any three of you, whereof the Archbishop of Canterbury, or one of the bishops above named, or Sir Francis Walsingham, Sir Gilbert Gerard, or some of the civilians, to be one, to inquire,.... as well by the oaths of twelve good and lawful men, as also by witnesses, and all other means and ways you can devise, of all offences, contempts, and misdemeanors .... committed contrary to the tenor of the said statutes; and also to inquire of all heretical opinions, seditious books, contempts, conspiracies, false rumors

[1] Strype's Whitgift, 134.

[2] Coke, Part V. p. 2. Strype's Annals, V. 260.

[3] 5 Eliz. Cap. I.

[4] 13 Eliz. Cap. XII.

or talks, slanderous words, and sayings contrary to the aforesaid laws, or any others ordained for the maintenance of religion, ... together with their abettors, counsellors, or coadjutors.

"And further, We do give full power to you, or any three of you, whereof the Archbishop of Canterbury, or one of the bishops mentioned, to be one .... to reform and punish all persons .... that obstinately absent from church, ... by the censures of the Church, or any other lawful ways and means; .... and to take order of your discretions, that the penalties and forfeitures limited by the Act of Uniformity .... be duly levied.

"And, We do further empower you, or any three of you, ... to reform all errors, heresies, schisms, abuses, offences, contempts, and enormities, which may lawfully be reformed by censures ecclesiastical, deprivation, or otherwise, according to the power limited by the laws, ordinances, and statutes of the realm.

"And we do further empower you, or any three, to call before you such as have ecclesiastical livings, and to deprive such of them as .... maintain any doctrine contrary to the Articles of Religion, ... which only concern the confession of the true faith and doctrine of the sacraments."

The next section authorizes the punishment of crimes against chastity, "by fine, imprisonment, censures of the Church, or by all or any of the said ways, as to them should appear most meet and convenient."

Also, "to call before you all persons suspected of any of the premises, ... to examine them on their corporal oaths; and if any are obstinate and disobedient either in not appearing .... or not obeying your orders and decrees, ... then to punish them .... by censures ecclesiastical, or by fine, according to your discretions; or to commit them to ward .... till .... by you delivered, and till they shall pay such costs .... as you shall think reasonable."

Also, "to command .... our officers by your letters to apprehend .... such as you shall think meet to be convened before you; and to take such bond as you shall think fit for their personal appearance; and, in case of refusal, to commit them to custody till you shall order their enlargement; and further to take such securities for their performance of your decrees as you shall think reasonable."

Except its date and the names of the persons whom it empowered, there was nothing new in this Commission; not even the authority to examine suspected persons upon their corporal oaths, and to fine and imprison such as should refuse. It seems, for the most part, to have been drawn after *a form* which had been framed when the first was issued; for it opens by referring to particular Acts of Parliament as the bases of its powers conferred; describes the same offences, and authorizes the same methods of procedure and the same punishments, as were described and authorized in former Commissions.

To sustain these assertions pointedly contradictory to the highest historical authorities of the present day, we are compelled to turn from the regular current of our narrative.

It has long been stated, and without being questioned, that "this Commission"—of 1583—"was made more arbitrary than any of the former, and conveyed more unlimited authority;"[1] that "the power to tender what was technically called the oath *ex officio* was contained for the first time in this Commission;"[2] or, in other words, that "the authority to the Commissioners to examine persons on their corporal oaths, which refers to the oath *ex officio mero*, was not in the first five Commissions."[3]

These statements seem to have been made on the authority of Robert Beal, clerk of Queen Elizabeth's Council, in a letter to Lord Burleigh, dated March 17th, 1592–3. In that letter he says: "In the first five Commissions ecclesiastical, there was no mention or warrant for them to proceed *ex officio* at all..... In this last Commission, there hath been an alteration, and a new clause inserted, to proceed by the oath of the party."[4]

Of the Commissions previous to that of the year 1583, it has been our fortune to meet with only two; those of the years 1559 and 1576. The first reads thus:—

"We .... by these presents do give our full power and authority to you, or six of you, ... to inquire as well by the oaths of twelve good and lawful men, as also by witnesses and other ways and means ye can devise, for all offences .... contrary to .... the said acts and statutes;"[5] .... and also of .... slanderous words .... against us, ... or against any the laws or

[1] Hume, III. 126.

[2] Hallam, 122.

[3] Neal, I. 161.

[4] Strype's Whitgift, 394.

[5] The Act of Uniformity and the Act of Supremacy; referred to in the previous section of the Commission.

statutes of this our realm;"[1] ".... to award such punishment to every offender .... as to your wisdoms and discretions, or six of you," shall seem meet;[2] ".... and to call before you, or six of you, ... such as you, or six of you, ... shall seem to be suspect persons in any of the premises; and also such witnesses, as you, or six of you, shall think to be called before you, or six of you ....; and them and every of them"—i. e. witnesses *and* suspect persons—"to examine *upon their corporal oath*," &c.[3]

The Commission of 1576 was issued to Archbishop Grindal and others. Concerning the oath *ex officio mero*, it contains the following clause: "We give full power and authority unto you, or three of you, to call before you every offender, ... and also such as by you shall seem to be suspect persons in any of the premises, ... and *him* or them to examine *upon their corporal oaths*," &c. Then follows a grant of the same power to punish, "according to their discretions," by censures ecclesiastical, by fine, and by imprisonment during the pleasure of the Commissioners, or any three of them, which we find in the

[1] Sec. III.

[2] The words "shall seem meet" are lacking in the copy before me; but are necessarily implied.

[3] Cardwell's Documentary Annals, I. 223 – 230.

Commenting upon this Commission, Dr. Cardwell says: "On a comparison with other warrants issued afterwards, as new powers or a change of Commissioners were wanted, it will appear that it was found necessary in *after times* to give the court the express power of *interrogating the accused party on oath*, a power which was exercised in the first instance"—i. e. by this Commission of 1559—"under the general clause of inquiring 'by all ways and means they could devise'"! This is very singular; as though "the express power," as though "*them and every of them to examine upon their corporal oath*," were *not* in the very Commission which Dr. Cardwell himself was editing!

Commission to Archbishop Parker and in that to Archbishop Whitgift.[1]

Thus we find that the Commission of 1559 was preferable to those of 1576 and 1583 in this particular only, that it constituted *six*, instead of *three*, Commissioners a quorum to adjudicate. In other particulars, we find no difference. For authorizing punishment at discretion, for authorizing arraignment upon mere suspicion, and for authorizing inquisition by corporal oath, — or oath of *mere office*, — all were *alike* exceptionable. It should be noted also, that the warrant for applying this oath is in the *same words* in *each* Commission, "to examine upon their corporal oaths." The last Primate of Queen Elizabeth craved no larger powers from his sovereign, and obtained no larger, than had been granted to his predecessors.

Mr. Beal was unquestionably a man thoroughly versed in the Roman and in the English law, — better than in the details of ecclesiastical Commissions, — and a man of truth. Yet, had he wished to do it, he could not have hoped to impose upon Lord Burleigh by what he himself knew to be a false statement, or did not suppose to be a true one. He was therefore deceived about the tenor and language of the two Commissions — before Whitgift's — which we have cited. This may be accounted for by the fact that the Commission of 1576 was not enrolled in Chancery,[2] — and perhaps that of 1559 was not; so that he had no better means of information than common rumor, touching an instrument drawn up sixteen or seventeen years before, — when he seems to have

[1] Strype's Grindal; Appendix, Bk. II. No. VI. pp. 64 – 70.

[2] Sir J. Mackintosh, III. 289. London edit. 1831.

been absent on the Continent,[1] — and under which the oath was rarely if ever enforced.[2]

We return to the Commission issued to Archbishop Whitgift and his colleagues. It should not be overlooked, that in this instrument the Commissioners are repeatedly and distinctly referred to "the tenor of the said several acts and statutes;" to "lawful ways and means;" to "the power and authority limited and appointed by the laws;" to "the Articles of Religion which *only* concern the confession of the true faith and doctrine of the sacraments." So far there was ostensible deference for law. But this deference becomes at least suspicious, when the instrument proceeds to authorize the arrest and prose-

[1] Strype's Whitgift; Appendix, p. 54.

[2] "Bishop Grindal," said Mr. Beal in the same letter to Lord Burleigh, "proceeded by the verdict of twelve men."

There is also other testimony which reaches back to 1561, and which conflicts with Beal's statement; for Bishop Aylmer said in 1591, in his own Court of Commission, "I have been Commissioner *thirty* years, and that clause of the Oath *was always inserted* in the Commissions." (Strype's Aylmer, 313.)

There had been two instances, one in the tenth, the other in the eighteenth year of the queen, in which the High Commissioners had attempted to enforce the oath; in each of which it was refused; in each, the refusal was punished by imprisonment; and in each, the prisoners, on a writ of *Habeas Corpus*, were enlarged by the Court of Common Pleas. (Coke's Reports, Part XII. p. 27.) Indeed, there was an earlier case than these two; that of the sayer and hearers of the Mass at Lady Carew's house. "Neither the priest nor any of his auditors, not so much as the kitchen-maid, will receive *any oath before us to answer to Articles*, but stoutly say they will not swear; and say they will neither accuse themselves nor none other." So wrote Grindal and Cox in 1562. (Haynes, 395.) They were undoubtedly of the High Commission.

These three cases are not exactly in point, because they do not show what was contained in the Commissions of the Commissioners; but they do show that in 1562, in 1568, and in 1576, the High Court of Commission *plied* the Oath.

cution of persons on mere suspicion; their inquisition by the corporal oath; their punishment discretionary by fine or by imprisonment; and also inquiry by any means which any three of the Commissioners could devise,—words which certainly comprehend every species of torture or other cruelty conceived or conceivable. With reference to these particulars, we have spoken of the Commission itself as *assuming* to confer very indefinite powers both inquisitorial and punitive. That such powers are here expressed is self-evident; and that they were exercised will sufficiently appear. Were they *conferred?* Unquestionably they were,—*if the sovereign herself had them* to confer.

The High Court of Commission had its only foundation in Section VIII. of the Act of Supremacy, entitled "An Act restoring to the Crown the ancient jurisdiction over the State Ecclesiastical and Spiritual." By this section, "*such* jurisdiction .... as might *lawfully* be exercised .... was united to the Imperial Crown of the Realm." By the same section, her Majesty was empowered to appoint Commissioners "to execute under her Highness" this her right of jurisdiction; or, in other words, "to correct and amend all errors, offences, and enormities, which might *lawfully* be corrected and amended; .... such persons *so* authorized having full power and authority, by virtue of the Act and of the said Letters Patent, to .... execute all the *Premises* according to the tenor and effect of the said Letters Patent." What, then, was the executive or judicial power conferred upon the Crown, and which it might delegate? The statute describes it. "The *lawful* exercise of power for reformation, order, and correction, of the ecclesiastical state and persons, and of errors, ... offences, contempts, and enormities." This *lawful* exercise, and in relation to such *ecclesiastical* offences only,[1] is what is meant by the words, "such persons *so* authorized shall have full power to execute all the premises."[2] The premises might be executed by the Commissioners; the premises, and nothing else. So far as *these* authorized fining, imprisoning, administering the corporal oath, and arrest of the body, so far the Commissioners were authorized by the Act, to fine, to imprison, to demand the oath, and to order arrest. But "the premises" did not *specify* any cases in which such judicial power might be exercised. Yet the word "lawful" restricted the Commissioners to "only such offences as might lawfully be reformed by the ecclesiastical law,"[3] and to such "proceedings or punishments concerning the lands, goods, or bodies of the subjects, as by the Crown aforetime had of right been put in use."[4] Such proceedings and punishments were, those prescribed by some law; as, for example, the law of Uniformity. Did any *law* authorize the corporal oath to be administered by an ecclesiastical court? or any arrest of the body by their command? or any fine or imprisonment? According to the Act, by *such* questions the powers of the court were to be determined; not by the question, whether this or that power was designated in their Commission? As the statute did not give the queen power by her Letters Patent to alter the proceedings of the ecclesiastical law,[5] therefore

[1] Coke, Part XII. p. 19.
[2] Ibid., p. 20.
[3] Ibid., p. 19.
[4] Ibid., p. 20.
[5] Ibid.

she could not *confer* by her Letters Patent to this court the power to arrest the body; because *citation*, not arrest, was the proper way to bring a subject before a court ecclesiastical.[1] "Nor could the court, in any case, punish any delinquent by fine or imprisonment, *unless they had authority so to do by Act of Parliament;*"[2] for the statute authorizing the appointment of Commissioners "did not give the queen absolute power by her Letters to prescribe *what manner* of proceedings or punishments" they might adopt; it authorized "no *innovation*" in either.[3] Thus — whatever might be comprised in the words of the Commission or Letters Patent — no authority to do otherwise than *lawfully* could be *conveyed*,[4] because the queen herself did not possess it; nor could she *alter* by her Commission, either her temporal or her ecclesiastical laws, nor their proceedings.[5]

So also, although the words of the Letters Patent and of the Act did authorize, or rather require, this court to proceed by the canon or ecclesiastical laws, yet, by the Act 25 Henry VIII. Cap. XIX., they could proceed by such only as did not conflict with the queen's prerogative or the laws of the realm; for all others were thereby made void. But more: "Their proceedings, though ever so consonant to Roman law, might not be repugnant to the fundamental maxims of municipal law."[6] In short, whatever the queen's Commission might say, her Commissioners had no authority to prosecute or to punish, in a single case, in

[1] Coke, Part XII. p. 89. Blackstone, III. 100.

[2] Coke, Part XII. p. 19.

[3] Ibid., p. 20.

[4] Ibid., pp. 49, 85.

[5] Ibid., pp. 19, 49.

[6] Blackstone, I. 83, 84; III. 87, 100. Coke, Part XII. p. 29.

any way, except as prescribed or permitted by the laws of the *realm*.

In respect to the oath *ex officio*, in particular. In certain suits — those involving personal claims, matrimony, and wills — the personal answer of a party himself upon oath, has ever been allowable by English law.[1] But the oath *ex officio*, or oath of purgation, used in the High Commission Court, was there applied "as well in criminal cases of ecclesiastical cognizance as in matters of civil right." By this mode of procedure, this Court obliged all persons against whom they thought proper to proceed, "to answer in cases of mere suspicion, and upon oath, to any matter however criminal which might be objected against themselves."[2] Even in those cases — mentioned above — in which a man might be examined upon his oath, the law did not require him to answer questions which should tend to the discovery of any crime;[3] nor might any man — ecclesiastical or temporal — be examined upon the secret thoughts of his heart, or of his secret opinion concerning any point of religion; but upon words or acts only.[4] Nor might any layman be thus examined, except in cases of matrimony and wills.[5] If, however, any man should *assent* to the oath, and take it *without exception*, it was not against the law to administer it, because not against his will.[6] But "if any person ecclesiastical was charged with anything punishable by law, he might not be examined upon

[1] Fuller, Bk. IX. pp. 183, 184. Blackstone, III. 447.

[2] Blackstone, III. 100, 447.

[3] Ibid., 447.

[4] Coke, Part XII. p. 26; XIII. p. 10.

[5] Ibid., Part XII. pp. 26, 28.

[6] Ibid., pp. 27, 28.

oath, because his oath would be evidence against him at common law," and because "it standeth not with the right order of justice nor good equity, that any person should be convict and put to the loss of his life, good name, or goods, unless by due accusation and witnesses, or by presentment, verdict, confession, or process of outlawry. Therefore, if any were compelled to answer upon his oath, where he ought not by law, this was oppression; and to do it incurred the penalty of the statute."[1] In two cases where the oath was refused, the refusal had already been justified by the temporal courts; and on the ground that the Commissioners had no right to demand it. In each of these decisions, it was also declared that they had no right to imprison. One case was in the tenth year of the queen; the other, in the eighteenth.[2] Thus the municipal law of the realm disallowed and even claimed to punish[3] such uses of the oath as were signified in the queen's ecclesiastical Commission. This being the case, the Commission did not *make* the uses lawful.

That this oath had been enforced by John Calvin in the Consistory of Geneva; that he even used it to pry into the secret opinions and intentions of those whom he convented; that he punished the refusal to answer, by deposition from the Gospel ministry and from the civil magistracy;[4] — the alle-

[1] Coke, Part XII. p. 27.

[2] Ibid.

[3] Fuller, Bk. IX. p. 183.

[4] Two cases were cited at the time, and are thus stated by Fuller, Bk. IX. pp. 185, 186. In their particulars they are singular.

"There was one Cumperel of Geneva, an ordained minister, who had a secret design *underhand* to place himself in the State of Berne; which in him was esteemed a heinous fault. The Consistory, coming at some notice hereof, ministered

gation of these things, in reply to those English disciples of Geneva who oppugned the oath, has been called "*argumentum ad hominem*," and said to be "striking the right string with a witness!"[1] But the Englishmen who objected to the oath, although partial to the Presbyterian Platform of Geneva, did not regard Calvin or his Consistory as impeccable, or as faultless models; nor were they at all involved in such proceedings. The question in England about this oath was, touching its fitness or unfitness, its right or its wrong, *under English law*; and therefore, to fling in the face of a Puritan the mal-practice of Geneva — though it might be well enough as a joke — was pointless and ill-sped as a missile; as a retort to *legal* objections, impertinent.

unto him an oath of *mere office* to answer to several questions. But because Cumperel answered not directly to those interrogatories (two whereof concerned the very cogitations of his heart), and because there was great presumption in *common fame*, the Consistory pronounced that they had just cause to depose him from the ministry.

"There was a wealthy widow living in Geneva in whose house there was a *dancing* held, which is a grievous crime in that Church, and condemned by their last form of Discipline. Amongst these dancers one was a Syndic (one of the four chief magistrates of the city); the other an Elder (Henrith by name) of the Church for that year. The matter coming to Calvin's ear, they were all convented before the Consistory, without any accuser or Party; and therefore of *mere office* put to their corporal Oaths to confess the Truth. The Elder pleaded for himself the words of Paul, — 'Receive not an accusation against an Elder, under two or three witnesses;' which would nothing bestead him, so that he was deposed from his eldership, and the Syndic from his magistracy until he should show some public testimony of his repentance."

The authorities cited by Fuller for these "memorable stories," are Calvin's own letters. Collier (VII. 62), citing *another* letter of Calvin, gives this addition. "Henrith was imprisoned for three days. The Syndic did penance, and so prevented his commitment. The others, being examined upon their oath, confessed they were at this dancing entertainment, upon which they were all sent to prison."

[1] Collier, VII. 62.

Although questioning by torture — that is, the rack — was freely employed during the reign of Elizabeth, and although the Government made no secret of its use,[1] yet it was utterly unknown in English *law*,[2] and was never used or thought of in the realm but as an engine *of State*. There is no reason, therefore, to suppose an intention, in one clause of the queen's Commission, of conveying the right to question by torture, although the words are capable of such a construction. And although torture was administered brutally by the underling minions of the Court of High Commission, there is no reason to suppose that the Court itself, or any of the Commissioners, ever commanded the Rack or the Little-Ease.

We have said that the queen husbanded her popularity, and left the odium of enforcing subscription to the "Three Articles" to "her Right Trusty and Right Well-beloved John, Archbishop of Canterbury." This remark is verified, negatively, by the Commission before us. While in this instrument she describes the duties of the Court, she is utterly silent about the "Three Articles" invented by his Grace. So obviously was forced subscription to them in the face of law, — so obviously, even to the masses, — that, while she was willing and desirous that it should be pressed by the Court, she would not suffer her regality to be implicated therein.

Such were the Letters Patent by which the High Court of Commission was renewed and organized. But these Letters were not sufficient to satisfy his Grace of Canterbury. He therefore tasked his inven-

[1] Hallam, 93, and note.

[2] Blackstone, IV. 326.

tion further; to create an auxiliary instrument which should give vigor and pregnancy to the oath of 'mere office,'—a compound-lever, having the Supremacy, the Statute, the Establishment, for its successive fulcra, and the oath for its motive power. It was "framed," apparently, in November, 1583; but not "drawn up"—by which we understand, arranged, completed, and put in play—until May, 1584.[1] It was particularly intended, we are told, to winnow *suspected* ministers; and to lay bare their smallest sins against the multifarious and minute orders of the Church ritual. Such men were first to be convented; then, to be sworn to answer truly, and in every particular, to—they knew not what; for *they might not know* the questions to be proposed until they had taken the oath.[2] It is impossible to appreciate the enormity of this proceeding without knowing the nature, and the very precise construction, of these interrogatories. We therefore give the points at which they aimed, from the Whitgift MSS., but in a condensed form. To refuse the oath was to incur fine and imprisonment at the will of the Court; to accept it, was to insure conviction by a clean disclosure of every clerical peccadillo. The information to be extorted is shown by the Articles interrogatory.

"By whom, and when, did you receive Orders? Were they conferred according to the English Book?"

"Do you *deem* and *judge* your Ordering to be lawful and not repugnant to the Word of God?"

"Wherein, and in what points, do you *deem* and

[1] Strype's Whitgift, 135. [2] Fuller, Bk. IX. p. 186.

judge the Book of Common Prayer other than a book godly, and virtuous, and agreeable to the Word of God?"

"Have you for the space of these three years, two years, one year, half a year, three, two or one month, last past, in any of your ministrations omitted to wear the surplice? How long? How often? For what cause, consideration, or intent?"

"Have you, within the time aforesaid, omitted the sign of the cross in baptism; or the words prescribed for the ordinance? Once? Oftener? How many times? Why?"

"Have you, within the time aforesaid, so neglected to baptize any child that it died without that sacrament? Whose child or children? When? Why?"

"Have you, within the time aforesaid, refused to use the ring, and the very words prescribed, in celebrating marriage? Who were the parties married? When? Where? Why?"

"Have you, within the time aforesaid, in any instance refused to use the form of thanksgiving for women after childbirth? In whose case? When? Where? Why?"

"Have you, within the time aforesaid, baptized any one infant in any other manner, or using any other words to godfathers and godmothers, than the manner or words prescribed in the Book of Common Prayer? In what cases? When? Where? Why?"

"Have you, within the time aforesaid, ever deviated, in whole or in part, from the form of Litany, or from the Lessons, or from the burial-service, prescribed in the said Book? particularly have you in the burial-service omitted the words, 'We commit earth to earth, in sure and certain hope of resurrection to eternal life'?[1] In what cases, in all these points? When? Where? Why?"

"Have you, within the time aforesaid, ever purposely omitted to use *any other* parts of the Book of Common Prayer as *being persuaded* that such parts are repugnant to the Word of God? What parts? Why?"

"Have you, within the time aforesaid, in any ministration, ever added, diminished, taken from, altered, and transposed manifoldly, at your own pleasure, sundry parts of the said Book? When? Where? Why?"

"Have you ever, within the time aforesaid, said or written, publicly or privately, anything against the Book, or against anything in it, as being repugnant to the Word of God, or as not proper to be used in the Church? What have you so said or written? When? Where? Why?"

"Do you at this present hold any or all of your former *opinions* against the Book? Do you purpose to continue such deviations from it as heretofore you have used? Have you used private conferences or conventicles for maintaining these your doings, or for encouraging others in a like disposition? When? Where? Why?"

"Have you ever been noted, presented, or detected publicly, to have been faulty in all and singular the premises? Have you ever been admonished,

[1] The Puritans objected to the use of these words, only when performing the burial-service for persons of immoral lives and principles, who had given no tokens of godly repentance.

officially, to reform? Have you refused, or deferred? When? Where? Why?"

"Have you been required to subscribe the Three Articles, and refused? To whom have you refused? How often? Do you persist in refusing?"

"Have you, without a license, preached, or read, or expounded the Scriptures, in public, or in private houses? When? Where?"[1]

Such was the style of inquisition under oath, which Whitgift projected; which Elizabeth "knew and allowed." Fifteen years before,—when there was commotion in her realm, and when "slanderous reports, specially from foreign parts, to the depraving that part of her government which concerned the ecclesiastical external policy of her realm"[2] were abroad,—she had proclaimed to the world: "We know not, nor have any meaning to allow, that any of our subjects should be molested, either by examination or inquisition, in any matter either of Faith, as long as they shall profess the Christian Faith . . . . or for matter of ceremonies, or any other external matters appertaining to the Christian Religion, as long as they shall in their outward conversation show themselves quiet and conformable, and not *manifestly* repugnant and obstinate to the laws . . . . for frequentation of Divine Service in the ordinary churches."[3] Now,—when intestine disturbance had ceased and foreign power was but little feared,—her subjects who *did* "frequent Divine Service in the ordinary churches," her subjects who were *not* "manifestly repugnant" to the laws for going to church, her

[1] Strype's Whitgift, Appendix, Bk. III. No. IV. pp. 49 – 52.

[2] Haynes, 591 *passim.*

[3] Ibid., 591, 592.

clergy who might be "*suspected*" — so ran her Commission — of any ecclesiastical fault, were to be "molested" flagrantly, grievously, and openly, "by examination or inquisition," not only "for matter of ceremonies and other externals appertaining to the Christian Religion," but even for "matter of faith" or opinion. If Elizabeth had changed her mind, she was not "*Semper Eadem.*" If she had not, she —

This, however, was comparatively a small matter. The Inquisition instituted by her Archbishop, with her "knowledge and allowance," wore a graver aspect. In every point of it, some offence against the letter of the law, or some offensive *opinion*, might be brought to light which would subject the respondent — if not to the loss of life — to the loss of good name or goods, of freehold or liberty, "otherwise than by the legal judgment of his peers, or by the law of the land."[1] But besides the inherent atrocity of a tribunal so arbitrary and so inquisitorial, there were wrongs naturally incident to its operation, and which gravely aggravated its tyranny.

For three hundred and sixty-eight years, it had been stipulated by solemn compact between the Crown and the People, that "no person should be put upon trial from rumor or suspicion alone, but upon evidence of lawful witnesses." The High Court of Commission set at naught this stipulation; a violation of natural and chartered right which could not fail of bitter fruit. They placed every Puritan minister at the mercy of every profligate. The votary of vice, or pleasure, or greed, could easily find grudge against the preacher of righteousness; malice could

[1] Magna Charta.

easily denounce its victim; the ear of the Court was always open to a charge of "suspicion;" and the "suspect person" was in their power. Then came the writ of citation, with its costs, — hard to be borne by country curates on stinted livings (or, sometimes, arrest without citation); then, "bonds for personal appearance," or a jail for safe keeping; then, "the Picklock of Conscience, — the oath;"[1] then, if self-convicted or silent, deprivation, or fine, or imprisonment. Yet, with all these antecedents of trial, and with all its ensnaring interrogation, the process of the Court was not complete. Although he should deny every charge and upon his oath, the respondent was *never* cleared upon his denial; and the Court often proceeded to a *second* trial, by the examination of witnesses.[2] Thus, however truthful and cautious he might be, the unfortunate man was thrown upon a new peril, — the risk of contradiction between himself and others by which he might be indicted for perjury. Such was the fiery trial — and, to protract it ever so long, fresh fuel could always be found — through which any single-minded, Christ-like curate in the realm might be forced to atone for a single, bygone, ceremonial sin, or to answer a single whisper of malice.

In its proceedings, the High Court of Commission acted upon, and sometimes exceeded, the letter of its Commission. In conflict with the temporal courts, — of right its supervisors, — but overshadowed by the august Supremacy of the Crown, it easily frightened the judges from uttering inhibitions upon its doings. Thus — in this instance — the ascendency of the

[1] Fuller, Bk. IX. p. 186. [2] Ibid.

queen's writ over the fundamental laws of her realm was, for a time, established; and three men therein named, at will and without let, might make havoc upon the pledged and sacred rights of Englishmen. "No person," — were the express words of the venerable Magna Charta, — "no person shall be put upon his trial from rumor or suspicion alone, but upon the evidence of lawful witnesses. No free man shall be taken, imprisoned, or disseized of his free tenement or liberties, or outlawed, or banished, or anywise hurt or injured, unless by legal judgment of his peers, or by the law of the land." This was musty paper in the eyes of the Commissioners. To resist them, therefore, was to resist despotism. To suffer at their hands, was to suffer under tyranny. And, however imperfectly the true principles of Liberty were then comprehended, they whose instinctive sense of natural rights and whose manly hearts, brought them into collision with this Court, were pouring their painful contributions upon that slowly rising tide which was destined to sweep Despotism away. The "contumacious" Puritan, braving this power, moaning in its dungeon, swinging on its gibbet, was in very truth a primitive apostle and martyr of an unwritten political gospel.

CHAPTER XV.

"SCANT CHARITABLE." (LORD BURLEIGH.)

THE COMMISSIONERS IN BAD REPUTE. — SIR FRANCIS KNOLLYS COMPLAINS OF SILENCING PREACHERS OF SOUND DOCTRINE. — A POLEMIC PASSAGE BETWEEN BEAL, CLERK OF THE COUNCIL, AND THE ARCHBISHOP. — HIS GRACE IGNORANT OF THE DOCUMENTS ON WHICH HE HAS BASED HIS PROCEEDINGS. — BEAL TRAVAILS WITH THE ARCHBISHOP BY LETTER. — BURLEIGH PRESSED BY MEN OF QUALITY TO STAY THE ARCHBISHOP'S "VEHEMENT PROCEEDINGS." — BURLEIGH COMMENDS EDWARD BRAYNE, A REFUSER OF SUBSCRIPTION, TO THE FAVOR OF HIS GRACE. — HE DISCOVERS WHITGIFT'S ARTICLES OF INQUISITION. — HIS SPIRITED REPREHENSION OF THEM. — HIS GRACE REPLIES; BUT "PASSES THE CONTROVERSY IN SILENCE." — BURLEIGH ANSWERS MILDLY, BUT CHARGES THE ARCHBISHOP WITH BREACH OF PROMISE; AND YIELDS BRAYNE'S CASE. — BRAYNE BEFORE THE COMMISSIONERS. — HIS FINAL APPEAL TO BURLEIGH; WHO REMONSTRATES AGAIN. — HIS GRACE VINDICATES THE OATH EX OFFICIO, AND HIMSELF. — COMPLAINS THAT MISLIKERS OF NON-CONFORMITY MISLIKE THAT NON-CONFORMISTS "SHOULD BE SUPPRESSED AND PUNISHED." — COMPLAINTS ACCUMULATE UPON THE COUNCIL-TABLE. — THE COUNCIL WRITE TO HIS GRACE AND THE BISHOP OF LONDON, COMPLAINING THAT GOOD MEN ARE PUT OUT OF THE MINISTRY AND BAD ONES PUT IN. — BURLEIGH FEARS THAT A BISHOP'S CHAIR MAKES AN UNWORLDLY MAN WORLDLY. — HIS GRACE THINKS THAT IT IS NOT THE CHAIR, BUT A BAD WAY OF GETTING INTO IT. — HE DECLARES THAT SEVERITY IS LAWFUL, USEFUL, AND CHARITABLE. — SO GENERAL A REPREHENSION OF THE ARCHBISHOP'S COURSE EXCITES HIS FEARS THAT THE QUEEN WILL BE WROUGHT AGAINST HIM. — THE TRUE GROUNDS OF THAT REPREHENSION. — THE QUEEN THE ONLY "REFUGE" AND SUPPORT OF HER PRIMATE.

1584.

A BAD odor was going out from Lambeth. By all but the despised Brownist, it was thought meet for humanity and acceptable to God, to manage the Church by statute; and heresy, with a rod of iron. But to pare away manhood, to anatomize opinion perforce, to rank the preacher of sound doctrine with the felon, to rule the Church *in contempt* of statute,—was odious, even in Elizabeth's day, to others than those who suffered. The wise men who formed her cabinet, Churchmen as they were, — Walsingham, Hatton, Burleigh,—had already begun to look doubtfully upon the measures of the new Primate. He was jealous of this; and was therefore disturbed when the gentlemen of Kent, at the close of their fruitless intercession for their ministers, had spoken of appealing to the queen or her Council. The very next day he wrote to her Majesty's Vice-chamberlain, Sir Christopher Hatton.

"I beseech your Honor to foresee (as much as in you lieth) that these ministers of Kent receive no encouragement from above; and (if need require) to signify this my petition to her Majesty. If these few, being of none account either for years, learning, or degree, ... shall be countenanced against the law, against me, and against all the rest of the preachers in my diocese, it will not be possible for me, either there or anywhere else, to do that good in procuring the peace of the Church, obedience and observance of good orders, which I am assured I shall bring to pass if I be suffered, without such overthwarts, to proceed as I have begun. Unless such contentious persons *were some way animated and backed*, they would not stand out as they do. . . . . Your Honor's as his own,

"JOHN CANTUAR."[1]

[1] Life of Hatton, 372.

There is something in this letter which would have been irrelevant in the text, but which deserves notice because difficult to be reconciled with facts. His lordship says, "I have in my diocese of Kent one hundred preachers and more, where-

It was not a groundless apprehension of the Archbishop, that the courtiers might be disaffected to his policy. "Your Grace's wisdom and learning doth know," wrote Sir Francis Knollys on the eighth day of June, "that by natural corruption, we her Majesty's subjects are in generality headily given to superstition and idolatry; which be, as it were, the arms of the Pope to draw us into his glittering kingdom of strong delusions..... And since this mighty enemy of God and of her Majesty, so full of treasonable practices, cannot be withstood, but by opening the mouths of preachers zealous and sound in doctrine,— although, as men, they have otherwise infirmities, as well in discretion as in judgment concerning politics and things indifferent,—therefore I do presume *again*, as I have done aforetime, most humbly to beseech your Grace *to open* the mouths of all zealous

of *ten* only, or thereabouts, have refused subscription." This was written on the ninth day of May, 1584. In February preceding, the Kentish ministers had appeared before him, — so much of "a multitude as imported conspiracy,"—*fourteen* in number. They had "refused to subscribe;" and his lordship had "suspended" them upon the spot. Could he have *forgotten* that there were so many? Or were fourteen "thereabouts" to ten? Their names are given by Strype (Life of Whitgift, p. 123), in a list of eighteen, four of whom belonged to the diocese of Rochester.

Such discrepancy, and under such circumstances, between the Archbishop's statement and the record, may well shake, if not destroy, confidence in his Schedule, rendered in June, 1584 (Strype's Whitgift, 155, and App. No. VII.) of the preachers in the Province of Canterbury who had "refused to yield conformity;" and also in his statement that "of these *the third* part were not suspended, but only admonished." He gives the whole number which had been returned to him of what he calls "Recusants" in the *Province*, forty-nine; adding, that there would not be many more unless in the dioceses of Norwich and Peterborough. One third part of forty-nine is sixteen, "or thereabouts;" thirteen of whom, according to his schedule, were in the single *diocese* of Canterbury, which (I suppose) comprised the county of Kent, in which he had himself "suspended fourteen."

preachers that be sound in doctrine, howsoever otherwise they *refuse to subscribe* to any tradition of man *not compellable by law*, or be infirm as before is said."[1]

There happened also a flurry between the Archbishop and the clerk of the Council; some incidents and words of which show not only how the wind was setting at court, but the tempers of the two men,—representatives of the Puritan and the Prelatic parties. Robert Beal was too old to be twitted with being a "boy;" too well read in divinity and in civil law to be openly charged with ignorance; and too high in her Majesty's confidence to be despised. He had given to the Archbishop a written remonstrance against the existing administration of Church affairs; and on the fifth day of May came to Lambeth to receive it again.[2] Some words had passed, in the course of which the Archbishop had refused to return the Paper. Mr. Beal replied to this:—

"When I delivered your lordship the writing, I did it *upon promise* to have it again and finish it, and to be better persuaded by some answer from your lordship. But to that which I wrote in eight days, I get no answer these eight weeks, more than '*ipse dixit;*' but no Scripture and no law."[3]

"I make no doubt you have a copy. If not, I will have it transcribed for you."

"My lord, I let pass your refusal; but will take it upon me to say at this present, that in persisting as you do in the execution of your lordship's Articles,

[1] Strype's Whitgift, Append., Bk. III. No. VIII. p. 62.

[2] Strype's Whitgift, 146.

[3] Strype's Whitgift, Appendix, p. 54.

you will be the overthrower of this Church, and a cause of tumult."

"Methinks it is not God's Spirit that moveth you, sir; for He worketh in man humility, patience, love. But your words declare you to be very arrogant, proud, impatient, and uncharitable."

"I had promise from your lordship to be better persuaded than my book did import, by some answer by your lordship. Albeit, I do now think that the bishops are never *able* to answer it; neither touching its points of divinity nor its points of law."

"Troth, sir! there be no great substance in it. It might very soon be answered. It maketh plain that neither your divinity nor your law be great."

"Seeing I seem in your lordship's eyes to be so base and contemptible and unmeet to deal in these causes, let me without arrogancy say something of myself. I have by the space of twenty-six years and upwards been a student of the civil laws, and long sith could have taken degree. And albeit, for lack of use my skill be impaired, yet would I be loath that the greatest doctor that is about your lordship could so teach me what law is, but that, with a little study, I could discern whether he say truly or no. In divinity, I think I have read as much as any chaplain your lordship hath. And when my book shall be finished and answered, let others judge thereof."

"I wish, sir, you were better advised in your *doings;* for in verity you be one of the principal causes of the waywardness of divers; because you give encouragement unto them to stand in the matter, telling them that the Articles shall be revoked shortly by the Council, and that my hands shall be stopped, and such like. This that you do, be bruited in every place, and is the only cause that so many do forbear to subscribe."

"It be an easy thing to charge a man in generality, my lord. But if it can be proved that I have counselled any one of the ministers that hath come up, to stand in the cause, but have not rather advised many by all humble and dutiful means to seek their relief at your lordship's hands, then will I be contented to submit myself to any punishment that her Majesty shall lay upon me."

The Puritan was heated; and he uttered more that was plain-spoken and unpalatable. In turn, the Archbishop's choler was up, and he retorted:—

"Sir, you do forget yourself. Your speeches be intolerable. You are a malapert; a maintainer of disorders; a mocker of preachers. I shall complain of you to her Majesty:" whereof Beal seemed to make small account, and so departed in great heat.[1]

But his lordship had let slip a confession — which told hard for one who was enforcing the Book of Common Prayer on the ground that it was established by law — that "he had *never seen* King Edward's Books of Common Prayer;"[2] the very Books upon which, by the terms of the statute, the *lawfulness* or *obligatory force* of the Book then used depended! Ignorant too, until taught by a Puritan, that it was said in the same Prayer-Book that "whosoever is baptized is undoubtedly saved"! *Is* it uncharitable to suppose that one thus unfamiliar with that for

[1] Strype's Whitgift, 146; Appendix, Bk. III. No. VI. *passim.*

[2] Strype's Whitgift, Appendix, p. 55.

whose legal authority and Biblical accuracy he was contending, did so for some *other* reason than that which he alleged?

The Clerk of the Council did not drop the controversy when he parted from his Grace; but, two days afterwards, wrote to him in his own vindication. After some words about "malapertness," he continued his letter thus:—

"But forsooth, concerning my mocking of sermons, let me be charged with particular matter; and if I do not sufficiently answer it, let me abide the pain. I know the bishop that would have had your lordship to complain of me to her Majesty was angry with me for saying that his sermon was a good sermon *for a bishop*. I know not well whether I said the words or no. But this I dare avouch,—that some of his sermons before her Majesty were such as prince, councillors, and all the rest of the auditory departed *with very evil satisfaction*, yea, *derision* of his doings. The like can I say of others; and of your lordship's chaplain that preached in the Court 8 March last, that having divided his text into four several parts, *never touched any of them*, but foolishly entered into other bye and impertinent matters. And what the opinion of those of her Majesty's Council and the Lord Bishop, that was then present, was, your lordship may understand from others. If, falsely and imprudently, such preachers allege and surmise things which are not found so, may not these things be misliked, and they told of it? Is not this to reduce the laity to the Popish ignorance? Are we only beasts? and is the Spirit of God and his good gifts only bestowed upon such as are termed of the clergy?

"I am not so malapert or obstinate but I will give place to truth; and, in the mean time, your lordship must pardon me if I be not by the nose led with any Pythagorical or Papal *ipse dixit*.....

"I see the preaching of Christ's blessed Word is little regarded; the people is untaught; the gentlemen known to be best affected to God and her Majesty are therewith grieved; the adversary to them both is comforted; Popery and Atheism increaseth; our enemies abroad are likely to lay hold on this opportunity to work their mischief. And therefore as hitherto the vigorous execution of these things"—preaching the Word and teaching the people—"hath been in a sort (in respect to the necessity of the State) *qualified and suspended*, so most of all (circumstances being duly considered) ought it to be now.[1] For howsoever small my learning and other gifts seem to your lordship to be, my knowledge of the State, the experience of my place, my being abroad, and my endeavor by reading and otherwise to come to knowledge of these matters, are such, that I dare, with a good conscience to God and her Majesty, say, that such is this State now that *if these proceedings go forward* as they have begun, both the Church and the Estate of the whole realm will receive great prejudice and hurt thereby, whatsoever your lordship thinketh otherwise.....

[1] That is: "As preaching and teaching have been curtailed, when we consider what grief to good men and what exultation to our enemies this policy has wrought, so much the greater reason do we see why this teaching and preaching should *be* again."

"As for Popery, I have detested it, and do still. I *fear the relapse of this realm into it,* whereof my conscience persuadeth me that *these actions are forerunners.* And it grieveth me not a little to have probably heard that the traitor Throckmorton, sith his commitment to the Tower, hath commended your lordship to be the only meetest bishop of this realm. The rest of that crew have conceived the same opinion and courage, not without cause; for *Popery is left untouched, or findeth more favor;* and those that instruct the people to beware of them *are put to silence,* so as the wolf may enter and make havoc of the flock at his pleasure.

"I am presently despatched from her Majesty to the Scottish queen..... But, by the way, I must tell your lordship that *she liketh very well* of your lordship's proceedings against the Puritans, whom she accounteth her mortal enemies; and *alloweth better* of the order that is meant to be established by *your lordship* in this Church than she doth of the Churches in France or Scotland; for that *here lacketh nothing but only the setting up of the Mass again.....*

"I have discharged the part of a Christian man and dutiful subject to her Majesty, to foretell your lordship of these things, and to beseech you, for the necessity of the time, to suffer the Church to enjoy that peace which it did at your coming to your place. ....The Lord Jesus give unto your lordship a true love and compassion of his Church,....that you may give a good account of the feeding of his sheep, which, *being bereft of their good shepherds, do want food, and are like to die both body and soul;* the penalty whereof, without remission, will be exacted at your lordship's hands. . . . . From my poor house at London, the vij^{h} of May, 1584. Your lordship's in all Christian and dutiful manner to command,

"ROBERT BEAL."[1]

Although this letter is not to be taken as an exponent of the views of the Lords of the Council, yet we may presume that Beal would not have ventured so far, had he not been aware of some degree of their sympathy. But this plain dealing wrought no change in his Grace. He was firm in the opinion that "mild kind of proceeding, with wilful persons in the ministry did them rather harm than good."[2]

In the mean time, the Lord Treasurer Burleigh was constantly beset with private petitions of ministers who were afflicted by the Archbishop and his colleagues in commission, but who were certified by persons worthy of credit, to be peaceable persons in their ministry.[3] Petitions likewise poured in upon him from their friends, "some of whom were of great name and quality."[4] At length he was daily charged by Councillors and public persons to have neglected his duty in "*not staying the Archbishop's proceedings,* so vehement and so *general* against ministers and preachers." To which upbraidings, his lordship had replied charitably — and honestly, no doubt — that "he thought the Archbishop was doing nothing which did not tend to maintain the religion established and to prevent schism." And when it was urged "what

[1] Strype's Whitgift, Append., Bk. III. No. VI.

[2] Strype's Whitgift, 155; Whitgift to Burleigh in June.

[3] Burleigh to Whitgift; Strype's Appendix, p. 63.

[4] Strype's Whitgift, 156.

a mighty scarcity there was of preachers in the realm, and what danger the queen's subjects were in of going back to Popery if these preachers should be suspended from their office," he had pointed to the Archbishop's schedule, showing how few had refused to yield to conformity; and to his written statement, that only "one third or thereabouts" of these few had been suspended.[1] The Lord Treasurer did not know all; but his eyes were soon opened.

In the latter part of May, two ministers of Cambridgeshire came upon a pilgrimage to London to seek relief from prelatic oppression. They had refused subscription to the "Three Articles," and had received two of the three canonical admonitions which usage required should precede suspension. They had petitioned the Archbishop that they might be excused from subscription, or be allowed longer time of grace. This had received no attention. After reaching London, they presented a Petition to the Lords of Council on the twenty-fourth day of May. In this Paper, they stated that they had taken the Oath of Supremacy and subscribed the Articles of Religion as required by statute; that they used the Book of Common Prayer, abhorred Popery, heresy, and schism, and were loyal to the queen; that they had been commanded to subscribe to things *not required by law,* some of which were against their consciences, some doubtful, and some of whose nature they were ignorant. "If," said they, "we offend against any law of the Church, or statute, we humbly crave such favor and clemency as is not contrary to law; but if this cannot be obtained, we submit our-

[1] Strype's Whitgift, 157; Appendix, p. 63.

selves to the censures of the law. We therefore most humbly beseech your Honors, that we may be freed from the subscription now urged upon us."[1]

Although he had always an inconceivable amount of business upon his hands, the Lord Treasurer's ear was always open to a cry. When it was possible, "he used to answer the poorest soul by word of mouth; appointing times and places."[2] It was but according to his custom, therefore, that these men by appointment waited upon his lordship a few days after their Petition had been received. But, to their astonishment, they met with a sharp reception.

"So, sirs!" he exclaimed, as they announced their names, "ye be the factious curates from Cambridgeshire! A right fair Petition yours touching 'your doubtful, fearful, distressed consciences, and your loyalty, and your obedience, and your poor people hungering for the bread of life.' I remember your words. And now, forsooth, it appeareth that ye go up and down the country making mischief, maugre your oily professions!"

The poor men were staggered. But Edward Brayne, who seems throughout this affair to have been the foremost of the two, replied, "Factious and mischievous, my lord! We do not think ourselves so chargeable."

"But I charge you."

"We humbly require at your lordship's hands only that we may be put upon trial, and so to receive punishment as shall appear."

"Hist, sirs! I did write to his Grace commending you to his favor; so much did your Petition move

[1] Brook, I. 289, 290. [2] Desid. Curiosa, Vol. I. Bk. I. p. 19.

me; and withal, a good report I had of your modesty and peaceableness. But anon his Grace hath wrot to me that ye be 'contentious, seditious, and persons vagrant.'"

"My lord, *whosoever* chargeth us so, we deny it."

"His Grace will so charge you. Go to him; go to him. So shall I afterward see what ye do deserve. Nor he, nor I, will judge you unheard. Howbeit,—howbeit,"—as though another thought had been suggested by the countenance and port of the men,—"perchance there be some ill report of misaffected informers.[1] An ye *be* good men and peaceable, take comfort. Ye will find favorable proceeding at his Grace's hands; and I hope so the more from my recommendation of your case. Come to me again."

The two ministers accordingly went their ways; and returned as he had bidden.

"Well, sirs! how hath it fared with you? How hath his Grace proceeded? As I said, I trow."

"We have been commanded to be examined by the Register."

His lordship mused a moment, and said dryly, "Whereof?"

"Of a great number of Articles, my lord. But we know them not, for we could have no copies."

"No matter. Ye may answer according to the truth."

"My lord, we are told that the Articles be so many in number, and so divers, as we be afraid to answer to them for fear of captious interpretations."

"Humph! the bishop saith the Puritan is captious. The Puritan saith the bishop is captious. An ye be

[1] Of "informers," see *ante*, p. 377, note.

all gone captious, woe worth the day! Go your ways again. I will look after this matter. An ye be good subjects I will befriend ye. An ye be *not*, I may bespeak your pardon—*when ye do amend*."

He did look after the matter, forthwith. First he sent for the Register, who brought him the Articles, which he read. Then he wrote to his Grace as follows, after having stated what we have given above:—

"It may please your Grace, I have thus by chance come to the sight of an instrument of twenty-four Articles of great length and curiosity, found in a Romish style, to examine all manner of ministers in this time without distinction of persons; which Articles are entitled '*Apud Lambeth May*, 1584, *to be executed ex Officio Mero*,' &c. Which I have read, and find so curiously penned, so full of branches and circumstances, as I think the Inquisitors of Spain use not so many questions to comprehend and to trap their preys.

"I know your canonists can defend these with all their particles; but surely, under your Grace's correction, this judicial and canonical sifting of poor ministers is not to edify or reform. And in charity, I think, they ought not to answer to all these nice points, except they were very notorious offenders in Papistry or heresy. Now, my good lord, bear with my scribbling. I write with the testimony of a good conscience. I desire the peace of the Church. I desire concord and unity in the exercise of our Religion. I favor no sensual and wilful recusants. But I conclude that, according to my simple judgment, this kind of proceeding is too much savoring of the Romish Inquisition; and is rather a device *to seek for* offenders, than to reform any. This is not the charitable instruction *that I thought was intended.* If those poor ministers should in some few points have any scrupulous conceptions meet to be removed, this is not a charitable way, to send them to answer to your common Register upon *so many Articles at one instant,* without any commodity of instruction by your Register, whose office is only to receive their answers. By which the parties are first subject to condemnation before they be taught their error.

"It may be, as I said, the canonists may maintain this proceeding by rules of their laws. But though all things be lawful, yet all are not expedient. I pray your Grace, bear *that one* (perchance a) fault, that I have willed them not to answer these Articles, except their consciences may suffer them. And yet I have sharply admonished them, that, if they be disturbers of the Church, they must be corrected. And yet upon your Grace's answer, I will leave them to your authority, as becometh me. Let not the cobbler go beyond his last. Neither will I put the sickle into another man's harvest. My paper teacheth me to end.

"First of July, 1584. Your Grace's at commandment,

"W. CECIL."[1]

"Your Grace must pardon my hasty writing; for I have done this *raptim.*"[2]

Two days afterwards, the Archbishop replied in a

[1] *Sic.*

[2] Strype's Whitgift, Append., Bk. III. No. IX. Fuller, Bk. IX. pp. 154–156.

tedious letter, of which we present the most important parts.

"My singular good lord, ... I have *by your lordship's advice* chosen this kind of proceeding with them, because I would not touch any for not subscribing only, but for breach of order in celebrating divine service, administering sacraments, and executing other ecclesiastical functions, according to their fancies, and not according to the form by law prescribed. Which neither your lordship, nor others, seemed to mislike, but to wish and require.....

"Touching the twenty-four Articles, ... I cannot but greatly marvel at your lordship's vehement speeches against them; seeing it is the ordinary course in other courts likewise; as in the Star-Chamber, the Court of the Marches" — Borders — "and other places..... I think these Articles to be more tolerable .... than those in other courts; because men are there oftentimes examined at the relation of a private man concerning private crimes. Whereas here men are only examined of their public acts in their public calling....[1]

"Your lordship writeth that the two for whom you speak are peaceable, observe the Book, and deny the

[1] By looking at the Articles of interrogatory, the reader will perceive that this is strangely untrue. "*Only* examined of their public *acts!*" How many questions touched their opinions? How many, also, touched the *intent* with which they did, or omitted to do?

But aside from this — what sort of *reasoning* is here? Whether a man's crime was public or private, official or non-official, mattered nothing. It did not touch the point of a man's criminating himself, which was the point at issue. Besides, a *public* crime admits, surely, of witnesses; so that there is no need of the monstrous extortion of a man's testimony against himself.

things whereof they are charged..... I do minister these Articles unto them .... that I may truly understand whether they are such men, or no, as they pretend to be; especially seeing that by public fame they are noted of the contrary, and one of them presented by the sworn men of his parish for his disorders.....

"I know your lordship desireth the peace of the Church. But how is it possible to be procured (after so long liberty and lack of discipline) if a few persons, *so meanly qualified* as most of them are, should be countenanced against the whole Estate of the clergy of greatest account for learning, steadiness, religion, and honesty; and open breakers and impugners of the laws, *young in years*, proud in conceit, contentious in disposition, be maintained against their superiors and governors seeking to reduce them to obedience? .... For my own part, I have done nothing in this matter which I do not think myself in duty and conscience bound to do; which her Majesty hath not *with earnest charge committed unto me*..... If your lordship do keep these two from answering according to the order set down, it will be of itself a setting at liberty of all the rest, and an undoing of all which hitherto hath been done. Neither shall I be able to do that which her Majesty expecteth at my hands and is now in very good forwardness. And therefore I beseech your lordship to leave them unto me.....

"From Croydon, the 3 of July, 1584. To your lordship most bound,

"JO. CANTUAR."[1]

[1] Strype's Whitgift, Appendix, Bk. III. No. X. Fuller, Bk. IX. pp. 156 – 159.

We suspend comment upon this letter, except to say — what charity whispers in our ear — that, at least, the Archbishop betrayed his culpable ignorance in alleging that the oath was used in the Star-Chamber as in the Court of Commission. True, it was used in the Star-Chamber and in Chancery; but with this heaven-wide difference, that a copy of the interrogations or articles, upon which the party was *to be* examined, was delivered to him "to the intent that he might know whether he ought by law to answer them."[1] The reader will perceive that "the point of seeking by examination to have these ministers accuse themselves, and then to punish them for their own confessions,"[2] — the whole burden of Burleigh's letter, — was not touched. Frivolous reasons and evasions did not satisfy the statesman; as is evident from his reply.

"I have received your Grace's long letter..... I perceive you are sharply moved to blame me and clear yourself. I know I have many faults, but I hope I have not given such cause of offence as your letter expresseth. I deny nothing that your Grace thinketh meet to proceed in with those whom you call factious..... *The controversy is passed, in your Grace's letter, in silence.*.... I say, your Grace *promised* me to deal only with such as violated[3] order, and to *charge* them therewith, — which I well allow of. But your Grace, *not* charging them with such faults, seeketh by examination to urge them to accuse themselves, and then I think you will punish them.[4] I

[1] Coke's Reports, Part XII. p. 26. Fuller, Bk. IX. p. 186.

[2] Strype's Whitgift, 160.

[3] In Strype "vilified."

[4] Fuller, Bk. IX. p. 159.

think your Grace's proceeding is — I will not say rigorous or captious, but I think it — scant charitable. .... I am content that your Grace and my Lord of London,[1] where I hear Brayne is, use him as your wisdoms shall think meet. If I had known his *fault*, I might be blamed for writing for him; but when by examination only it is meant to sift him with twenty-four Articles, I have cause to pity the poor man. Your Grace's, as friendly as ever,

"WILL: BURLEIGH."[2]

On Friday — it seems to have been the fourth day of July, the day after the date of the Archbishop's letter — Brayne and his brother in affliction presented themselves at Lambeth palace, but were denied access to his Grace. On Saturday, they went thither again; when they were admitted, and found themselves in presence of the High Commission. The Archbishop immediately ordered them to go before his Secretary, Mr. Hartwell, and make their answers. To the Secretary's apartment they went; but he told them "*precisely* that he could not by any means that day take their answer." But, lest the delay should seem to be a fault of his own, Brayne went to Mr. Hartwell again in the afternoon, when he was called in before his lordship and two of his colleagues in Commission, who were a sufficient number to constitute a court. Being required to take the oath, he refused, unless it might please his Grace that he should first have the Articles before him, and alone, that he might write his answers with his own

[1] The two chief ecclesiastical Commissioners.

[2] Strype's Whitgift, 160.

hand. This was denied. The Archbishop then gave him a grave exhortation, and closed with his canonical admonitions upon the spot,—once, twice, thrice,—and by then ordering a registry to be made of his "*Refusal with contempt.*"[1]

"God knoweth," wrote the poor man to Lord Burleigh on the sixth day of the month,—"God knoweth how far any contempt was from my heart; and I trust my words and behavior will witness the same." In this same letter he gave the Lord Treasurer the narrative of proceedings which we have stated above; and wrote further:—

"We fear lest our repair for relief to your good lordship hath procured us his harder opinion and dealing at his Grace's hands.... My lord, my estate is poor, my charges great, the time of my attendance upon the Commissioners uncertain, and I am perplexed through doubt of further troubles. I therefore beseech your lordship to succor a poor man whose refuge is unto you; who would gladly satisfy his Grace with any duty which *God's law, or man's law, or common humanity* requireth. And so, leaving the means of succor unto your honorable compassion, I beseech the Lord Jesus to bless your lordship with all manner of graces, and many honorable days."[2]

[1] Brook adds, "and suspended him from the ministry." Perhaps so. Probably; else why the three canonical admonitions? Yet I find no authority for this. I confine myself to Brayne's own statement; and the more scrupulously because, if the Archbishop *did* then suspend him, he must have violated a distinct promise in his letter of July 3d to Lord Burleigh,—"I will not proceed to *any sentence* against them, until I have made your Lordship privy to *their answers*, and further conferred with you thereof" (Strype's Whitgift, Append., p. 66); a sentence which I have omitted in the text.

[2] Strype's Whitgift, 163.

His lordship immediately wrote beneath this the following, and sent the Paper to the Dean of Westminster, one of the Commissioners: —

"Master Dean, I cannot but receive poor men's complaints; and yet I use to suspend my opinion. If these poor men be worse used at my Lord of Canterbury's hands, or his officers, I shall be sorry. The fault or lack is mine, not theirs. When you have read this, return it to me again."[1]

"When the good prelate," says honest Mr. Strype, — and for his honesty we thank him, — "when the good prelate came to know this from the Dean, or some other way, it did not a little afflict him."[2] Wherefore, on the fifteenth day of the month, he despatched three long documents to the Lord Burleigh; one containing reasons for proceeding in ecclesiastical Commission by the oath *ex officio;* another, stating inconveniences of not so proceeding; and a third, in the form of a letter, in vindication of himself. The first consisted, in substance, of statements purely *ex cathedra;* that "the ministering of such Articles was so clear by law that it was never *hitherto* called in doubt;" that it had been practised; that "it was consistent with law, reason, and charity, for a man" — to be forced? — "to accuse himself;" with charity, "because none are in this manner to be proceeded against, but whom their own speeches or acts, the public fame, and some of credit, shall denounce and signify;"[3] and that it was an admirable

[1] Strype's Whitgift, 164.

[2] Ibid.

[3] Was the Archbishop as ignorant of the very Commission under which he was acting, as of the Book of Common Prayer, and of the process of the Star-Chamber? Did he, or did he not, know that the Com-

contrivance for the detection and conviction of "these singular persons" who were so few in the Province of Canterbury, that "there were but *hundreds* of them to *thousands* of Conformists,"[1] and who, in comparison, "were far inferior for excellence of gift in learning, discretion, and considerate zeal."

The sum of the second Paper was, — that in eight particulars it would *make more trouble*, especially to the bishops, to convict by witnesses, than to make a man convict himself. "Weighty Papers," says his biographer!

We give the most spirited parts of the third Paper in his own words: —

"My singular good lord, God knoweth how desirous I have been .... to satisfy your lordship in all things, and to have my doings approved by you..... I have risen early and set up late to write unto you objections and answers. I have not done the like to any man. And shall I now say, that I have lost my labor? Or shall my just dealing with two of the most disordered ministers in a whole diocese .... cause you so to think and speak of my doings and of myself? No man living should have made me believe it. My lord, an old friend is better than a new; and I trust your lordship will not so lightly cast off your old friends for any of these new-fangled and factious sectaries.....

mission professedly empowered the Court "to call before them all persons *suspected* of any of the premises, and to *examine* them on their corporal oaths"?

[1] In June, the Archbishop's census of the righteous and the wicked gave — so far as ascertained — only forty-nine "singular persons" to only seven hundred and eighty-six not singular. Now, in July, two and a half score, "or thereabouts," had grown to indefinite hundreds; and three fourths — "or thereabouts" — of one thousand to indefinite thousands.

"Your lordship seemeth to charge me with breach of promise touching my manner of proceeding; whereof I am no way guilty. But I *have altered my first course* of dealing with them for not subscribing only, and chosen this *only to satisfy your lordship*. . . . .

"Your lordship further seemeth to burthen me with *wilfulness*. . . . . I appeal to your own conscience. There is a difference betwixt wilfulness and constancy. I have taken upon me the defence of the religion and rites of the Church, ... the reducing the ministers thereof to uniformity and obedience. Herein I intend to be constant, ... wherein your lordship and others ought, as I take it, to help me. It is more than strange that a man in my place, dealing by so good warranties as I do, should be so hardly used; and, for not yielding, be counted wilful. . . . . If my friends herein forsake me, I trust God will not; nor her Majesty; who have laid the charge on me, and are able to protect me.

"But of all other things it most grieveth me, that your lordship should say the two ministers fare the worse because you sent them. Had your lordship ever any cause to think so of me? . . . . I have rather occasion to complain to your lordship of yourself, that upon so small occasion you will so hardly conceive of me; and, as it were, countenance persons so meanly qualified in so evil a cause against me, their Ordinary, and your lordship's long-tried friend. It hath not been so in times past; and now it should not, least of all. . . . .

"I have sent unto you, herein closed, certain reasons to justify the manner of my proceeding, which I marvel should be so much misliked. . . . .

Truly I must proceed this way, or not at all..... And now, my singular good lord, I heartily pray you not to be carried away, either from the cause, or from myself, upon unjust surmises or clamors; lest thereby you be some occasion of that confusion which, hereafter, you will be sorry for..... To conclude, I am your lordship's most assured; neither do I doubt the continuance of your good affection towards me; which I heartily desire, as God himself knoweth, to whose tuition I commit you. From Croydon, the 15 of July, 1584. To your lordship most bound,

"JO. CANTUAR."[1]

We shall see that "the Lord Treasurer, with all the labor and pains of the Archbishop, was not convinced of the justness and blamelessness of the proceedings."[2] Nor could his Grace shake off his apprehensions of a counter influence from the Court; nor was the opposition which he encountered there slight — as appear by a letter written two days afterwards, to Sir Christopher Hatton, who had offered to befriend his Grace with the queen;[3] and "whose great friendship and courtesy, most honorably offered, he was most bold to use, especially at this time, in the public cause of the Church and State;"[4] but who, notwithstanding, was on the eve of subscribing a stinging rebuke of the ecclesiastical administration.

"Right Honorable, I give you most hearty thanks for that friendly message .... by Mr. Kemp. I shall think myself bound unto you therefor, as long as I

[1] Strype's Whitgift, Append., Bk. III. No. XI. Fuller, Bk. IX. p. 160.

[2] Strype's Whitgift, 165.

[3] Ibid., 224.

[4] Whitgift to Hatton, May 9th, 1584; Life of Hatton, 372.

live. It hath not a little comforted me, in respect of some unkind speeches lately received from those who, I little thought, of all others would have taken offence against me only for doing my duty..... I marvel how it should come to pass that the selfsame persons which will seem to wish peace and uniformity in the Church, and to mislike of the contentious and disobedient sort, cannot abide that anything should be done against them; wishing rather that the whole ministry of this land should be discountenanced and discouraged, than a few wayward persons, of no account in comparison, should be suppressed and punished. Men, in executing of laws according to their duties, were wont to be encouraged and backed by such as now, in this weighty service, do partly impugn the due course of justice. It falleth out in these days clean contrary. Disobedient and wilful persons (I will term them no worse) are animated, laws contemned, her Majesty's will and pleasure not regarded, and the executors thereof, in word and deed abused..... Your Honor, in offering me that great courtesy, offered unto me as great a pleasure as I can desire. Her Majesty must be my refuge, and I beseech you that I may use you as a means, when occasion shall serve; whereof I assure myself, and there rest."[1]

But the wrongs inflicted upon the Church by the Archbishop's policy were so gross and palpable, that even Hatton could not befriend him at the Council Board, or withhold remonstrance. Complaints and petitions had accumulated there from different coun-

[1] Life of Hatton, 380; Whitgift to Hatton, July 17th, 1584. Fuller, Bk. IX. p. 154.

ties, of proceedings against a *great number* of the clergy, — *all of whom were preachers.* But the Council — perhaps through the intervention of the Vice-Chamberlain — had forborne to examine these complaints minutely; arguing that the Archbishop and the Bishop of London would surely stay and temper their ecclesiastical officers, at least from silencing such as were efficient instructors of their people against the insidious arts of Popery.[1] But in September, apparently, there came from the county of Essex a complaint so grave, that the Council were roused to action. The inhabitants of Malden wrote as follows: —

"Since our ministers have been taken from us for not subscribing to certain Articles, neither confirmed by the law of God *nor of the land,* we have none left but such as we can prove unfit for the office. They are altogether ignorant; having been either Popish priests, or shiftless men thrust in upon the ministry when they knew not how else to live, — serving-men and the basest of all sorts; and what is most lamentable, as they are men of no gifts, so they are of no common honesty, but rioters, dicers, drunkards, and such like, of offensive lives. These are the men that are now supported; the men, too, whose reports and suggestions against others are readily received and admitted. Hence it hath come to pass that Papists, heretics, and other enemies to God and the queen are increased to multitudes, and we ourselves are in danger of being insulted. We therefore humbly beseech your Honors, in the bowels of Jesus Christ, to be a means of restoring our godly and faithful

[1] Strype's Whitgift, 166.

ministers. So shall we and many thousands of her Majesty's subjects continue our daily supplications to Almighty God."[1]

On the twentieth day of September, the following letter was despatched from the Council Chamber, addressed to his Grace of Canterbury and the Lord Bishop of London:—

"After our hearty commendations to both your lordships: Hearing of late of the lamentable state of the Church in Essex; of a great number of zealous and learned preachers there suspended; of places for the most part without any ministry of preaching, prayers, and sacraments; of certain appointed in some places to those void rooms, neither of learning nor of good name; of a great number in other places of that county occupying the cures, but notoriously unfit, most for lack of learning, and many chargeable with enormous faults, as drunkenness, filthiness of life, gaming at cards, haunting of ale-houses, and such like; and having heard in a general sort, *out of many parts*, of the like; yet to the intent that we might not be deceived with these generalities of reports, we have sought to be informed of some particulars,— namely, of some parts of Essex. And having received the same credibly in writing, we have thought it our duty, for the remedy hereof, without intermeddling with your jurisdiction ecclesiastical, to make report unto your lordships as persons that ought most especially to have regard thereto. Therefore we have sent herewith a catalogue of the names of persons of sundry natures and conditions. One sort,

[1] Neal, I. 159.

reported to be learned and zealous, and good preachers, deprived and suspended. The other sort, a number of persons having cures, being far unmeet for any offices in the Church, for their many defects and imperfections, yet continued without reprehension or other proceeding against them. In a third sort, a number having double livings with a cure, and not resident upon their cures; enjoying the benefit of their benefices, without any personal attendance upon their cures. Against all these sorts of lewd, evil, unprofitable, and corrupt members we hear of no inquisition, nor any kind of proceeding to the reformation of those horrible offences in the Church; but yet of great diligence, yea, and extremity, used against those that are known diligent preachers. Now therefore we, for the discharge of our duties being by our vocation under her Majesty bound to be careful that the universal realm may be well governed, do most earnestly desire your lordships to take some charitable consideration of these causes; that the people of the realm may not be deprived of their pastors, being diligent, learned, and zealous, *though in some points ceremonial,* they may seem doubtful, — only in conscience, and not of wilfulness; nor that their cures be suffered to be vacant without good pastors; nor that such as be placed in the rooms of cures be insufficient for learning, or unmeet for their conversation. And though the notes we send you be only of parsons belonging to Essex, yet we pray you to look into the rest of the country in many other dioceses; for we have and do hear daily of the like in generality in many other places..... And so we bid your lordships right heartily farewell.

From Oatlands, the 20th of September. Your lordship's loving friends,

"WILL. BURLEIGH.	A. WARWICK.
C. HOWARD.	CHR. HATTON.
GEO. SHREWSBURY.	R. LEICESTER.
I. CROFT.	FRA. WALSINGHAM."[1]

Knollys's name does not appear, because "casually absent from the Council Board."

To this the Archbishop replied on the 27th,—"That he could not make full answer, because of the absence of the Bishop of London; that he hoped the information to be in most parts unjust; that if the ministers were such as the schedule reported, they were worthy to be grievously punished, and that he would not be slack therein; that none or few had been detected or presented for any such misdemeanors; that the few silenced preachers there whom he knew were factious, and such disquieters as he could not suffer, without further conformity, to execute the ministry."[2]

It is noticeable that we find nothing on record to show that the bishops ever corrected the evils complained of by the Council.

Before the month had expired, the Lord Treasurer wrote to the Archbishop: "There are to be new bishops placed in the six vacant chairs. I wish—but I cannot hope it—that the Church may take that good thereby that it hath need of. Your Grace must pardon me; for I see such worldliness in many that were otherwise affected before they came to

[1] Strype's Whitgift, 166, 167. Fuller, Bk. IX. pp. 151, 152.

[2] Strype's Whitgift, 167, 168. Fuller, Bk. IX. pp. 152, 153.

cathedral churches, that *I fear the places alter the men.* .... I mean nothing in any conceit to your Grace. For notwithstanding I have varied in my poor opinion from your Grace in that by your order simple men[1] have been rather sought by inquisition to be found offenders, than upon their facts condemned, yet I affirm that, for all this, I differ not from your Grace in amity and love."[2]

"It is not the chair that maketh the alteration, if any there be," replied his Grace, "but the unlawful means of coming by it..... I doubt not but as good men, even at this day, possess some of these chairs as ever did in any age; although I will not justify all, *nor yet many*, of them..... For my manner of proceeding against these kind of men who would seem most *pure*, I am as yet fully persuaded that it is both lawful, useful, and charitable; neither can I devise how otherwise to deal to work any good effect..... Not severity, but lenity, hath bred this schism in the Church..... The accusation of severity is the least thing I fear. If I be able to answer to the contrary fault, I shall find myself well apaid."[3]

So the two ended their discussion; professedly on friendly terms, but as wide apart as at the beginning in their views of prelatic severity and holy inquisition. This particular topic was, for the most part, thrust aside by the preparation for Parliament, which, just now, engrossed the attention of statesmen and prelates. In particular cases, however, others had occasion to interfere with the keen administration of the Precisian prelates; as Walsingham, in the case of

[1] That is, "undesigning;" or, perhaps, "harmless."

[2] Strype's Whitgift, 171, 172.

[3] Ibid., 172.

one imprisoned a year for refusing subscription; and the whole Council, in another case of false imprisonment by a prelate during a series of years.[1]

We have preferred — at the risk of being tedious — that the parties in this commotion should represent their own doings and opinions by their own words. The Papers which we have so freely quoted have taken us away from the company of the oppressed themselves, into a more dispassionate circle; and show us — what it is worth our while to know —

[1] The first case here alluded to was that of Lever Wood, one of the fourteen Kentish ministers, mentioned in a previous chapter, who had waited upon the Archbishop at Lambeth, and whom he had immediately suspended. He, with some others of them, was also thrown into prison, where he remained a year, when he was released. Soon after, he secured the good-will of Walsingham, who wrote to the Archbishop that he would be favorable to him; meaning, doubtless, that he would take off his suspension. His Grace refused, because Wood was only willing to subscribe so far as the law required; "his meaning being," wrote the Archbishop, "that the law requireth no *such* subscription. And again," his Grace continued, "in saying that he will always use the Book of Common Prayer, and none else, his meaning is, that he will use but so much of the Book as pleaseth him."

Brook and Neal say that he was *released* upon thus subscribing. But the correspondence between Walsingham and Whitgift shows otherwise. (Fuller, Bk. IX. p. 162. Strype's Whitgift, 227. Neal, I. 177. Brook, I. 444.) Strype gives this case under the year 1585.

The other case was that of Barnaby Benison, a minister of London. In 1579, he had been imprisoned by Bishop Aylmer for an alleged ceremonial informality in his marriage, two weeks before; although the specifications upon which he was committed were proved to the Bishop to be false in fact, by Dr. Hammond and John Fox, who had been eyewitnesses. Yet the Bishop would not release him. In November, 1584, after having been spoiled of his "household stuff" and his library, being greatly damaged in his Freehold, and living in prison five years at his own charges, he succeeded in gaining the ear of the Privy Council. In closing his petition he said: "Wherefore I most humbly beseech your godly Honors, for the everlasting love of God, ... to be a means that my pitiful cry may be heard, ... and that I, being now half dead, may recover again to get a poor living with the

how the oppression was regarded by those whom it did not touch. Not to the suffering Puritan only, but to the wise, the reflecting, the satisfied *Churchmen of the time* — the measures of the Archbishop were offensive. Not only Beal, but Burleigh; not only Walsingham, but Hatton; not only the Church-Puritan Knollys, but the Lord Chancellor Bromley, entered their repeated protests against the severities of the prelates.[1] Nor were these protests expressive of their own sentiments alone. Among the courtiers generally, the like sentiments obtained; and to such

little learning which God has given me."

The Lords of the Council immediately wrote to Bishop Aylmer as follows: —

"Whereas Barnaby Benison, minister, has given us to understand the great hindrance he has received by your hard dealing with him and his long imprisonment, for which *if he should bring his action of false imprisonment he should recover damages, which would touch your lordship's credit,* — We, therefore, have thought fit to require your lordship to use some consideration towards him, in giving him *some sum of money to repay the wrong* you have done him, and in respect of the hindrance he hath incurred by your hard dealing towards him. Therefore, praying your lordship to deal with the poor man, that he may have occasion to turn his complaint into giving us a good report of your charitable dealing, we bid you heartily farewell. Hampton Court, Nov. 14, 1584." Signed by Warwick, Knollys, Mildmay, Walsingham, Burleigh, Bromley (Lord Chancellor), Bedford, Leicester, Croft, and Hatton.

Bishop Aylmer replied, by begging their lordships "to consider his poor estate" — only seventeen thousand pounds, equal to at least twice that sum now-a-days — "and to allow it to be referred to himself, either to bestow upon Benison some small benefice, or otherwise to help him as opportunity should offer." This is the end of the story.

In comparing the above statement, derived from Neal, with what Strype says, one will be very much perplexed, unless he discards Strype's tale altogether. This I have done, because it is *very* evident that he knew but little about it. (Strype's Aylmer, 194, 209. Neal, I. 169. Brook, I. 294. Hallam, 123.

[1] It has been supposed, and not without reason, that the Paper which Beal laid before the Archbishop was drawn up and presented at the suggestion, or with the privity, of the Council; in truth, but a protest of theirs, or of some of them, over the name and in the name of their Clerk.

a degree that his Grace of Canterbury confessed that he "had some cause to fear the worse;" to fear that her Majesty herself might be wrought to frown upon him, by "the information which might be made to her of his dealings."[1] Instead of finding himself "encouraged and backed" by statesmen, and courtiers, and men "of great name and quality," he bitterly exclaimed, in his letter to Hatton, "it falleth out in these days *clean contrary;*" and, despairing of other countenance, he added, "*Her Majesty* must be my refuge." And when imploring her Majesty herself "not to be drawn into any misliking of his doings by any information," he avowed that "he had incurred the evil speeches and slanderous reports of *every man.*"[2]

We repeat it, then,—a bad odor was going out from Lambeth; offensive not to the Puritan only, but to the Churchman; not to statesmen and courtiers only, but to the gentry,[3] and to all—except the prelates—who were accustomed to lay righteousness to the line and judgment to the plummet. We cannot concur with the charitable censure,—"Whitgift was only upon a level with his age."[4] Upon his own testimony, we find him below it.

But *what* was it which gave offence to the age? It was not that the Archbishop used his authority to secure uniformity; for he himself counted among his opponents "the selfsame persons who *wished* for uniformity." Uniformity, in some sense, was a duty con-

[1] Whitgift to the Queen; Strype's Whitgift, 169.

[2] Ibid.

[3] "The gentlemen known to be best affected towards God and her Majesty are therewith grieved," said Beal in his letter to the Archbishop.

[4] Marsden; "Early Puritans," 129.

ceded by Puritans and Churchmen alike. Nor was it merely, that he was *too* severe in carrying out this conceded principle, or in executing a law. Nor was it merely, or pre-eminently, that "good preachers and other godly disposed were molested (under *color* of law) for things not so much against the *matter and very meaning* of the law, as in some *show* swerving from the *letter* thereof."[1] Nor was it merely, or mainly, that the rights of conscience were invaded; or, in other words, that "the people of the realm were deprived of diligent, learned, and zealous pastors, who were of doubtful conformity only in some ceremonial points, and that from conscience, and not wilfulness."[2] None of these things were overlooked; but they did not constitute the *gravamen* of the Archbishop's offence. Had he done all these only, he would hardly have raised, at the outset, a universal cry of reprobation.

That which *first* brought upon Whitgift a rebuke so resolute and uncompromising that he quailed under it, was "his flat argument from authority;"[3] his self-constituted "Decree" requiring a solemn assent to the "Three Articles" of his own framing; a Decree for which he had not even "the color of law." When this outrage upon the manhood and rights of free-born Englishmen became known to them, both Burleigh and Walsingham protested. They met him face to face, foot to foot. Nor did they cease to wrestle with him until he "chose" to recede; until he saw fit "not to touch any for *not subscribing only;*"[4]

[1] *Ante*, p. 377, note; letter of the Council.

[2] The Council's letter; *ante*, p. 435.

[3] Fuller, Bk. IX. p. 170.

[4] Whitgift to Burleigh, July 3d; *ante*, p. 423.

until he had "*promised* to deal *only* with such as violated order, and to *charge* them with it;"[1] until "he had *forborne* to suspend or deprive any man in any cure for not subscribing only."[2] So much of a change was it for the better, when the Primate seemed to yield his Decree for Law, when he "altered his *first* course of dealing for not subscribing only," that the Lord Treasurer was content; believing that he would do nothing but what the law allowed, and only that which "should tend to maintain the religion established and to prevent schism."[3]

That which *next* roused the indignation of men generally, and of Lord Burleigh particularly, was — that the Primate had only abandoned a lesser outrage for a greater; had ceased to inflict ecclesiastical punishments for not subscribing, only to adopt inquisition by oath; that his Grace, "*not* charging the ministers with faults of order, sought, by examination, to urge them to accuse themselves;"[4] that, "by his order, they were rather sought by inquisition to be found offenders, than upon their facts condemned."[5] Wherein, wrote an eyewitness, "the true professors and ministers of the Word are at this present *more* subject to all kind of inquisition and persecution than either *Papist, atheist,* or whatsoever *profane or dissolute* person."[6] What must have been Lord Burleigh's surprise! "This," he exclaimed, "is not the charitable instruction that *I thought was intended*" when "your Grace promised me to deal only with such as

[1] Burleigh to Whitgift, July 4th; *ante*, p. 425.

[2] Whitgift to Walsingham; Fuller, Bk. IX. p. 162.

[3] Strype's Whitgift, Append., 63.

[4] Burleigh to Whitgift, July 4th; *ante*, p. 425.

[5] See *ante*, p. 437.

[6] Faunt to Bacon; Birch, I. 47.

violated order, and to *charge* them therewith." And what must have been his lordship's indignation when the Archbishop replied, "I have chosen *this* kind of proceeding by your lordship's advice"! "only to satisfy your lordship"!

It was this going from bad to worse; from too severe discipline "under color of law," to an arbitrary enforcing of subscription; and then, from subscription to inquisition — which the Lord Treasurer opposed so sternly and uncompromisingly; to such a degree, that his Grace trembled lest his lordship should "be carried away either from the cause or from himself;" lest he might "cast off an old friend for new-fangled and factious sectaries." It was this, which woke so strong and wide-spread disgust, that Councillors and other public persons clamored *daily* against Burleigh that "he did not stay the Archbishop's proceedings;" a disgust so general and rigid, that his Grace "incurred the evil speeches of *every man*," and looked for refuge *only* to her Majesty. It was priestly tyranny; a thing of unearthly birth, pestiferous on English soil, odious to English hearts, and damned by English law. It was priestly tyranny; liveried at Lambeth to go about in parishes, — like an ill-visaged, flat-footed, gnome, — with a scowl for pastors and a smile for Papists, with a cudgel for preachers and livings for tipplers. It was priestly tyranny; christened by the Primate to save "ceremonial points," and perpetrating outrage at the risk of Religion and the Crown. It was *this*, that galled Elizabeth's Councillors and made her wise men mad.

But if such was the thing, and such its aspect, and

such its odium, why did Burleigh and his colleagues utter only dissuasions, entreaties, and remonstrances? Why did they not clip the Archbishop's "illegal stretch of power"? Why did not they—the constitutional guardians of the public weal—heed the dictates of their moral sense and of humanity, by interdicting that examination by oath "so repugnant to the rules of English law and to the principles of natural equity"?[1] The will was in *each;* and we find the Archbishop himself, as well as those who reproached Burleigh, recognizing the power, as existing in *the body.* Burleigh was slow "to put his sickle into another man's harvest;" and "the extensive jurisdiction improvidently (?) granted to the ecclesiastical Commissioners, and which the queen was not at all likely to recall, placed Whitgift beyond the control of the temporal administration."[2]

But these are only answers in part; and do not satisfy us. We naturally ask, In a case which outraged alike the laws of England and the axioms of equity, had her Councillors no powers of persuasion over her Majesty? In some matters—none. "*Her* ministers of State acted"—authoritatively—"more by her princely rules and judgments than by their own wills and appetites." She compelled them to; and this supremacy in her Council Chamber "she observed to the last;" and, "to the last she was absolute enough in her own resolutions."[3] In *this* case "she was not likely to recall" a specific office expressly granted, and held her "resolution" beyond the reach or hope of persuasion, because the grant,

[1] Hallam, 122.

[2] Ibid., 123.

[3] Fragmenta Regalia; Phœnix, I. 184, 185.

not new, was intentional, *provident*, and for a paramount object.

With this affair Elizabeth's grand policy was interwoven. It should be remembered, that from her accession to the throne she had regarded it of the first political importance to retain the papistical features of the Establishment; that it was with her a *fundamental* "resolution" to conciliate her Catholic subjects by reducing, as far as possible, the visible differences between the Church of England and the Church of Rome. And, though she ratified the most terrible bills in Parliament against traitorous Papists, and sanctioned their most terrible butchery upon the scaffold, "this resolution" she never abated. Now — with her throne firmly established at home, with her name respected and her power feared abroad, and with a Primate after her own heart — she found herself, for the first time, able to sustain her resolution, and execute her policy with vigor. With *her*, it was no "improvident jurisdiction," but a sagacious one, which she had "granted to the ecclesiastical Commissioners," with Whitgift at their head. *This* grant and *this* Prelate were her first complete machinery for the prosecution of her policy. "Her Black Husband," as she called him,[1] had received executive charge from the lips of his Mistress less than twelve months ago; but in that time he had wrought with all conjugal fidelity. He was just now developing the despotic energies of the Establishment. He was just now perfecting its despotic features. "Popery was left untouched, or found more favor." One after another, Protestant preachers were silenced; and

[1] Paule's Whitgift, Sec. 114, p. 78.

their number fast dwindling toward the royal standard, — "three or four to a county." Papists and profligates were placed in their steads. The order, the formalism, the energy, the bigotry, the cruelty, the very Inquisition, of Rome,—all — all — were reflected as by a mirror from the face of the English Church. "The meetest bishop in the realm!" said a Catholic conspirator on his way to the scaffold. "Nothing is lacking," exclaimed the Scottish Queen exultingly, "but only the setting up of the Mass again!"

What could Elizabeth's Councillors do, against this favorite policy, this tide of success, and this masculine will?

CHAPTER XVI.

THE PARLIAMENT OF 1584-5.

The Puritans and the Primate prepare for Parliament. — The First Gathering of the Commons House elect; their Qualification; their Choice of Speaker. — The Puritans' View of their Condition. — Sampson sends to Burleigh certain Puritan "Petitions," with his own "Supplication Prefatory" to them. — Petitions introduced in the Commons. — Dr. Turner's "Bill and Book;" refused by the House. — A Committee to review and digest the Petitions, and to request the Lords to join in the same. — Parliament adjourned for forty-four Days. — The Archbishop's Travails with the Queen and with the Lord Treasurer. — Parliament reassemble. — Fresh Petitions. — The Articles of Petitions as prepared by the Committee. — The Answer of the Lords Temporal. — The Answer of the Lords Spiritual. — The Commons excited by this Answer. — Divers Bills for Church Reform introduced. — The Queen inhibits these Proceedings. — The Commons persist. — The Archbishop informs the Queen, that, notwithstanding her late Charge, the Commons are dangerously employed. — She sends them a Reprimand, and lays her imperative Inhibition upon the Speaker. — The Puritans petition the Convocation. — They petition the Archbishop by a Paper entitled "Means to settle Quietness in the Church." — His Answer. — The Queen's Speech at the Close of Parliament. — The Measure of Reform asked. — The Wisdom of the Puritans in this, and in their First Step towards it. — Their Resoluteness. — Their Political Sagacity.

The plaints of ministers and people, the remonstrances of courtiers, the indignant murmurings of "public persons," had been unavailing. The High Court of Commission retracted nothing. The Puritans, therefore, resolved to intercede with Parliament for relief, in some measure at least, from the arbitrary proceedings by which they were oppressed. To prepare for this, they published the positions which they assumed.

The first, — That the measures adopted by the Archbishop were emphatically tyrannical; emphatically his own; against the peace and spiritual weal of the Church; against the wishes of some of the bishops; and against the whole *current of public opinion.* This position was "writ about Parliament time,"[1] and was published under the title of "The Practice of the Prelates."[2]

Their second position, announced in another Tract, was, — That the measures urged by his Grace and

[1] Strype's Annals, V. 291.

[2] To justify my description of this pamphlet, I copy a fragment; making only such transposition of words as is necessary to make clear the writer's meaning.

"Howsoever some hard dealings here and there have been showed towards some particular good men, ... none ever dealt so generally against the whole ministry, and so eagerly *against the stream and light of all men's judgments* in so learned an age, as the author of those articles set forth lately," — for "who can deny that they came forth from the humor of one man . . . . against the tide of the advice of many of his own coat? . . . . But came this *alone* of himself? . . . . To thrust out godly and learned preachers (the only" ones, "in a manner, who are found to stand up like men against swarming Jesuits and busy traitors), *this* reach most certainly must needs be drawn out of the very inward closets of hell. . . . . The intent hereof, as they would have men believe, is peace. But who of those men who have refused subscription have ever dealt disorderly or tumultuously? Who of them, in word or deed, ever gave out any just suspicion of unpeaceable dealing? Nay; have they not, more than any, striven for peace, — in their ministry; in their writings; in their example? If, for so long a time, their discipline hath been sought for by them never disorderly, but by all lawful and dutiful means, what use may this new device" of the Three Articles, "have? Verily, what use, but for the Archbishop's exercising tyranny upon his fellow-ministers, upon a mere ambition, and for the starving up of many thousands of souls, by depriving them that refuse subscription, and discouraging thereby other godly and sufficient men from entering into the ministry?" (Strype's Whitgift, 122.) Strype here mentions this Book under the date of 1583; but in his Annals he says that it was "writ about Parliament time," which was in 1584.

his colleagues in commission were contrary to certain acts of Parliament, to certain of her Majesty's injunctions, and to certain canons of the Church; a position so notoriously tenable, that it was assailed only as a gross imitation of the sin of Ham in exposing his father's nakedness.[1]

The Archbishop also was girding up his loins; preparing to meet the bills and petitions which the Puritans were about to introduce to Parliament, and he was "very glad," he said, "that the notes" of them, which Sir Christopher Hatton sent to him early in November, "did prove so frivolous."[2] What "frivolities" were, in his lordship's estimation, will appear when we ourselves examine the petitions.

The royal summons for a new Parliament had appointed Monday, the twenty-third day of November, for their assembling. Accordingly, in the forenoon of that day, her Majesty proceeded from her palace of Whitehall to the cathedral church of Westminster, escorted by the Lords and others in royal state. Here they were occupied, until nearly two o'clock in the afternoon, by a sermon, and by the other religious exercises usual upon like occasions.[3]

While these solemnities were in progress, the knights, citizens, burgesses, and barons, members

[1] Strype's Annals, V. 338.

This Treatise, or Tract, against the discipline of the Church was entitled, "An Abstract of certain Acts of Parliament, of certain her Majesty's Injunctions, of certain Canons," &c. (Strype's Annals, V. 411.) It was "put forth without name of author or printer." (Ibid., 338.) Mr. Neal (I. 172), in ascribing the printing of it to Henry Denham, has mistaken the printer of "The Answer" to it, for the printer of "The Abstract." (Ibid., 411.)

[2] Strype's Annals, V. 331, 332. Life of Hatton, 371.

[3] D'Ewes, 311, 332.

elect of the House of Commons, had flocked irregularly to the Parliament-House, and were waiting to be qualified according to law, by openly receiving and pronouncing the Oath of Supremacy before the Lord High Steward of England, or such as he might depute for the purpose.[1] Nearly all were country gentlemen, who had heard but little, in their rural homes, of the political news of the day; and who — with the exception of seven or eight who had before been members of the Commons[2] — had had but little familiarity with questions of State, and none with Parliamentary forms. Yet they were far from being "unfit to exercise a powerful part in the government, even in difficult State questions;"[3] for their lack of political data and of Parliamentary experience might be rapidly supplied by that good sense, clear perception, and manly honesty, which have always characterized the rural gentry of England. For the first time to take their places in the High Council of the nation, strangers to its usages, and knowing little of its duties, it is not surprising that they felt the embarrassment of a situation so new and so grave. As yet unorganized and without business, they were of course a confused assembly, "making strange noises" as they walked about, or as they discussed "in troops and out of all order" the miscellaneous topics suggested by the place and the occasion.[4]

After what seemed a long time, it was announced that the noble Earl of Leicester, Lord High Steward of the realm, was in waiting in the anteroom to

[1] 5 Eliz. Cap. I. Sec. XIII.

[2] Fleetwood to Burleigh; Wright's Eliz. II. 243.

[3] Wright; Introd., p. xxvi.

[4] Fleetwood to Burleigh.

receive the oath of those of her Majesty's Council who had been chosen and returned from different counties into the House of Commons. Whereupon the Right Honorables, — Sir Francis Knollys, Treasurer of her Majesty's Household; Sir James Croft, Comptroller of her Majesty's Household; Sir Walter Mildmay, Chancellor of the Exchequer, — leaving the others, repaired unto his lordship, and "then and there before him did take and pronounce the oath according to the statute in that behalf made and provided. Which done, the said Lord Steward departed into the lower end of the room called the White Hall, or Court of Requests, and then also did the Right Honorable Mr. Secretary Walsingham, returned one of the Knights for the County of Surrey, likewise take and pronounce the said oath before his lordship." These "Right Honorable Personages" being thus qualified by the Lord Steward himself, the rest of the Commons were then called into the old White Hall, that the names of so many as had been returned into the Crown Office, being read from the roll, might be thereon checked as each proved his presence by his answer. This done, his lordship deputed the drudgery of the occasion to the Right Honorables whom he had just qualified; and so took his departure.[1]

Then commenced the tedious process of "openly receiving and pronouncing," one by one, the oath required by the statute. This continued until two o'clock, when it was interrupted by a notice "that her Majesty with divers of the Lords spiritual and temporal were then already set in the Upper House,

[1] D'Ewes, 332. Wright, II. 243.

and there expected them."[1] Whereupon, they who had sworn immediately repaired to the Chamber of the Lords; while the others, of whom was Fleetwood, the Recorder of London, were compelled to "lose the Oration made by my Lord Chancellor" Bromley, and all the pageant of opening the Parliament;[2] for to assume by word or act to be a member thereof before having "pronounced" the oath, was to forfeit the right of membership and to incur other pains and penalties.[3]

The usual ceremonies having transpired in the Chamber of Lords, the Commons returned to their own House, where they seated themselves with all decorum,—the residue having been sworn,—and waited in silence to know what they should do next. After a little time, Sir Francis Knollys rose and reminded his colleagues that the Lord Chancellor, in her Majesty's name, had just directed them to proceed to the choice of their Speaker; and further added, that himself did well allow of Mr. Serjeant Puckering as a very able person and fit to undergo the office, but that any one who had a mind to, might make another nomination. Now Mr. Serjeant Puckering and Mr. Recorder Fleetwood sat side by side; the former drooping his eyes, and the latter,—who seems to have had a cit's contempt for his less polished brethren from the country,—finding that no one responded, said to his companions around him, "Cry, Puckering!" "Cry, Puckering!" Then he and they beginning, the cry ran through the whole. Whereupon Mr. Treasurer again rose, and put the

[1] D'Ewes, 332.

[2] Fleetwood to Burleigh.

[3] 5 Eliz. Cap. I. Sec. XIII.

question in form that they would announce the name of whom they would have for Speaker. Upon which there was a general voice for Puckering, and no one seemed to dissent. Mr. Serjeant Puckering then stood up, and, "in a modest and humble speech," said that he was not able to fill "a place of so great charge and weight." No notice being taken of this, Mr. Recorder again took it upon himself to hasten matters, and requested Mr. Treasurer and Mr. Comptroller, as being two of the most eminent Personages of the House, to conduct Mr. Serjeant to the Chair and to put him in it; to which the Speaker elect quietly submitted. Mr. Recorder remarked, by the by, that "they should have set him there either before his speech, or else at the beginning, and that his speech should have been before the cheer," — a criticism which, for want of understanding, we do not appreciate.[1]

On Thursday, with the customary formalities, this act of the Commons was publicly ratified in the Upper House by her Majesty; upon whose decision, John Puckering, Serjeant at Law, "submitted himself to the undergoing of the said Prolocutorship." Thus the capacity of the Commons for business was perfected.

It was not a sense of misfortune or of suffering merely, but a sense of wrong, under which the Puritans writhed. It was not that the hand of power was laid so heavily upon *them*, but that it was laid upon them in the face of natural and chartered rights, in the face also of both the common

[1] D'Ewes, 333, and Fleetwood's letter compared.

and the statute law; that this was done by the imposition of the "Three Articles," by the imposition of the *ex officio* oath, by the imposition of the Book of Common Prayer. In reference to this latter point, it is important, as a matter of justice, to note and to bear in mind, that the Book at this time in use differed from that described and ordained by the Act of Uniformity; to remember that these differences were specially offensive to the Puritans, as seeming to favor false doctrine and superstition; and, that they were required to adopt these *differences* in their public ministrations. In other words, we must bear in mind, that, so far as *these* things were concerned, they were punished, "under color of law," for *not* disobeying the law.[1]

[1] This point, I have before noticed only incidentally. Its importance — as revealing the true position of the Puritans, who at this time were really contending, not for liberty of conscience only, but for a fundamental principle of civil liberty — requires more special attention. I therefore quote the following from a Tract addressed to Archbishop Whitgift, and published while the Parliament of 1584–5 was in session. It was entitled, "Means how to settle a godly and charitable quietness in the Church," and is registered in Strype's Life of Whitgift, p. 196; and — with the Archbishop's answers — in the Appendix, Bk. III. No. XVI.

"In the first Book printed in the beginning of her Majesty's reign, the Apocrypha was left out; and was after, *without warrant of law, and contrary to the statute* (which alloweth but three alterations) inserted. . . . . In King Edward's second Book, there was a note which left the sign of the cross in the sacrament of Baptism, and certain other indifferent rites, to be used or not used: Which note ought to have been printed in her Majesty's Book, and was *none* of the alterations *appointed by statute.* And all that was in King Edward's second Book, besides the three alterations mentioned in the statute, ought to be in her Majesty's Book, and is warranted by law."

Thus we see how pointedly, openly, and vehemently, the Puritans resisted ecclesiastical exactions *as an infringement of their legal rights;* and the notorious facts on the ground of which they did so.

The Statute of Uniformity describes the Book of Common Prayer thereby established, as "the Book

To the honor of the Puritans, they understood these things too well, and had too much manhood, tamely to submit without remonstrance, and without at least peaceable efforts to recover protection. Suspensions, deprivations, fines, imprisonments, — past, present, and in prospect, — did not, as was intended, daunt them; but, as was not intended, aroused them. Under all contumely and wrong, their spirit was unbroken; and, in the name of Law, and invoking Law, they resolved to leave no means untried with Parliament which might afford relief.

A better man, a greater linguist, a more complete scholar, or a more accomplished orator than Thomas Sampson, could hardly be found in the realm.[1] Although deprived, on account of his non-conformity, of his Deanery in the University of Oxford, and pensioned on a pittance of ten pounds a year as Lecturer in Whittingham College in London, he still commanded universal respect. In 1573, he had addressed two letters to the Lord Treasurer Burleigh, which that statesman respectfully and kindly entertained, upon the deformity which attached to the Protestant Church of England by being "governed by such canons, customs, and officials as those by which antichrist did rule his synagogue."[2] He was now sixty-seven years of age, poor, paralytic, but still retaining the Mastership of Leicester Hospital, to

authorized in the Fifth and Sixth years of the reign of King Edward the Sixth, with one alteration or addition of certain Lessons to be used on every Sunday in the year, and the form of the Litany altered and corrected, and two sentences only added in the delivery of the Sacrament to the Communicants, *and none other or otherwise.*" (1 Eliz. Cap. II. Sec. II.)

[1] Brook, I. 377, 378.

[2] Strype's Annals, III. 392 – 395. Strype's Parker, Appendix, p. 177.

which he had been presented when his infirmity of body compelled him to resign his Lecture.[1] In March last, he had again addressed his lordship, "in secret sort," expressing his "many thoughts of the state of the Church of England;" and suggesting certain measures for her further reformation, by which particularly her spiritual lack might be supplied. "In these," said he, "I presume not as an admonisher, nor do I prescribe as a lawmaker, or as an instructor of lawmakers. But as an humble supplicant in the cause of the Church, I do present these poor petitions of my heart to the view and correction of your Honor, to your godly wisdom, and to the zealous care of God, which I pray may possess your lordship's heart. And I pray your Honor to give me leave to put these small sticks as little matches to kindle the fire of God in your heart." These thoughts and suggestions were described as "petitions to be humbly offered unto the queen and Parliament for the help of the poor untaught people of this realm, and for the reforming of some other disorders which are in it." On the tenth day of November, in view of "the drawing near of Parliament," he wrote again, commending his petitions, "revised and somewhat altered, to his lordship's hands, ... to do that herein that may best serve God's glory and the good of the Church of England."[2]

So far as our own purpose is concerned, the burden of these petitions is sufficiently indicated in their title; especially as his lordship seems only to have used

[1] Brook, I. 379, 382.

The order of events does not correspond with the statement in Wood's Athenæ. See *ante*, Vol. I. p. 234, note 1.

[2] Strype's Whitgift, 184.

them "in secret sort."[1] But accompanying them was a "Prefatory Supplication" by Dr. Sampson, to the queen, the Council, and the High Court of Parliament,—a Paper worthy of more than a passing notice, because it reveals that religious poverty which was partly induced by a ruthless discipline, and which greatly stimulated the Puritans to press reform.

"We, who are thousands of poor untaught people of England, ... do show .... that where there is, and hath been, now many years, a blessed liberty given to preach and hear the Gospel of Jesus Christ, ... yet so it is, that we your said suppliants, are sore pinched with a great scarcity..... In very many of our congregations, we have none who do break the bread of life unto us; we have none that do diligently teach us the holy Word of God..... We have not the comfortable preaching of the kingdom of God joined with the ministry of the sacraments .... where we do dwell; and therefore some of us are driven to seek the same .... where we do not dwell. .... We have some pastors .... not resident on their benefices. Some are licensed to be double, if not treble, beneficed men. Some are occupied in other affairs..... Our bishops, so far from giving a meet remedy for these our griefs, do rather daily increase them; for they do daily make numbers of ministers .... which are so dumb that they neither can, do, nor

[1] They consist of thirty-four Articles; and are preserved by Strype in his Annals, VI. 278, Appendix, Bk. I. No. XXXIX. They contain various devices, by no means impracticable, for providing a general supply of competent and resident ministers; and propose wholesome checks upon the ecclesiastical government of bishops, modelled somewhat upon the Presbyterian plan.

will speak anything in the congregation .... more than they are compelled to read out of a printed book..... If men do contend to set up a reading ministry in place of a preaching, they do not regard how the Lord hath ordained a preaching ministry for the profitable edifying of his Church..... A number of them do read in no better sort than some young scholars could do which were newly taken out of some English school. Truly, this their reading is so rude in some places among us, that they seem themselves scarce to understand that which they do read..... Whereas, by God's grace, there are in some places good teachers among us (which are, in comparison of them who are no teachers at all, very few), these few do receive great discouragement and discredit; yea, and some of them are displaced, not because they do not teach us painfully and truly, but for an old continued quarrel of *conformity* in such ceremonies as men have devised, which have not in them any power to edify us. ....We do humbly beseech you to understand that this hard handling of our good pastors doth cast us into great distresses..... For when our bishops do deprive our preaching pastors and do stop their mouths .... they do indeed stick us with a dart of death. They take from us the bread of life..... Verily, we have great need of such pastors..... We have no need at all of such idle ceremonies as do not edify us in true godliness..... To take preachings from us, and to give us instead a bare reading with a sort of idle and unprofitable ceremonies, is to take from us the bread of life which God hath prepared, and to feed us after the device of man, with unprofitable hearing and looking; *unprofitable,* because our dulness is not thereby quickened, or our minds stirred to understand the mind of God.....

"Some of ourselves.... who do labor quietly to resort where the preaching of the Word is comfortably joined with the ministry of the sacraments, are for this our doing molested by our idle shepherds and such officers as do favor them..... We fear that some of our men which are called to receive the charge of a church, do think more, that they are called to the commodity of a house, glebe lands, tithes, and of their Easter book, than to take the care and charge of souls. Such pastors we have. We do neither envy, nor deny to pay, that which is *due to them;* but we desire that they may be commanded *to give to us our due,* which in their idleness and worldliness they do withhold.....

"There are whole thousands of us left untaught; yea, by trial it will be found, that there are in England whole thousands of parishes destitute of this necessary help to salvation; that is, of diligent preaching and teaching..... So of this want of preaching we do complain. This penury of preaching breedeth in us a penury of faith, which doth both greatly pinch us, and put us in danger. It doth also constrain us at this time to make this our humble complaint.

"In tender consideration whereof and for redress of these griefs.... we do humbly beseech you.... not only graciously to consider of the premises, but also of these our humble petitions hereunto annexed; which we do present to your godly wisdoms, not as prescribers, but as most humble suitors..... And that both you may govern us, and we obey you, thoroughly, according to His blessed will, we do pray God, our Heavenly Father, even in the name of Jesus Christ."[1]

Penury of preaching a subject of complaint! It was the very marrow of her Majesty's policy! It had been the very aim of her charge to Grindal; and the aim of her charge to Whitgift. "To *reduce* the number of preachers" (as well as to please the Papists) was a very reason why she was *so* exacting of uniformity; "enforcing the points of law upon the breach or omission of *every tittle* of the Book of Common Prayer;"[2] a very reason why preaching ministers were required to avow the Book to be consonant, in all its parts, with God's; a very reason why they were offered the alternative of self-conviction under oath, or of ecclesiastical censure and other penalties for its refusal. Effectual means for reducing the number! Effectual means for preventing recruits! The "husband" was an efficient servant. Nothing — save statistical tables — could better have proved his success, than this very "complaint of the penury of preaching." Her Majesty's policy ran counter to its prayer. The staff was in her own hands.

Thus, by their printed books, and by these large Papers "in a secret sort," the Puritans had operated beforehand for their direct movements upon the Parliament. They seem also to have been assiduous in soliciting and counselling its members during the session.[3]

[1] Strype's Annals, V. 321 – 329.

[2] "Means to settle quietness in the Church;" Strype's Whitgift, 196.

[3] Fuller, Bk. IX. pp. 173, 175. Collier, VII. 33.

The first-fruits of their influence appeared in the House of Commons on the fourteenth day of December; when Sir Thomas Lucy introduced a Petition touching the liberty of godly preachers; Sir Edward Dymock, another for their continuing to exercise their ministry; and Mr. Gates, a third "for the speedy supply of able and sufficient men into divers places now destitute, and void of the ordinary means of salvation." Soon after, Dr. Peter Turner,[1] a zealous man in religious and in political affairs,[2] presented a bill and a book which, he said, "had been framed by godly and learned ministers, and did tend to the glory of God, the safety of her Majesty, and the good of the Commonwealth." These he asked permission to read.[3]

The bill was entitled, "An Act concerning the subscription of ministers." Its tenor was as follows: "That no other subscription but what is enjoined by 13 Eliz. Cap. XII. be required of any minister or preacher in the Church of England; and that the refusing to subscribe any other Articles shall not be any cause for the archbishops or bishops, or any other persons having ecclesiastical jurisdiction, to refuse any of the said ministers to any ecclesiastical office, function, or dignity; but that the said archbishops, &c. shall institute, induct, admit, and invest, or cause to be instituted, &c., such persons as shall be

[1] He was a son of the late Dr. Turner, Dean of Wells, who had so strong an antipathy to the authority vested in the bishops of the English Church, that he used to call them, in humorous derision, "white-coat-and-tippet gentlemen." A more grave expression of his dislike to spiritual lordship has been quoted. (*Ante*, Vol. I. p. 410, note 2.)

[2] Brook, I. 132.

[3] D'Ewes, 339.

presented by the lawful patrons, notwithstanding their refusal to subscribe any other Articles not set down in the statute 13 Elizabeth. And that no minister for the future shall be suspended, deprived, or otherwise molested in body or goods, by virtue of any ecclesiastical jurisdiction, but only in the cases of obstinately and wilfully defending any heresies condemned by the express Word of God, or their dissolute lives, which shall be proved by two credible witnesses, or by their own voluntary confession."[1]

The book was a Presbyterian liturgy; and was entitled, "A Book of the Form of Common Prayers, Administration of the Sacraments, &c;" to which was appended a Petition to her Majesty that it might be established by law. The rubric of this book left each minister at liberty to adopt the prayers prescribed, or to substitute the impulses of his own heart.[2]

Probably the House had some knowledge of these Papers, or at least of the latter; for they were successfully opposed by Sir Francis Knollys and Sir Christopher Hatton, and "it was at length resolved,

[1] Neal, I. 172.

[2] Collier, VII. 34.

I have adopted Neal's description of Dr. Turner's bill; and Collier's, of his book, though with some hesitation. Neal's is embraced in quotation marks, but he does not give his authority. Nor does Collier; although he refers — rather blindly, as to his points — to a sermon of Dr. Bancroft and to his book, "Dangerous Positions." Neal contradicts Collier as to the substance of Dr. Turner's book; by saying, that "it consisted of thirty-four Articles of complaint, but by advice of the House the substance of the (I understand him to mean '*its*') petitions was reduced by the ministers in sixteen Articles." In this (if I have understood him rightly) he has followed Strype (Life of Whitgift, 177), who says that the bill and the book "were reduced into a Petition consisting of sixteen Articles." Both are mistaken. Both

that the said book and bill should not be read." It is evident from the doings of the House afterwards, that they were rejected because considered injudicious at the outset of their proceedings; not because disliked in their substance. But touching the three Petitions presented by the other members, both the Treasurer and the Vice-Chamberlain declared their belief "that her Majesty would take some speedy order concerning the same." There the matter rested for the present.[1]

Two days afterwards, some motions were made in the House touching these Petitions, and "many arguments ensued." At last, upon motion of Sir Walter Mildmay, Chancellor of the Exchequer, it was resolved, "That Committees should be appointed to view over the said Petitions which concerned the liberty of some ministers, and the placing of others in places that wanted; and to reduce the contents of the same into some particular Heads of Articles," with instructions to the Committees to impart the same, so reduced, unto the Lords, with "request to their lordships to join the Commons in such further course as should be thought meet."[2] The course thought

disagree with the Journal of the House, which I shall strictly follow in the text.

The fact that Dr. Turner was not allowed to read his bill and book, is sufficient to show that the House would not have reduced *them* into Articles; for however they may have liked them, they regarded their proposal at present impolitic. Collier's statement harmonizes with this. For both these reasons, I have accepted Collier's description of the *book*. Neal seems to have been confused by Dr. Sampson's thirty-four Articles; which, however, he does not mention; "out of which," says Strype, "(*it may be*) the Commons drew up their petitions reducing them to the number of sixteen." (Annals, V. 321.)

[1] D'Ewes, 339.

[2] Ibid., 340.

meet by the Committees was,—"to exhibit these Petitions and grievances by way of *humble suit to the queen;*" and in *this* they requested the Lords to join them?[1]

On the twenty-first day of December, the Committee, just returning from a conference with the Upper House, stated that their lordships had "feelingly expressed" their sorrow for the grievances set forth in the Petitions, and had "resolved that those lords who were of her Majesty's Privy Council should move her Highness to know her Majesty's pleasure

[1] Strype's Whitgift, 177. Hallam, 127. D'Ewes, 344. Strype has truthfully reduced to few and plain, the many and somewhat obscure words of the Journal.

I have been the more careful to express myself on this point because Mr. Hume (III. 125) says, that "the Commons, a majority of whom were Puritans or inclined to that sect, were content to proceed by way of humble petition; and that *not* addressed to her Majesty, ... but to *the House of Lords.*" From this misapprehension, he argues the pusillanimity of the Puritans; that "they were overawed by the queen's authority;" that "the severe reprimands which they had already, in former sessions, met with from the throne, deterred them from introducing *any bill* concerning Religion"! There were but seven or eight who had had a chance to be reprimanded in any former session. Besides, there were bills enough concerning Religion introduced by this Puritan House, as will appear. Again, bills were sometimes couched in the language of petitions. Witness the Preamble to Cap. I. passed at this very session: "At the humble suit and earnest petition and desire of the Lords spiritual and temporal, and the Commons, in this present Parliament assembled, ... Be it enacted," &c.; also the speech of Mr. Speaker Puckering to the queen, in which he calls bills which have passed both Houses "petitions." The Act 1 Eliz. Cap. I. is *all* petition. Neal (I. 174), Strype in his Life of Whitgift (187), and Camden (308), call these same petitions of the Commons "a bill."

Another error of Hume, though of less importance, is significant. He says on the same page, that it was proof of the prevalency of the Puritans among the Commons, that they passed a bill for the reverent observance of Sunday. So they did. So also did the Lords (D'Ewes, 322), who, he rightly observes, had "a contrary spirit" to that of Puritanism. Each House passed *the same* bill.

therein, before they proceed any further in the matter."[1]

Immediately after this the Parliament was adjourned, by Letters Patent from the queen, until the fourth day of February. "Which done, Sir Christopher Hatton moved the House to join in most humble and earnest prayer unto Almighty God for the long and prosperous preservation of her Majesty, with thankful acknowledgment of his infinite benefits to the realm through the mediation of her Highness' ministry under Him." He said also that he had in his hand a written prayer to that effect, which, if it pleased them to follow and say after him, he would read. And then, "every one kneeling upon his knees, the said Mr. Vice-Chamberlain begun the said prayer, which being ended every one departed away for that time until the said day of adjournment."[2]

The Archbishop of Canterbury was in a flutter. Although forewarned that some attempt was to be made to disturb the current of Church affairs, he had not been prepared for a scheme so large and so exceptionable as that proposed by the Commons. The very day after its announcement, he betook himself to her Majesty with a draught "of divers things that called for amendment....; wherein (with the rest of the bishops) he prudently took the best course to oblige the queen; who, as she looked upon herself to have the supreme government and care of her Church's affairs under God, so she disliked to have her Parliaments, consisting of laymen, to meddle in Church matters." The Archbishop's Paper — de-

[1] D'Ewes, 345. [2] Ibid., 346.

signed, in part, to pacify the restless — provided for but a partial remedy of but few of the evils complained of by the Puritans.[1]

In less than a week after Parliament had adjourned, he also addressed the Lord Treasurer; stirring him up against "needless innovation, liberty, and the overthrow of government, especially in the ecclesiastical state; beseeching his lordship to believe that he stood so much in these matters only for conscience' sake and duty to the Church;" and reminding him that it was wise "to confirm her Highness in the laws and orders established, and that her Majesty loved not to hear of innovations."[2]

On Thursday, the fourth day of February, the Parliament resumed their session, as they had suspended it, with prayer; and then, without other solemnity or pomp, as though the adjournment had been only for a day, "fell to the reading of bills and to other business." Fresh Petitions were presented to the House from the people in different counties respecting abuses in the ministry and some prelatic disorders; but they were laid aside until answer should be received from the Lords respecting the like Petitions already under consideration.[3] This answer was given on the twenty-second day of the month. Upon announcing the fact to the House on the same day, Sir Francis Knollys said, "It so much passeth my capacity to conceive and understand all the effect of their lordships' answer, that I will not undertake to make a report of it; but will leave it to others who can

[1] Sparrow, 193 - 198. Strype's Whitgift, 185; Appendix, p. 76.

[2] Strype's Whitgift, 183.

[3] D'Ewes, 349.

better remember and deliver it." Sir Walter Mildmay said the same in substance; but proposed that all the Committee "should meet in the afternoon, and, helping each other's memories, set down the substance and effect of the answer"—which had been given chiefly by his Grace of Canterbury—"as near as they could, and then signify the same unto the House to-morrow:" which was agreed to by the House.[1] But they did not report on the morrow; nor on the next day, but on the twenty-fifth; from which we infer that even their united memories were baffled, and that they waited for *another* answer, which was drawn up by his Grace of York (Sandys), and which constituted their report to the House.

But it is time to state the "particular Heads or Articles" into which the Committee (appointed for the purpose on the sixteenth day of December) had reduced the Petitions presented by Sir Thomas Lucy, Sir Edward Dymock, and Mr. Gates, and which they had "offered to the consideration of the Right Honorable the Lords spiritual and temporal of the Higher House."

Articles I. and II. were for the suspension from the ministry of such as were not qualified according to the statute of the thirteenth year of Elizabeth, and according to an Article of the Convocation of 1575.

Article III. That "none should hereafter be admitted to the ministry but such as shall be sufficiently furnished with gifts for so high and earnest a charge."

Article IV. That, "Whereas in the Book of ordain-

[1] D'Ewes, 354.

ing ministers it is prescribed that the bishops, with the priests present, shall lay hands severally upon the head of every one that receiveth ordination, without mention of any certain number of priests: And, Whereas in a statute of 21 Henry VIII. it is affirmed that a bishop must occupy six chaplains at giving Orders, — it may be considered whether it may be meet to provide that no bishop shall ordain but in public and with the assistance of at least six other ministers of good repute."

Article V. Whether some provision may be made that none be admitted to be a minister, but in a vacant benefice in the diocese of the ordaining bishop, or to some certain place where such minister is to be a preacher, &c.

Article VI. Whether it might be provided, that none be preferred to any benefice with cure of souls, ... without notice before given to the parishes where they take charge, and reasonable time allowed to discover and object any defect in conversation of life in the person to be placed.

Article VII. "That it may be considered, Whether this favor may be shewed, that hereafter no oath or subscription be tendered to any that is to enter into the ministry .... but such as be expressly prescribed by the statutes, save an oath to try whether the person is to enter the benefice corruptly or incorruptly."

Article VIII. "Whereas sundry ministers .... have of late years been grieved with indictments in temporal courts, and molested by some exercising ecclesiastical jurisdictions, for omitting some small portions" of, "or some ceremony prescribed in, the Book of Common Prayer," .... it may be considered whether "some good and charitable means may be .... devised, that such ministers as in the public service .... do use the Book of Common Prayer, ... and none other, be not from henceforth called in question for omission or change of some portion or rite, *as is aforesaid,* so their doings therein be void of contempt."

Article IX. Whether "it might please the archbishops and bishops to take to their own hearings, with .... assistance, ... the causes of complaint against any known preacher, ... and to proceed .... with as little discredit to the person .... as may be."

Article X. For the restoration to their former charges, or at least liberty to preach, for such as have been suspended or deprived for only refusing to subscribe such Articles as have lately been tendered, or for such like things.

Article XI. "That the Fathers aforesaid would forbear their examinations *ex officio mero* of godly and learned preachers not detected of open offence of life or for public maintaining of error, and only deal with them for such matters as shall be detected in them. And that her Majesty's Commissioners for causes ecclesiastical be required .... to forbear the like proceedings against such preachers, and not to call any of them out of the diocese where he dwelleth, except for some notable offence. ...."

Article XII. For common exercises or conferences for the better increase of knowledge in ministers.

Article XIII. Against the abuse of excommunication.

Article XIV. That, nevertheless, excommunication

for enormous crimes be executed; yet not by chancellors, &c., but by the bishops themselves.

Article XV. That licenses of non-residence cease; and likewise licenses of Pluralities.

Article XVI. "That none having license of non-residence" on their cures "shall enjoy it hereafter except he depute an able and sufficient preacher to serve the cure," &c.[1]

The answers of the Lords touching these petitions, "in which the House of Commons had desired their lordships *to join with them*," were reported on the twenty-fifth day of the month, by Sir Francis Knollys, as follows:[2]—

"The Lord Treasurer in general made answer, That the Lords did conceive many of the Articles to be unnecessary, that others of them were already provided for"—by the action of the present Convocation—"and that the Uniformity of Common Prayer had been established by Parliament."[3]

The Archbishop of York, Dr. Sandys, in the name of the Lords Bishops, made an answer at large. This answer we state, from The Journal of Parliament;[4] qualifying it however (and as indicated) by an answer given in writing by his Grace of Canterbury "soon after" that which was given by the Archbishop of York,[5] and by another from Cooper, Bishop of Winton, or Winchester.[6] There was another—for the Articles made no small stir among the Lords of the

[1] D'Ewes, 357-359. Strype's Whitgift, Appendix, pp. 70-73. Fuller, Bk. IX. p. 189.

[2] D'Ewes, 357.

[3] D'Ewes, 359. Strype's Whitgift, 177.

[4] D'Ewes, 359, 360; also, Strype's Whitgift, 177-179.

[5] Strype's Whitgift, 180; and Appendix, p. 73.

[6] Ibid., 187. Strype's Annals, V. 329, 336.

Clergy — seemingly given by the bishops collectively at their Convocation,[1] but which it will be unnecessary to notice.[2]

"The first and second Articles cannot be allowed; because divers unqualified persons are dispensed with by law;"[a] — for "though the statute of 13 Elizabeth requireth that none be made a minister unless able to give an account of his faith in Latin, yet it addeth, '*or* have special gift and ability to be a preacher;' which 'or,' being a disjunctive, giveth scope to the admittance of Lack-Latin ministers; because divers parishes would be left destitute of ministers; and because it was against charity to send such ministers with their families a begging which had dedicated themselves to the ministry and had not any other trade whereby to live."[a c]

"The third Article is confessed to be very necessary."

"The fourth is utterly disallowed,[a] for divers causes needless to be rehearsed. As they have the thing, why contend they with us about the manner? We shall observe the laws therein,"[b] albeit "there is no law now in force that requireth the certain number of six preachers[3] at the making of ministers."[b c]

"The fifth Article is allowed, so far as the avoiding of vagrant ministers,"[a] by which is meant, "ministers without some certain stay of living;[b] but dis-

[1] Strype's Annals, V. 329; VI. 302, Bk. I. No. XL.

[2] In my statement of this answer, I interweave with Bishop Sandys's answer, which appears in the Journal of Parliament, the answers of Whitgift and of Cooper to the several Articles. The first, or Sandys's, I designate by *a;* Whitgift's, by *b;* and Cooper's, by *c*.

[3] *Sic.*

allowed so far as it concerneth Deans, Prebendaries, and such like." [b c]

"The sixth is disallowed, as favoring controversies and dissensions." [a] 'It smelleth of popularity and of popular elections, long ago justly abrogated for the tumultuousness thereof, and indeed intolerable in a settled state and where there is a Christian magistrate. Moreover, it doth prejudice the patron's right; doth alter many laws; and will not work the effect intended, as the party presented will usually be unknown to the parish." [b c]

"The seventh is utterly misliked; for even bishops must take the oath of canonical obedience to their metropolitan; and as for subscription to the 'Three Articles,' it is doubtless lawful." [a]

"The eighth and ninth are utterly disallowed, as freeing ministers from jurisdiction temporal and even from that of bishops themselves" [a] "*in effect;* their authority being so restrained." [b]

"The tenth may not be allowed; because deprivation is often necessarily used *in terrorem;*" [a] and because "the punishment is just, and may be removed by submission, — for honest and godly ministers are not molested, but arrogant and factious persons, opposing themselves to laws and framing new platforms, are bridled and restrained according to law. [b]

"The eleventh is misliked." [a] "Examination *ex officio mero* is lawful, usual, and necessary; necessary because either the bishop must dismiss the preacher upon his single denial of the fact, or else, *ex officio,* put him to his oath;" [b] "necessary especially, because in many places these men have so framed their parishioners that, although they clean alter the order of service and administration of the sacraments, they will never complain of them." [c]

"To the twelfth Article it is answered, that the Lords spiritual will take order for such exercises;" [a] "not however to be like those called prophecies, but others more private." [b]

"Touching the thirteenth and fourteenth; the bishops purpose to be more strait in the matter," [b] and intend that hereafter no excommunication shall be sent out but for adultery and some other weighty cause." [a]

The fifteenth and sixteenth, the Archbishop of York acknowledged "to stand with good reason; especially the proviso for godly and sufficient curates." But the Archbishop of Canterbury said, that "Pluralities could not be taken away without discouraging the best sort of ministers, and taking away the reward of learning." [1]

"By these petitions," he sneeringly added, "it may appear that these *holy ones* disdain to be under any government, civil or ecclesiastical; but to do even what they list, without controlment. These petitions bewray their meanings." [2]

[1] Neal adopts only the Answer to these petitions by the pen of Winchester; under the impression that it was given in the name of the bishops. It does not appear that Dr. Cooper drew it up for any other purpose than his own satisfaction; or, perhaps, to be read by him in the Upper House of Parliament, or, of Convocation. (See Strype's Whitgift, 187.)

On the other hand, we have it distinctly testified, repeatedly, and uniformly, that *the Answer* given to the Committee of the Commons was given by Sandys, and was given by him in the name of the Lords spiritual, "whom in all that he said he but personated." (See D'Ewes, 359, 360, and Strype's Whitgift, 177, 179.) Consequently, the reader who may chance to compare my version with Neal's will find great dissimilarity.

[2] Strype's Whitgift, Appendix, p. 74.

But Archbishop Sandys — in his remote Province more exposed to rude attacks from the ill-affected, both Catholics and Puritans, than were his Grace of Canterbury and the Bishop of London under the immediate shadow of the throne, and even now smarting, like a flayed man, from an infamous plot of his enemies [1] — was more wary and courteous in the conclusion of his answer. "I fear," said he, "that *some* of the House of Commons be too ready to think and speak hardly of the ancient and godly Order of Bishops; yet would I desire them that they will be pleased to think well of me, and of the rest of my brethren *now living*, if not in respect of our places, yet for charity sake, and for that some of us were preachers when many of the House of Commons were in their cradles." [2]

We do not understand this as the petulant language of supercilious age, but as prompted by the

[1] In May, 1581, Archbishop Sandys had been the victim of a trick to extort money; a trick the more likely to be successful with men of the sacred profession, because of their usual lack of worldly wisdom; but still more, because it peculiarly involves that which is a peculiar treasure to *them*, — a good name. It is sufficient to say, that, while Sir Robert Stapleton, a knight of Yorkshire, with two men his accomplices, were the plotters, *a woman* was the chief actor. The innocent but terrified Archbishop was speedily fleeced of six hundred pounds sterling; and it was not until he found his tormentors proceeding to extortion upon extortion, with no prospect of a limit, that he gained wisdom enough and courage enough to reveal the matter to the Council. Stapleton was suffering imprisonment in the Tower for his villany, when Archbishop Sandys penned the words which follow in the text. (Strype's Annals, V. 142-158; fol. ed., III. 98-110.) Even "the judicious Hooker" was the subject of a like imposition, though less gross. There is an unsatisfactory reference, in a general way, to the "trepanning" of this good man, in Izaak Walton's Memoir of him prefixed to his Works, page 73. I have somewhere met with the particulars; but my memory fails to tell me where.

[2] D'Ewes, 360. Strype's Whitgift, 179.

honorable yet tremulous respect of a veteran for his own gray hairs; as the subdued words of one whose dim eye moistened as he pathetically alluded to the fresh graves of his revered and beloved companions.

Mr. Treasurer's report of the answer delivered by the Archbishop of York roused the spirit of the House. So far were they from tamely acquiescing; so far from being "deterred by the severe reprimands with which, in former sessions, the Commons had met from the throne;"[1] so far from thinking "that those matters were too high for them to attempt of themselves," that the report was no sooner rendered, than "Mr. Speaker!" "Mr. Speaker!" was heard in various quarters from members who had sprang to their feet. Many motions were made, and "sundry long speeches" followed. At last the House, resolved to push this matter of ecclesiastical reform, directed the same Committee "to select such grave members of the House as were learned in divinity, in the common laws of the realm, and in the canon law, and to confer together with them in the Exchequer Chamber on the afternoon of the next day, concerning the answer of the Lords; and after such conference and consideration had, then to resolve for further proceeding therein as then shall be thought meetest by the House."[2]

In the very deficient journal of the Commons, we find, to be sure, only one other mention of this con-

[1] Hume, III. 125. Hume's "they" is here changed for "the Commons." There were but seven or eight who had been members "in former sessions."

[2] D'Ewes, 360.

ference, and that an incidental one.[1] Yet this action of the House was by no means a vapid bluster. "As that former bill"—the sixteen petitions—"succeeded not, other bills relating to ecclesiastical matters were devised and brought into the House; and all to clip the wings of the bishops and to weaken (if not destroy) their Courts."[2] The very next day—February 26th—so impatient were the House, a bill was read and committed, without waiting for the consultation with "the select grave members," against unlawful licenses to marry.[3] On the same day was read for the second time another bill,—very significant; and, as such, a public verification of our statements above about the *illegal* practices of the hierarchy,—a bill "for swearing bishops and archbishops, in Chancery and King's Bench, that *they should act nothing contrary to the common law of England.*"[4] On the sixth day of March, another for "avoiding the multiplicity of excommunications," was committed upon the third reading.[5] On the eighteenth of the month, a bill for the better execution of the statute of the thirteenth year of her Majesty for reformation of certain disorders in ministers of the Church, was read for the first time.[6] We find no description of it; yet it can hardly be doubted that it provided against subscriptions required, under color of that statute, to other articles than "the Articles of Religion, which only concerned the true Christian Faith and the doctrine of the sacraments." The next day it was

[1] D'Ewes, 361.

[2] Strype's Life of Whitgift, p. 187.

[3] D'Ewes, 360.

[4] Strype's Whitgift, 187. D'Ewes, 361. Camden, 308.

[5] D'Ewes, 364.

[6] Ibid., 370.

read the second time and committed. On the twentieth of the month, a new bill was substituted, read twice, ordered to be engrossed, and, on the *next* day, read the third time, largely argued, and passed.[1]

It should be particularly noted, however, that *before* the passage — if not before the introduction — of this bill, "the queen, uneasy at their thus meddling in these matters, had sent to them a charge not to deal in causes of the Church."[2] Yet the House persisted; passed this bill so pointedly (if our supposition of its contents is correct) against the favorite policy of the prelates and the Crown; and, on the twenty-third of the month, sent it up to the Lords.[3]

On the same day that it passed the Commons, a bill against excessive fees and taxations in ecclesiastical courts was read the second time and committed.[4]

On the twenty-third, they also passed a bill "for the qualification of ministers;"[5] and another had been "brought in" for restoring of discipline in the Church. The latter was "for abolishing the canon law and all the spiritual courts, and for bringing the probates of wills and all civil business into the courts of Westminster Hall, and for appointing a presbytery or eldership in each parish," — not interfering at all with the Church regimen established, — "which, to-

[1] D'Ewes, 371.

[2] Strype's Whitgift, 187, 198 (and, below in this chapter, Whitgift's letter to the queen); 212, Beal's persistence in the House.

It would seem that a like commandment was given, in the queen's name, to the Speaker of the House by the Lord Chancellor at the opening of the Parliament, (D'Ewes, 345,) though no mention of it is made in the notice of the Chancellor's speech.

[3] D'Ewes, 326.

[4] Ibid., 371.

[5] Strype's Whitgift, 198.

gether with the minister, should determine the spiritual business of the parish, with an appeal to higher judicatories in cases of complaint."[1]

The bill for the qualification of ministers was, "to annul all Popish ordinations, and to disqualify such ministers as were not capable of preaching, or who might be convicted of profaneness or any kind of immorality, — allowing, however, the deprived minister a sufficient maintenance; a reasonable consideration not granted, in like cases, by the bishops. It also provided for a careful examination and trial of the qualifications of candidates for the ministry by the bishop, assisted by twelve of the laity; and for making the election or consent of the people necessary to any one's induction to the pastoral charge."[2]

"Specious bills" were also brought in against pluralities and non-residences;[3] but at what time during the session does not appear.[4] The one against pluralities created the greatest excitement. His Grace of Canterbury drew up a statement of the "inconveniences" which would ensue should it become a law; and Sir Francis Knollys, a counter statement.[5]

[1] Neal, I. 174.

[2] Ibid.

It is to be regretted that Mr. Neal does not give us his authority for his description of this bill; as he does, for the bill of discipline. It is so remarkable, that I could not have adopted it, were it not supported in part by a single clause in the letter of Archbishop Whitgift, about to be introduced.

[3] Strype's Whitgift, 192.

[4] That these three bills last named are not mentioned in D'Ewes's Journal argues nothing. For, as Mr. Hallam justly remarks (153, note), "we cannot rely upon negative inferences as to proceedings in Parliament at this period." A very large and important part of the Journals, as given by D'Ewes, consists of matters gathered from authentic sources other than the Journals as kept from time to time by "the very greatly negligent" Clerks.

[5] It was argued by the bishops: The supporters of this bill say that non-residence is *malum in se*. But

The bill drew forth "a very pathetical address to the queen from the Convocation," entitled "A petition to the queen that the bill against pluralities pass not;" in which they styled themselves her Majesty's "poor, distressed supplicants," and represented the bill as consisting, not only of "great indignities, injuries, and absurdities," but "of hypocrisy as great."[1]

"In the mean time the bill passed the Commons and was sent up to the Lords, where the two Archbishops and the Bishop of Winchester made long speeches, showing that neither the Cathedrals nor Professors in the Universities could subsist without Pluralities. To prove this, they produced a list of the small value of many ecclesiastical livings. To which it was replied, that there were many suspended preachers who would be glad of the smallest of those livings, if they might have them without molestation; however, that it was more proper to go upon ways and means for the augmentation of smaller livings than to suffer the poor people to perish for lack of knowledge, while the incumbents were indulged in

it allows one man to have two benefices being but three miles apart. So that the bill doth allow *malum in se.*

Sir Francis Knollys replied: Non-residence is not *malum in se.* But the pastor, not to feed his flock, is. One man may feed two flocks but three miles apart. Therefore, one man *may* have two benefices without committing *malum in se.*

It was objected to the bill, that parents would not send their children to study divinity, if they could not hope for plurality of benefices; but Sir Francis answered: "Good men will desire rather to feed their flocks than to get their wool or their milk."

It was objected that resident preachers could not be had for all the parishes, for there were nine thousand in the realm, and but three thousand preachers. "But," answered Sir Francis, "you can, thus and so, soon turn your readers into preachers; and the Universities will soon furnish more, if you furnish suitable livings." (Strype's Whitgift, 193, 194.)

[1] Strype's Whitgift, 193, 194.

idleness and sloth. But the weight of the Bench of Bishops, with the Court interest, threw out the bill."[1]

By all these proceedings, the Archbishop was "closely affected." The day after the bill for the qualification of ministers passed the Lower House, he again appealed to the queen.

"May it please your Majesty to be advertised, That notwithstanding the charge of late given by your Highness to the Lower House of Parliament for dealing in causes of the Church; albeit also, according to your Majesty's good liking, we have set down order"—in Convocation—"for the admitting of meet men in the ministry hereafter, yet they have passed a bill in that House yesterday touching that matter. Which, besides other inconveniences (as namely, the trial of the minister's sufficiency by twelve laymen, and such like), hath this also,—that if it pass by Parliament, it cannot hereafter but in Parliament be altered, whatsoever necessity shall urge thereunto. Which I am persuaded in short time shall appear; considering the multitude of livings not fit for men so qualified by reason of the smallness thereof. Whereas if it is but as a canon from us by your Majesty's authority, it may be observed or altered at your pleasure.

"They have also passed a bill giving liberty to marry at all times of the year without restraint, contrary to the old canons continually observed among us; and containing matter which tendeth to the slander of this Church as having hitherto maintained an error.[2]

[1] Neal, I. 174.

[2] "But," says Mr. Neal judi-

"There is likewise now in hand in the same House, a bill concerning ecclesiastical courts and visitation of bishops. Which may reach to the overthrow of ecclesiastical jurisdiction and study of the civil laws. The pretence of the bill is against excessive fees and exactions in ecclesiastical courts. Which fees are none other than have been of long time accustomed to be taken..... I therefore most humbly beseech your Majesty to continue your gracious goodness towards us, who with all humility submit ourselves to your Highness, and cease not daily to pray for your happy state and long and prosperous reign over us. From Lambeth the 24th of March, 1584"–5.

"Your Majesty's Chaplain and daily Orator, most bound,

"JO. CANTUAR."[1]

Her Majesty was sufficiently inclined to the prayer of the Archbishop; for "she pitied him because she trusted him, and had thereby eased herself, by laying the burden of all her clergy-cares upon his shoulders."[2] Besides, the prayer was but asking her "to verify her own motto,— *Semper Eadem*;"[3] it was but playing upon her "jealousy of her Parliament's encroaching upon her Supremacy in Spirituals."[4] Immediately upon receiving this letter she sent a Message to the Commons reprimanding them for attempting what belonged to herself alone, and what

ciously, "many of the canons are contrary to the canon of Scripture;" and "is it, then, a slander to the Church of England, or to any Protestant Church, to say she is fallible?" (Neal, I. 175.)

[1] Strype's Whitgift, 198. Fuller, Bk. IX. p. 174.

[2] Hooker, I. 41; Walton's Life of Hooker.

[3] Fuller, ibid.

[4] Strype's Whitgift, 207.

she had forbidden by her previous Message. She ordered them "to stay any further proceeding in the debating of.... reformation.... in the Church;"[1] and commanded the Speaker "to see that no bills touching reformation in causes ecclesiastical should be exhibited, and, if any such were exhibited, she commanded him upon his allegiance not to read them."[2] This sharp and imperative Message was obeyed; but the Puritan party in the Commons had already done, apparently, all that they wished to do in the way of framing and discussing such bills. In the Lords, the influence of the Crown and the Mitre predominated; and all special efforts at reform were dashed there, except a bill for the better observance of the Sabbath, which the queen herself rejected after it had passed *both* Houses.[3]

The Puritans plied other means of relief. They presented a Petition at the door of the Convocation House. It was rejected. They published "An Apology to the Church and Humble Suit to the High Court of Parliament." It was of no avail.[4] They then publicly addressed the Archbishop himself in a printed Paper (already mentioned), entitled, "Means how to settle a godly and charitable quietness in the Church." The points — or rather, the petitions — of this Paper, his lordship answered. These answers, his biographer says, "are very well worthy the con-

[1] Puckering to the Queen; Strype's Annals, VI. 359.

[2] Neal, I. 174.

The speech of Puckering at the close of Parliament is the only authority I find for this message. Mr. Neal gives us more; which I have used, because it was probably true. But again we have reason to complain, that, for a statement of importance, he does not give his authority, — only quotation marks.

[3] Strype's Annals, V. 429.

[4] Neal, I. 175.

sidering."[1] We think they are; and therefore quote the most worthy.

To their petition that the articles *ex officio* might be forborne, he replied by simply denying every legal and historical fact which they gave as their reasons.

They petitioned that the ministers suspended or deprived might be suffered to preach on condition of a bond to the following effect: not to preach error or schism, not to inveigh against the Book of Common Prayer, the Articles of Religion, the Book of Ordination, or the Prelacy, but solely to teach Christ crucified, to uphold and maintain the order of the Church, and to withstand those who should not. "I do not mislike of the bond," the Archbishop answered; "but he that shall enter into it and yet refuse to subscribe, in my opinion is either a mere hypocrite or a very wilful fellow; for this condition indeed containeth more than doth the subscription." We confess astonishment at the obliquity of vision which could see *more* in such a bond than in avowing that "the Book of Common Prayer and the Book of Ordination contained *nothing* contrary to the Word of God."

They also petitioned, "That no ministers be enforced to read any piece of the Apocrypha in the Service; seeing in the first book printed in the beginning of her Majesty's reign, the same is left out, and *was after* (without warrant of law, and contrary to the statute which alloweth *but three* alterations) *inserted*."

His lordship simply replied, that it had been accounted part of the Bible in the purest time of the Church; that it was in the calendar[2] of King Ed-

[1] Strype's Whitgift, 197.

[2] "The calendars are not of the

ward's latter Book; and that it was printed in the first *year* of her Majesty's reign,—evading the point in their petition, that it was not in the queen's first *Book*, and evading their other point, that it was inserted contrary to the statute.[1]

To their petition not to be enforced to use the sign of the cross in baptism, seeing in King Edward's second Book a note left it to be used or not used, his lordship denied that there was such a note in that Book. Had he *seen* King Edward's Books of Common Prayer" since his controversy with Beal? Had he *discovered*, since his conversation with the ministers belonging to the diocese of Chichester, *what was in* the queen's Book?[2]

To their petition that his Grace would forbear urging the precise wearing of the gown, the surplice, &c., he answered, "The law urgeth it, and decency doth require it. But some, being ashamed of their calling, or not daring to displease their *dames* at home and abroad, had rather go like mere laymen or ruffians, than wear the apparel prescribed." We think *this* answer, at least, "worth considering;" but unsavory.[3]

The consideration of certain acts passed by this Parliament we reserve.

On Saturday, the twenty-seventh day of March, immediately after morning prayers, her Majesty ordered the Commons, through their Speaker, not to

substance of the Book," the Archbishop had said. (*Ante*, Chap. XIII. p. 357.)

[1] *Ante*, p. 454, note; also, Vol. I. p. 427, note 4.

[2] *Ante*, Chap. XV. p. 413, and Chap. XIII. p. 359.

[3] Strype's Whitgift, Append., Bk. III. No. XVI.

sit that day; but to come together on Monday when she would signify "her further pleasure."[1] This was but a sign of that royal *dis*-pleasure to which she soon gave open expression. On the afternoon of Monday, being notified that her Majesty with her Lords waited their attendance in the Upper House, there to prorogue the Parliament, the Commons repaired thither. We give a few sentences only from the Speaker's address to the queen; some of which throw light upon her memorable speech in reply,—so prominent in all our histories of the time.

"Our firm hope is that your Majesty will, by your strait commandment to your clergy, continue your care to see, and command, that such abuses as are crept into the Church by the negligence of the ministers may be speedily reformed, to the honor of Almighty God, and to your own immortal praise, and comfort of your subjects.

"May it please your Majesty to yield your royal assent to such petitions[2] .... as have been .... determined and conceived in writing, with uniform consent of the Lords spiritual and temporal, and us your Commons, in this your Parliament assembled. Wherein your Majesty shall do no less than pertaineth to the authority which you have, like to God Almighty; who, as He giveth life and being to all his creatures great and small, so your Majesty shall give life and continuance to the fruits of our consultations, as well to the small as to the great; without which your royal assent with your own breath, the same shall become without life and sense, and all of our labors

[1] D'Ewes, 373.

[2] Bills. *Ante*, p. 464, note 1.

therein lost, and our expectations therein made frustrate.

"For defence of your Majesty's noble person, and for revenge of any act imaginate against your Majesty we have by a form of law, if it shall like your Majesty to assent thereunto, given a testimony to the whole world how dear the safety of your life is to us. And this I do assure your Majesty, that we, your most loving subjects, were most willing to have extended this ordinance to a far straiter course, as we thought the same meet for your safety, and for terrifying of all persons not well willing to you, if otherwise we had not understood that your Majesty's pleasure was that it should not be extended to any straiter points than it is."[1]

After the ceremony of her Majesty's answers to the several bills, she addressed her Parliament in the following "most pious and gracious speech": —

"My Lords, and ye of the Lower House, my silence must not injure the owner thereof so much as to suppose a substitute sufficient to render you the thanks that my heart yieldeth you, not so much for the safe keeping of my life for which your care appears so manifest,[2] as for the neglecting your private future peril not regarding other way than my present state. No prince, I confess, can be surer tied or faster bound than I am with the link of your good-will; and" — I — "can for that but yield a heart and a head to seek forever all your best.

"Yet one thing toucheth me so near as I may not

[1] Strype's Annals, VI. Appendix, No. LI. pp. 359, 360.

[2] In the Act referred to by the Speaker, and just passed, "For the surety of her Majesty's most royal person."

overskip,—Religion; the ground on which all other matters ought to take root, and"—which—"being corrupted, may mar all the tree. And"—I may not overlook—"that there be some fault-finders with the Order of the clergy, which so may make a slander to myself and the Church whose overruler God hath made me, whose negligence cannot be excused if any schisms or errors heretical were suffered.

"Thus much I must say, that some faults and negligences may grow and be, as in all other great charges it happeneth. And what vocation, without? All which, if you, my Lords of the clergy, do not amend, I mean to depose you. Look ye, therefore, well to your charges. This may be amended without heedless or open exclamations.

"I am supposed to have many studies; but most, philosophical.[1] I must yield this to be true, that I suppose few that be no Professors have read more. And I need not tell you that I am so simple that I understand not, nor so forgetful that I remember not. And yet amidst my many volumes I hope God's Book hath not been my seldomest lectures, in which we find—that which by reason, for my part we ought to believe—that, seeing so great wickedness and griefs in the world in which we live but as wayfaring pilgrims, we must suppose that God would never have made us, but for a better place, and of more comfort, than we find here. I know no creature that breatheth whose life standeth hourly in more peril for it than mine own,—who entered not into my state without fight[2] of manifold dangers of life and Crown,

[1] "By which, I suppose she meant —theological." Hume, III. 127.

[2] In Stow, "fight." In D'Ewes, "sight."

as one that had the mightiest and greatest to wrestle with. Then it followeth — that I regarded it" — my *Crown* — "so much, as I left my *life* behind my care. And so, you see, that you wrong me too much, if any such there be, as doubt[1] my coldness in that behalf; for if I were not persuaded that mine were the true way of God's will,[2] God forbid that I should live to prescribe it to you.

"Take you heed lest Ecclesiastes say not too true, 'They that fear the hoary frost, the snow shall fall upon them.' I see many over-bold with God Almighty; making too many scannings of his blessed Will; as lawyers do, with human Testaments. The presumption is so great, as I may not suffer it. Yet mind I not hereby to animate Romanists (which, what adversaries they be to mine estate, is sufficiently known) nor tolerate new-fangleness. I mean to guide them both by God's holy true Rule.

"In both parts be perils; and of the latter, I must pronounce them dangerous to a kingly rule, — to have every man, according to his own censure, to make a doom of the validity and privity of his prince's government, with a common veil and cover of God's Word, whose followers must not be judged but by private men's exposition. God defend you from such a ruler that so evil will guide you.

"Now I conclude, that your love and care neither is nor shall be bestowed upon a careless prince, but such as but for your good-will passeth as little for this world as he who careth the least: With thanks for your free Subsidy, — a manifest show of the abundance of your good-wills, — the which I assure you,

[1] Suspect.

[2] "*Truth* of God's will," Stow.

but to be employed to your weal, I could be better pleased to return than receive."[1]

The Parliament was then prorogued until the twentieth day of May; and, after repeated further prorogations, was dissolved on the fifteenth day of September, 1586.

The Journal of this House of Commons is barren of incident and of debate. Yet in the mere entries of motions and bills, in the Petitions, and in the answer to them, when collated with the other Papers which have been produced, we find much which claims our scrutiny and commands our respect.

The reform projected by the Puritans was no light affair; nor was it so radical as some have supposed. Much as they desired it, they were too wise to ask for an ecclesiastical revolution. They did not ask for the abolition of prelacy. They did not ask that the prelates should be divested of their temporal lordships, their revenues, or their worldly pomp. They did not ask for a favorable consideration of Presbytery. They did not ask for any change of ecclesiastical government.[2] They did not ask even to be freed from the ecclesiastical censures and other penalties prescribed by the statutes.

[1] D'Ewes, 328. Stow, 702.

[2] Their fourth Article did not propose a change of ecclesiastical government; and their references there to the Book of Ordination (See Sparrow, 158), and to the statute of 21 Henry VIII., prove it. Mr. Hume, by changing the word "ministers," in the Article, to "Presbyters," perverts its meaning, leads his reader to suppose that the Puritans asked for the substitution of Presbytery, — or, at least, for its grafting upon Episcopacy, — and charges them with a foolish "demand," of which they were innocent, that "a change of ecclesiastical government should be introduced." (Hume, III. 125.)

They did ask that the ecclesiastical government, as established, might be restrained to its proper limits. They asked that, instead of being prosecuted in the temporal Courts for every the least petty omission or addition in the service of public worship; "things," even in the opinion of the Privy Council, "not so much against the matter and very meaning of the law, as in some show swerving from the letter thereof," — instead of being "subjected to the malice of cavilling, sophistical lawyers enforcing the points of law;" they might, upon *cause* of complaint, be proceeded against by the bishops; and so they were distinctly understood.[1] They asked to be freed from the suffering and odium of suspension and deprivation for only refusing to subscribe to Articles not prescribed by law. They asked that the examination *ex officio mero* might be forborne. They asked to be freed from arbitrary impositions, from the abuse of power, from illegal exactions and illegal punishments. They asked that their rights as citizens might be respected, and their chartered liberties be preserved intact. They asked that the spiritual famine in the land might be relieved, and that the ministry of reconciliation might not be disgraced by the incompetent and desecrated by the immoral. These were no

[1] Archbishop Whitgift objected that the eighth and ninth articles proposed to free ministers from the jurisdiction of the bishops, "*in effect*, their authority being so restrained." Cooper was more ingenuous. His words were: "The eighth petition desires a dispensation from the temporal judge. The ninth, the like from chancellors, &c. . . . . But whereto this tendeth is most evident. For if those ministers . . . . had once wrested themselves from the authority of chancellors and such like, they would shortly wring themselves from the bishops too, *before whom already they limit*, by this petition, *how they will* be dealt withal." Strype's Whitgift, 189.

childish or "fantastic" petitions. They were the petitions of men; of Christian men; of men whose Christian honor was touched by the degradation of the sacred office, whose Christian compassion was moved, to its very depths, by the cries of those who lacked the Bread of Life. They were the petitions of men who appreciated the necessity of law and of penalty; of men who—however their perceptions of religious liberty were beclouded—were beginning to appreciate, in some important measure, the nature, the value, and the means of civil liberty; of men who were contending for rights; of men who were resenting oppression. The entire burden of their remonstrance was, not the government, but the misgovernment, of the prelates; and the entire burden of their petitions was, that this misgovernment, in its various departments, might be corrected.

But these were grave matters. The ramifications of prelatic power were so extensive, its wrongs to the Church of Christ and to the free citizen of England were so many, that no little wisdom was requisite to remedy the evils without disturbing the system. The Puritans were wise enough to be aware of this, and they acted accordingly. They acted like men who comprehended alike the difficulties and the importance of reform; like men enlisted and girded for the right, but feeling after the wisdom equal to their work. They were neither bashful nor exorbitant in their requests; neither timid nor conceited; neither witless nor hot-headed. Therefore when they went forward, it was sagaciously; not planting the foot without seeing and feeling their ground. The first step in their movement in the House of

Commons, singular as it may seem to us and liable as it is to be misrepresented, was simply according to Parliamentary usage in peculiar cases.

When any question of great moment and peculiar delicacy arose, it was often thought proper to proceed with more than ordinary deliberation; and, first of all, to bring into consultation Queen, Lords, and Commons. The initiatory step towards this seems to have been expected from the Lower House. How, and how soon, to deal with the Duke of Norfolk? was such a question before the Parliament of 1572. Therefore, it was moved in the Commons, "Whether it were convenient that this House and the Lords should *join in petition to move the Queen's Majesty*" for his execution. Accordingly, "request was made, that it might please their lordships in petition thereof unto her Highness to join with this House."[1] Was there anything sycophantic or craven-hearted in this? any fear of her Majesty's displeasure? How to proceed with the Queen of Scots? was such a question before the same Parliament. Therefore, in this matter also, they proceeded by *joint petition* to her Majesty "for the speedy execution of the Scottish Queen."[2] But who ever dreamed that this proposition might incur her Majesty's displeasure? The subject of The Succession had been considered, during the whole reign, as of the greatest magnitude, and — considering her Majesty's sensitiveness — one of peculiar delicacy. Therefore, when it was again broached by Peter Wentworth in the Lower House of Parliament in 1592–3, it was by "a petition desiring the Lords of the Upper House to be *suppliants with* them of the

[1] D'Ewes, 206, 214.

[2] Ibid., 207–219.

Lower House to her Majesty for entailing the Succession of the Crown."[1] But who ever said, or who ever dreamed, then or since, that Peter Wentworth was afraid? that Peter Wentworth took this course of procedure being "overawed by the queen's authority?" Perhaps other like cases might be found. But these are enough to show the usage of Parliament. They show, that a request from the Commons to the Lords to join them in petition to the queen, signified only that the subject-matter proposed for petition called for the concerted wisdom of Parliament; that it was of such moment and delicacy as to make desirable a mutual comparison of views between the Crown, the Lords, and the Commons, *before* devising and draughting any particular course of action. Thus in the case before us. The subject of ecclesiastical reform, as it lay in the minds of the Puritans, was of great moment and peculiar delicacy. It was commensurate with the combined and deliberate wisdom of her Majesty, her Lords, and her Commons. Therefore, the latter *prudentially* initiated their movement by requesting the Lords to join with them in petition.

It was not to be supposed that the bishops, whose authority the petitioners proposed to circumscribe, and to whose proceedings they took exceptions, would readily consent to be shorn of their greatness or to be responsible at law. Nor did they, as we have seen. But this did not check the Commons. No sooner were they repulsed in their preliminary measure — that is, no sooner had the Lords refused, for the reasons given, to join in petition to the queen

[1] D'Ewes, 470.

— than the Commons threw themselves upon their own resources for wisdom, and upon their own rights, and introduced bill after bill aiming, for the most part, at the same particulars of reform as those indicated in their petitions, "and all to clip the wings of the bishops and to weaken (if not destroy) their courts." Nor did they, within their own doors, enter upon these matters without a high-spirited determination to speak their own minds and to assert *their own* prerogatives. Robert Beal, who had wrestled so with his Grace of Canterbury, was a member of the House; and *he* was not "overawed by the queen's authority;" but "openly spake of matters of ecclesiastical jurisdiction, &c., contrary to her Majesty's express pleasure, afore delivered. For which he was also committed."[1]

We have said, that the Commons in these petitions discovered some just notions of the value, the nature, and the means of civil liberty. They proposed to correct the misgovernment of the bishops. By what means? By encompassing their authority *with checks*, — a fundamental provision for a free and equitable

[1] Strype's Whitgift, 212.

Mr. Hume says, that the Commons in their petitions, "entreated the reverend Fathers to think of some law for the remedy of abuses of excommunication; implying that those matters were too high for the Commons themselves to attempt."

But, on the sixth day of March, they introduced a bill on this very matter; for "avoiding the multiplicity of excommunications." If Mr. Hume is correct, they must have advanced in their own estimate of themselves, and in real altitude, since the offering of their petitions.

I leave the reader to judge between my views expressed in the following text, and these other words of Mr. Hume: "The Commons, in making their general application *to the Prelates*, as well as in some particular articles of their petition, showed themselves wholly ignorant, no less than the queen, of the principles of liberty and a legal constitution."

government. The nature and source of these checks, show that they who proposed them had no dim or untrue view of that liberty which coexists with authority, and which flourishes only under its shadow; and no dim or irrational view of the Popular element as the true corrective of Power and the hale constituent of Liberty. It was the theory of the prelates, that the government of a Church should correspond to that of the State in which it was planted; and on this ground they justified the constitution of the Church of England. Falsely,—because, while, in the Civil Government, the Popular element had its representation in the House of Commons, there was no corresponding representation in the government of the Church. The people had no voice. The laity held no check upon the prelatic Lords. It was this defect which the Puritan Commons were now seeking to supply. It was this check which they were seeking to provide.

This appears in the fourth Article of the Petition, which sought to check the bishops from ordaining unworthy men, by imposing the co-operation of the inferior clergy.

It appears in the sixth Article, requiring the approval of the people before the induction of a curate.

It appears in the bill for restoring discipline in the Church; in its provision for an eldership in each parish, which, together with the minister should constitute an inferior ecclesiastical court (from which there might be appeal) to determine the spiritual business of the parish.

It appears in the bill for the qualification of ministers; in its provision for a careful examination of candidates for the ministry by the bishop and twelve laymen; and in its provision that no one should be inducted to a pastoral charge without the election or consent of the people.

Such are the facts on which we base a special esteem for *this* House of Commons,—their perception of legal wrongs; their Parliamentary prudence in moving reform; their unfaltering persistence by themselves when rebuffed by the Lords; their calm but resolute proceeding notwithstanding the queen's first inhibition; and, above all, their sagacious recognition of the true source of civil liberty, their statesmanlike estimate of an oligarchy and of the true antidote to its evils.

The bishops had been efficient teachers of principles they would have kept hid. The Puritans were rapid learners. The stroke of steel develops the latent spark; the abuse of power, the light and spirit of Liberty.

CHAPTER XVII.

THE PARLIAMENT OF 1584-5. (THE CATHOLICS.)

Edward Arden executed for plotting against the Queen's Life. — Gregory Martin's "Treatise of Schism." — William Carter tried and executed for publishing it. — Apprehensions and Cautionary Measures of the Queen's Ministers about a Catholic Invasion of England. — Throckmorton's Conspiracy discovered. — His Revelations of a Foreign Plot. — Mendoza, the Spanish Ambassador, sent away as an Accomplice of Throckmorton. — The Queen sends a special Minister to Spain to explain the Matter. — He is refused a Hearing by Philip. — Throckmorton's Trial. — English Refugees in Paris plot against their Queen. — Sir Edward Stafford's Conference about them with Henry of France. — Throckmorton executed. — Stafford advertised of a Plot to assassinate Elizabeth. — The Plan for an Invasion of England clearly revealed. — The Leicester Association formed, for the Safety of the Queen. — The solemn Bond of the Associators. — The Queen of Scots offers to subscribe the Bond, on Conditions. — Parliament adopt the Substance of the Bond in "an Act for the Surety of her Majesty's most royal Person." — The Points of the Act. — Its just and humane Difference from the Bond. — The Bond to be limited and interpreted by the Act. — The "Act against Jesuits and Seminary Priests." — The Queen the Modifier of the first Act. — The Action of the Commons on both Bills, deliberate. — The Conspiracy of William ap Harry for the Murder of the Queen. — He is returned a Member of the House of Commons. — Vehemently opposes the Bill against Jesuits and Seminary Priests. — Is put in Ward for Contempt of the House. — Is restored to his Seat through the Queen's Mediation. — His Intent to assassinate her discovered. — His Arrest and Confessions. — The Commons "disable him to be a Member of the House." — On his Trial, he ratifies and retracts his Confessions. — His Execution.

In the autumn of 1583, a young gentleman from Elstow, in Warwickshire, while journeying in great haste towards London, was arrested for having made murderous attacks, on his way, upon certain unoffending persons. This John Somerville was a Catholic, whose religious enthusiasm had been inflamed to frenzy by brooding over Jesuitical invectives against excommunicated princes, — one of which, probably, was "a treatise" soon to be mentioned. Upon his arrest, he at once avowed that his soul was athirst for Protestant blood, and that he was then on a holy errand to shed that of Queen Elizabeth. He also implicated his own wife, Edward Arden, — a gentleman of an ancient family in Warwickshire, — and Maria Arden (the parents of his wife), and Hugh Hall, a missionary priest, as being privy to his designs. Under ordinary circumstances, a confession so bold, so needless, so willing, so surely suicidal, and so terribly involving his own household, taken in connection with the wild behavior for which he was arrested, might have suggested that he was a lunatic to be pitied and cared for, rather than a criminal to be punished. But, in her relations to the Catholic world at large, and in regard to the succession, England was *not* 'in ordinary circumstances;' and in December all these persons were tried and condemned for High Treason. On the third day after their conviction, Somerville strangled himself in Newgate; and on the fourth day — December the twentieth — Arden suffered as a traitor at Smithfield. The rest of the family and the priest were pardoned.

This tragedy "was generally imputed to the malice of the Earl of Leicester," who sought Arden's life for the same reason for which Ahab sought Naboth's; and also, for the same for which Haman sought Mordecai's. But besides refusing the Earl his homage and his land, Arden had tormented him by discussing his adulterous sins. The singular facts, that all but

Arden and the suicide were pardoned, and that the coveted land came into the Earl's possession, leave little room to doubt that this "terrestrial Lucifer" had coolly used the misfortune of a religious monomaniac to gratify his own avarice and lordly pride.[1] However, the trial and execution left also no slight impression among the people that the purpose of Somerville was at best but an index of what was passing in *sane* Catholic minds.

In 1578, Gregory Martin, a scholar of Oxford, but then a Professor of Divinity in the missionary college at Rheims, published a book entitled "A Treatise of Schism." It contained the following passage: "If our gentlewomen would follow the godly and constant wisdom of Judith, they might destroy Holofernes, the Master Heretic, and amass all his retinue, and never defile their religion by communicating with them in any small point." The author, we are told, was giving "instances from the Old Testament of persons who had refused to participate in any kind of worship which they deemed unlawful."

In 1580, this book was reprinted in England by William Carter, a bookseller. On the tenth day of January, 1583–4, he was indicted, for doing so, on a charge of High Treason. It was contended for the Crown, that by Holofernes, the master heretic, the queen was designated; and her assassination, by the destruction of Holofernes; in other words, that this crime was really suggested and — quickly enough — would be understood to be, by a fit mind; although, standing in a discourse about not defiling one's religion by tampering with heresy, the passage might

[1] Stow, 698. Camden, 289. Lingard, VIII. 179, 180.

so easily admit of an innocent construction that a zealot might venture to disperse it. Carter protested that *he* had never taken it in a bad sense; that it could not have been so intended, for the writer's whole object was to warn his brethren against schism; that the argument was simply, "as Judith abstained from the meats of Holofernes, so ought the faithful to abstain from communicating in heretical worship, for by *so* doing — by constancy in their religion and the rejection of a schismatic service — they would destroy Holofernes, *or Satan*, the author of heresy." Unfortunately for this defence, an English Court could not see how any one might hope to destroy *Satan* by rejecting a schismatic service; nor could they fail to see that the way in which Judith — the pattern — *did* destroy Holofernes was, — by cutting off his head. Carter was convicted; and on the next day was executed at Tyburn.[1] This event of course increased the public apprehensions for the queen's life.

For two or three years the Privy Council had had reason to suspect that the Catholic project for an invasion of England had been revived; that the Duke of Guise — kinsman of the Scottish Queen — had been soliciting the Pope and certain princes for forces; that one of these princes was pledged to the enterprise; and that the Duke would be furnished with men and money so soon as things should be in readiness in England.[2] The indignity with which Philip of Spain had for a long time treated the

[1] Stow, 698. Fuller, Bk. IX. p. 169. Strype's Annals, V. 407. Lingard, VIII. Appendix, note G.

[2] Holingshed, IV. 607.

ambassadors of the English Queen[1] had naturally excited suspicion — to say nothing of other causes — that *he* was the pledged Prince-patron of the Duke of Guise. Of course, the overthrow of the established religion and of Elizabeth, the recovery of the realm to Popery and Mary, were the objects aimed at.[2] Philip's power, already formidable, and yet upon the flood, was seriously estimated;[3] and under these circumstances the English Government had grounds for real apprehension and the most careful vigilance.

"Practices at home concurred, both for time and other circumstances, with those — not few or feeble — abroad." "The Seminaries were busy everywhere, drawing away the queen's subjects to Popery;" and "the young gentlemen were going over in heaps out of all places, and most by creeks and in fisher-boats, carrying with them great provision of all necessaries;" and large preparations of shipping by the Spanish King had already begun to attract attention.[4]

Under these circumstances, the queen's ministers considered themselves justified in vigorous, and even in rigorous and extreme cautionary measures. "Subtle ways were taken to try how men stood affected. Counterfeit letters were privily sent, in the names of the Queen of Scots and of the fugitives, and left in the houses of Papists. Spies were sent abroad up and down the country to take notice of people's discourse and to lay hold on their words. Reporters of vain and idle stories were admitted and credited.

[1] Holingshed, IV. 625.

[2] Strype's Annals, V. 277, 278.

[3] Camden, 305.

[4] Strype's Annals, V. 278. Birch, I. 41; Faunt to Bacon.

Hereupon many were brought into suspicion;"[1] "divers were taken up and imprisoned for refusing the Oath of Supremacy;"[2] others, because they had been ensnared into something indictable as treason; and others, doubtless, on mere suspicion. "The prisons were full of them."[3] For the Catholics, "it was become intolerable to continue in England."[4]

Among others, the watchful agents of Walsingham had had special regard to one Francis Throckmorton of Chester, of whom secret intelligence had been given that he was a messenger between the Queen of Scots and her friends. But for lack of sufficient proof, no steps were taken for his arrest for several months; none until — at some time soon after September, 1583[5] — "some proof more apparent fell out," when he was arrested.[6] Papers were found in his house strongly indicating preparations for an invasion of the realm. After being examined repeat-

[1] Camden, 294.

[2] Strype's Annals, V. 276.

[3] Birch, I. 41. Strype's Aylmer, 106.

[4] Hallam, 96.

[5] Holingshed, IV. 608.

[6] I pay no attention to the statement of Camden, Hume, and Lingard, that this arrest was immediately occasioned by an intercepted letter from, or to, the Queen of Scots, because of the peculiarly indefinite language quoted in the text; because such a letter — a strong incident — is nowhere alluded to in the Papers before me; and because the official document on which I rely says: "At the time of Throckmorton's apprehension there was no knowledge or doubt," i. e. suspicion — for "knowledge" and "doubt," in our use of the latter word, could not thus stand together — "had of these treasons, or of his privity unto them; but only an information and suspicion .... of some practice between him and the Scottish Queen." (Holingshed, IV. 540.)

The point is of but little historical importance, except as this peculiar use of the word "doubt" confirms the construction which I have put upon it as used by the Earl of Essex on his death-bed. So also does that clause in the queen's speech at the close of this Parliament: "You wrong me too much (if any such there be) as *doubt*" — suspect — "my coldness in that behalf."

edly by the Privy Council, and giving no satisfaction touching the various "causes and matters against him," he was put to the rack. The first trial was unavailing; but, being laid upon the engine again, after an intermission of nine days,[1] "he yielded to confess anything he knew; whereupon he was loosed."[2] He then confessed that everything was prepared abroad for the invasion of England; that the enterprise was sustained by the Duke of Guise, who had been persuaded by the Pope and the King of Spain[3] to act as generalissimo; that it was also sustained by the Queen of Scots, and by her confederates in France, in Spain, in Rome, and in England; that its objects were to force a toleration for Catholics or to dethrone her Majesty, and chiefly to set at liberty the Queen of Scots; that they were only waiting for assured co-operation in England, and for assurance against peril to the person of Queen Mary; that he himself had been engaged in this matter both abroad and at home; and that, at home, he had found an adviser in Mendoza, the Spanish ambassador, who zealously aided the plot.[4]

[1] Lingard, VIII. 182, note.

[2] It is useless to talk of a man being only "somewhat pinched, although not much" by the rack; as the writer of this "Declaration" does. Neither is it worth while to exaggerate facts which, at the best, were bad enough. This Dr. Lingard does; unless he had unquestionable authority to contradict, on a simple matter of fact, the published documents of the queen's ministers, from which I derive my statement. Such unquestionable authority he does not give. He says: "Throckmorton had *thrice* suffered the rack without making any disclosure; when he was *again* led to that engine of torture he confessed," &c. (Vol. VIII. p. 181.)

[3] Holingshed, IV. 545; Throckmorton's Declaration to the queen.

[4] For the particulars of this statement respecting Throckmorton, for which I have not made citations, I refer to the "Declaration" published (by the Council doubtless) in June, 1584, in Holingshed, IV.

Very soon after Throckmorton's arrest, Thomas Lord Paget and Charles Arundel, both of them Papists who seem to have been connected with his designs, fled to France.[1] Soon after this, Henry Percy, Earl of Northumberland; Philip Howard, Earl of Arundel, a professed Papist and eldest son of the unfortunate Duke of Norfolk; his Countess; his uncle; and his brother — all being implicated by Throckmorton's confession — were repeatedly subjected to examination before the Council; and perhaps consigned to private custody.[2]

As soon as it had been made patent, by Throckmorton's confession, "by witness clearer than noonday, and by arguments beyond all exception, that the Spanish ambassador was a most diligent head and ringleader to disturb the quiet state of the commonwealth by soliciting the minds of the English Papists to make a rebellion,"[3] he was requested to honor the Council with his presence; where he was "charged with these dangerous practices, and it was made patent to him how and by whom" this was known.[4] Hot words of crimination and recrimination ensued;[5] but no denial of the facts. Her Majesty, "therefore, caused him in very gentle sort to be content within some reasonable time to depart out of

536-539; to the statement made by Popham, the queen's attorney, in 1585, in the Court of the Star-Chamber, by command of the Lord Chancellor (Ibid. 605-607); and to Queen Elizabeth's "Declaration," published in 1585. (Ibid. 625.)

[1] Camden, 294.

[2] Lingard, VIII. 180. Echard, 845.

[3] The Queen's Letter to Philip of Spain; Strype's Annals, VI. 242, 243, Appendix, No. XXVI.

[4] Queen's Declaration; Holingshed, IV. 626.

[5] Camden, 296. Rapin, II. 118.

the realm."[1] Mendoza, complaining loudly of this order as an infringement of his official privilege, retired to Paris, where he busied himself in patronizing the refugees and others who were there plotting against England.[2] To prevent any umbrage at an act which, unexplained, would have had the aspect of diplomatic discourtesy, Queen Elizabeth immediately despatched William Wade, a Clerk of the Council, as a special messenger to the Court of Spain, and the bearer of a letter to the monarch giving her reasons for sending away his minister. This letter was dated at Westminster on the fourteenth day of January, 1583–4.[3] Upon his arrival at the Spanish Court, Mr. Wade was directed to communicate the subject of his embassy to his Majesty's Council; which he "flatly refused" to do, urging that it was customary, even in war, that the ambassador of a prince should be received by the prince in person.[4] At the same time the Council "would not permit him to come to the king their master's presence;"[5] and so Mr. Wade was fain to return without a hearing.[6]

On the twenty-first day of May, 1584, Throckmorton was brought to his trial for High Treason in the Guildhall of the city of London. He here pleaded that he was not indictable for his offences, because, by the statute of the thirteenth of the

[1] Queen's Declaration; Holingshed, IV. 626.

[2] Camden, 296. Strype's Annals, V. 228, 314. Birch, I. 45. Lingard, VIII. 182.

[3] Birch, I. 45. Camden, 296. Holingshed, IV. 625; Queen's Declaration.

[4] Camden, 296.

[5] Queen's Declaration; Holingshed, IV. 625, 626. Birch, I. 45.

[6] Camden, 297. Elizabeth's Letter to Philip is in Strype's Annals, VI. Appendix, No. XXVI.

queen it was provided that no one should be arraigned for any of the treasons therein specified and committed within her Majesty's dominions, unless indicted within six months after his offence, which time had more than expired since his arrest; and because the same Act further provided, that the offence charged should be proved by two witnesses upon oath, and in the presence of the prisoner and the Court, unless the party arraigned should willingly and without violence confess the same,[1] which he had not done. The Court replied, that his treasons were not of the sort mentioned in that statute; but were punishable by a statute of the twenty-fifth of Edward III., which admitted no such limitation of time or proof. Upon this, he declared his confession to have been an utter fiction, adopted only that he might not be again put to the torture. He was then found guilty upon the statute of Edward; and received sentence to be drawn, hanged, bowelled, and quartered.[2]

In the mean time, the Lord Paget and Charles Arundel, with other English refugees, were known to be plotting in Paris against their queen and country; although Sir Edward Stafford, Queen Elizabeth's ambassador there, "could by no means discover *what* they were contriving." By direction of his Court, he therefore made a request of Henry that they and others like them might be removed out of France; assuring his Majesty, however, that his queen was content that those of her subjects who were in France for conscience of religion only should remain unmolested, to pray for his Majesty and his Estate, seeing

[1] 13 Eliz. Cap. I. Secs. VIII, IX.

[2] Stow, 698. Holingshed, IV. 536, 543. Camden, 298.

their consciences would not suffer them to pray for her. At the same time Sir Edward added his own private conviction, that the *political* refugees and plotters, for whose surrender only he asked, would pray more in a quarter of an hour for the King of Spain than in a year for his Majesty. This seemed to move Henry, — that his cousin of Spain should rob him of prayer, — for he immediately asked Sir Edward for a list of the obnoxious Englishmen; received it graciously; and promised to consider the subject with advisers.[1] To this — afterward — it was replied, That "if they" — the Pagets, Arundel, Morgan, and others — "attempted anything in France, the king would punish them according to law; but if they *had* attempted anything in England, the king could not take cognizance thereof, nor proceed against them by law; *for all kingdoms were free for fugitives*."[2]

The announcement of this application to Henry and of its gracious reception — the king's answer had not yet been given — must have been received in London about the first of June. We can only conjecture — what is probable — that the fact was made known to Throckmorton, and perhaps with some embellishments. But, whether influenced by this or not, on the fourth day of June he sent a written submission to her Majesty, and also a written confession of his treasonable practices; the same, in substance, as that which he had given in terror of the rack.[3] But it availed him nothing. On the tenth day of July he was taken from the Tower to the Old Bailey without Newgate, where he was delivered to the

[1] Stafford to Walsingham, May 23, 1584; Murdin, 400.

[2] Camden, 296.

[3] Holingshed, IV. 543 – 547.

Sheriffs of London, and drawn thence on a hurdle to Tyburn, where he again asserted upon the gallows his innocence of the crimes he had twice confessed.[1] He then suffered the awful sentence of the law.

Two confessions and two denials may fairly be considered to neutralize each other. But, however unfairly the confessions may have been obtained, however unfairly the trial may have been conducted, and however *unproven* were the charges against him, yet — in taking into account that his intimacy with Mendoza, who did not deny the truth of his confession, was well known; that his intimacy with Englishmen and others now abroad and conspiring with the Guise, was well known; and that it was also well known that her Majesty had been assured by friendly princes and by her ambassadors in foreign Courts,[2] that the plot of the Guise, the Pope, and the Spanish King, was a verity — we can hardly doubt that the Court had circumstantial evidence corroborative of his confession, and, in connection with it, sufficient to convince them of his guilt.[3]

The birds had hardly bared the bones of this victim of the law, when Sir Edward Stafford received secret information, from different sources, that a desperate plot was now on foot for the assassination of Elizabeth; or — as he expressed it in a letter dated the twenty-seventh day of July — "that the same

[1] Holingshed, IV. 548. Camden, 298. Lingard, VIII. 182.

[2] Holingshed, IV. 541.

[3] It being once admitted, that Throckmorton had held fraternity with the Lord Paget, Charles Arundel, and Mendoza, his collusion with them in treason — as also that of the Howards and the Countess of Arundel — is put beyond all question by the letter of Thomas Morgan to Mary, Queen of Scots, dated "last of March, 1586." It is in Murdin, pp. 481 - 502.

practice that hath been executed upon the Prince of Orange, there are more than two or three practisers about to exercise upon her Majesty and some others, and especially her Majesty; and that to be done within these two months..... But it may be it is not so. But howsoever it be, it is necessary.... for her Majesty to take good heed and have care of herself more than ordinary; for there must no doubt be had that she is the chief mark they shoot at; and seeing there were men knowing enough to enchant a man .... to kill the Prince of Orange, and a knave desperate enough to do it, we must think that hereafter anything may be done..... Therefore God, I pray Him, with His mighty hand, preserve her Majesty."[1]

During this same summer, all doubts about a conspiracy for invasion and for insurrection were removed. Certain Papers had been found in possession of a Scottish Jesuit, named Chreicton, while on a voyage to Scotland. To prevent their seizure, he had torn them in pieces and thrown them overboard; but, landsman as he was, he had thrown them *against* the wind which threw them back again, when they were secured. They were sent to Mr. Wade, who put them together and read a complete revelation, in the Italian language, of the new design of the Pope, the Guises, and Philip of Spain, for invading England; and also an unqualified declaration that it was "certainly known, not surmised, that all the Catholic lords and gentry in the northern parts of England would join the foreign forces, and that the priests dispersed throughout the realm were able to control the other Catholics as they should be ordered."[2]

[1] Murdin, 414. [2] Holingshed, IV. 608. Camden, 299.

Such had been the events which, in the short space of nine or ten months, had occurred in rapid succession, — the mad-brained attempt of Somerville; the distribution of the "Treatise of Schism;" accumulating signs of another "Holy League;" the conspiracy of Throckmorton; the perfidy of Mendoza; the plottings of English Catholic refugees; their despairing resolve to murder Elizabeth; the ominous assassination of William of Orange; and, finally the veil lifted clear from the confederacy of the Guises, and the whole Catholic population of England brought under suspicion — which, indeed, they did not merit — of rebellious intent. All these things, it was seen, had a common origin, — Popery; a common watchword, — "the Queen of Scots!" a common aim, — the ruin of Elizabeth and a religious revolution.

We have stated these things, and with some particularity, because they were remarkable in themselves, remarkable for their family resemblance, and remarkable for their conflux; but, more especially, because, had we omitted to notice and to confirm them, we should have done great injustice to the Parliament whose Acts now claim our attention.

For their enemies, Queen Elizabeth and her ministers had hearts of oak. For a quarter of a century, they had warded blows without recoil and without a wound; they had acquired sagacity and gained confidence with every expiring year; they had husbanded wealth by frugality, and the elements of greatness, with an honorable pride; until, no longer a sanctuary barely sufficing the Faith which had fled to the horns of her altar, England had become a bulwark; and the Refugee, her champion; until she was as much respected for her power as hated for her religion. Thus the tokens of new assault which had just been so rapidly revealed found Queen Elizabeth and her Councillors undaunted. At the same time, the Government and the people read these tokens gravely. They interpreted them truly. By the cadence of the wind, and by the mischiefs it had just now assayed, they measured the circuit and the violence of the coming storm. In short, the apprehensions of the whole nation were soberly aroused by these indications of a hostile crusade; and it was with this rational estimate of these ominous events — perhaps with a feverish apprehension also of the evils they portended — that the Parliament was summoned and assembled. From their position, we must view their acts.

The first precautionary measure was in the form of a voluntary association to provide for the safety of the queen. It seems to have been set on foot by the Earl of Leicester,[1] and to have been first formed in the Council Chamber early in October. On the twenty-seventh day of that month, the Lord Treasurer wrote to Lord Cobham as follows: "I doubt not but your lordship hath lately heard how, upon a consultation in the Council, it was accorded that there should be a bond of an union, or association, made by such noblemen and others, principal gentlemen and officers, as should like thereof, voluntarily to bind themselves to her Majesty, and every one to the other, for defence and safety of her Majesty's person against all her evil willers; whereupon all the Council have already accorded, subscribed, and sealed,

[1] Sidney Papers, II. 49. Camden, 300.

such a bond as I do herewith send your lordship a true copy thereof. And there are like made by all the Judges, Serjeants, and principal officers at Westminster. The like is made by the Gentlemen and Justices of Peace in sundry counties." Lord Burleigh closed by suggesting that Cobham should subscribe the bond before coming to London to attend the Parliament; but in courtly words, "it is a matter that I leave to your own consideration."[1]

The bond was a touchstone. To refuse it, for any reason, must have subjected one to a dangerous imputation; and no partisan of Mary could subscribe it without a solemn hypocrisy upon which few would care to venture, or without the public renunciation of a princess dear as their religion to their hearts. Thus it was with a purpose and with a meaning, that Lord Burleigh commended the matter to the "consideration" of Cobham, who was "not evil inclined" toward the Queen of Scots.[2] Voluntary or not voluntary as the Association may have been, and for the most part doubtless was, he must have been a bold man who would decline it; and a daring man who would sign it, if true in heart to Mary. That its "reasons and causes" were the matters which we have narrated above, the bond itself declares. After a solemn Preamble, it proceeds:—

"We, whose names are or shall be subscribed to this Writing, ... finding *lately*, by divers depositions, confessions, and sundry advertisements out of foreign parts from credible persons well known to her Majesty's Council and to divers others, that for the furtherance of some pretended title to the Crown, it hath

[1] Lodge, II. 299, 300. [2] Murdin, 489; Morgan to Queen Mary.

been manifested, that the life of our gracious Sovereign hath been most dangerously designed against, ... do, for these reasons and causes before alleged, ... by this Writing make manifest our bounden duties to our Sovereign Lady for her safety.

"And to that end, we and every one of us, first calling to witness the name of Almighty God, do voluntarily .... bind ourselves, every one of us to the other, ... and do hereby vow and promise by the Majesty of Almighty God, that with our whole powers, bodies, lives, and goods, and with our children and servants, we and every of us will .... withstand, pursue, and offend, as well by force of arms as by all other means of revenge, all manner of persons, ... and their abettors, that shall attempt any act, or counsel or consent to anything that shall tend to the harm of her Majesty's royal person; and will never desist from all manner of forcible pursuit against such persons to the utter extermination of them.....

"And if any such wicked attempt .... shall be taken in hand, ... we do not only bind ourselves, both jointly and severally, never to allow, accept, or favor any such pretended successor *by* whom, or *for* whom, any such detestable act shall be attempted or committed, ... But do also further vow and protest, as we are most bound, in the presence of the Eternal and Everlasting God, to prosecute such person or persons to death, with our joint and particular forces, and to act the utmost revenge upon them that by any means we or any of us can devise and do, or cause to be devised and done, for their utter overthrow and extirpation.

"And .... we do also testify by this Writing, that

we do confirm the contents hereof by our oaths corporally taken upon the Holy Evangelists, with this express condition, That no one of us shall.... separate from this Association or fail in the prosecution thereof.... upon pain of being by the rest of us prosecuted and suppressed as perjured persons, and as public enemies to God, our queen, and to our native country; to which punishment and pains we do voluntarily submit ourselves..... In witness of all which premises to be inviolably kept, we do to this Writing put our Hands and Seals; and shall be most ready to accept and admit any others hereafter to this Society and Association."[1]

When this Association was made known to the unhappy Mary, her heart sank; for she saw at once that it "was made for her ruin and undoing;"[2] for the least movement of her friends in her behalf would expose her to its curse; and so would even any rumor of such a movement which might be maliciously set afloat by her enemies. Notwithstanding, she herself offered to subscribe the bond, "provided her liberty might be granted her; provided she might be assured of Elizabeth's sincere affection and love; and provided nothing should be done to prejudice her, her son, and their heirs, in the succession, before such time as they were heard in an assembly of the Estates of England."[3]

The loyalty of the nation towards Elizabeth, never faint, was roused by recent events to fervid zeal. This fact, in connection with the statements in Lord Burleigh's letter to Lord Cobham, justifies the belief

[1] Hargrave's State Trials, I. p. 143.

[2] Camden, 303.

[3] Ibid., 300.

that the bond received general subscription throughout the realm from the nobility and gentry.

The Parliament manifested the same sense of the queen's peril, and the same zeal for her protection. The first Act of the Twenty-seventh of Elizabeth which appears upon the Statute-Book, gave a legal sanction, but only in part, to this Association. It was entitled, "An Act for Provision to be made for the Surety of her Majesty's most Royal Person, and the continuance of the Realm in Peace." Premising, as its reason, that sundry wicked plots had of late been devised, both without and within the realm, against her Highness's person, and to the ruin of the Commonwealth, it enacted:

That if any open invasion or rebellion should occur, or if any act should be attempted tending to the hurt of her Majesty's person, *by* or *for* any pretender to the Crown; or if anything should be compassed or imagined tending to the hurt of her person, by, or with the privity of, any such pretender, then certain Commissioners should examine, and give judgment upon, such offences:

And that all persons, against whom such judgment should pass, should be excluded and disabled from the Succession:

And that all her Highness's subjects might lawfully pursue to death all persons, their aiders, abettors, and comforters, by whom, or by whose means, assent, or privity, any such invasion or rebellion, or other thing against her Majesty's person, should have been adjudged, as before provided, to have been made, attempted, or imagined.

The same disability and outlawry were also ordained against the like persons, in case any such act detestable should be *executed* against the queen's person whereby her life should be taken away.

By this first section, which contains the burden and object of the statute, should any attempt be made against her Majesty's Crown or person, and in behalf of the Queen of Scots, the latter would be, *ipso facto*, absolutely excluded from the Succession; but she would *not* be obnoxious — as by the engagement of the Association she *might seem* to be — to the vengeance of death at any man's hand unless *privy* to such attempt; nor would she be so disabled, nor she or any other person so outlawed, until the Commissioners had pronounced judgment against them. Thus there were two essential, just, and humane points of difference between the statute and the bond. Wherefore the statute further enacted, That every article and sentence contained in the bond of the Association lately formed should, in all things, be expounded and adjudged according to the true intent and meaning of the Act, and not otherwise, nor against any other person or persons.

The only other Act of this Parliament which claims our notice is the second, entitled, "An Act against Jesuits, Seminary priests, and other such like disobedient persons." It enacted:

That all Jesuits and priests made or ordained either without or within any of her Majesty's dominions, by any authority from the See of Rome, and since the twenty-fourth day of June, 1559, should depart from the realm within forty days after the end of the present session of Parliament:

That any Jesuit, priest, or other ecclesiastical person, born within the realm and ordained as, and since the time, aforesaid, who should be within the realm after the said forty days, should be adjudged guilty of High Treason, and suffer accordingly; excepting only — and only for six months and on their bonds for good behavior — such as might be too ill to depart without imminent danger of life, and such as should submit by taking the Oath of Supremacy:

That any person who should, after the said forty days, wittingly and willingly comfort, aid, relieve, or maintain, any such ecclesiastical person as aforesaid, the latter being not imprisoned, should suffer death as a felon:

That every her Majesty's subjects, not such persons ecclesiastic as aforesaid, but of, or brought up in, any foreign Catholic college, who should not return within six months after Proclamation in that behalf to be made, or who, returning, should not, within two days after his return, submit himself by taking the Oath of Supremacy, should be adjudged guilty of High Treason and suffer accordingly:

That persons sending abroad money or other relief, wittingly and willingly, to or for any such ecclesiastical person as aforesaid, or to or for any such college, should incur the penalty of a præmunire:

That parents sending their children abroad, after the said forty days, without license from her Majesty or four of her Council, should forfeit for each offence an hundred pounds:

That every of the queen's subjects who, after the said forty days, should know any such Jesuit or priest as aforesaid to be within the realm contrary to this Act, and should not discover him within twelve days after such knowledge, but willingly conceal his knowledge, should suffer fine and imprisonment at the queen's pleasure;

That if any person submitting by oath as aforesaid, should, within ten years after such submission, come within ten miles of her Majesty without special license from her Highness under her own hand, he should have no benefit of such submission.[1]

It is due to the good name of Queen Elizabeth to state, that the clauses in the Act for the surety of her person, by which it so humanely differed from the bond, and by which the bond itself was *perforce* qualified, were inserted by her commandment, — "her pleasure signified," was equivalent, — and probably originated in her own mind. A bill to the same general effect, but without directing the adjudication by Commissioners, had been introduced in the Commons, and upon the second reading had been ordered to be engrossed.[2] At this point, her Majesty interfered; expressing to the House her pleasure that "all persons barred or disabled by force of the law as it then

[1] Dr. Lingard omits to state that no part of this Act touched any priest in the realm who had received ordination from authority of the See of Rome *before* the twenty-fourth day of June, 1559. This omission *might* be attributed to — a censurable ? — oversight. But it looks much like disingenuousness, when we find that in four other instances, at least, he seriously libels the act by unpardonable and material omissions.

But more. He has *added* something, — That children sent to seminaries abroad "should be disabled from inheriting the property of their parents." So also says Camden.

Camden also says, that the statute enacted that any one suspected to be a Jesuit or priest as aforesaid, who should not submit himself to examination, should be imprisoned until he should submit himself. Neither is this in the statute. (See Lingard, VIII. 188. Camden, 309.)

[2] D'Ewes, 340.

was" — that is, in the bill — "should be first called to answer and be heard what they had to say in excuse of themselves before they shall be prejudiced in their pretended right or titles: And also, that her Majesty would take away the proviso in the law, by which any of those subjects which have taken the oath of the Association might any way hereafter by any possibility be touched in conscience."[1] The latter clause is somewhat obscure; but seems to guard against the obligation which might by possibility be found to arise of acting the penalty of death — as by the letter of the bond — upon some one *not privy* to rebellion, invasion, or harm of her Majesty's person. Upon receiving this intimation of the queen's "most loving and merciful disposition," the House framed a new bill, "according to the purport of her Majesty's pleasure."[2]

It is due also to the House of Commons — for through that body only were the Puritans responsible for these two Acts — to say that neither of the bills were passed rashly, impulsively, under a panic, or under the influence of religious passion. The bill for her Majesty's safety was introduced on the fourteenth day of December, was reconstructed, and did not pass until the thirteenth day of March.[3] The bill against priests was introduced before the fifteenth day of December; conferred upon by committees of both Houses; discussed; amended; committed; discussed again; conferred upon again; amended again; and did not pass until the nineteenth day of March.[4] Even the astounding discovery, while the

[1] D'Ewes, 341.

[2] Ibid.; and the Speaker's speech, *ante*, Chap. XVI.

[3] D'Ewes, 339, 367 *bis*.

[4] Ibid., 340, 352, 365 *bis*, 366, 367, 370.

bills were in progress, that one of their own members was party to a plot for the queen's murder, did not disturb the counsels of the Commons, or precipitate their final action. If in either Act, or if in both, there is anything which merits reprobation, it lies against these Puritans with unmitigated force; for, what they did was done coolly, deliberately, and with a clear understanding of its aim and of its probable consequences.

The merits or demerits of the case may be indicated, when we shall have finished the tale of aggressions on the one hand, and of defensive provisions on the other.

"What should I care for her?" exclaimed William ap Harry. "What hath she done for me? Have I not spent ten thousand marks since I knew her service, and never had a penny by her?" [1]

The words were hotly spoken; and were a comprehensive expression of passion which had accumulated during a long dialogue about the government of Elizabeth. They were addressed to Edmund Neville alone, and at his lodgings in the White Friars, early in the month of August, 1584.

"Now out upon thee, cousin mine, for the rarest piece of ingratitude in England," replied Neville. "Verily I do blush for thy mother's blood; seeing thee showing thyself a person so greatly miscontent; and hearing thee so vehemently inveighing against thy liege Lady! Did she not give thee thy life?"

Neville spoke with a sly leer which betrayed his

[1] Holingshed, IV. 568.

humor and his lurking irony. There was a sting too in his allusion to ap Harry's mother, who came into the world in a left-handed way, as much indebted (at least) to the priesthood for the first wail of life as for the last hope in death. Through this mother, however, ap Harry claimed kindred to Neville.[1] Moreover, there was an allusion, by no means soothing, to a passage in ap Harry's history; for he had tried to murder his creditor to cancel a debt, and had been rescued from the gallows only by the pardon of the queen.[2] Ap Harry colored; but swallowing resentment, he replied between his teeth:—

"My life! It be no felony, I trow, to cudgel a two-for-a-farthing knave for going to law, like a Jew, for borrowed money. Wherefore, I, doing only what a gentleman should to chastise a huckster's insolence, and it being called burglary in the books, but being no burglary out of the books, *ergo* my life was no forfeit. Troth; it may be *said* she gave me my life. But *I* say, as the case stood, it had been tyranny to take it; and I fear me it is little less yet. If it please her graciously to look into my discontentments, would to Jesus Christ she were about it, for I am weary of it."

"My faith!" exclaimed the other, whom these last words had touched, "the more service to her Majesty, the less bounty and the more discontentments." Me set as a watch-dog upon Father Persons whiles he abode in Rouen;[3] you going as his lordship's spy from London to Paris, from Paris to Venice; from Venice to Rome, from Rome to Lyons, and again to

[1] Holingshed, IV. 580, 581.
[2] Ibid., 581, 582. Hargrave's State Trials, I. 122, note.
[3] Lingard, VIII. 191.

Paris and London,—and what booteth it to you or to me? Nay, I bethink; *you* are to have the Mastership of St. Catherine's."[1]

"Zounds! 't is refused me; and a pension too, which her Majesty did offer.[2] Ay, ay; what booteth it to serve a queen or to pray to her Council? I say, I be weary of it. Wherefore, three weeks sithence I did leave the Court at Greenwich utterly rejected; discontent; careless of myself; and here am I in London, poverty pinching me like a devil, and neglect making me mad. Assure yourself as I assure myself."

"Of what?"

"Of this, that during *this* time and state, you shall never receive contentment. Does not the Earl of Westmoreland still remain convict of High Treason, and proscribed?[3] Is not Robert Cecil in actual possession of his estate?[4] And think you the Lord Burleigh, when the Earl shall chance to die, will bid his own eldest son give place, that Edmund Neville may be restored in blood, and take the inheritance and title of Lord Latimer? Fie! I tell thee, during *this* time and regiment, thou wilt never receive contentment."

The words annoyed Neville; for Cecil in possession of the Westmoreland estates did indeed augur badly for his own expectations. He was too much disturbed to reply. Ap Harry, enjoying for a moment his chagrin, resumed: "Sith I know you to be honorably descended and a man of resolution, if you will

[1] Holingshed, IV. 564. Strype's Annals, V. 367.

[2] Holingshed, IV. 562, 564, 568.

[3] Camden, 135, 136.

[4] Lingard, VIII. 192.

give me assurance, either to join with me or not betray me, I will deliver unto you the only means to do yourself good."

"I will, I will," said Neville, starting to his feet and pressing his hand upon his forehead. "But not now; not now. I will go to your house tomorrow."

Ap Harry politely took the hint; and retired chuckling and satisfied.

It will be perceived, that the interlocutors were needy adventurers; both seeking office or emolument from a princess proverbially careful of her purse. Both were Catholics; but both feigned loyalty. Neville was in impatient expectation of the death of Westmoreland, one of the rebel earls in the insurrection of 1569, now an old man, attainted, living in the Netherlands upon a slender pension from Spain. Neville hoped, by his death and the royal grace, to be restored to his birthright possessions as Westmoreland's next heir male, and to the title of Lord Latimer.[1]

William ap Harry was the son of Harry ap David, an alehouse keeper in North Wales. In other words, William was the son of Harry, who was the son of David. Hereafter we recognize his Anglicized name, William Parry, and his title of Doctor of Law.[2] He had pretended to act upon the continent for Lord Burleigh, as a spy upon the Catholics; but had been reconciled while there to the Romish Church, had leagued with conspirators against England, and had even taken a solemn vow to murder Elizabeth.[3]

[1] Holingshed, IV. 569. Camden, 305.

[2] Holingshed, IV. 580, 582.

[3] Ibid., 562, 566, 567, 568.

Neville was true to his word, and the next day found him at Parry's house in Fetter Lane.

"Cousin," said he with a resolute air, "let us *do* somewhat, sith we can *have* nothing."

"Ha! methought you would hit upon what I have in my head; and right gladly do I hear your words. I will join with you in anything, for I do know you to be a good Catholic."

"It did need but little brain to understand,—'*this time and state.*'"

"I knew, my lord,"—so Parry chose to tickle him with his expected title,—"I knew you had both brain and stomach. But I protest before God, that three reasons principally do induce me to enter into this action which I intend to discover unto you: the replanting of religion; the preferring of the Scotch title; and the advancement of justice, wonderfully corrupted in this Commonwealth."

Upon this the two fell into long discourse, of which we need only say, that it was for the deliverance of Mary and the introduction of foreign forces. Neville thought the delivery of the royal captive easy, "presuming upon his credit and kindred in the north;" while Parry "thought it dangerous to her, and impossible to men of their fortunes" to achieve, even were it not dangerous.

"Could Berwick be taken," said Neville, "we should hold a key to England, a chance for retreat or recruits by sea, and a people on our northern flank who would bid us God-speed, mayhap."

"Troth, a good point to reach; a good, to hold. And, if I be not deceived, by the taking of Queenboro' castle, we shall hinder the passage of the queen's ships forth of the river."

Neville making no reply, Parry, grasping his hand, broke out impetuously, "Tush! all this about castles and ships and foreign forces, is nothing. If men were resolute, there is another manner of enterprise of much more moment and much easier to perform; an act more honorable and profitable unto us and the Catholics' commonwealth, and withal meritorious to God and the world."

"What?"

"Will you join in it with me?"

"In anything. Name it."

"Will you vow to join?"

"I will. By my soul, I do. Name it; name it."

"Nay," replied Parry, coolly, "the case requireth a deeper vow. Do nothing rashly, my lord. Think of the matter. Sleep over it. Then, if you will, we will covenant in God's name."

The next morning the conference was renewed by Neville, who came to Parry's lodging and repeated his offer. He then took his oath upon the Bible, to conceal and constantly to pursue the enterprise for the advancement of religion.[1] Parry then told him in plain terms, that his scheme and his determination were to kill Queen Elizabeth. "Wherein," said he, "if you will go with me, I will lose my life, or deliver my country from her tyrannous government."

"Such an enterprise, good cousin, is not to *my* contentment. It be a matter of great charge both of soul and body."

"You doubt, my lord, that it be not meritorious? that it be damnable?"

"Troth."

[1] Holingshed, IV. 569.

"Hast seen Doctor Allen's book against the Lord Burleigh's book, entitled 'Justice of England'? It hath at this present been sent to me out of France; and redoubleth my former conceits. Every word in it is a warrant. It teacheth that kings may be excommunicated, deprived, and violently handled. It proveth that all wars civil or foreign, undertaken for Religion, is honorable."[1]

"No, I have not seen it; nor do I believe that authority."

"Well, my lord, I would have you satisfied on this point; and I do much respect your conscience. But what will you say if I show further authority than this, even from Rome itself; a plain dispensation for the killing of her, wherein you shall find it meritorious?"

"Good doctor, when you shall show it me, I shall think it very strange, when I shall see one to hold that for meritorious which another holdeth for damnable."

"Well, my lord, do me but the favor to think upon

[1] Holingshed, IV. 567, 569.

Dr. Lingard says (VIII. 193, note), "It has been supposed that Allen's book, to which he alluded in his confession, justified and recommended the murder of heretical princes. This is a mistake. Allen wrote no such work. Parry referred to Allen's answer to Burleigh."

Of what consequence is it to *what* book of Allen's he referred? And of what use is it for Dr. Lingard to say, "Allen wrote no such work," when we have Parry's description of *some* work of Allen's such as is described in the text? Who must have known best *what* Parry had read from Allen's pen, — Parry himself? or Dr. Lingard? I prefer the reader's (Parry's) testimony to that of the historian; and therefore say, with my witness, "Allen *did* write such a work." See Strype's Annals, VI. 368, Appendix, No. LIV.; containing "expressions in Dr. Allen's book;" "an answer to the Justice of England." (Ibid., V. 450.) This book did not *in express terms* (so far as quoted by Strype) justify "the *murder* of heretical princes." This was left for inference. Parry understood it.

it till to-morrow; and if a certain man be in the town, I will not fail to show you the thing itself. And if he be not, he will be, within these five or six days; at which time, if it please you to meet me in Chanon Row, we may there receive the sacrament to be true to each other; and then I will discover unto you both the party and the thing itself."

"Think better of it, I pray you, doctor; for I repeat, it be a matter of great charge both of soul and body."

"My lord! I would to God you were as perfectly persuaded in it as I am; for then undoubtedly you should do God great service."

The next meeting of these conspirators, of which we have any account, was about ten days after, at which time Neville had evidently abated his conscientiousness; for during the whole conversation, it will be seen, he made slight objection on this score to Parry's scheme, and dwelt chiefly on its impracticability.

The "plain dispensation from Rome itself for killing the queen" had doubtless been shown to him in the mean time (Dr. Allen's book certainly had), and had wrought upon him. It was a letter from the Cardinal of Como, the Roman Secretary of State, dated January, 1583–4; which, while for prudence sake, it was expressed in words which might be construed as "no more than a civil answer to a general offer of service, and which made not the remotest" — cognizable — "allusion to the murder,"[1] was yet (interpreted by what had before passed between him and the Cardinal[2]) a letter, to use Parry's own words, "whereby

[1] Lingard, VIII. 191. [2] Holingshed, IV. 567 *bis*, 568.

I found the enterprise commended and allowed, and myself absolved in his Holiness's name of all my sins, and willed to go forward in the name of God. It confirmed my resolution to kill the queen, and made it clear in my conscience that it was lawful and meritorious."[1]

But to return. From Parry's lodgings, the two walked into the fields, where he renewed his determination to kill her Majesty; "for," said he, "she is

[1] The following is a translation of the Cardinal's letter: "Monsignor: the Holiness of our Lord hath seen the letter of your Signory of the first, with the assurance included, and can but commend the good disposition and resolution which you write towards the service and benefit public: Wherein his Holiness doth exhort you to persevere, with causing to bring forth the effects which your Signory promiseth. And to the end you may be so much more holpen by that good Spirit which hath moved you thereunto, his Blessedness do grant to you plenary indulgence and remission of all your sins, according to your request; assuring you that, besides the merit that you shall receive therefor in heaven, his Holiness will further make himself debtor, to reacknowledge the deservings of your Signory in the best manner he can: And that so much the more, in that your Signory useth the greater modesty, in not pretending anything. Put, therefore, to effect your holy and honorable thoughts, and attend your health. And to conclude, I offer myself unto you heartily, and do desire all good and happy success." (Holingshed, IV. 573. Hargrave's State Trials, I. 125. Strype's Annals, V. 361; fol. ed. III. 249.

To Dr. Lingard's comment (quoted above) I add what he also says in a note on the same page; viz. "The Pope grants the indulgence, which Parry had asked for, that which was usually granted to persons on their reconciliation." These comments of the Catholic historian, no impartial reader can accept after scrutinizing the letter of the Cardinal. They cannot weigh at all against Parry's own exposition which I have quoted from Holingshed and Hargrave. The Cardinal's letter is just such an one as common prudence would have suggested; the intent of the murder being presupposed. It is of the same character, and for the same reason of the same character, as the passage which I have before quoted in this chapter as explanatory of Gregory Martin's Treatise of Schism about dealing with *Satan* as Judith dealt with Holofernes.

To Lingard's words—"that which was usually granted to persons on their reconciliation"—Dr. Nares, singularly enough, *adds as Lingard's words* (comp. *ante*, page 64 of this volume, note) what I cannot find

most unworthy to live. And I do wonder that you should have scruples therein. She hath sought your ruin and overthrow; why should you not then seek to revenge it?"[1]

"I confess," replied Neville, "that my case is hard; but yet am I not so desperate as to revenge it upon *myself*, which must be the event of so unhonest and unpossible an enterprise."

"Unpossible, my lord! I wonder at you; for in truth there is not anything more easy. You are no courtier, and therefore know not her customs of walking with small train, and often in the garden very privately. At such time myself may easily have access unto her; and you also when you are known at Court."

Neville gave a sign of incredulity.

"You doubt? How easily I might have done it already! I can have as good opportunity again."

"Prithee, how mightest have done it?"

"At that present when I did return into England in January last, I wrote to the Court that I had a special service to discover to her Majesty. Which I did more to prepare access and credit, than for any care I had of her person; though I were fully

on Lingard's page, viz. "a remission of canonical censures incurred by *former* offences." (Life and Times of Burleigh, III. 247.) Aside from the very singular manner (I confess I cannot understand some such things in the volumes of the Regius Professor) in which he criticises words which he attributes to Lingard, but which seem to be his own, Dr. Nares has (on page 249) some strictures upon the Cardinal's letter which are worthy of consideration, but are too extended to be quoted here. It is enough for Dr. Lingard to bear the burden of *his own* disingenuousness and misrepresentations.

[1] This is obscure. Unless it refers to the *just* attainder of Westmoreland, through which Neville suffered, there was some fact, necessary to explain it, of which I am ignorant.

resolved never to touch her (notwithstanding any warrant) if, by any device, persuasion or policy, she might be wrought to deal more graciously with the Catholics than she doth, or by our manner of proceeding in Parliament meaneth to do, for anything yet seen.[1] I came to the Court; prayed audience; and had it."

"Ha!"

"At large."

"To what import?"

"That in Paris, under pretence of ill-will to her Highness, but really to gain knowledge of her enemies' devices, I did get conference with certain Jesuits and other ministers of the Pope, and especially with Thomas Morgan, a fugitive; by all of whom — after that I had waded so far in pretence as by oath and vow to promise the taking away of her life — I learned that there was a design to murder her presently."[2]

"By the Mass! didst tell thine own plot?"

"To make the way easier to accomplish it. That I might gain her confidence and have to know my person, that she might not be mistrustful at sight of me in the garden or palace. For the same cause, and as a proof of my truth, I did show her the letter of the Cardinal of Como. So have my conferences with her been many times and most private, there being never

[1] To the same purport were Parry's words in his letter of confession to Burleigh and Leicester dated 18th Feb. 1584-5. "The matter .... digested and resolved in England, if it had not been prevented by accusation, or by her Majesty's greater lenity, and more gracious usage of her Catholic subjects." (Hargrave's State Trials, I. 125.)

[2] Holingshed, IV. 561, 562, 567. Camden, 306.

a person present, save one of her Majesty's Council; and he, out of earshot."

"Private! and didst not strike!"

"Did I not say I was determined never to do so, if either policy, practice, persuasion, or motion in Parliament could prevail? I feared to be tempted; and therefore, always, when I came near her, I left my dagger at home. By this only did I let myself; albeit I was greatly troubled when I looked upon her Majesty, for my vows to slay her were in heaven, my promises to do it were on earth, and the case of the Catholics little bettered."

"How took she it?"

"Doubtfully; and I departed with fear. Yet after, she did profess to conceive of my fidelity, and did speak to me of a pension; and quoth she, 'never a Catholic shall be troubled for religion or supremacy, so long as they live like good subjects.' Whereby I mistrusted that her Majesty is given to understand,[1] that none *is* troubled for the one or the other. Thus have I prepared the way; for I can come at her Majesty without suspect. I wait only that you may be my sworn helper, and for fit opportunity. And I have come to you to join me herein, because I do hold you the only man of England like to perform it, in respect of your valor."

"I must first know how you can execute the enterprise."

"At Greenwich where she walketh privately, or with small train. I will strike her there. Upon the fact, we must have a barge ready to carry us with speed down the river, where we will have a ship

[1] In the Chronicle, "is borne in hand."

ready to transport us if it be needful. But, upon my head, we shall never be followed so far."

"How will you escape forth of the garden? You shall not be permitted to carry any men with you, and the gates will then be locked. Neither can you carry a dag without suspicion."

"As for a dag, I care not. My dagger is enough. And as for mine escaping, those that shall be with her will be so busy about her, as I shall find opportunity enough to escape, if you be there ready with the barge to receive me."

"Now by the holy rood! it be a foul act to butcher a queen in a corner! I will none of it. And yet my heart serveth me to strike off her head in the field."

"Then let it rest till her coming to St. James. Meanwhile, let us furnish ourselves with men and horses fit for the purpose. Each of us may keep eight or ten men without suspect. Then can we beset her on horseback with eight or ten horses when she shall ride abroad about St. James, or some other like place. For my part, I shall find good fellows that will follow me. It is much that so many resolute men may do upon the sudden, being well appointed with each his case of dags. If they were an hundred waited upon her, they were not able to save her; you coming on the one side and I on the other, and discharging our dags upon her; it were unhappy if we should both miss her. But if our dags fail, I shall bestir me well with a sword ere she shall escape me."

This plan was finally "resolved upon" *by both.*[1] Soon after, her Majesty came to St. James; when

[1] Holingshed, IV. 569.

Parry revived his former discourse with Neville of killing her Majesty, and that with great earnestness and importunity. Other like interviews succeeded. But, after all, it was concluded, first to try what might be done in Parliament,[1] which would doubtless be assembled before long.[2]

In the mean time Parry had contrived to be chosen and returned a member of the House of Commons for the Borough of Queenboro' (because it was nigh to Queenboro' castle?) in the county of Kent. Of course, in becoming qualified for his seat, he took the Oath of Supremacy.

Upon the third reading of the bill against Jesuits and priests, on the seventeenth day of December, Parry was the only one who opposed it, which he did vehemently; alleging that it was fraught with "treasons, blood, danger, despair, terror, and confiscations." These assertions, he said, "he could prove and justify by good reasons; which, nevertheless, he would reveal only to her Majesty." This speech, for "its unseemly manner and unfitting, reproachful words," was

[1] Holingshed, IV. 569.

[2] My narrative of this conspiracy might have been sustained by references, step by step. As I have omitted them (for obvious reasons), I take occasion to say that, as far as the nature of the case would admit, it is only a connected collocation of the very words of the principal documents in the case; namely, Neville's written declaration before Leicester, Hatton, and Walsingham, and Parry's confession before Hunsdon, Hatton, and Walsingham, which describe the different interviews between the conspirators. The former is in Holingshed, IV. 464 – 466. The latter, in the same volume, 466 – 470; and in Hargrave's State Trials, I. 122 – 124. From these are derived the accounts of the affair given by Camden, Rapin, Strype, and others.

I have occasionally used the language of Holingshed's Continuator; and also that of a Paper printed at the time by C. Barker, printer to her Majesty. (See Holingshed, IV. 580 – 587.) In these instances, I think, I have uniformly given reference.

considered a "contempt;" and Dr. Parry was immediately ordered to an outer apartment in custody of the Sergeant, while the House should consider his behavior. Upon his recall, being demanded "what reasons he could yield for his words," he declared that he still chose to conceal them. Upon which he was committed to ward, for further consideration of his case by the House.

The next day, the queen, by a message, approved the course they had taken; but advised that, upon his humble submission, they should pass over the matter, inasmuch as he had discovered his reasons to some of her Majesty's Council and partly to the satisfaction of herself. The House acquiesced; and, upon his confession and apology, Parry was restored to his seat.[1]

The nature of his communication to the Council we can only conjecture. But, from his own declaration afterwards,[2] it would seem that in his Speech he had in mind, and alluded to,[3] her Majesty's words, that "no Catholic should be troubled for religion or supremacy while he lived a good subject;" that he took occasion, through the Council, that she should "be borne in hand"—other than he "mistrusted" she was—that they *were* troubled for both. It would seem, too, that before the Council he may have "prayed hearing of her Majesty to move her to take compassion upon her Catholic subjects."[4] Had the hearing been granted while he was yet flushed by the excitement occasioned by the bill, it is hardly to be doubted that he would have made his murderous attempt.

1 D'Ewes, 340-342.

2 Holingshed, IV. 568.

3 His words are, "after a sort avowed."

4 Holingshed, IV. 569, 570.

Whether because the revelations of the last summer had rendered access to her Majesty more difficult than before, or for other reasons, Parry and Neville suffered their plan to slumber for the present. During the holiday recess of Parliament (probably), news was received of the death of Charles Neville, the last of the Earls of Westmoreland.[1] Edmund Neville's hopes of recovering, through the grace of the queen, the estates and title which would have fallen to him but for Westmoreland's attainder, were now revived; and he sought to win her Majesty by "discharging his conscience."[2] On the eighth day of February — the fourth, after the reassembling of Parliament — he made known to her Majesty, through one of her courtiers, all that had passed between himself and Parry;[3] giving, of course, his own version of the facts; and professing to have been so touched by remorse as to have abjured the plot.[4]

Until this time, the queen had wholly concealed the nature of Parry's private communications; but now made them known to certain of her Council.[5] By her directions, Neville was immediately examined by the Earl of Leicester and Sir Christopher Hatton. On the same evening, Parry was easily induced to a confidential interview with Sir Francis Walsingham at his house, on matters which concerned her Majesty highly, and in which he (in her Majesty's opinion) was peculiarly fitted to deal, because of his extraordinary and devoted loyalty. Once within Walsingham's toils, he was quickly entangled in his own talk,[6]

[1] Camden, 304.

[2] Holingshed, IV. 565.

[3] Ibid., 562.

[4] D'Ewes, 356.

[5] Holingshed, IV. 562, 577, 578.

[6] Lloyd says (page 516): "Wal-

though as yet unconsciously; was detained under the Secretary's roof, whither he had gone only to play the counsellor; was entangled deeper in the same net the next day; and, in the evening, at the house of Leicester, before the Earl, Hatton, and Walsingham, and face to face with Neville, was entangled deeper still. Yet he stoutly denied the declarations of his accomplice and accuser. Whereupon he was committed to the Tower.[1]

Two days afterwards, in presence of Hunsdon, Hatton, and Walsingham, he made a full confession of his treasonable intents and practices; and, on the thirteenth day of the month transmitted the same, in his own handwriting, to the Court.[2] With this confession, Neville's written declaration corresponded as to the main facts of their treasonable conferences; but it was verbose touching his own abhorrence and *refusal* of the plot. These asseverations, however, weigh but little against one stubborn fact, — he made no disclosure of the plot during six months; or, — to use the significant language of Parry, — "Belike the land and dignity of Westmoreland *bred* this conscience in him to discover a treason in February, contrived and agreed upon in August:" "in which space

singham's training of Parry who designed the murder of Elizabeth, the admitting of him, under pretence of discovering a plot, to the queen's presence, and then letting him go where he would, only on the security of a dark sentinel set over him, was a piece of reach and hazard beyond common apprehension."

This is hardly consistent with the narrative as it appears in Holingshed. If that is correct, Walsingham had no knowledge, at the time, of what was Parry's errand; nor do we find that he suspected him. It may be that Lloyd regarded Neville as nothing worse than "a dark sentinel." See *ante*, p. 44, note.

[1] Holingshed, IV. 562, 563.

[2] Ibid., 566. Hargrave's State Trials, I. 122.

her Majesty and ten princes in different provinces might have been killed."[1]

On the fourteenth day of the month, Parry wrote a letter to the queen, in which he described his confession as voluntary, and Neville as a sworn party in the design, of which, "in his very soul," he himself had repented. These points in his letter were published, but other important parts omitted, by the queen's ministers.[2]

On the eighteenth of the month, he wrote a letter to Lord Burleigh and the Earl of Leicester, in which he confessed that he deserved death for having "vowed the death of his natural queen;" "although commended and warranted by his Holiness the Pope." The burden of the letter was a prayer for pardon.[3]

On the same day, by vote of the Commons in Parliament, he was "disabled to be any longer a member of the House;" and by the same vote a warrant was ordered for a writ to the Sheriff of Kent for choosing and returning another Burgess in his stead.[4]

When arraigned on the twenty-fifth day of the month, his indictment charged him with having conspired, not only to depose the queen, "but also to bring her Highness to death." When called upon to

[1] Holingshed, IV. 569 *bis*. Hargrave's State Trials, I. 124 *bis*.

[2] By mistake, Mr. Hallam (page 97, note) calls this letter "a speech made upon the scaffold." He adds, "it contained some very good advice to her," — the queen. Some of this good advice was as follows: "Last of all, forget the glorious title of *supreme governor*. Trouble none that refuse to swear it; for that cannot agree with your sex. Luther and Calvin did not allow it. The Puritans smile at it, and the Catholic world doth condemn it. . . . . And lastly and ever, good madam, be good to your obedient Catholic subjects. For the bad I speak not." (Strype's Annals, VI. 338, 339.)

[3] Holingshed, IV. 571. Hargrave's State Trials, I. 125.

[4] D'Ewes, 352.

answer, he said, "I do confess that I am guilty of all that is contained in the indictment; I do confess it in manner and form as it is comprised therein." A little while after, "I never intended to kill Queen Elizabeth. I appeal to her own knowledge and to my Lord Treasurer's and Master Secretary's."

Again, "after he had particularly viewed every leaf" of his confession in the presence of the Court, he declared it to be true, and that it was "made freely and willingly of himself, without any extort means used to draw it from him." A little while after, "Your Honors know how my confession upon mine examination was extorted."

When remonstrated with for such gross contradictions, he only repeated wildly, "I never meant to kill her! I never meant to kill her! I will lay my blood upon Queen Elizabeth and you, before God and the world!" These and other words, "I do not see that I must die, because I am not *settled*," were what the Court called "dark speeches;" and when called upon to explain his meaning, he replied by another equally dark, "Look into your study, and into your new books, and you shall find what I mean." The wretched man's brain reeled. Such contradictions, appeals, "dark speeches," and wild imprecations as came from his lips in the hour of an awful reckoning, show clearly enough a distraught state induced by suddenly realizing the hopelessness of his condition and the terribleness of his doom.

When the sentence of the law was pronounced upon him, in which each horrid particular of his execution was given with revolting minuteness, and which closed with the usual formula, "And God have mercy on thy soul," despair wrung from him a frantic cry: "I do here summon Queen Elizabeth to answer for my blood before God!" By order of the Court, the Lieutenant of the Tower instantly removed him from the bar; and he was transferred to his prison amidst the imprecations of the multitude.[1]

On the second day of March, 1584–5, he was drawn upon an hurdle from Tower Hill through the midst of the city of London to the Palace yard at Westminster. Upon the scaffold he "avowed his innocency" (shriven and absolved?); declaring, "for any evil thought that ever I had to harm the queen, it never came into my mind; she knoweth it, and her own conscience can tell her so." At last, "he was turned from the ladder; and after *one swing* was cut down. When his bowels were taken out, he gave a great groan."[2] Thus in sight of the Parliament-House, where he had but just now sat an honored representative of loyal constituents, this deluded fanatic suffered the dreadful penalty for Treason.

[1] Holingshed, IV. 574 – 579. Hargrave's State Trials, I. 121 – 128.

[2] Holingshed, IV. 580. Hargrave's State Trials, I. 128. Strype's Annals, V. 364.

END OF VOL. II.

www.ingramcontent.com/pod-product-compliance
Lightning Source LLC
LaVergne TN
LVHW021303110826
845150LV00003B/466
* 9 7 8 1 4 2 5 5 6 0 3 1 7 *